INDUSTRIAL
QUALITY
CONTROL

INDUSTRIAL QUALITY CONTROL

Harvey C. Charbonneau
General Motors Institute

Gordon L. Webster
General Motors Institute

PRENTICE-HALL, INC.,
Englewood Cliffs, New Jersey 07632

Library of Congress Cataloging in Publication Data

CHARBONNEAU, HARVEY C   date–
    Industrial quality control.

    Includes index.
    1. Quality control.   I. Webster, Gordon L.,
date–   joint author.   II. Title.
TS156.C43   658.5′6   77–13904
ISBN 0–13–464255–4

© 1978 by Prentice-Hall, Inc.,
Englewood Cliffs, N.J. 07632

Printed in the United States of America

10 9 8 7 6 5 4 3 2 1

PRENTICE-HALL INTERNATIONAL, INC., *London*
PRENTICE-HALL OF AUSTRALIA PTY. LIMITED, *Sydney*
PRENTICE-HALL OF CANADA, LTD., *Toronto*
PRENTICE-HALL OF INDIA PRIVATE LIMITED, *New Delhi*
PRENTICE-HALL OF JAPAN, INC., *Tokyo*
PRENTICE-HALL OF SOUTHEAST ASIA PTE. LTD., *Singapore*
WHITEHALL BOOKS LIMITED, *Wellington, New Zealand*

To Jane and Martha

CONTENTS

PREFACE

This is intended as a basic text in quality control. An attempt has been made to eliminate much of the mathematical jargon that often does more to confuse than clarify. The text is designed for those who may sometime be expected to perform—not inform. Experience with using it at General Motors indicates that these objectives have been achieved.

Portions of the text were based on sessions written by Robert W. Aamoth, formerly an Associate Professor of Industrial Engineering at General Motors Institute. Essentially, however, the material is a culmination of what has been used in some form or other during the many years which the authors taught at GMI.

All example data are fictitious and should not be attributed to the automobile industry.

It is hoped that the text will provide guidance and help to those unfamiliar with either quality control or statistical applications. Where useful, procedures have been included to simplify the application of "statistical tools," since they are generally appreciated by the practical practitioner. Mentioned in the text is the statistical quality control slide rule, developed at GMI in the early 1950's. These slide rules are available from Graphic Calculator Co., Barrington, Illinois.

HARVEY C. CHARBONNEAU

Flint, Michigan

GORDON L. WEBSTER

INDUSTRIAL

QUALITY

CONTROL

CHAPTER ONE | VARIATION CONCEPTS AND ANALYSIS

Statistical methods are analytical tools used to evaluate men, materials, machines, or processes. Evaluations obtained by these methods assist in maintaining desired results by using past history to predict capabilities or trends. Such analytical methods are management tools which furnish data to all levels of supervision for appropriate action.

Some advantages of statistical techniques in interpreting engineering data and controlling manufactured products are

- More uniform quality at a higher level
- Less waste by reduction of rework and scrap
- Improved inspection by better planning and better execution
- Higher production of good parts per man per machine hour
- Improved design tolerancing
- Better plant relations through coordinated efforts

Control through statistical methods differs from the procedure of manufacturing a product according to schedule and then sorting the product into acceptable and nonacceptable lots. Eventually these control methods help to decide

- When the process is operating at a satisfactory level
- When the process level is not satisfactory and corrective action is required to prevent the manufacture of unacceptable products

The underlying cause for the differences in product reliability and quality is variation. Thus variation is the real reason for using statistical methods. Variation has been defined as "the difference between things which might otherwise be thought to be alike because they were produced under conditions which were as nearly alike as it is possible to make them."

1

PRINCIPLES UNDERLYING VARIATION

1. *No two things are exactly alike*. Experience has proven that things are never identical. Each individual, for example, has characteristics which differ from all others. Even such things as "two peas in a pod" have slight differences if examined closely enough. Likewise, no two parts are precisely identical. Blueprint tolerances result from engineers recognizing this fact. Although it is impossible to make interchangeable parts precisely identical, it is desirable to keep variations as small as possible.

2. *Variation in a product or process can be measured*. Two pins, two castings, or two hinges when manufactured may look just alike—but are they? With a suitable comparator, micrometer, or air gage, a difference can be measured. In fact, if the measurement unit is small enough, each part can be shown to be different from the next. This difference or variation is important when it has some effect on the functioning of the part being produced.

3. *Individual outcomes are not predictable*. Can it be reliably predicted whether the next flip of a coin will turn up heads or tails? With what assurance can one predict, to the tenth of a millimeter, the outside diameter of the next part coming from a machine? Even the most learned fingerprint expert cannot describe the identifying characteristics of the index finger of the next person he meets. Exactly predicting such things would be contrary to common sense, since if many items are measured or enumerated, a dissimilarity of individual outcomes will be evident. Serious mistakes in decisions can be made by examining only one or two items.

4. *Groups of things form patterns with definite characteristics*. Pour out a cupful of sugar on the table. Can an accurate prediction be made concerning where a particular grain will fall? No! Yet if this procedure were repeated again and again, the same pattern, or the same representative mound, would appear each time. Similarly, if supposedly identical parts from a process are carefully measured for a given dimension and are counted and arranged in order of size, a definite pattern will be revealed. This general characterizing pattern will also repeat with another group from the same productive process. A variation pattern example is the measurement tally of outside shaft diameters, shown in Figure 1-1. A variation pattern is also obtained by throwing two dice 50 times and recording the results in a tally form, as shown in Figure 1-2.

0.26003–0.26007	II
0.25998–0.26002	⌶⌶⌶ I
0.25993–0.25997	⌶⌶⌶ ⌶⌶⌶ IIII
0.25988–0.25992	⌶⌶⌶ ⌶⌶⌶ ⌶⌶⌶ ⌶⌶⌶ III
0.25983–0.25987	⌶⌶⌶ ⌶⌶⌶ ⌶⌶⌶ ⌶⌶⌶ ⌶⌶⌶ II
0.25978–0.25982	⌶⌶⌶ ⌶⌶⌶ ⌶⌶⌶ IIII
0.25973–0.25977	⌶⌶⌶ ⌶⌶⌶
0.25968–0.25972	⌶⌶⌶ I
0.25963–0.25967	III

Fig. 1-1 Tally of measurements

12	I
11	I
10	⌶⌶⌶
9	⌶⌶⌶
8	⌶⌶⌶ III
7	⌶⌶⌶ ⌶⌶⌶ I
6	⌶⌶⌶ II
5	⌶⌶⌶ I
4	IIII
3	II
2	I

Fig. 1-2 Frequency distribution for dice

5. *Sources of variation.* Variation is attributed to two different sources. One, called *chance*, results from inherent changes in the process such as variations in raw material, changing atmospheric conditions, room vibration, and backlash in equipment. The other, called *assignable*, consists of correctable errors. These errors may be such details as basic changes in materials, incorrect processing temperature or tool speeds, operator errors, or damage to equipment. Variations due to chance, being beyond control, give rise to a characteristic bell-shaped pattern. Variations due to assignable sources tend to distort this pattern. There are infinite assignable sources of variation in a manufacturing process. However, they can all be classified into these categories:

- Man
- Machine
- Material
- Measurement

If the process is functioning in a stable manner, these contribute to chance variation and are indistinguishable from one another. If they can be identified and the magnitude reduced or eliminated, the amount of product variation will be reduced. Since all variation cannot be eliminated, an attempt is made to reduce the amount contributed by each source: the operator doing the job, the machine or process performing the work, the substance from which the piece is made, and the devices gaging the work. For example, the substitution of an automatic machine for one that is manually operated tends to reduce the first source. However, variation resulting from operating disturbances—dirt, deflection, wear, workpiece variation, and workpiece mutilation— is still involved in the last three sources. Phrasing it differently, even though the process appears to be invariable, some variation still exists. Variation from piece to piece is accepted as inevitable, but control of variation is based on studying the variation pattern. Statistical methods are techniques for evaluating process variations, determining whether chance or assignable sources are present, and predicting the future.

POPULATIONS AND SAMPLES

Referring again to Figures 1-1 and 1-2, these data sets would be considered as samples from a population. The shaft measurements' population could consist of all shafts produced in the past, present, and future and would, for all practical purposes, never be completely known. Similarly, the dice population would be generated by infinitely many throws.

From a logical standpoint populations are only academically interesting, since the totality of objects or measurements is usually not available. Decisions must be made utilizing samples, or population subsets, and statistical methods embody a set of techniques employed in assisting in these decisions and/or predictions.

Other obvious reasons for sampling involve cost, the time involved in collecting information, situations where destructive testing is employed, and particularly product engineering testing where limited prototypes are available. When predictions are based on sampling results, risk elements exist, and a large part of statistical analysis is expressing these risks quantitatively.

In theoretical situations it is possible to make deductive inferences which involve enumerating sampling results from a known population. When samples are employed an opposite procedure is involved; that is, inferences are made about the population from the samples. Measures used to describe population characteristics are referred to as *parameters* and wherever possible are denoted by Greek letters; measures used to describe sample characteristics are referred to as *statistics* and are denoted by Roman letters. These concepts are explained more explicitly in other sections where their application and understanding are pertinent.

TYPES OF DATA

A meaningful step in data analysis is arranging the observed values. When these values are listed in numerical order and frequency, the array is called a frequency distribution. The frequency distribution displays the sample data collected. Its chief value lies in the information it reveals about the distribution form.

Variation analysis, using different procedures, can be applied to almost any data. Two general data types are encountered.

Discrete Data

When the data can take on only a particular set of values, that is, each observation can assume only given values and no observations can exist between these values, they are called discrete. For example, assembly defects must be an integral number, 0, 1, 2, or 3. A half defect or $1\frac{1}{4}$ defects cannot exist, except as an average value. Summing spots on the upturned faces of two dice is discrete data. Figure 1-8 portrays discrete data using defects which were observed on an assembly.

Continuous Data

Continuous data can take on any potential value within a given range. Within this range the only restriction on the particular value is the measuring limitation. The data appear to vary in jumps as discrete data do, but this characteristic is one artificially imposed by the measurement instrument capability. For example, shaft diameter may be measured by a vernier scale as 0.410 inch, by a tenth micrometer as 0.4096 inch, or by an air gage as 0.40958 inch.

CONSTRUCTING A FREQUENCY DISTRIBUTION

When recording a series of measurements, it is common practice to tabulate successive readings, as shown in Figure 1-3. This method has merit only when gaging order is important. It is immediately apparent that the same data in a frequency tally (Figure 1-4) reveal much more informa-

Fig. 1-3

INSPECTOR'S REPORT
Thickness of Steel Sheets

0.114	0.118	0.111	0.108	0.115	0.105	0.115	0.114	0.107	0.108
0.110	0.103	0.113	0.114	0.110	0.111	0.108	0.116	0.108	0.111
0.104	0.113	0.114	0.115	0.112	0.108	0.109	0.109	0.112	0.108
0.111	0.111	0.107	0.113	0.111	0.104	0.108	0.116	0.110	0.116
0.113	0.111	0.108	0.110	0.109	0.110	0.112	0.111	0.109	0.113
0.106	0.109	0.107	0.107	0.110	0.107	0.105	0.111	0.111	0.110
0.115	0.108	0.112	0.112	0.112	0.111	0.109	0.112	0.112	0.114
0.107	0.113	0.117	0.106	0.110	0.111	0.112	0.114	0.111	0.110
0.112	0.110	0.110	0.109	0.114	0.110	0.113	0.110	0.110	0.112
0.107	0.109	0.111	0.116	0.106	0.114	0.113	0.109	0.106	0.110
0.112	0.107	0.117	0.116	0.115	0.106	0.106	0.109	0.105	0.113
0.108	0.113	0.110	0.111	0.110	0.114	0.112	0.112	0.110	0.108
0.114	0.111	0.109	0.110	0.111	0.114	0.104	0.111	0.109	0.114
0.112	0.111	0.107	0.108	0.112	0.108	0.109	0.117	0.105	0.113
0.114	0.106	0.115	0.108	0.113	0.113	0.115	0.113	0.109	0.112
0.110	0.111	0.109	0.112	0.113	0.110	0.111	0.111	0.112	0.112
0.108	0.115	0.109	0.109	0.111	0.116	0.114	0.107	0.113	0.107
0.109	0.111	0.111	0.112	0.112	0.109	0.109	0.107	0.112	0.113
0.114	0.106	0.112	0.113	0.113	0.111	0.110	0.108	0.107	0.109
0.109	0.111	0.110	0.115	0.109	0.105	0.110	0.108	0.109	0.108
0.110	0.110	0.108	0.113	0.108	0.107	0.105	0.108	0.113	0.107
0.113	0.114	0.115	0.106	0.110	0.106	0.112	0.105	0.110	0.109

FREQUENCY TALLY
Thickness of Steel Sheets

0.118	I
0.117	III
0.116	HHT I
0.115	HHT HHT
0.114	HHT HHT HHT I
0.113	HHT HHT HHT HHT II
0.112	HHT HHT HHT HHT HHT
0.111	HHT HHT HHT HHT HHT II
0.110	HHT HHT HHT HHT HHT III
0.109	HHT HHT HHT HHT HHT
0.108	HHT HHT HHT HHT I
0.107	HHT HHT HHT
0.106	HHT HHT
0.105	HHT II
0.104	III
0.103	I

Number of measurements

Fig. 1-4

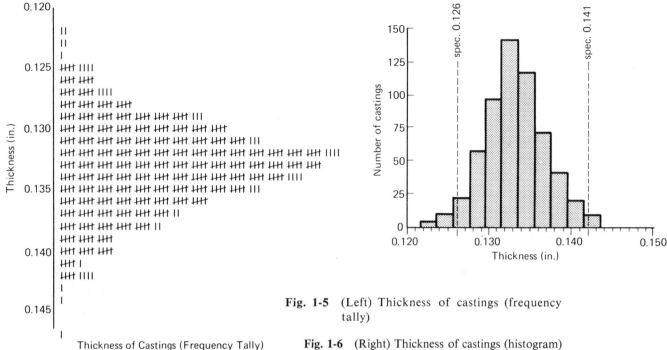

Fig. 1-5 (Left) Thickness of castings (frequency tally)

Thickness of Castings (Frequency Tally)

Fig. 1-6 (Right) Thickness of castings (histogram)

tion about the variation pattern than the tabular information does. The frequency tally is the recommended method for compiling data except when measurement order is important.

The frequency tally is constructed by

1. Determining the largest and the smallest readings in the data.

2. Tabulating in a column all values from the largest to the smallest.

3. Tallying beside these columnar figures the number of observations for each value.

A sample from an industrial operation shows how a process has performed over a specific time period. The frequency tally provides a picture of the variation pattern. A histogram, or bar chart, may be considered as a special frequency distribution form and portrays the same information as the tally chart. However, if the sample is large with low frequencies for some values or if the sample is small with a large spread, this pattern may be distorted, limiting its usefulness. (See Figures 1-5, 1-6, and 1-7.) It is essential that some method for grouping the data be devised to provide a more compact variation pattern. Steps to follow in constructing a histogram are given in the appendix to this chapter.

Fig. 1-7 Frequency tallies—door lock key torque

Ungrouped		Grouped	
Torque (lb-in.)	Tally	Torque (lb-in.) (class midpoints)	Tally
20	||	19	||||
19	|	16	₥ ₥ ₥ ₥ ₥ |
18	|	13	₥ ₥ ₥ ₥ ₥ ₥ ₥
17	₥	10	₥ ₥ ₥ ₥ ₥ ||
16	₥ ₥ |||	7	₥ |||
15	₥ |||		
14	₥		
13	₥ ₥ |||		
12	₥ ₥ ₥ ||		
11	₥ ₥ ||||		
10	||||		
9	₥ ||||		
8	₥ |		
7	|		
6	|		

5

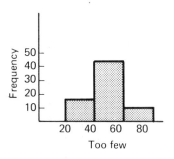
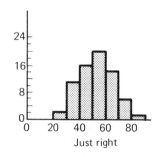
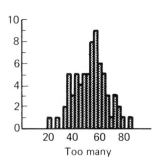

Fig. 1-8 Class interval effect on histogram shape

To reveal as much as possible about the distribution, the number of class intervals in histogram construction must be selected carefully. If the number is too small or too large, the population's estimated true shape may be obscured (Figure 1-8).

The bases of the histogram rectangles are always equal and one class interval in width. All measurements within any class interval are characterized by the midpoint of that interval. Each rectangle height is proportional to the class frequency in such a way that the histogram total area is proportional to the total frequency.

Theoretically, a discrete data histogram would consist only of variable-height, infinitely thin lines, erected at discrete intervals. However, the practical approach is to present these data using bar graphs (Figure 1-9).

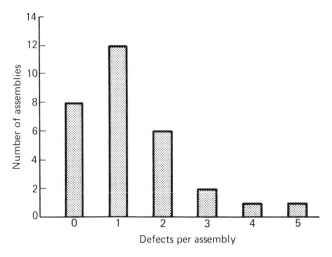

Fig. 1-9 Histogram of discrete data

ANALYSIS WITH THE HISTOGRAM

After constructing the histogram, draw in the specifications. It will then quickly answer three questions:

- Is the product consistent with previous checks?
- Is the product well centered?
- Does it appear that the product is meeting engineering specifications?

Referring to Figures 1-5 and 1-6, note that the histogram is roughly symmetrical, which indicates that the overall process is normal and that variations may be due to chance; the average is close to the specification midpoint, implying that the process is well centered; and the spread is greater than the specification limits, indicating that the process will have to be improved, that the tolerance is unrealistic, or that both must be adjusted.

Histograms often reveal, without elaborate analysis, much information about the process or product under observation and, because they are easily understood by operating personnel, can materially aid in making improvements. The histogram may be used for such purposes as

- Assessing material strengths
- Evaluating processes
- Indicating the necessity for corrective action
- Measuring the effects of corrective action
- Determining machine capabilities
- Portraying life characteristics
- Comparing operators
- Comparing materials
- Comparing vendors
- Comparing products

The simple histogram is helpful in making an analysis, but its use is limited because

- It requires many measurements
- It does not take time into consideration
- It does not separate the two kinds of variation—variation due to chance and variation due to assignable factors
- It does not show trends

Essentially, a histogram is a *postmortem* picture in that it portrays a situation that has already occurred. For illustrating variation patterns or for indicating shift or improvement, the histogram is unexcelled. But one precaution should be observed; a histogram will hide more than it reveals if control is not exercised. Note in Figure 1-10 that the frequency distribution summing the day's run fails to reveal the shift in the process over the time period shown.

Fig. 1-10   Frequency distribution study

Periodic sampling

	8:00	9:00	10:00	11:00	1:00	
0.825–0.830						Summation of
0.830–0.835						day's samples
0.835–0.840	Lower specification					
0.840–0.845						
0.845–0.850	I					I
0.850–0.855	IIII	I				HHT
0.855–0.860	HHT HHT I	III	II			HHT HHT HHT I
0.860–0.865	HHT HHT III	HHT III	HHT	II		HHT HHT HHT HHT HHT III
0.865–0.870	HHT IIII	HHT III	HHT III	HHT I	I	HHT HHT HHT HHT HHT HHT II
0.870–0.875	II	IIII	HHT I	HHT IIII	HHT I	HHT HHT HHT HHT HHT II
0.875–0.880		I	III	HHT I	HHT IIII	HHT HHT HHT HHT
0.880–0.885	Upper specification	I	II	HHT II	HHT HHT	
0.885–0.890				II	II	
0.890–0.895						

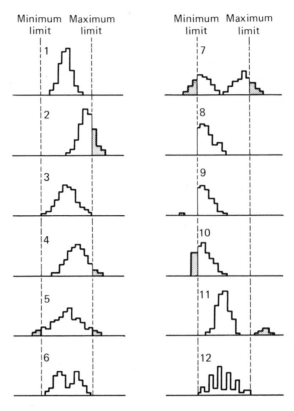

Fig. 1-11 Typical examples of variation

VARIATION EXAMPLES

In Figure 1-11, 12 typical variation examples are shown using histograms. They might be explained as follows:

1. An ideal situation where the spread is substantially within the specified limits and the distribution is well centered.

2. The distribution is off-center with parts outside the upper limit.

3. A distribution with a spread approximately the same as the specification limits, well centered and satisfactory.

4. A distribution with a spread approximately the same as example 3 which has drifted off-center with parts beyond specification.

5. A distribution with a spread greater than the specification limits with parts outside both limits.

6. A bimodal distribution suggesting that two different machines, two different materials, or two different products are involved.

7. A double distribution with a total spread greater than example 6 resulting in increased rework and/or scrap.

8. A process operating off-center where pieces have been 100 percent inspected and the defective ones removed. This could also indicate eccentricity readings or some other variable where only positive values can be measured.

9. A process resembling example 8 in which 100 percent inspection has not been entirely effective.

10. A process similar to example 8 or 9 indicating a salvage limit, a gage set up incorrectly, or an operator having difficulty deciding borderline cases.

11. A well-centered principal distribution with another small distribution that may be the result of including setup pieces in the lot.

12. A distribution where the operator has favored certain readings because the gaging was inadequate or difficult to interpret.

FREQUENCY DISTRIBUTION DATA CALCULATIONS

A histogram may be described by its central tendency and its spread or variation. The measures commonly used to describe central tendency are

1. *Mean:* the sample values summed and divided by the number observed; the arithmetic average; the center of gravity for the distribution.

2. *Median:* the center value when all observed values are placed in the order of size; the fiftieth percentile value; the value dividing the distribution exactly in half.

3. *Mode:* the most frequently occurring value; the highest bar in a histogram.

The measures commonly used to describe spread or variation are

1. *Variance:* the deviations from the mean squared, summed, and divided by one less than the sample size.

2. *Standard deviation:* the positive square root of the variance.

3. *Range:* the difference between the largest and the smallest value in the sample.

For distributional analysis, the mean and the standard deviation are the characteristics normally used. For the variables control chart considered in Chapter 7, the mean and range are used.

Using the algebraic symbol X to represent any single value, the following equations are used for calculation:

$$\text{The mean} = \bar{X} = \frac{\text{Sum of sample values}}{\text{Sample size}} = \frac{\sum X}{n}$$

$$\text{The variance} = s^2 = \frac{\text{The sum of the squared deviations from the mean}}{\text{The sample size minus 1}}$$

$$= \frac{\sum (X - \bar{X})^2}{n - 1} = \frac{\sum X^2 - (\sum X)^2/n}{n - 1} = \frac{n \sum X^2 - (\sum X)^2}{n(n - 1)}$$

$$\text{The standard deviation} = s = \text{The square root of the variance}$$

$$= \sqrt{\frac{\sum X^2 - (\sum X)^2/n}{n - 1}}$$

$$\text{The range} = R = \text{Largest minus smallest value}$$

$$= X_L - X_s$$

EXAMPLE PROBLEM (UNCODED DATA)

The procedure for calculating the sample mean and standard deviation using a simple problem with five values is shown below:

Step	Action Taken	Symbol	Result
1	Record sample size	n	5
2	Record values	X	0.197
			0.188
			0.184
			0.205
			0.201
3	Sum the values	$\sum X$	0.975
4	Sum the squared values	$\sum X^2$	0.190435
5	Square step 3 result	$(\sum X)^2 = (0.975)^2$	0.950625
6	Divide step 5 result by sample size	$\dfrac{(\sum X)^2}{n} = \dfrac{0.950625}{5}$	0.190125
7	Subtract step 6 result from step 4 result and divide difference by sample size minus 1	$\dfrac{\sum X^2 - (\sum X)^2/n}{n-1} = s^2$ $= \dfrac{0.190435 - 0.190125}{5-1}$	0.000077
8	Take square root of step 7	$\sqrt{s^2} = s$ $= \sqrt{0.000077}$	0.0088
9	Divide step 3 result by step 1 result	$\bar{x} = \dfrac{\sum X}{n} = \dfrac{0.975}{5}$	0.195

Fig. 1-12 Calculation of average and standard deviation, coded data method

Upper Class Limits	Class Midpoint, x_m	Tally	Frequency, f	d	fd	fd²
0.1925						
	0.192		4	5	20	100
0.1915						
	0.191		6	4	24	96
0.1905						
	0.190		7	3	21	63
0.1895						
	0.189		14	2	28	56
0.1885						
	0.188		15	1	15	15
0.1875						
	0.187		27	0	0	0
0.1865						
	0.186		15	−1	−15	15
0.1855						
	0.185		10	−2	−20	40
0.1845						
	0.184		7	−3	−21	63
0.1835						
	0.183		8	−4	−32	128
0.1825						
	0.182		2	−5	−10	50
0.1815						
			115		−98 + 108 = 10	626
			n		Σfd	Σfd²

Code: $d = \dfrac{X_m - A}{i}$

where A = midpoint of class with highest frequency
i = interval between class midpoints or class limits

For larger samples or when an electronic calculator is not available, these calculations become laborious. They can be simplified by grouping and coding the data and following the procedure shown in Figure 1-12. When the calculations are completed they must be decoded to return them to their original measurement units.

EXAMPLE PROBLEM (GROUPED AND CODED DATA)

Step	Action Taken	Symbol	Result
1	Record data on form similar to Figure 1-12		
2	Code data in d column	$d = \dfrac{X_m - A}{i}$	See Fig. 1-12
3	Fill in fd column		See Fig. 1-12
4	Fill in fd^2 column		See Fig. 1-12
5	Record sample size	n	115
6	Sum the fd column	$\sum fd$	10
7	Sum the fd^2 column	$\sum fd^2$	626
8	Square step 6 result and divide by the sample size	$\dfrac{(\sum fd)^2}{n} = \dfrac{(10)^2}{115}$	0.8696
9	Subtract step 8 result from step 7 result and divide difference by sample size minus 1	$\dfrac{\sum fd^2 - (\sum fd)^2/n}{n-1}$ $= \dfrac{626 - 0.8696}{115 - 1}$	5.4836
10	Take square root of step 9 result	$\sqrt{s^2} = s$ $= \sqrt{5.4836}$	2.3417
11	Decode step 9 result by multiplying standard deviation by class interval	$(i)(s) = (0.001)(2.3417)$	0.0023
12	Divide step 6 result by step 1 result	$\dfrac{\sum fd}{n} = \dfrac{10}{115}$	0.0870
13	Decode step 12 result by multiplying step 12 result by class interval and adding A to product	$\bar{X} = (i)\dfrac{\sum fd}{n} + A$ $= (0.001)(0.0870)$ $+ 0.187$	0.18787 or 0.1879

APPENDIX 1 CHAPTER 1 | A PROCEDURE FOR CONSTRUCTING A HISTOGRAM

A histogram is constructed to show the general variation pattern inherent in data. It should be constructed precisely, even though some arbitrary decisions must be made. The shape can be altered by varying the class size and class width. To have some consistency in construction, the following guidelines are recommended.

PRECONSTRUCTION STEPS

1. Determine the range of the data by subtracting the smallest observed measurement from the largest and designate it as R.

    EXAMPLE 1

    Largest observed measurement = 1.1185 inches

    Smallest observed measurement = 1.1030 inches

    R = 1.1185 inches — 1.1030 inches = 0.0155 inch

    EXAMPLE 2

    Largest observed measurement = 51,500 kilograms

    Smallest observed measurement = 39,700 kilograms

    R = 51,500 kilograms — 39,700 kilograms = 11,800 kilograms

2. Record the measurement unit (MU) used. This is usually controlled by the measuring instrument least count.

    EXAMPLE 1

    MU = 0.0001 inch

    EXAMPLE 2

    MU = 100 kilograms

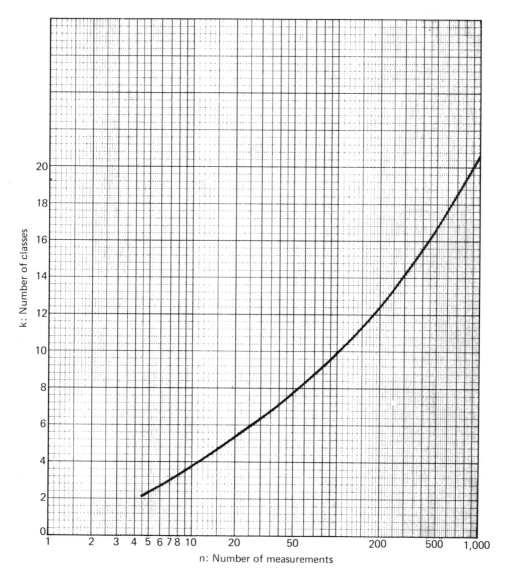

Fig. 1A1-1 Graph to determine k

3. Determine the number of classes and the class width.
    a. The number of classes, k, is dependent on the total measurements, n.
    b. Obtain the preferred number of classes, k, from the graph shown in Figure 1A1-1.

    EXAMPLE 1
    $$n = 50$$
    $$k = 7.7 \text{ or } 8 \text{ classes}$$

    EXAMPLE 2
    $$n = 100$$
    $$k = 9.9 \text{ or } 10 \text{ classes}$$

    c. Calculate the class width by dividing the range, R, by the preferred number of classes, k.

    EXAMPLE 1
    $$\frac{R}{k} = \frac{0.0155 \text{ inch}}{8} = 0.0019375 \text{ inch}$$

    EXAMPLE 2
    $$\frac{R}{k} = \frac{11,800 \text{ kilograms}}{10} = 1,180 \text{ kilograms}$$

d. The class width selected should be an odd-numbered multiple of the measurement unit, MU. This value should preferably be close to the class width calculated in step 3c.

EXAMPLE 1

MU = 0.0001 inch

Class width = 0.0019 inch or 0.0021 inch   (odd-numbered multiple is 19 or 21, respectively)

EXAMPLE 2

MU = 100 kilograms

Class width = 1,100 kilograms or 1,300 kilograms   (odd-numbered multiple is 11 or 13, respectively)

4. Establish the class midpoints and class limits.
   a. The first class midpoint should be located near the largest observed measurement. If possible, it should also be a convenient increment.

EXAMPLE 1

First class midpoint = 1.1185 inches

EXAMPLE 2

First class midpoint = 51,500 kilograms

   b. Always make the class widths equal in size.
   c. Express the class limits in terms which are one-half unit beyond the accuracy of the original measurement unit. This avoids plotting an observed measurement on a class limit. If the procedure under step 3 is followed correctly, this will be done automatically.

EXAMPLE 1

First class midpoint = 1.1185 inches

The class width is 0.0019 inch. Limits for the first class would be

$$1.1185 \pm \frac{0.0019}{2}$$

or

$$1.1185 \pm 0.00095$$

Midpoints and class limits for the entire data set are

| | Class Limits | |
Midpoints	Lower	Upper
1.1185	1.11755	1.11945
1.1166	1.11565	1.11755
1.1147	1.11375	1.11565
1.1128	1.11185	1.11375
1.1109	1.10995	1.11185
1.1090	1.10805	1.10995
1.1071	1.10615	1.10805
1.1052	1.10425	1.10615
1.1033	1.10235	1.10425

This results in one more class than originally determined in step 3b (eight) due to dropping 0.0000375 inch. Using 0.0021 inch would give the following:

| | Class Limits | |
Midpoints	Lower	Upper
1.1185	1.11745	1.11955
1.1164	1.11535	1.11745
1.1143	1.11325	1.11535
1.1122	1.11115	1.11325
1.1101	1.10905	1.11115
1.1080	1.10695	1.10905
1.1059	1.10485	1.10695
1.1038	1.10275	1.10485

EXAMPLE 2

First class midpoint = 51,500 kilograms

The class width is 1,300 kilograms. Limits for the first class would be

$$51,500 \pm \frac{1,300}{2}$$

or

$$51,500 \pm 650$$

Midpoints and class limits for entire data set are

| | Class Limits | |
Midpoints	Lower	Upper
51,500	50,850	52,150
50,200	49,550	50,850
48,900	48,250	49,550
47,600	46,950	48,250
46,300	45,650	46,950
45,000	44,350	45,650
43,700	43,050	44,350
42,400	41,750	43,050
41,100	40,450	41,750
39,800	39,150	40,450

Note: Both class limits are seldom used, since the lower limit in one class is the same as the upper limit in the next class. The examples showed both limits for illustrative purposes only.

CONSTRUCTING THE HISTOGRAM

1. Determine the axes for the graph.
   a. The frequency scale on the vertical axis should slightly exceed the largest class frequency.
   b. The measurement scale along the horizontal axis should be at regular intervals which are independent of the class width.

2. Draw the graph.
   a. Mark off classes.
   b. Draw rectangles with heights corresponding to the measurement frequencies in that class.
3. Title the histogram.
   a. Give an overall title.
   b. Identify each axis.

EXAMPLE PROBLEM

To illustrate the procedure for constructing a histogram and the difference in shapes which can be obtained using different class widths and midpoints, consider the following data:

Out-of-Balance Ounce-Inches After Rough-Turn Bullard: 50 Random Readings

21	10	23	25	22
28	26	12	26	18
15	24	14	27	27
32	26	5	25	13
26	28	25	24	27
27	30	27	22	15
23	28	26	19	24
15	28	35	20	28
23	14	29	25	20
25	34	23	24	25

Preconstruction Steps

1. $R = 35 - 5 = 30$.
2. MU = 1 ounce-inch.
3. a. $n = 50$.   c. $R/k = \frac{30}{8} = 3.75$.
   b. $k = 7.7$ or 8.   d. Use either 3 or 5.
4. Class midpoints and class limits (three different starting midpoints are shown for each class width):

C.W. = 3

	Class Limits			*Class Limits*			*Class Limits*	
Midpoints	*Lower*	*Upper*	*Midpoints*	*Lower*	*Upper*	*Midpoints*	*Lower*	*Upper*
34	32.5	35.5	35	33.5	36.5	36	34.5	37.5
31	29.5	32.5	32	30.5	33.5	33	31.5	34.5
28	26.5	29.5	29	27.5	30.5	30	28.5	31.5
25	23.5	26.5	26	24.5	27.5	27	25.5	28.5
22	20.5	23.5	23	21.5	24.5	24	22.5	25.5
19	17.5	20.5	20	18.5	21.5	21	19.5	22.5
16	14.5	17.5	17	15.5	18.5	18	16.5	19.5
13	11.5	14.5	14	12.5	15.5	15	13.5	16.5
10	8.5	11.5	11	9.5	12.5	12	10.5	13.5
7	5.5	8.5	8	6.5	9.5	9	7.5	10.5
4	2.5	5.5	5	3.5	6.5	6	4.5	7.5

C.W. = 5

	Class Limits			Class Limits			Class Limits	
Midpoints	Lower	Upper	Midpoints	Lower	Upper	Midpoints	Lower	Upper
33	30.5	35.5	35	32.5	37.5	37	34.5	39.5
28	25.5	30.5	30	27.5	32.5	32	29.5	34.5
23	20.5	25.5	25	22.5	27.5	27	24.5	29.5
18	15.5	20.5	20	17.5	22.5	22	19.5	24.5
13	10.5	15.5	15	12.5	17.5	17	14.5	19.5
8	5.5	10.5	10	7.5	12.5	12	9.5	14.5
3	0.5	5.5	5	2.5	7.5	7	4.5	9.5

Constructing the Histogram

The histograms based on these midpoints and classes are shown in Figures 1A1-2 and 1A1-3.

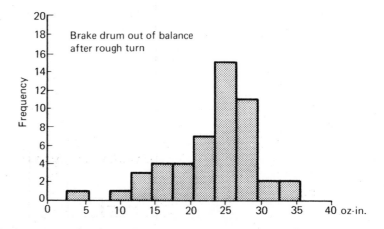

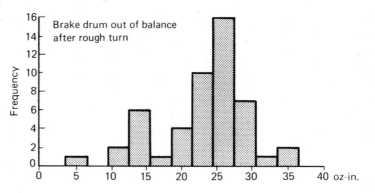

Fig. 1A1-2 Histogram—brake drum data (C.W. = 3)

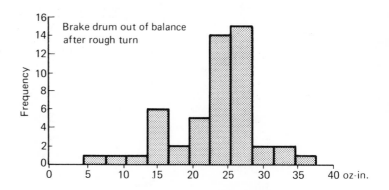

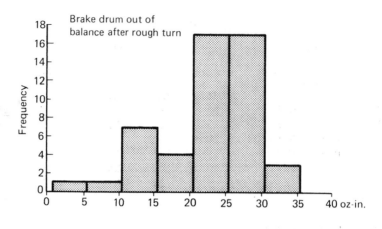

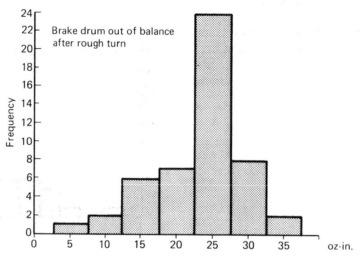

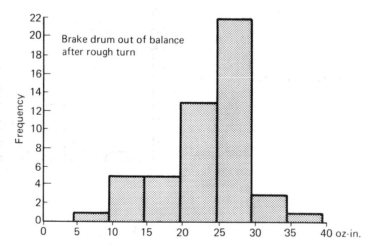

Fig. 1A1-3   Histogram—brake drum data (C.W. = 5)

CHAPTER TWO | PROBABILITY

In the building industry the *footing* is the foundation upon which a house, apartment, or plant is constructed. Similarly in statistics, probability is the foundation upon which the mathematical theory that has been and continues to be developed is constructed. This chapter will not attempt to present probability in a rigorous form, but will provide some basic concepts and theorems useful for the general practitioner.

The earliest recorded reference to probability occurred about 1654 when the French mathematician Blaise Pascal was asked to calculate the fair odds in a dice game. Chronologically, from that point, in 1662, Captain Graunt constructed life tables from the London death registers; in 1693, Halley developed a table to use in calculating annuities; Gauss' work followed in astronomy and surveying; and in the present century, K. Pearson and R. A. Fisher brought the theory into science, agriculture, and commerce.

GENERAL EXAMPLES

The word *probability* or *chance* is frequently used in everyday conversation, and people know vaguely what it means. For instance, reference is made to

- The chance that a person will win at cards or that a team will win at football
- The probability that it will rain today
- The chance that a person will live to his one-hundredth birthday

In these cases interest is in a future event where the outcome is uncertain and about which a prediction is desired. Sometimes a rough qualitative statement is made:

- It is very likely that it will rain today.
- A man has less chance than a woman to live 100 years, although either has a slim chance.

19

At other times, the tendency is to be on the numerical side:

- There is a fifty-fifty chance to win the game.
- The odds are two to one that it will rain today.

Such statements are quite clear and understandable, but what is actually meant when the words *probable*, *likely* or *chance* are used? How many things happen by pure chance? In statistics the words *probability*, *likelihood*, and *chance* have the same meaning and can be used interchangeably.

SPECIFIC APPROACHES

There are three approaches that can be used in determining probabilities: the classical, the frequency or empirical, and the subjective or personalistic. The classical is the ratio of the ways an event *can* occur to the total ways for all possible cases. The empirical is the limiting value for the relative frequency of the ways an event *does* occur as the trials increase indefinitely. The personalistic is a quantification of uncertainty representing the extent to which a person *believes* a statement based on his background knowledge, his access to available information, and his interpretation of the data obtained.

The classical approach applies only when all possible outcomes can be enumerated and where all outcomes are assumed equally likely, for example, coin tossing, rolling dice, and card games. The empirical approach can also be applied to the preceding, although practically it is used whenever probability statements are based on collected data. The personalistic approach can be used with the two preceding ones but in addition deals with unique events such as the probability that Cleopatra was a blond or the events mentioned in the book *Chariot of the Gods*. If large quantities of data are available, all three approaches will usually result in similar answers.

BASIC MATHEMATICS

Essentially, classical and empirical probability statements differ only in the ways in which the ratios are obtained. The probability statement for the event E is

- Classical

$$P[E] = \frac{\text{Ways } E \text{ can occur}}{\text{Total ways for all possible cases}}$$

- Empirical

$$P[E] = \frac{\text{Ways } E \text{ did occur}}{\text{Total trials}}$$

For example, in coin tossing, the event E could be a head.

- Classical

$$P[\text{head}] = \frac{\text{Ways a head can occur}}{\text{Total ways (head or tail)}} = \frac{1}{2} = 0.50$$

- Empirical

$$P[\text{head}] = \frac{\text{Ways head did occur}}{\text{Total tosses}} = \frac{7}{10} = 0.7$$

$$P[\text{head}] = \frac{488}{1,000} = 0.488$$

The estimate will obviously get closer to the true probability as the total tosses increase. Thus if 6,000 tosses were made, the result might be

$$P[\text{head}] = \frac{488 + 518 + 508 + 483 + 496 + 503}{6 \times 1,000} = \frac{2,996}{6,000} = 0.499$$

In industrial applications, empirical rather than classical probability estimates are usually made since the prediction is based on a sample result. For example, if 100 pieces were selected from a machining process and 10 failed to conform to the specifications, it would be estimated that 10 percent defective parts were being produced.

PROBABILITIES WHEN EVENTS ARE COMBINED

Combined events imply that the outcomes can be categorized into more than a single classification. When this exists, the compound probability can be determined from precise mathematical relationships. Before presenting these, however, two definitions are needed:

1. *Mutually exclusive event::* Two or more events are mutually exclusive if they cannot occur simultaneously.
2. *Independent events:* Two or more events are independent if the occurrence of one has no effect on the other's occurrence.

Note: There is a danger that mutually exclusive events may be confused with independent events. This can result from the expression "has no effect on the other's occurrence." On a single toss, a head and a tail are mutually exclusive, whereas on two successive tosses, they are independent. Set theory or Venn diagrams are required to explain the concept more completely.

THE ADDITION LAW

Mutually exclusive events. If the probability that an event is in class A is $P[A]$ and if the probability that an event is in class B is $P[B]$, then if A and B cannot occur simultaneously, the probability that the event is in either class A or class B (exclusive *or*) is

$$P[A \text{ or } B] = P[A] + P[B]$$

The coin toss can be used for illustration:

$$P[\text{head or tail}] = P[\text{head}] + P[\text{tail}] = \frac{1}{2} + \frac{1}{2} = 1$$

Nonmutually exclusive events. If the probability that an event is in class A is $P[A]$ and if the probability that an event is in class B is $P[B]$, then if A and B can occur simultaneously, the probability that the event is in class A or class B or both (inclusive *or*) is

$$P[A \text{ or } B] = P[A] + P[B] - P[A \text{ and } B]$$

As an illustration, suppose two coins are tossed:

$$P[\text{head on first coin or head on second coin}]$$
$$= P[\text{head on first coin}] + P[\text{head on second coin}]$$
$$- P[\text{head on first coin and head on second coin}]$$
$$= \frac{1}{2} + \frac{1}{2} - \frac{1}{4} = \frac{3}{4}(\text{HH, HT, TH, TT})$$

THE MULTIPLICATION LAW

Independent events. If the probability that an event is in class A is $P[A]$ and the probability that an event is in class B is $P[B]$ and if A and B are independent, then the probability that both A and B will happen, known as their joint probability, is obtained by multiplying their individual probabilities:

$$P[A \text{ and } B] = P[A] \times P[B]$$

Continuing with two coins as an example,

$$P[\text{head on first coin and head on second coin}]$$
$$= P[\text{head on first coin}] \times P[\text{head on second coin}]$$
$$= \frac{1}{2} \times \frac{1}{2} = \frac{1}{4}$$

Nonindependent events. If the probability that an event is in class A is $P[A]$ and the probability that an event is in class B is $P[B]$ and if A and B are not independent, then the probability that both A and B will happen, known as their joint probability, is obtained by multiplying $P[A]$ times $P[B$ given that A has occurred$]$ or by multiplying $P[B]$ times $P[A$ given that B has occurred$]$:

$$P[A \text{ and } B] = P[A] \times P[B/A]$$

or

$$P[B \text{ and } A] = P[B] \times P[A/B]$$

Since coins can no longer be used to illustrate this concept, consider a box which contains 20 balls: 3 white, 7 red, and 10 blue. If 2 balls are drawn in succession and the first ball is not returned to the box before the second is drawn, then the events are dependent. The probability that 2 white balls will be drawn is

$$P[\text{white and white}] = P[\text{white on first draw}]$$
$$\times P[\text{white on second draw given white on first draw}]$$
$$= \frac{3}{20} \times \frac{2}{19} = \frac{6}{380} = 0.0158$$

For comparison, if the draws are independent (the first ball is replaced), then

$$P[\text{white and white}] = \frac{3}{20} \times \frac{3}{20} = \frac{9}{400} = 0.0225$$

Both the multiplication and addition laws can be extended for more than two events.

GENERAL PROPERTIES

There are three properties which apply when working with probabilities:

1. Any event has a probability which is a number between 0 and 1:

$$0 \leq P[E] \leq 1$$

2. Probabilities for all possible mutually exclusive events add up to 1:

$$\sum_{i=1}^{n} P[E_i] = 1$$

3. Since the sum of only two possible mutually exclusive events is 1, the probability that E will not occur is

$$P[\text{not } E] = 1 - P[E]$$

This is also referred to as the complementary event.

RANDOMNESS AND PROBABILITY

In tossing a coin it was noted that it had two sides, a head and a tail and, consequently, that the probability of a head was one-half. However, it is more interesting to know that if an unbiased coin is tossed in a *random manner*, a head will come up about as often as a tail. There is no influence on the outcome, nor is any outcome influenced by a previous outcome.

Randomness is difficult to define. It can more easily be explained by defining nonrandomness. For instance, if the coin were always laid tail down, flipped over twice in the air, caught, and laid on the back of the hand, this would not be a random toss. Similarly, in inspecting incoming shipments, if the boxes were packed in such a manner that all defective pieces were on the bottom and the sample were drawn from the top, the selection would not be a random one.

A point to remember is that probabilities predict what will happen *in the long run*. They give an expected result for many trials, not just for a few. If a coin is tossed many times, the prediction is that about half the time it will turn up heads. If a large volume is produced by a machine, it can be predicted that over a 1-year period, 2 percent will be defective.

Determining the precise sample size required for a specific application is beyond the scope of this text. Suffice it to say that in some opinion polls 400 is considered adequate, while in work sampling the number may go as high as 10,000.

Since quality may be considered the degree to which a process or a product meets the specifications, it may be affected by a change in any process variable. That is, quality becomes a function of one or several process characteristics. If the process is operating in a random manner, the quality level can be accurately predicted. What is desirable then is to be able to determine a change in quality or a change in a variable which will affect quality as soon as it happens. The ability to understand and effectively utilize probability concepts is essential for all practicing engineers.

CHAPTER THREE | ANALYSIS TECHNIQUES FOR CONTINUOUS DATA

As indicated previously, a histogram is a graphical picture using continuous data and may be used for predictive purposes. It gives probability estimates and indicates a variation pattern for the population from which the sample was taken.

PROBABILITY PREDICTIONS

The histogram appears as adjacent rectangles placed along a common base line and is so constructed that the rectangle widths are all equal. Each rectangle represents a group or measurement class; its height indicates the measurement frequency in that class. Since the class widths are equal, the rectangle area also represents the class frequency. Similarly, the total histogram area represents the total frequency.

A probability prediction can be made using the above information and the histogram of distance measurements shown in Figure 3-1. For example, it is possible to estimate the probability that a pilot hole distance will measure 0.185 inch, as a fraction, by dividing the rectangle area centered at 0.185 inch by the total area of the histogram. (Since this is continuous data, it is not theoretically correct to estimate the probability for such a specific value as exactly 0.185. It is done here to illustrate a concept.)

$$P[\text{distance} = 0.185 \text{ inch}] = \frac{10 \text{ units of area}}{115 \text{ units of area}} = 0.087$$

Similarly, the estimated probability that a distance will measure 0.188 or 0.189 inch equals

$$P[\text{distance} = 0.188 \text{ or } 0.189 \text{ inch}] = \frac{15 \text{ area units} + 14 \text{ area units}}{115 \text{ area units}} = 0.251$$

Probabilities may also be estimated from a cumulative frequency distribution, which is another statistical technique. The sample cumulative distribution, in graphical form, is a monotonically increasing broken line. Construction steps are as follows:

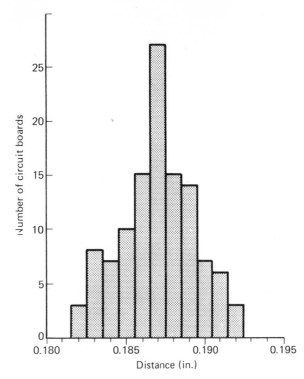

Fig. 3-1 Histogram of distances—pilot hole to edge of circuit board

1. Arrange the sample data as in constructing a histogram.

2. In a column adjacent to the frequency column, cumulate the frequency by classes.

3. Calculate the cumulative fraction values by dividing each value determined in step 2 by the total sample size.

4. Label a conveniently read measurement scale along the horizontal axis in accordance with the class values.

5. Label a scale on the vertical axis (either as a decimal from 0.00 to 1.00 or as a percentage from 0.00 to 100.0).

6. Plot the upper class limits on the horizontal axis against the cumulative decimal fraction or percentage frequencies on the vertical axis.

7. Connect each point with a straight line.

8. Title the axes and the graph.

Figure 3-2 shows the necessary calculations for constructing a cumulative frequency distribution.

Fig. 3-2

Upper Class Limit	Frequency Below Limit	Cumulative Frequency	Cumulative Decimal Fraction	Cumulative Percent
0.1815	0	0	0.0	0.0
0.1825	3	3	0.026	2.6
0.1835	8	11	0.096	9.6
0.1845	7	18	0.157	15.7
0.1855	10	28	0.243	24.3
0.1865	15	43	0.374	37.4
0.1875	27	70	0.610	61.0
0.1885	15	85	0.740	74.0
0.1895	14	99	0.860	86.0
0.1905	7	106	0.922	92.2
0.1915	6	112	0.975	97.5
0.1925	3	115	1.000	100.0

25

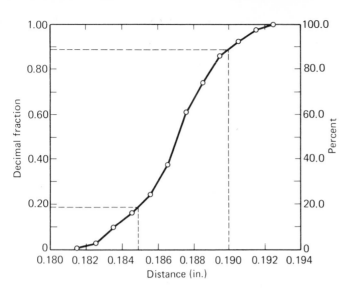

Fig. 3-3   Cumulative frequency distribution

The cumulative frequency distribution (Figure 3-3) is then constructed using the appropriate columns from Figure 3-2. (Refer to step 6.) Probability estimates using this graph are cumulative, for example,

$$P[\text{distance is less than } 0.185 \text{ inch}] = 0.180 \text{ approximately}$$
$$P[\text{distance is less than } 0.190 \text{ inch}] = 0.890 \text{ approximately}$$
$$P[\text{distance exceeds } 0.190 \text{ inch}] = 1.000 - 0.890 = 0.110 \text{ approximately}$$

PROBABILITY DISTRIBUTIONS

Histograms constructed from sample measurements do not show the exact population pattern and will vary from sample to sample. A truer population picture can be obtained by taking larger samples and measuring to a more accurate degree. In so doing, the histogram will show more and narrower rectangles, until the distribution can be represented by a smooth curve (Figure 3-4).

If the smooth curve is now plotted against a relative frequency scale, the resultant figure is called a probability distribution curve. This distribution is used when the vertical scale is changed to a relative frequency scale, making the area under the curve equal to one unit which represents the total probability. Consequently, the probability that a distance measurement would be between 0.182 and 0.185 inch is the shaded area under the curve in Figure 3-5, between the vertical lines at these two values. This area, and hence the desired probability, can be obtained mathematically. Although probability distribution varieties number in the hundreds, relatively few are employed in statistical analysis, and probability tables have been compiled for these.

Fig. 3-4   Histogram—large sample

Fig. 3-5   Probability distribution curve

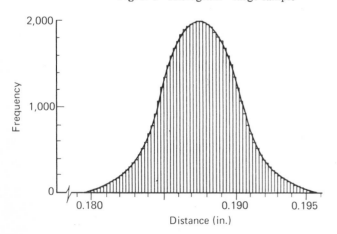

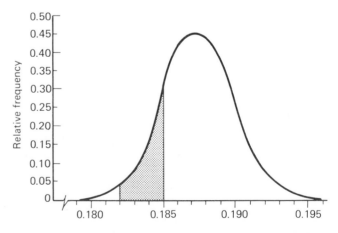

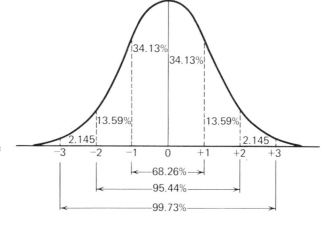

Fig. 3-6 Standardized normal curve

THE NORMAL PROBABILITY DISTRIBUTION

In variation patterns, the natural tendency is for the sample measurements to cluster about the center or average value. This pattern is so universal in industry and nature that a general bell-shaped curve can be formed over the frequency distribution or histogram. A special bell-shaped curve is called the Gaussian or normal curve (Figure 3-6). If a histogram approximates this form, the sample is usually considered to be from a normal distribution.

The normal curve, in the strict sense, is a theoretical one, absolutely symmetrical about its mean. It is precisely defined by designating its two parameters the mean (μ) and the standard deviation (σ). Thus, changing either one or both of these parameters defines a different normal curve. The curve extends to infinity in both directions. Generally, the normal curve is considered to portray variation which is due to chance. Most data occurring in engineering and manufacturing are considered to follow this pattern.

In Figure 3-6 the area under the theoretical normal curve is divided into six zones, three on each side of the mean. Each zone is one standard deviation in width. Theory shows, and practice confirms, that in a controlled operation 99.73 percent of the values will lie between limits set by taking the mean (μ) plus and minus three standard deviations (σ). It should be emphasized that this statement is completely valid only when the population parameters are known.

The curve in Figure 3-6 is usually described as the standardized normal distribution. Since each population could conceivably have a different mean and standard deviation, there are theoretically an infinite number of normal distribution curves. Standardizing the normal distribution results in one curve which is applicable to any data set that can be characterized by this distribution. The numerical values shown on the curve base line (Figure 3-6) represent what are termed standard Z values. These values result when the random variable, X, is expressed as a deviation from the mean, μ, measured as multiples of its standard deviation σ. The equation is

$$Z = \frac{X - \mu}{\sigma}$$

As can be observed, when $X = \mu$, $Z = 0$, or the distribution mean is at 0, and when $X = \sigma$, $Z = 1$. The quantity Z has the following properties:

1. It is dimensionless, since all measurement units cancel.

2. The numbers are small, since 99.73 percent of the X values have a resulting Z value between $+3$ and -3.

3. Only one cumulative probability table is required, since any normal random variable X can always be reduced to a corresponding Z value.

27

Previously it was indicated that the area under a probability distribution curve can be used to estimate the probabilities that given X values will occur. To determine these probabilities for a normal distribution, the standard Z values are calculated using a specified X value and reference is made to a table of areas under the normal curve (see Figure 3-9).

EXAMPLE PROBLEMS

1. The specifications on the outside diameter for a pump motor shaft seal are 1.515 and 1.525 inches. The population mean (μ) is 1.5202 inches, and the standard deviation (σ) is 0.0020 inch. What percent of the seals will be within specifications?

Given

$$\mu = 1.5202$$
$$\sigma = 0.0020$$

calculate Z for the upper limit,

$$Z = \frac{X - \mu}{\sigma}$$

Substituting the upper limit for X,

$$Z = \frac{1.525 - 1.5202}{0.0020} = \frac{0.0048}{0.0020} = 2.4$$

From Figure 3-2,

$$P(X \geq 1.525) = P(Z \geq 2.4) = 0.0082$$

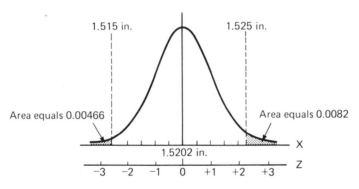

Fig. 3-7 Standardized normal curve— pump motor shaft seals

(Refer to Figure 3-7.) Calculate Z for the lower limit,

$$Z = \frac{X - \mu}{\sigma}$$

Substituting the lower limit for X,

$$Z = \frac{1.515 - 1.5202}{0.0020} = \frac{-0.0052}{0.002} = -2.6$$

Since Figure 3-9 shows only positive Z values, consider the -2.6 as positive, and use the tabulated value 0.00466. This is the probability that the size will be less than 1.515, or

$$P[X \leq 1.515] = P[Z \leq -2.6] = 0.00466$$

(Refer to Figure 3-7.)

Adding these two outside areas together and subtracting from one, gives the probability that the shaft seal diameters will be produced within specifications:

$$0.00466 + 0.0082 = 0.01286$$
$$1 - 0.01286 = 0.98714 \text{ or } 98.714 \text{ percent}$$

2. A steering pot joint angle in excess of 12 degrees might cause a steering failure in the field. From a large quantity of data the mean (μ) was estimated at 9.95 degrees and the standard deviation (σ) at 1.03 degrees. What is the probability of exceeding 12 degrees?

Given

$$\mu = 9.95 \text{ degrees}$$
$$\sigma = 1.03 \text{ degrees}$$
$$\text{Upper specification} = 12 \text{ degrees}$$

calculate Z,

$$Z = \frac{X - \mu}{\sigma}$$

Substituting the specification for X,

$$Z = \frac{12 - 9.95}{1.03} = \frac{2.05}{1.03} = 1.99$$

From Figure 3-9,

$$P[X \geq 12 \text{ degrees}] = P[Z \geq 1.99] = 0.0233$$

Therefore 2.33 percent will be produced beyond specification. (See Figure 3-8.)

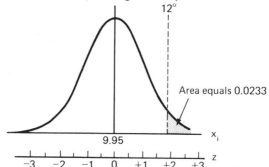

Fig. 3-8 Standardized normal curve—pot joint angle

NORMAL PROBABILITY PAPER

Since considerable time is involved in constructing a histogram, in calculating the average and the standard deviation, and in determining percentages, a quicker method for obtaining the same information is desirable. Such a method is available using normal probability paper (abbreviated NOPP). One scale on NOPP is the usual linear scale. The other is a probability scale, so arranged that when cumulative frequencies, as percentages, are plotted against the measured variable, the normal curve becomes a straight line. See Appendix 1.

NOPP is also used to test the assumption that a sample has been taken from a normal population. If the points plotted on this graph paper can be reasonably fitted by a straight line, it is concluded that the sample came from a normal population. In addition, if sample data points fall in approximately a straight line, the mean and the standard deviation are readily obtained graphically.

$$\int_Z^\infty \frac{1}{2\pi} e^{-x^2} \; dx = \alpha$$

Z_α	.00	.01	.02	.03	.04	.05	.06	.07	.08	.09
0.0	.5000	.4960	.4920	.4880	.4840	.4801	.4761	.4721	.4681	.4641
0.1	.4602	.4562	.4522	.4483	.4443	.4404	.4364	.4325	.4286	.4247
0.2	.4207	.4168	.4129	.4090	.4052	.4013	.3974	.3936	.3897	.3859
0.3	.3821	.3783	.3745	.3707	.3669	.3632	.3594	.3557	.3520	.3483
0.4	.3446	.3409	.3372	.3336	.3300	.3264	.3228	.3192	.3156	.3121
0.5	.3085	.3050	.3015	.2981	.2946	.2912	.2877	.2843	.2810	.2776
0.6	.2743	.2709	.2676	.2643	.2611	.2578	.2546	.2514	.2483	.2451
0.7	.2420	.2389	.2358	.2327	.2296	.2266	.2236	.2206	.2177	.2148
0.8	.2119	.2090	.2061	.2033	.2005	.1977	.1949	.1922	.1894	.1867
0.9	.1841	.1814	.1788	.1762	.1736	.1711	.1685	.1660	.1635	.1611
1.0	.1587	.1562	.1539	.1515	.1492	.1469	.1446	.1423	.1401	.1379
1.1	.1357	.1335	.1314	.1292	.1271	.1251	.1230	.1210	.1190	.1170
1.2	.1151	.1131	.1112	.1093	.1075	.1056	.1038	.1020	.1003	.0985
1.3	.0968	.0951	.0934	.0918	.0901	.0885	.0869	.0853	.0838	.0823
1.4	.0808	.0793	.0778	.0764	.0749	.0735	.0721	.0708	.0694	.0681
1.5	.0668	.0655	.0643	.0630	.0618	.0606	.0594	.0582	.0571	.0559
1.6	.0548	.0537	.0526	.0516	.0505	.0495	.0485	.0475	.0465	.0455
1.7	.0446	.0436	.0427	.0418	.0409	.0401	.0392	.0384	.0375	.0367
1.8	.0359	.0351	.0344	.0336	.0329	.0322	.0314	.0307	.0301	.0294
1.9	.0287	.0281	0274	.0268	.0262	.0256	.0250	.0244	.0239	.0233
2.0	.0228	.0222	.0217	.0212	.0207	.0202	.0197	.0192	.0188	.0183
2.1	.0179	.0174	.0170	.0166	.0162	.0158	.0154	.0150	.0146	.0143
2.2	.0139	.0136	.0132	.0129	.0125	.0122	.0119	.0116	.0113	.0110
2.3	.0107	.0104	.0102	.00990	.00964	.00939	.00914	.00889	.00866	.00842
2.4	.00820	.00798	.00776	.00755	.00734	.00714	.00695	.00676	.00657	.00639
2.5	.00621	.00604	.00587	.00570	.00554	.00539	.00523	.00508	.00494	.00480
2.6	.00466	.00453	.00440	.00427	.00415	.00402	.00391	.00379	.00368	.00357
2.7	.00347	.00336	.00326	.00317	.00307	.00298	.00289	.00280	.00272	.00264
2.8	.00256	.00248	.00240	.00233	.00226	.00219	.00212	.00205	.00199	.00193
2.9	.00187	.00181	.00175	.00169	.00164	.00159	.00154	.00149	.00144	.00139

Z	.0	.1	.2	.3	.4	.5	.6	.7	.8	.9
3	.00135	.0^{3}968	.0^{3}687	.0^{3}483	.0^{3}337	.0^{3}233	.0^{3}159	.0^{3}108	.0^{4}723	.0^{4}481
4	.0^{4}317	.0^{4}207	.0^{4}133	.0^{5}854	.0^{5}541	.0^{5}340	.0^{5}211	.0^{5}130	.0^{6}793	.0^{6}479
5	.0^{6}287	.0^{6}170	.0^{7}996	.0^{7}579	.0^{7}333	.0^{7}190	.0^{7}107	.0^{8}599	.0^{8}332	.0^{8}182
6	.0^{9}987	.0^{9}530	.0^{9}282	.0^{9}149	.0^{10}777	.0^{10}402	.0^{10}206	.0^{10}104	.0^{11}523	.0^{11}260

Fig. 3-9   Areas under the normal curve from Z to ∞

APPENDIX 1
CHAPTER 3

STEP-BY-STEP PROCEDURE FOR PLOTTING ON NORMAL PROBABILITY PAPER

This analysis procedure uses a special graph paper, abbreviated NOPP, for evaluating continuous data. On this graph paper the measured variable, or the midpoint of grouped measurements, is plotted on the linear scale against the accumulative percent plotted on the normal probability scale.

The construction and analysis procedure consists of the following steps:

A. Measure and record the data and calculate the percentages.

   1. Obtain a work sheet similar to that in Figure 3A1-1.
   2. Record cell midpoints in the midpoint column.
   3. Tally the readings on your work sheet.
   4. Compile the frequency in column (1). (See Figure 3A1-2.)
   5. Accumulate column (1) in column (2).
      a. Transfer the first value in column (1) to the same line in column (2).
      b. Add three values: [first value, column (2)] + [first value, column (1)] + [second value, column (1)].
      c. Record this sum on the second line of column (2).
      d. Repeat this U adding with the next lines: [second value, column (2)] + [second value, column (1)] + [third value, column (1)] = [third value, column (2)], etc.
      e. Check: The last value recorded in column (2) must equal twice the sum of column (1); if it does not, an error in calculations has been made (Figure 3A1-3).
   6. Divide each value in column (2) by twice the total of column (1).
   7. Record the quotient, as a percentage, in column (3) (Figure 3A1-4).
      a. Above 90 percent and below 10 percent, round off to the nearest 0.1 percent.
      b. Between 10 percent and 90 percent, round off to the nearest whole percent. (This value is the estimated accumulative percentage of the sample from the extreme measurement up to the corresponding value recorded in the "midpoint" column.)

CALCULATION SHEET FOR NORMAL PROBABILITY PAPER

Part No._____Name_____Specification_____

Mach. No._____Tool_____ Oper._____Dept._____Zero_____

Study Information_____

Unit of Measurement_____

Midpoint	Tally	Frequency Col (1)	Accumulate Col (1) in Col (2)	Col (2) Expressed as a %
Totals				

Fig. 3A1-1

CALCULATION SHEET FOR NORMAL PROBABILITY PAPER

Part No._____Name_____Specification_____

Mach. No._____Tool_____ Oper._____Dept._____Zero_____

Study Information_____

Unit of Measurement_____

Midpoint	Tally	Frequency Col (1)	Accumulate Col (1) in Col (2)	Col (2) Expressed as a %
	Step ②			
	Step ③	Step ④		
0.3685	I	1		
0.3690	II	2		
0.3695	IIII	4		
0.3700	IIII IIII IIII I	16		
0.3705	IIII IIII IIII IIII I	21		
0.3710	IIII IIII IIII IIII IIII IIII	30		
0.3715	IIII IIII II	12		
0.3720	IIII I	6		
0.3725	IIII I	6		
0.3730	II	2		
Totals		100		

Fig. 3A1-2

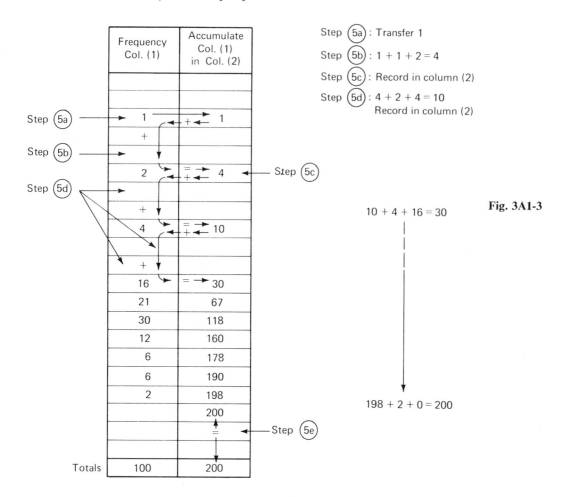

Step (5a) : Transfer 1

Step (5b) : 1 + 1 + 2 = 4

Step (5c) : Record in column (2)

Step (5d) : 4 + 2 + 4 = 10
Record in column (2)

10 + 4 + 16 = 30

198 + 2 + 0 = 200

Fig. 3A1-3

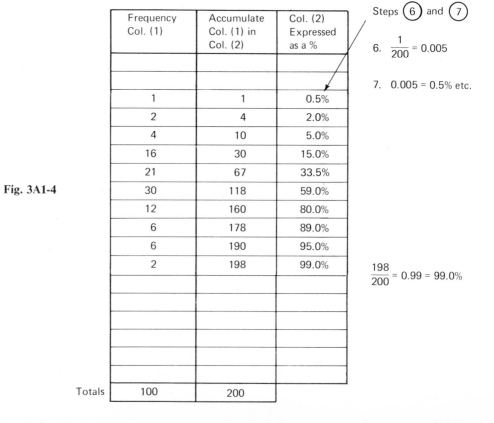

Steps (6) and (7)

6. $\dfrac{1}{200} = 0.005$

7. 0.005 = 0.5% etc.

$\dfrac{198}{200} = 0.99 = 99.0\%$

Fig. 3A1-4

Frequency Col. (1)	Accumulate Col. (1) in Col. (2)	Col. (2) Expressed as a %
1	1	0.5%
2	4	2.0%
4	10	5.0%
16	30	15.0%
21	67	33.5%
30	118	59.0%
12	160	80.0%
6	178	89.0%
6	190	95.0%
2	198	99.0%
Totals 100	200	

B.   Plot the data and determine the line of best fit.

1.   Lay out the measurement or the midpoint value scale on the linear scale of NOPP with values increasing from left to right.

2.   Plot the midpoint values on the linear scale against the corresponding accumulative percentage on the probability scale.

   a.   If the midpoint values recorded on the work sheet increase in value from top to bottom, plot against the "percent under" probability scale (see Figure 3A1-5).

   b.   If the midpoint values decrease from top to bottom, plot against the "percent over" probability scale.

Fig. 3A1-5

NORMAL PROBABILITY PAPER

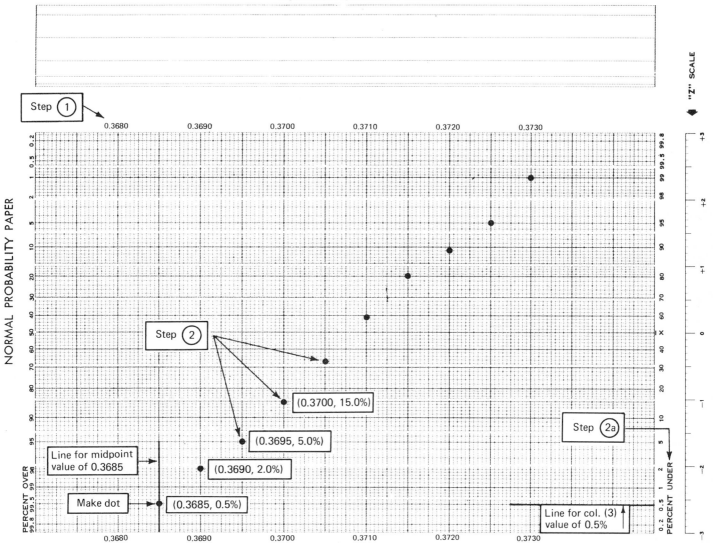

3. Draw a straight line that best fits the plotted points, giving less preference to out-lying points than to the ones in the center (Figure 3A1-6).

4. Find the mean, $\bar{X}$, of the sample as that value where the 50 percent or $\bar{X}$ line intersects the diagonal *line of best fit*.

5. Determine the standard deviation, s, of the sample using the auxiliary Z scale at the right: Divide the difference in the intercepts at $Z = 2$ and $Z = -2$ by the whole number 4 to obtain one standard deviation (see Figure 3A1-6).

Fig. 3A1-6

NORMAL PROBABILITY PAPER

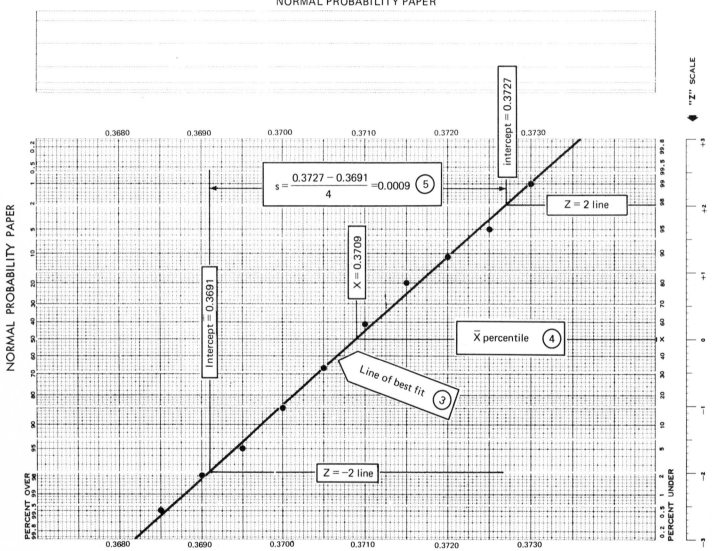

6. Construct the bell-shaped curve at the top.
   a. Locate the intersection of each half Z value (from −3 to +3) on the line of best fit.
   b. Successively project the above intersections on the line of best fit to the lines on the upper grid.
   c. Draw a smooth curve through the projected locations on the upper grid (Figure 3A1-7).

Fig. 3A1-7

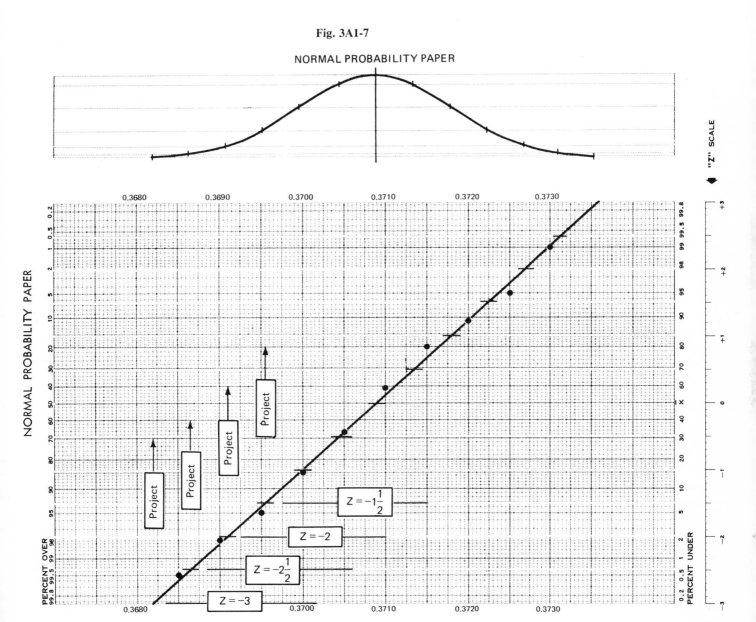

C. Construct confidence bands about the line of best fit.

1. Select a desired confidence factor—90, 95, or 99 percent.
2. Enter column (1) of the accompanying table of factors with the sample size, and from column E select the corresponding value.
3. Multiply the value obtained in step 2 by your value of s, previously determined.
4. On the $\bar{X}$ (or 50 percent) line of NOPP, mark off with an $\times$ the distance calculated in step 2 (E times s) on either side of the sample mean. These points are called $\bar{X}_{max}$ and $\bar{X}_{min}$, respectively (Figure 3A1-8).
5. Divide the sample standard deviation, s, by U, the value obtained in the third column in the table of factors. This is called S_{max}.
6. Divide s by L, obtained from the final column in the table. This is S_{min}.

Fig. 3A1-8

NORMAL PROBABILITY PAPER

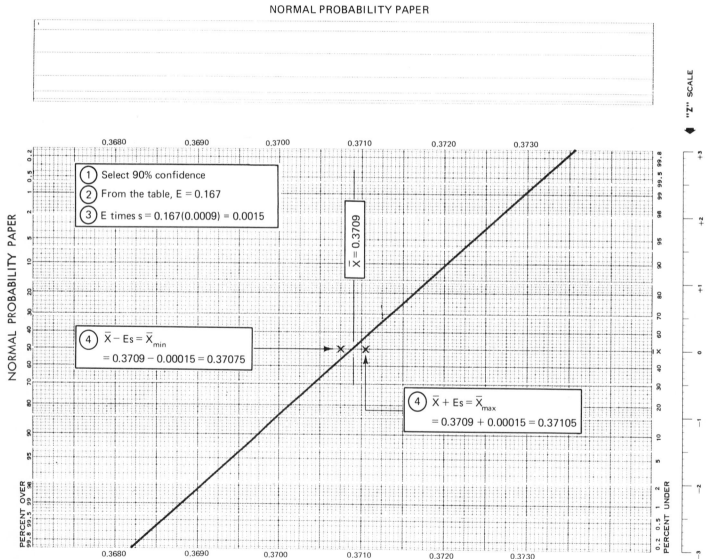

7. Locate the following four points:
   a. Add S_{max} to $\bar{X}_{max}$. Plot this value at the 84th percentile on the "percent under" scale. This is point A.
   b. Add S_{min} to $\bar{X}_{min}$. Plot this value at the 84th percentile on the "percent under" scale. This is point B.
   c. Subtract S_{min} from $\bar{X}_{max}$. Plot this value at the 16th percentile on the "percent under" scale. This is point C.
   d. Subtract S_{max} from $\bar{X}_{min}$. Plot this value at the 16th percentile on the "percent under" scale. This is point D.

8. Construct the confidence bands by drawing the following four straight lines: $\bar{X}_{max}$ through A and through C, and $\bar{X}_{min}$ through B and through D (Figure 3A1-9).

Fig. 3A1-9

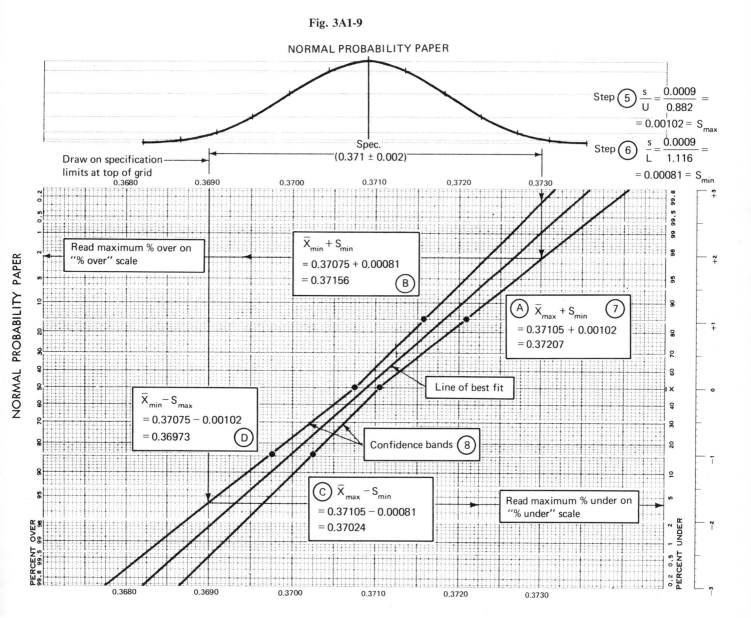

40

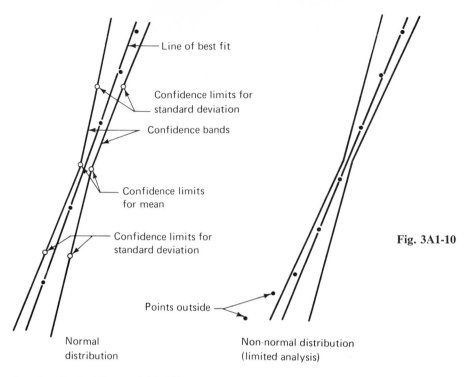

Fig. 3A1-10

Normal
distribution

Non-normal distribution
(limited analysis)

9. Analysis (Figure 3A1-10).

   a. If any of the plotted sample points fall outside the confidence lines, the sampled population is suspected to be nonnormal.

   b. Where this occurs, construct a new line of best fit, compute new confidence bands, and observe the sample plottings.

   c. If the plottings still fall outside the confidence bands after two or three tries, the population is concluded to be nonnormal.

   d. When all plotted points fall within the confidence bands, the population is assumed to be normal with the mean and standard deviation values estimated.

Torque	Cum. %
3	3
4	10
5	16
6	22
7	30
8	41
9	51
10	55
11	62
13	70
14	77
16	83
19	87
20	91
22	93
28	95
29	97
30	99

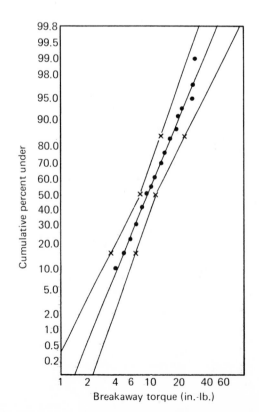

Fig. 3A1-11 Log normal probability plot —visor vertical operating effort

ADDENDUM | PROCEDURE FOR PLOTTING ON LOGARITHMIC NORMAL PROBABILITY PAPER

On logarithmic normal probability paper, LOG-NOPP, the linear scale has been replaced with a logarithmic scale. The measured variable is plotted here on the log scale against the cumulative percent plotted on the probability scale. LOG-NOPP may be used when the plot on NOPP resembles a logarithmic curve.

The construction and analysis procedure is similar to NOPP:

1. Obtain cumulative percentages as with NOPP.
2. Plot the data and determine the line of best fit in a similar manner.
3. The data are analyzed differently.
   a. The measurement value for the 50th percentile, call it $X_{0.50}$, is the mean of log X, but the median of X, $\bar{X}$, cannot be obtained graphically.
   b. S_X cannot be obtained graphically.

$$S_{\log x} = \log (X_{0.50}) - \log (X_{0.16})$$

4. Determine the six points for constructing confidence bands by

$$X_a: \quad \text{antilog} [\log (X_{5.50}) + E \cdot S_{\log x} = \overline{\log X_{\max}}]$$
$$X_b: \quad \text{antilog} [\log (X_{0.50}) - E \cdot S_{\log x} = \overline{\log X_{\min}}]$$
$$A: \quad \text{antilog} [\overline{\log X_{\max}} + S_{\max}]$$
$$B: \quad \text{antilog} [\overline{\log X_{\min}} + S_{\min}]$$
$$C: \quad \text{antilog} [\overline{\log X_{\max}} - S_{\min}]$$
$$D: \quad \text{antilog} [\overline{\log X_{\min}} - S_{\max}]$$

where

$$S_{\max} = \frac{S_{\log x}}{U} \qquad S_{\min} = \frac{S_{\log x}}{L}$$

EXAMPLE

From the graph, the X value at 50 percent, $X_{0.50}$, $= 9.25$ and the X value at 15 percent, $X_{0.16}$, $= 5.10$.

$$\overline{\log X} = \log (9.25) = 0.9661$$
$$S_{\log x} = \log (9.25) - \log (5.10) = 0.9661 - 0.7076$$
$$= 0.2585$$

For 95 percent confidence bands with a sample size of 50,

$$\overline{\log X}_{max} = [0.9661 + (0.284)(0.2585)]$$
$$= (1.0395)$$
$$X_a = \text{antilog } (1.0395) = 10.95$$
$$\overline{\log X}_{min} = [0.9661 - 0.0735]$$
$$= (0.8925)$$
$$X_b = \text{antilog } (0.8925) = 7.807$$
$$S_{max} = \frac{0.2585}{0.803} = 0.322$$
$$S_{min} = \frac{0.2585}{1.197} = 0.216$$

A: $\quad$ antilog $(1.0395 + 0.322) = $ antilog (1.3615)
$$= 22.9$$

B: $\quad$ antilog $(0.8925 + 0.216) = $ antilog (1.1085)
$$= 12.84$$

C: $\quad$ antilog $(1.0395 - 0.216) = $ antilog (0.8235)
$$= 6.66$$

D: $\quad$ antilog $(0.8925 - 0.322) = $ antilog (0.5205)
$$= 3.72$$

Plot the following: $\quad$ At 50 percent X_a and X_b.
$\qquad\qquad\qquad\quad$ At 84 percent, A and B.
$\qquad\qquad\qquad\quad$ At 16 percent, C and D.

Table of Factors for Confidence Interval on NOPP

Sample Size (*n*)	90% Confidence			95% Confidence			99% Confidence		
	E	*U*	*L*	*E*	*U*	*L*	*E*	*U*	*L*
2	4.465	0.0627	1.960	8.986	0.031	2.240	45.019	0.0063	2.807
3	1.686	0.227	1.731	2.484	0.159	1.920	5.730	0.022	2.302
4	1.176	0.342	1.613	1.591	0.268	1.765	2.920	0.154	2.066
5	0.953	0.422	1.525	1.243	0.348	1.666	2.059	0.227	1.930
6	0.823	0.480	1.490	1.050	0.408	1.594	1.646	0.287	1.828
7	0.743	0.523	1.449	0.925	0.454	1.549	1.401	0.336	1.756
8	0.670	0.557	1.419	0.836	0.491	1.512	1.237	0.376	1.703
9	0.620	0.584	1.392	0.769	0.522	1.479	1.118	0.409	1.658
10	0.580	0.608	1.370	0.715	0.548	1.453	1.028	0.438	1.619
11	0.546	0.628	1.353	0.672	0.570	1.432	0.955	0.465	1.587
12	0.518	0.644	1.338	0.635	0.589	1.411	0.897	0.486	1.561
13	0.494	0.660	1.323	0.604	0.605	1.393	0.847	0.506	1.536
14	0.473	0.673	1.313	0.577	0.621	1.378	0.805	0.524	1.514
15	0.455	0.685	1.301	0.554	0.634	1.365	0.769	0.539	1.495
16	0.438	0.696	1.291	0.533	0.646	1.354	0.721	0.554	1.479
17	0.423	0.705	1.282	0.514	0.657	1.342	0.708	0.567	1.464
18	0.410	0.712	1.274	0.497	0.667	1.333	0.683	0.579	1.449
19	0.398	0.722	1.267	0.482	0.676	1.323	0.660	0.589	1.438
20	0.387	0.729	1.259	0.468	0.685	1.316	0.640	0.600	1.425
21	0.376	0.738	1.253	0.455	0.692	1.308	0.620	0.610	1.414
22	0.367	0.743	1.248	0.443	0.700	1.300	0.604	0.618	1.404
23	0.358	0.748	1.241	0.432	0.707	1.293	0.588	0.627	1.395
24	0.350	0.755	1.237	0.422	0.713	1.287	0.573	0.634	1.386
25	0.342	0.758	1.231	0.413	0.719	1.281	0.560	0.642	1.378
26	0.335	0.764	1.228	0.404	0.724	1.274	0.547	0.648	1.370
27	0.328	0.770	1.224	0.396	0.728	1.269	0.535	0.656	1.363
28	0.322	0.774	1.219	0.388	0.735	1.265	0.524	0.661	1.355
29	0.316	0.777	1.214	0.380	0.739	1.261	0.513	0.668	1.350
30	0.310	0.781	1.212	0.373	0.743	1.255	0.503	0.672	1.343
31	0.305	0.785	1.208	0.367	0.748	1.252	0.494	0.678	1.338
32	0.300	0.789	1.205	0.360	0.751	1.247	0.485	0.684	1.332
33	0.295	0.792	1.202	0.355	0.756	1.244	0.477	0.687	1.326
34	0.290	0.796	1.198	0.349	0.759	1.239	0.469	0.692	1.321
35	0.286	0.799	1.196	0.343	0.763	1.237	0.461	0.697	1.317
36	0.282	0.802	1.193	0.338	0.767	1.233	0.454	0.701	1.312
37	0.277	0.804	1.190	0.333	0.769	1.229	0.447	0.705	1.308
38	0.274	0.807	1.188	0.329	0.773	1.227	0.440	0.709	1.304
39	0.270	0.809	1.185	0.324	0.776	1.224	0.434	0.713	1.300
40	0.266	0.812	1.183	0.320	0.779	1.221	0.428	0.716	1.296
41	0.263	0.814	1.181	0.316	0.781	1.218	0.422	0.719	1.292
42	0.260	0.816	1.178	0.312	0.784	1.216	0.417	0.722	1.289
43	0.257	0.818	1.176	0.308	0.787	1.213	0.411	0.725	1.284
44	0.253	0.821	1.174	0.304	0.789	1.210	0.406	0.730	1.281
45	0.250	0.823	1.173	0.300	0.792	1.208	0.401	0.732	1.278

Table of Factors for Confidence Interval on NOPP (Continued)

Sample Size (n)	90% Confidence			95% Confidence			99% Confidence		
	E	U	L	E	U	L	E	U	L
46	0.248	0.825	1.171	0.297	0.794	1.206	0.396	0.735	1.276
47	0.245	0.826	1.168	0.294	0.797	1.203	0.392	0.737	1.272
48	0.242	0.829	1.167	0.290	0.799	1.201	0.387	0.741	1.269
49	0.240	0.830	1.165	0.287	0.801	1.199	0.383	0.743	1.266
50	0.237	0.832	1.163	0.284	0.803	1.197	0.379	0.745	1.263
55	0.226	0.840	1.156	0.270	0.812	1.188	0.360	0.758	1.251
60	0.216	0.847	1.149	0.258	0.820	1.180	0.344	0.768	1.240
65	0.206	0.853	1.143	0.246	0.827	1.173	0.325	0.777	1.230
70	0.198	0.859	1.138	0.237	0.833	1.166	0.314	0.785	1.222
75	0.192	0.864	1.134	0.229	0.839	1.161	0.304	0.792	1.214
80	0.186	0.868	1.129	0.222	0.844	1.156	0.295	0.799	1.207
85	0.180	0.872	1.125	0.216	0.849	1.151	0.286	0.805	1.201
90	0.175	0.875	1.122	0.210	0.853	1.146	0.279	0.810	1.195
95	0.171	0.879	1.118	0.204	0.857	1.142	0.272	0.815	1.190
100	0.167	0.882	1.116	0.199	0.861	1.139	0.266	0.820	1.185
125	0.147	0.895	1.109	0.175	0.876	1.130	0.230	0.838	1.171
150	0.134	0.904	1.099	0.160	0.886	1.118	0.210	0.852	1.155
175	0.124	0.911	1.091	0.148	0.895	1.109	0.195	0.863	1.143
200	0.116	0.917	1.085	0.138	0.901	1.102	0.182	0.872	1.134
225	0.110	0.922	1.080	0.131	0.907	1.095	0.172	0.879	1.126
250	0.104	0.926	1.076	0.124	0.912	1.091	0.163	0.885	1.119
275	0.099	0.929	1.072	0.118	0.916	1.086	0.155	0.891	1.113
300	0.095	0.933	1.069	0.113	0.920	1.082	0.149	0.896	1.108
325	0.091	0.935	1.066	0.109	0.923	1.079	0.143	0.899	1.104
350	0.088	0.937	1.064	0.105	0.926	1.076	0.138	0.903	1.100
375	0.085	0.940	1.062	0.101	0.928	1.073	0.133	0.906	1.096
400	0.082	0.941	1.060	0.098	0.931	1.071	0.129	0.909	1.093
425	0.080	0.943	1.058	0.095	0.933	1.069	0.125	0.912	1.091
450	0.078	0.945	1.056	0.092	0.935	1.067	0.121	0.915	1.088
475	0.075	0.946	1.054	0.090	0.936	1.065	0.118	0.917	1.085
500	0.074	0.948	1.053	0.088	0.938	1.070	0.115	0.919	1.083

APPENDIX 2
CHAPTER 3

MIRROR IMAGE
TECHNIQUE

The mean and standard deviation can be calculated for any data set regardless of what shape it has. For example, $\bar{X}$ and s could be determined for any distribution in Figure 1-11. Using these two statistics, however, to evaluate a distribution which is not relatively normal may give results which are misleading. When the nonnormality existing is skewness, a technique that transforms a nonsymmetrical distribution to a symmetrical one, called the *mirror image* method, is extremely useful.

The data in Figure 3A2-1 will be used to illustrate the differences that can be obtained, following first the procedure in Chapter 1 and then applying the mirror image technique and comparing results. In each case the percent beyond specifications will be estimated.

Fig. 3A2-1 Camshaft runout data; specification: 0.002 inch maximum

T.I.R.	Tally	Frequency
0.000	JHT	5
0.001	JHT JHT JHT JHT JHT II	27
0.002	JHT JHT II	12
0.003	JHT	5
0.004	I	1
		—
		50

HISTOGRAM

The data from Figure 3A2-1 are shown in histogram form in Figure 3A2-2. The shape would tend to indicate that the data might be nonnormal. This is generally characteristic of runout data, since readings less than zero are not possible. A side comment should be made concerning the number of class intervals shown. With 50 readings, 8 intervals are specified from Figure 1A1-1. It would appear that the measuring equipment least count is 0.001 inch, which is unusual with a 0.002-inch specification. Normal practice would dictate one-tenth of 0.002 inch for least count, or 0.0002 inch. This could have an effect on the distribution shape. Referring to the

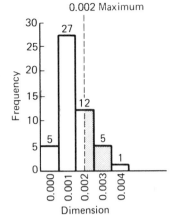

Fig. 3A2-2 Histogram—camshaft runout

histogram, note the shaded area beyond 0.002 inch. Assuming that the 12 frequency in the 0.002-inch class is distributed equally over the class, then one-half the frequency, or 6, would be beyond the specification. This plus the 5 in the 0.003-inch class and the 1 in the 0.004-inch class gives 12 out of 50, or 24 percent beyond specification. This is a rough approximation, not recommended for actual practice. It indicates what exists in the sample but not necessarily what may be true for the population.

CALCULATING AVERAGE AND STANDARD DEVIATION

The average and standard deviation for these data are determined as follows:

Class Interval	Tally	f	d	fd	fd^2
0.000	1111	5	-1	-5	5
0.001	1111 1111 1111 1111 1111 11	27	0	0	0
0.002	1111 1111 11	12	$+1$	$+12$	12
0.003	1111	5	$+2$	$+10$	20
0.004	1	1	$+3$	$+3$	9
	Totals	50		20	46

$$\bar{X} = A + \frac{i \sum fd}{n}$$

$$= 0.001 + \frac{(0.001)(20)}{50}$$

$$= 0.001 + 0.0004$$

$$= 0.0014$$

$$s = i \frac{\sqrt{\sum fd^2 - (\sum fd)^2/n}}{n-1}$$

$$= 0.001 \frac{\sqrt{46 - (20)^2/50}}{50 - 1}$$

$$= (0.001)(0.8806)$$

$$= 0.00088$$

PERCENT BEYOND SPECIFICATION

The preceding values calculated for the average and standard deviation can be used to estimate the percent of the camshafts expected to exceed 0.002-inch runout. This involves calculating the standardized normal deviate:

$$Z = \frac{\text{Specification limit} - \bar{X}}{s}$$

For the camshaft data,

$$Z = \frac{0.002 - 0.0014}{0.00088} = 0.68$$

Referring to the normal area tables,

$$P[X > 0.002] = P[Z > 0.68] = 0.2483$$

The estimated percent beyond specifications, then, is 24.83 percent, essentially the same value estimated by counting. The similarity should not be relied on, however. This technique also assumes that the data are distributed normally, which, as previously stated, is questionable. Figure 3A2-3 shows the analysis schematically.

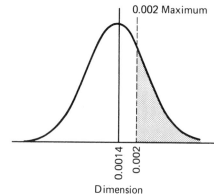

Fig. 3A2-3 Normal distribution—camshaft runout

PROCEDURE FOR MIRROR IMAGE METHOD

As stated earlier, the mirror image method transforms a nonsymmetrical into a symmetrical distribution. This is accomplished by generating a new distribution about the zero origin class interval (mode) and then calculating the mean and standard deviation in the usual manner.

Step 1. Select the class interval with the greatest frequency (mode class) and establish it as the zero origin class *A*.

Step 2. Duplicate the cell frequencies, from the zero origin class in the skewness direction, on the nonskewed side of the zero origin class. This results in a symmetric frequency distribution table. What was the distribution's nonskewed side is now a *mirror image* of the skewed side. (See Figure 3A2-4.)

Step 3. Calculate the mean and standard deviation for the new distribution(s).

Fig. 3A2-4 Mirror image—camshaft runout

Original Data		Mirror Image		
Midpoint	Tally	Midpoint	Tally	d
0.000	ЖТ	−0.002	I	−3
0.001	ЖТ ЖТ ЖТ ЖТ ЖТ II	−0.001	ЖТ	−2
0.002	ЖТ ЖТ II	0.000	ЖТ ЖТ II	−1
0.003	ЖТ	0.001	ЖТ ЖТ ЖТ ЖТ ЖТ II	0 (Origin cell)
0.004	I	0.002	ЖТ ЖТ II	+1
		0.003	ЖТ	+2
		0.004	I	+3
Midpoint	Tally	Midpoint	Tally	d
0.000	ЖТ	0.000	ЖТ	−1
0.001	ЖТ ЖТ ЖТ ЖТ ЖТ II	0.001	ЖТ ЖТ ЖТ ЖТ ЖТ II	0
0.002	ЖТ ЖТ II	0.002	ЖТ	+1
0.003	ЖТ			
0.004	I			

Class Interval	Tally	f	d	fd	fd^2
−0.002	1	1	−3	−3	9
−0.001	1111	5	−2	−10	20
0.000	1111 1111 11	12	−1	−12	12
0.001	1111 1111 1111 1111 1111 11	27	0	0	0
0.002	1111 1111 11	12	+1	+12	12
0.003	1111	5	+2	+10	20
0.004	1	1	+3	+3	9
	Totals	63		0	82

$$\bar{X} = A + \frac{i(\sum fd)}{n} = 0.001 + \frac{(0.001)(0)}{64} = 0.001$$

$$s_1 = i\sqrt{\frac{\sum fd^2 - (\sum fd)^2/n}{n-1}} = (0.001)\sqrt{\frac{82 - (0)^2/63}{62}}$$

$$= 0.00115 = 0.0012$$

Class Interval	Tally	f	d	fd	fd^2
0.000	1111	5	−1	−5	5
0.001	1111 1111 1111 1111 1111 11	27	0	0	0
0.002	1111	5	+1	+5	5
	Totals	37		0	10

$$\bar{X} = A + \frac{i(\sum fd)}{n} = 0.001 + \frac{(0.001)(0)}{37} = 0.001$$

$$s_2 = i\sqrt{\frac{\sum fd^2 - (\sum fd)^2/n}{n-1}} = 0.001\sqrt{\frac{10 - (0)^2/37}{36}}$$

$$= 0.0005$$

The second standard deviation was calculated to demonstrate that this can be done for each side. For the example problem, only s_1 will be needed. As before, another estimate can now be made for the percent of the camshafts expected to exceed the 0.002-inch specification:

$$Z = \frac{\text{Specification limit} - \bar{X}}{s}$$

or

$$Z = \frac{0.002 - 0.001}{0.0012} = 0.83$$

Referring to the normal area tables,

$$P[X > 0.002] = P[Z > 0.83] = 0.2033$$

The estimated percent beyond specifications is now 20.33 percent. This compares to the approximately 24 percent estimated by the two previous methods. However, this last estimate should be more accurate since the mirror image distribution more closely resembles the normal curve. This is shown schematically in Figure 3A2-5.

Fig. 3A2-5 Normal distribution—camshaft runout

CHAPTER FOUR | ANALYSIS TECHNIQUES FOR DISCRETE DATA

The laws or rules used in making probability predictions from samples differ with the data type. When the sample observations are classified as discrete data, that is, observations which can vary only in jumps as in counting, a discrete probability distribution is used for predicting. Discrete data are obtained when each successive evaluation is classified as belonging to two (or perhaps more) possible outcomes and the number in each classification is recorded. Quality conformance measurements resulting in two outcomes are acceptable or unacceptable (good or bad). In reliability evaluation, the outcomes are designated success or failure. Current word usage, in either case, is tending toward *conforming* and *nonconforming*. The variation encountered when the sample outcomes are tabulated is properly described by a discrete probability rule or distribution. The two discrete distributions most often used are the binomial and the Poisson.

BINOMIAL PROBABILITY DISTRIBUTION

The binomial distribution is used when the measured data result from independent evaluations, where each measurement results in either a success or a failure and where the true probability of success remains constant from sample to sample.

Examples are

1. A plating machine operator checks five finished pieces from a batch. In repeated five-piece samples the number of acceptable parts will vary. What probabilities can be associated with the different possible outcomes?

2. Eight window lift mechanisms are each required to cycle 50,000 times. The number failing is the observed outcome. What is the probability of 0 (or 1, or 2, . . . , 8) failures?

3. There are 10 new engineers assigned to the engineering department. Each Friday, one engineer is chosen by lot to work overtime on Saturday. Of these engineers a fixed proportion have had considerable training in statistical techniques. On three Saturdays during the past two months a statistical analysis was necessary. Considering only these Saturdays, what is the probability that statistically trained engineers were available all three (or exactly two, or just one, or zero) times?

In the preceding examples, each sample required several identical repeated actions called trials. In the plating inspection example, a trial involved inspecting a single piece. The outcome was an acceptable or an unacceptable piece. In the second example, a trial was a reliability test on one mechanism. The outcome was a success or a failure. In the third example, a trial was selecting one engineer to work overtime. The outcome was an engineer with or without statistical training.

To qualify as a binomial experiment, a sample must have four properties:

1. A number of trials specified.

2. The outcome for each trial, a "success" or a "failure."

3. The probability of "success" identical for all trials.

4. Each trial independent.

These properties can be explained in relation to the previous examples.

1. In most applications, the sample size is fixed in advance. Thus, if a five-piece sample from the plater is always examined or an eight-piece sample is always placed on reliability test, the specified unsuccessful outcome probabilities can be predicted. An alternative procedure where the sample size is *not* fixed and where binomial rules will *not* apply would be the following: Sample until an unacceptable piece is found. In this case the sample size would obviously vary.

2. Binomial trials imply two outcomes, for the word *binomial* means "two names." The outcome for each observation (evaluation or inspection) must fall into one of two categories, although the trial may be repeated many times. Each plated part is either acceptable or unacceptable; each mechanism either survives or fails.

3. For each successive trial, the probability of a failure (or an unacceptable piece, or an engineer not trained in statistics) must remain the same. The symbol p is used to represent this probability, whether or not its true value is known. For a given manufacturing process, the fraction of unacceptable plated pieces or the number of mechanisms failing a known test should be a constant as long as the process has not changed.

4. If trials are independent, a compound probability can be calculated by multiplying the individual probabilities. Commonly expressed, independent trials have no relationship to each other; a previous outcome will not affect a subsequent outcome. In the third example, the engineer's selection by lot assures independence.

A binomial experiment could be conducted to compare actual sampling results against what might be expected based on past experience. A predetermined sample size would be selected (five parts, eight mechanisms, three Saturdays) and the total failures observed (unacceptable plated pieces, test failures, Saturdays when a statistical analyst was not available). To predict what would be anticipated in the trial outcomes requires a formula for calculating the probability for exactly zero (or one, or two, . . . , or n) failures, assuming that p, the failure probability for an individual trial, is constant.

Using the plating example as an illustration, suppose that an inspector is sampling from a tub containing 10,000 pieces and further that historical information indicates that 90 percent are acceptable and 10 percent are unacceptable. If a single piece is drawn randomly from this tub, then

$$P[\text{1 failure or unacceptable piece}] = 0.10 = p$$

$$P[\text{1 success}] = 0.90 = 1 - 0.10 = 1 - p$$

If two successive random draws are made, the probability that both pieces will be unacceptable can be determined using the multiplication law of probability:

$$P[\text{2 failures}] = P[\text{1 failure and 1 failure}] = 0.1 \times 0.1$$
$$= 0.01 = p^2$$

Likewise,

$$P[\text{5 failures}] = 0.1^5 = 0.00001 = p^5$$

Similarly, the probability for two successful draws is

$$P[\text{2 successes}] = 0.9 \times 0.9$$
$$= 0.81 = (1 - p)^2$$

Furthermore, the probability of two successes or two failures in two draws can be determined using the addition law, since an individual piece cannot be acceptable and unacceptable at the same time. Therefore a success and a failure are called mutually exclusive outcomes for $P[\text{success and failure on a single draw}] = 0$:

$$P[\text{2 failures or 2 successes}] = P[\text{2 failures}] + P[\text{2 successes}]$$
$$= 0.01 + 0.81 = 0.82$$
$$= p^2 + (1 - p)^2$$

Then $1.00 - 0.82$ represents the probability that the two draws are not alike. But this difference can happen in two ways: a success first and then a failure, or a failure and then a success. This probability is then

$$P[(\text{1 success and 1 failure}) \text{ or } (\text{1 failure and 1 success})]$$
$$= P[\text{1 success and 1 failure}] + P[\text{1 failure and 1 success}]$$
$$= P[\text{1 success}] \times P[\text{1 failure}] + P[\text{1 failure}] \times P[\text{1 success}]$$
$$= 2 \{P[\text{1 failure}] \times P[\text{1 success}]\}$$
$$= 2 \times 0.1 \times 0.9 = 0.18$$

There are thus three possible outcome combinations when two successive draws are made. Their probabilities can be summed and written as

$$0.01 + 0.18 + 0.81 = 1.00 \quad \text{which is also } 0.1^2 + 2(0.1 \times 0.9) + 0.9^2$$
$$= p^2 + 2p(1 - p) + (1 - p)^2$$

When $1 - p$ is called q, this statement can be recognized as $(p + q)^2$. In like manner, if three successive draws are made, the various outcomes could be three failures, or two failures and one success in three orderings, or one failure and two successes in three orderings, or three successes. Then the binomial expression $(p + q)^3$ applies:

$$(p + q)^3 = p^3 + 3p^2q + 3pq^2 + q^3$$
$$= p^3 + 3p^2(1 - p) + 3p(1 - p)^2 + (1 - p)^3$$
$$= 0.1^3 + 3 \times 0.1^2 \times 0.9 + 3 \times 0.1 \times 0.9^2 + 0.9^3$$
$$= 1.000$$

A general formula for the binomial expands $(p + q)^n$. Each term in the expansion is the probability for a specific combination of successes and failures. Let X represent the failure per sample. X is then a variable and can be zero (or one, or two, ..., or n) if the experiment is repeated n times. The probability formula for calculating X failures in n when the single failure probability p is constant follows:

$$P[X \text{ failures}] = \frac{n!}{X!(n-X)!}p^x(1-p)^{n-x}$$

In this formula $n!$ is read n factorial and means

$$n! = n \times (n-1) \times (n-2) \times (n-3) \times \cdots \times 3 \times 2 \times 1$$

For example,

$$5! = 5 \times 4 \times 3 \times 2 \times 1 = 120$$

If $n = 8$ and $X = 5$,

$$(n - X)! = (8 - 5)! = 3! = 3 \times 2 \times 1 = 6$$

The expression $n!/[X!(n-X)!]$ determines the ways in which X failures and $n - X$ successes can be drawn.

To illustrate the general formula application, consider again the plating situation. Calculating the probability that zero unacceptable items would occur in five pieces,

$$P[0 \text{ failures}] = \frac{5!}{0!(5-0)!} \times 0.10^0 \times 0.90^5$$
$$= 1 \times 1 \times 0.59049 = 0.59049$$

While these probabilities are relatively easy to calculate for small n values and convenient p values such as 0.5, they are laborious to evaluate in most situations. It must also be recognized that n can take on any value from one to infinity and that p varies between zero and one. Binomial tables, which simplify obtaining these probabilities, are available but not readily so. However, due to the many values which n and p can assume, a relatively complete table results in a large volume. For illustrative purposes, some tabulated binomial values (1,000 times the probability) appear in Figure 4-1.

Fig. 4-1 Binomial probabilities

n	x	.01	0.5	.10	.20	.30	.40	p .50	.60	.70	.80	.90	.95	.99	x
2	0	980	902	810	640	490	360	250	160	090	040	010	002	0+	0
	1	020	095	180	320	420	480	500	480	420	320	180	095	020	1
	2	0+	002	010	040	090	160	250	360	490	640	810	902	980	2
3	0	970'	857	729	512	343	216	125	064	027	008	001	0+	0+	0
	1	029	135	243	384	441	432	375	288	189	096	027	007	0+	1
	2	0+	007	027	096	189	288	375	432	441	384	243	135	029	2
	3	0+	0+	001	008	027	064	125	216	343	512	729	857	970	3
4	0	961	815	656	410	240	130	000	026	008	002	0+	0+	0+	0
	1	039	171	292	410	412	346	250	154	076	026	004	0+	0+	1
	2	001	014	048	154	265	346	375	346	265	154	049	014	001	2
	3	0+	0+	004	026	076	154	250	346	412	410	292	171	039	3
	4	0+	0+	0+	002	008	026	062	130	240	410	656	815	961	4
5	0	951	774	590	328	168	078	031	010	002	0+	0+	0+	0+	0
	1	048	204	328	410	360	259	156	077	028	006	0+	0+	0+	1
	2	001	021	073	205	309	346	312	230	132	051	008	001	0+	2
	3	0+	001	008	051	132	230	312	346	309	205	073	021	001	3
	4	0+	0+	0+	006	028	077	156	259	360	410	328	204	048	4
	5	0+	0+	0+	0+	002	010	031	078	168	328	590	774	951	5

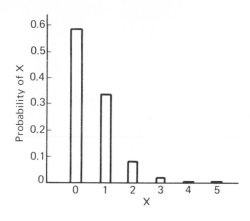

Fig. 4-2 Plated part failures

With $n = 5$ and $p = 0.1$, the individual probabilities for $X = 0, 1, 2, 3, 4$, or 5 are 0.590, 0.328, 0.073, 0.008, 0+, and 0+, respectively. (See Figure 4-2.) It will be recalled that the actual value for $X = 5$ was 0.00001 and that for $X = 0$ it was 0.59049.

Figure 4-3 portrays additional examples showing how the binomial distribution changes when n and p vary.

It will be recalled that the normal distribution had two parameters, the mean (μ) and the standard deviation (σ). The binomial distribution also has a mean and standard deviation. The defining parameters in this case are n and p. The mean or average is n times p (np), and the standard deviation is $\sqrt{np(1 - p)}$. Chapter 6 will amplify their application with respect to attribute control charts, and Chapter 7 will use this distribution in connection with sampling plans.

Fig. 4-3 Binomial distributions (vertical axis is probability of X)

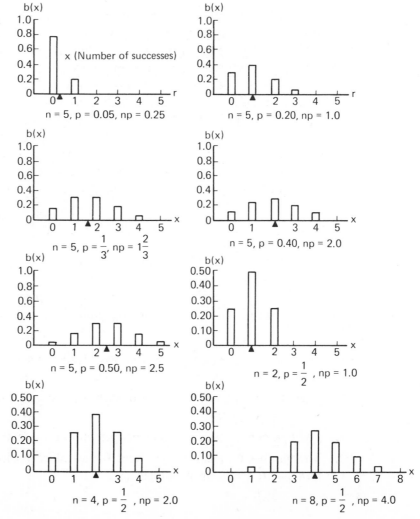

BINOMIAL PROBABILITY PAPER

A useful shortcut in statistical analysis is a graphical solution. Graphical methods are faster, have the advantage of visually presenting the facts, and are sufficiently accurate for most practical purposes. Special graph paper called binomial probability paper, or BIPP, has been devised by Frederick Mosteller and John Tukey. The procedure for using BIPP is included in Appendix 1 to this chapter. Applications are presented in the chapters on attribute control charts and sampling.

POISSON PROBABILITY DISTRIBUTION

The Poisson distribution is used when, within the area of opportunity specified, theoretically infinite "successes" (or failures) can occur. For example, if lightning flashes in a storm having an unspecified duration were counted, the *area of opportunity* is the storm itself, and the lightning flashes theoretically could be infinite in number. However, the area of opportunity could be changed to a sufficiently small time interval such that the result would be either zero or one flash within that interval. A different example for an area of opportunity could be a radiator core, which when water-tested would not leak or would have one or more leaks. Likewise, while the area is the radiator core, this could be reduced to an extent such that each unit would contain zero or one leak. In both cases, when the unit (time or area) is made sufficiently small, the occurrences divided by the total units would represent a fraction defective. It should be realized that this is not only impractical but that also the information generated would usually be worthless. It is impractical because the manipulation of data could involve an enormous "cut and try" analysis after the initial data collection to have the unit small enough to either contain or not contain the flash or leak. The worthlessness can be attributed to the fact that the next storm or core might require a smaller unit to accommodate its particular data. Therefore the simpler approach is to treat both the radiator and the storm as a unit. This is where the Poisson probability distribution has its applicability: merely counting the occurrences within a specified area of opportunity. In summary, this distribution is used when there are a great many opportunities for something to occur, yet the likelihood for any given opportunity is relatively small, and when the average occurrence is constant for a specified area of opportunity. The area of opportunity may not only be time or physical area, as mentioned, but can also be such characteristics as weight, volume, or length. The formula for the Poisson distribution is

$$P[X \text{ occurrences}] = \frac{m^x}{X!}e^{-m}$$

where m = average number of occurrences per unit,
$e = 2.71828\ldots.$

Note that n is not involved in the formula; thus the probability for all possible outcomes is calculable when the average occurrences (m) is known. Examples where the Poisson distribution applies include

1. The number of errors in the window-raising mechanism alignment on each four-door automobile.
2. The number of paint drops per 0.00015 square inch (the microscope aperture) in electrostatic painting.
3. The number of lost-time accidents per month in a manufacturing plant.
4. The number of vacancies per year for an office position in a business due either to retirement, death, or incompetency.

In these examples the possible alignment errors, or paint drops, or lost-time accidents, or vacancies per year are potentially large but tend to occur with a relatively low frequency. The area of opportunity within which the event could occur remains unchanged: one four-door automobile, 0.00015 square inch, 1 month, 1 year.

Example 2 referred to paint drops per unit area. The data collected with the calculation for its mean are shown in Figure 4-4.

Number of Paint Drops (X)	Frequency (f)	fx
0	7	0
1	21	21
2	24	48
3	27	81
4	16	64
5	11	55
6	8	48
7	3	21
8	1	8
9	2	18
Totals	120	364

$$m = \frac{\Sigma\, fx}{\Sigma\, f} = \frac{364}{120} = 3.09 = 3.1$$

Fig. 4-4 Paint drop data

To illustrate the formula application, the probability that $X = 2$ is calculated as follows, based on the mean (3.1) for the data in Figure 4-4:

$$P[X = 2] = \frac{(3.1)^2}{2!} \times 2.71828^{-3.1}$$

$$= \frac{(9.61)(0.045049)}{1 \times 2} = 0.216461$$

While this is simpler than the binomial calculation, it is still laborious when numerous probabilities are required. Poisson probability tables are less extensive than relatively complete binomial tables, and a set is included in Appendix 2 to this chapter. Their use can be demonstrated using the paint drop data. The specific mean (3.1) is not found in the table; therefore interpolation between 3.0 and 3.2 is required. The theoretical probabilities are shown in Figure 4-5.

Fig. 4-5 Poisson probabilities for paint drop data

Number of Occurrences (X)	P [X Occurrences]
0	0.0455
1	0.1395
2	0.2165 (0.216461 calculated)
3	0.2235
4	0.1730
5	0.1075
6	0.055
7	0.025
8	0.0095
9	0.0035
10	0.0015

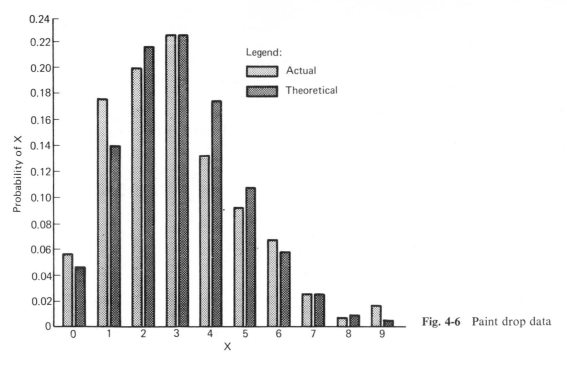

Fig. 4-6 Paint drop data

For comparative purposes the Poisson and observed probabilities are plotted in histogram form in Figure 4-6.

The binomial distribution has two parameters n and p, with mean np and standard deviation $\sqrt{np(1-p)}$. The Poisson distribution, however, has only one parameter, which is the average number of occurrences per unit, m. The standard deviation is simply $\sqrt{m}$. Chapter 6 will amplify this with respect to attribute control charts, and Chapter 9 will use this distribution in connection with sampling plans.

POISSON APPROXIMATION TO THE BINOMIAL

The Poisson distribution is used extensively when approximations to binomial probabilities are suitable. These are obtained by equating the binomial mean to the Poisson mean:

$$\text{Binomial mean, } np = \text{Poisson mean, } m$$

This approximation is not always applicable but is considered justifiably accurate whenever

$$p \text{ is less than } 0.1 \ (p \leq 0.1)$$

and

$$n \text{ times } p \text{ is less than } 5 \ (np \leq 5)$$

Using the plating example cited earlier, the sample size was 5 and the mean (p) was 0.10. This gives $n \times p$ equal to 5×0.1 or 0.5, which is m. Although both conditions specified above are not theoretically satisfied, the table probabilities for the binomial and Poisson distributions given in Figure 4-7 will illustrate its application.

As can be observed, the differences in probabilities are relatively small, and, since both conditions were marginally met, the Poisson distribution can be considered sufficiently accurate for all practical purposes.

Fig. 4-7 Binomial and Poisson comparison

| X | Probability of X | |
	Binomial	Poisson
0	0.590	0.607
1	0.328	0.303
2	0.073	0.076
3	0.008	0.012
4	0.0+	0.002
5	0.0+	0.0+

NORMAL APPROXIMATION TO THE BINOMIAL

The advantage in using the normal distribution as an approximation to the binomial distribution is that normal tables are readily available and simple. Similar to the Poisson use, these avoid the lengthy calculations involved in obtaining the binomial probabilities. This approximation is applicable when

p is greater than or equal to 0.1 ($p \geq 0.1$)

and

n times p is greater than or equals 5 ($np \geq 5$)

Since the binomial is a discrete distribution and the normal is continuous, a correction for discontinuity should be made to improve the approximation accuracy. To find the probability for X or less, set

$$Z = \frac{\dfrac{X + 0.5}{n} - p}{\sigma_p} = \frac{\dfrac{X + 0.5}{n} - p}{\sqrt{\dfrac{p(1-p)}{n}}}$$

To find the probability for X or more, set

$$Z = \frac{\dfrac{X - 0.5}{n} - p}{\sigma_p} = \frac{\dfrac{X - 0.5}{n} - p}{\sqrt{\dfrac{p(1-p)}{n}}}$$

APPENDIX 1 CHAPTER 4 | STEP-BY-STEP PROCEDURE FOR PLOTTING ON BINOMIAL PROBABILITY PAPER

Binomial probability paper, or BIPP, is a special graph paper devised for use with discrete data. On this paper it is customary to plot the number of successes (or conforming or acceptable outcomes) on the horizontal axis and the number of failures (or nonconforming outcomes or defectives) along the vertical axis. Both axes of this graph paper are scaled with the square root of the plotted number.

In plotting BIPP:

1. Plot the true probability of success, that fraction of success obtained from long-run testing (call it the population parameter, P), as a straight line from the origin through the point (100 times P, $100Q$). $Q = 1.00 - P$ (see Figure 4A1-1). The line thus plotted represents all combinations of points for any sample size, n, that have this fraction of P success.

2. Plot the sample results as a small triangle with coordinates at three points (Figure 4A1-2):
   a. (Number of successes, number of failures), i.e., (s, f).
   b. $(s + 1, f)$.
   c. $(s, f + 1)$.
   (This plotting is a continuity adjustment which can be ignored for large sample sizes.)

3. Probabilities on the graph are measured as perpendicular distances between points and lines and compared with the scale at the top of the graph entitled "probability scale" (Figure 4A1-1). The relationships between probabilities and scale values are shown in the following table:

Associated Probabilities

Scale Value	Probability
1.28	0.20
1.64	0.10
1.96	0.05
2.33	0.02
2.57	0.01
2.81	0.005
3.09	0.002
3.29	0.001

Fig. 4A1-1

BINOMIAL PROBABILITY PAPER

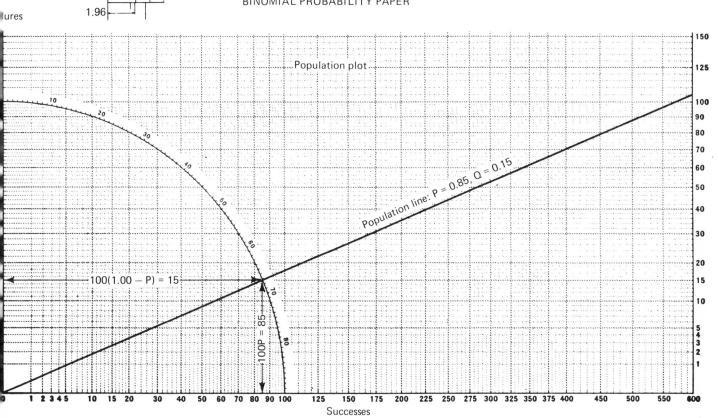

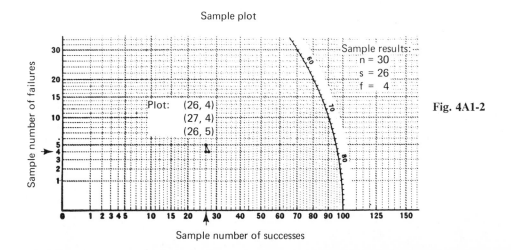

Fig. 4A1-2

SAMPLE PROBLEMS ON BIPP

The solutions to many problems can be obtained quite accurately through graphical means on BIPP. A sharp pencil and a good straightedge are the necessary tools for precision.

EXAMPLE 1

A test has been averaging 4 percent failures. A random sample of 25 is found to contain 3 failures. Is this sufficient evidence to judge that the parts are worse than average?
Steps in solution:

1. Decide on the risk level or error allowable and mark off the associated distance on the upper probability scale.

2. Plot the test average as the parameter by drawing a line from the origin through the point [(100 × 0.96), (100 × 0.04)].

3. Plot the sample result: the points (22, 3), (23, 3), and (22, 4).

4. Measure the perpendicular distance from the midpoint of the hypotenuse of the sample triangle to the line.

5. Compare this distance with that distance previously marked along the probability scale. If the measured perpendicular distance is greater than the marked probability scale distance, conclude that the parts are worse than average; otherwise, conclude that no real change has occurred (Figure 4A1-3).

Fig. 4A1-3

BINOMIAL PROBABILITY PAPER

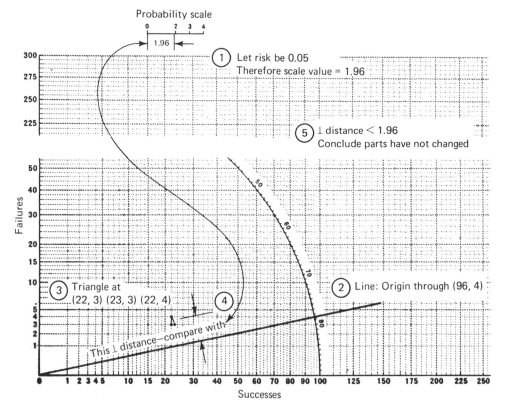

60

EXAMPLE 2

A process was sampled before and after a modified design was placed into effect. Before the change the sample showed 15 (X_1) nonconforming from the sample of 200 (n_1). After the change a sample of 100 (n_2) yielded only 5 (X_2) nonconforming. Has the design alteration significantly changed the rate of nonconformance?

Steps in solution:

1. Decide on the risk level or error allowable and mark off the associated distance on the upper scale.

2. The population line will be associated with an average fraction nonconformance, p. Plot the population line from the origin through the points $[(n_1 + n_2) - (X_1 + X_2)]$ and $(X_1 + X_2)$.

3. Plot the first sample point.

4. Plot the second sample point.

5. Find the sum of the perpendicular distances of the points to the population line. Multiply this sum by $\frac{1}{\sqrt{2}} = (0.7)$.

6. Compare this resultant, 0.7 sum, with the distance marked on the upper scale. If the 0.7 sum distance is greater than the scale distance, assume that the design change has a significant effect. If 0.7 sum is less, conclude that no change has occurred (Figure 4A1-4).

Fig. 4A1-4

BINOMIAL PROBABILITY PAPER

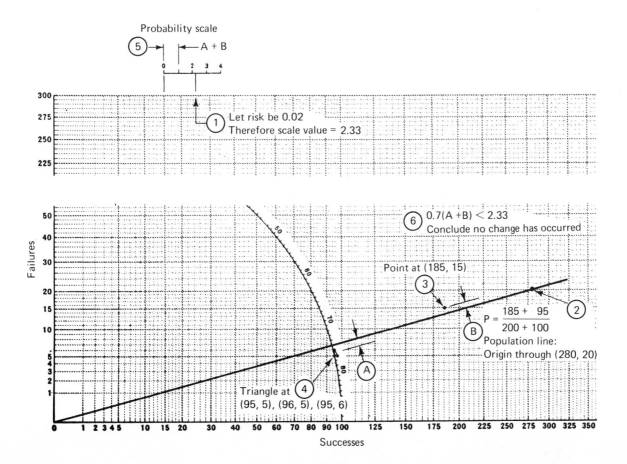

EXAMPLE 3

A life test of 8,000 cycles on a sample of 30 pieces resulted in 2 failures. What are confidence limits for the true probability of failure, Q? (Confidence limits define an interval which will include the population parameter a selected percent of the time.)

Steps in solution:

1. Select the level of confidence desired.

2. Plot the sample.

3. Draw arcs with a radius corresponding to

$$1.00 - \text{Confidence value}$$

with centers at $(s, f + 1)$ and $(s + 1, f)$.

4. Draw lines from the origin tangent to the two arcs.

5. Determine the two points where the tangent lines cross the quarter circle. Read the confidence limits on the failure scale (Figure 4A1-5).

Fig. 4A1-5

BINOMIAL PROBABILITY PAPER

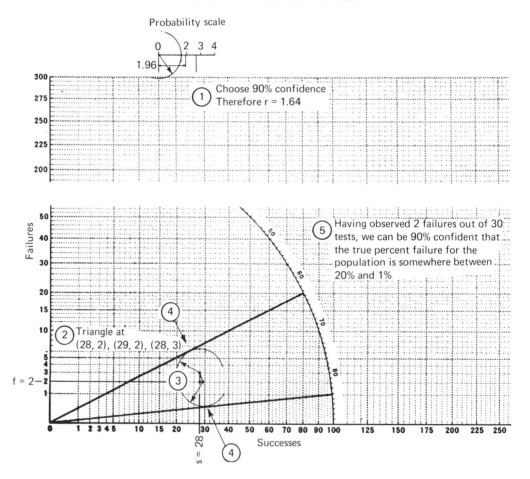

APPENDIX 2
CHAPTER 4

SUMMATION OF TERMS OF
THE POISSON DISTRIBUTION[†]

1,000 times probability of c or r or X or less occurrences of event that has average number of occurrences equal to m or $\bar{c}$ or np.

m or $\bar{c}$ or np \ c or r or X	0	1	2	3	4	5	6	7	8	9
0.02	980	1,000								
0.04	961	999	1,000							
0.06	942	998	1,000							
0.08	923	997	1,000							
0.10	905	995	1,000							
0.15	861	990	999	1,000						
0.20	819	982	999	1,000						
0.25	779	974	998	1,000						
0.30	741	963	996	1,000						
0.35	705	951	994	1,000						
0.40	670	938	992	999	1,000					
0.45	638	925	989	999	1,000					
0.50	607	910	986	998	1,000					
0.55	577	894	982	998	1,000					
0.60	549	878	977	997	1,000					
0.65	522	861	972	996	999	1,000				
0.70	497	844	966	994	999	1,000				
0.75	472	827	959	993	999	1,000				
0.80	449	809	953	991	999	1,000				
0.85	427	791	945	989	998	1,000				
0.90	407	772	937	987	998	1,000				

[†]From E. L. Grant, *Statistical Quality Control*, McGraw-Hill Book Company, New York, 1946.

m or $\bar{c}$ or np \ *c or r or X*	0	1	2	3	4	5	6	7	8	9
0.95	387	754	929	984	997	1,000				
1.00	368	736	920	981	996	999	1,000			
1.1	333	699	900	974	995	999	1,000			
1.2	301	663	879	966	992	998	1,000			
1.3	273	627	857	957	989	998	1,000			
1.4	247	592	833	946	986	997	999	1,000		
1.5	223	558	809	934	981	996	999	1,000		
1.6	202	525	783	921	976	994	999	1,000		
1.7	183	493	757	907	970	992	998	1,000		
1.8	165	463	731	891	964	990	997	999	1,000	
1.9	150	434	704	875	956	987	997	999	1,000	
2.0	135	406	677	857	947	983	995	999	1,000	
2.2	111	355	623	819	928	975	993	998	1,000	
2.4	091	308	570	779	904	964	988	997	999	1,000
2.6	074	267	518	736	877	951	983	995	999	1,000
2.8	061	231	469	692	848	935	976	992	998	999
3.0	050	199	423	647	815	916	966	988	996	999
3.2	041	171	380	603	781	895	955	983	994	998
3.4	033	147	340	558	744	871	942	977	992	997
3.6	027	126	303	515	706	844	927	969	988	996
3.8	022	107	269	473	668	816	909	960	984	994
4.0	018	092	238	433	629	785	889	949	979	992
4.2	015	078	210	395	590	753	867	936	972	989
4.4	012	066	185	359	551	720	844	921	964	985
4.6	010	056	163	326	513	686	818	905	955	980
4.8	008	048	143	294	476	651	791	887	944	975
5.0	007	040	125	265	440	616	762	867	932	968
5.2	006	034	109	238	406	581	732	845	918	960
5.4	005	029	095	213	373	546	702	822	903	951
5.6	004	024	082	191	342	512	670	797	886	941
5.8	003	021	072	170	313	478	638	771	867	929
6.0	002	017	062	151	285	446	606	744	847	916

	10	11	12	13	14	15	16
2.8	1,000						
3.0	1,000						
3.2	1,000						
3.4	999	1,000					
3.6	999	1,000					
3.8	998	999	1,000				
4.0	997	999	1,000				
4.2	996	999	1,000				
4.4	994	998	999	1,000			
4.6	992	997	999	1,000			
4.8	990	996	999	1,000			
5.0	986	995	998	999	1,000		
5.2	982	993	997	999	1,000		
5.4	977	990	996	999	1,000		
5.6	972	988	995	998	999	1,000	
5.8	965	984	993	997	999	1,000	
6.0	957	980	991	996	999	999	1,000

	0	1	2	3	4	5	6	7	8	9
6.2	002	015	054	134	259	414	574	716	826	902
6.4	002	012	046	119	235	384	542	687	803	886
6.6	001	010	040	105	213	355	511	658	780	869
6.8	001	009	034	093	192	327	480	628	755	850
7.0	001	007	030	082	173	301	450	599	729	830
7.2	001	006	025	072	156	276	420	569	703	810
7.4	001	005	022	063	140	253	392	539	676	788
7.6	001	004	019	055	125	231	365	510	648	765
7.8	000	004	016	048	112	210	338	481	620	741
8.0	000	003	014	042	100	191	313	453	593	717
8.5	000	002	009	030	074	150	256	386	523	653
9.0	000	001	006	021	055	116	207	324	456	587
9.5	000	001	004	015	040	089	165	269	392	522
10.0	000	000	003	010	029	067	130	220	333	458

	10	11	12	13	14	15	16	17	18	19
6.2	949	975	989	995	998	999	1,000			
6.4	939	969	986	994	997	999	1,000			
6.6	927	963	982	992	997	999	999	1,000		
6.8	915	955	978	990	996	998	999	1,000		
7.0	901	947	973	987	994	998	999	1,000		
7.2	887	937	967	984	993	997	999	999	1,000	
7.4	871	926	961	980	991	996	998	999	1,000	
7.6	854	915	954	976	989	995	998	999	1,000	
7.8	835	902	945	971	986	993	997	999	1,000	
8.0	816	888	936	966	983	992	996	998	999	1,000
8.5	763	849	909	949	973	986	993	997	999	999
9.0	706	803	876	926	959	978	989	995	998	999
9.5	645	752	836	898	940	967	982	991	996	998
10.0	583	697	792	863	917	951	973	986	993	997

	20	21	22
8.5	1,000		
9.0	1,000		
9.5	999	1,000	
10.0	998	999	1,000

	0	1	2	3	4	5	6	7	8	9
10.5	000	000	002	007	021	050	102	179	279	397
11.0	000	000	001	005	015	038	079	143	232	341
11.5	000	000	001	003	011	028	060	114	191	289
12.0	000	000	001	002	008	020	046	090	155	242
12.5	000	000	000	002	005	015	035	070	125	201
13.0	000	000	000	001	004	011	026	054	100	166
13.5	000	000	000	001	003	008	019	041	079	135
14.0	000	000	000	000	002	006	014	032	062	109
14.5	000	000	000	000	001	004	010	024	048	088
15.0	000	000	000	000	001	003	008	018	037	070

	10	11	12	13	14	15	16	17	18	19
10.5	521	639	742	825	888	932	960	978	988	994
11.0	460	579	689	781	854	907	944	968	982	991
11.5	402	520	633	733	815	878	924	954	973	986
12.0	347	462	576	682	772	844	899	937	963	979
12.5	297	406	519	628	725	806	869	916	948	969
13.0	252	353	463	573	675	764	835	890	930	957
13.5	211	304	409	518	623	718	798	861	908	942
14.0	176	260	358	464	570	669	756	827	883	923
14.5	145	220	311	413	518	619	711	790	853	901
15.0	118	185	268	363	466	568	664	749	819	875

	20	21	22	23	24	25	26	27	28	29
10.5	997	999	999	1,000						
11.0	995	998	999	1,000						
11.5	992	996	998	999	1,000					
12.0	988	994	997	999	999	1,000				
12.5	983	991	995	998	999	999	1,000			
13.0	975	986	992	996	998	999	1,000			
13.5	965	980	989	994	997	998	999	1,000		
14.0	952	971	983	991	995	997	999	999	1,000	
14.5	936	960	976	986	992	996	998	999	999	1,000
15.0	917	947	967	981	989	994	997	998	999	1,000

	4	5	6	7	8	9	10	11	12	13
16	000	001	004	010	022	043	077	127	193	275
17	000	001	002	005	013	026	049	085	135	201
18	000	000	001	003	007	015	030	055	092	143
19	000	000	001	002	004	009	018	035	061	098
20	000	000	000	001	002	005	011	021	039	066
21	000	000	000	000	001	003	006	013	025	043
22	000	000	000	000	001	002	004	008	015	028
23	000	000	000	000	000	001	002	004	009	017
24	000	000	000	000	000	000	001	003	005	011
25	000	000	000	000	000	000	001	001	003	006

	14	15	16	17	18	19	20	21	22	23
16	368	467	566	659	742	812	868	911	942	963
17	281	371	468	564	655	736	805	861	905	937
18	208	287	375	469	562	651	731	799	855	899
19	150	215	292	378	469	561	647	725	793	849
20	105	157	221	297	381	470	559	644	721	787
21	072	111	163	227	302	384	471	558	640	716
22	048	077	117	169	232	306	387	472	556	637
23	031	052	082	123	175	238	310	389	472	555
24	020	034	056	087	128	180	243	314	392	473
25	012	022	038	060	092	134	185	247	318	394

	24	25	26	27	28	29	30	31	32	33
16	978	987	993	996	998	999	999	1,000		
17	959	975	985	991	995	997	999	999	1,000	
18	932	955	972	983	990	994	997	998	999	1,000
19	893	927	951	969	980	988	993	996	998	999
20	843	888	922	948	966	978	987	992	995	997
21	782	838	883	917	944	963	976	985	991	994
22	712	777	832	877	913	940	959	973	983	989
23	635	708	772	827	873	908	936	956	971	981
24	554	632	704	768	823	868	904	932	953	969
25	473	553	629	700	763	818	863	900	929	950

	34	35	36	37	38	39	40	41	42	43
19	999	1,000								
20	999	999	1,000							
21	997	998	999	999	1,000					
22	994	996	998	999	999	1,000				
23	988	993	996	997	999	999	1,000			
24	979	987	992	995	997	998	999	999	1,000	
25	966	978	985	991	994	997	998	999	999	1,000

CHAPTER FIVE | CONTROL CHART CONCEPTS

The control chart is a tool used primarily for analyzing data, either discrete or continuous, which are generated over a time period. The concept was evolved by Dr. Walter A. Shewhart, Bell Telephone Laboratories, in 1924. At that time he suggested the chart could fulfill three basic functions:

1. To define a goal for an operation.
2. To aid in the attainment of that goal.
3. To judge whether the goal had been reached.

The control chart can be utilized by product engineering to record and analyze test data, by accounting to analyze costs, by process engineering to determine machine and process capabilities, by production engineering to monitor operations, and by inspection and quality control to report scrap and rework and to analyze incoming material quality. As such, it may be considered among the most versatile tools in statistical methods.

CONTROL CHART PHILOSOPHY

While the term *control* chart has been universally accepted and used, it must be understood at the outset that the chart does not actually control anything. It simply provides a basis for action and is effective only if those responsible for making decisions act upon the information which the chart reveals.

Adequate control requires a means for continuously monitoring repetitive operations. The control could be simply periodically reviewing histograms or frequency distributions. Histograms, however, require relatively large samples, whereas control charts can frequently accomplish as much and more with small samples.

Chance variations, when plotted against time, will behave in a random manner; they will show no cycles, runs, or definite patterns. In like manner, random samples from a constant-

68

cause system will differ purely by chance. The variation or spread, produced solely by chance causes, can in general be predicted after an initial sample series has been studied. Knowing the probability distribution pattern aids in predicting the variation anticipated for a great many measurements.

For instance, if a certain size sample is drawn from a chance source at regular intervals and sample statistics (such as fraction defective, average, or range) are calculated, these statistics (like the original measurements) will vary according to a definite pattern. For this sample series, the average and standard deviation for each statistic can be computed. This information and knowledge of probability distributions can be used to estimate the group behavior for each sample statistic. This is done by calculating the grand average and measuring plus and minus some standard deviation multiple from this value to obtain the control limits. Thus a chart constructed with the vertical scale calibrated in units corresponding to the statistic, with a horizontal scale marked according to time, and with horizontal lines drawn through the grand average and the control limits can be called a control chart for that statistic. Figure 5-1 shows a conceptual control chart.

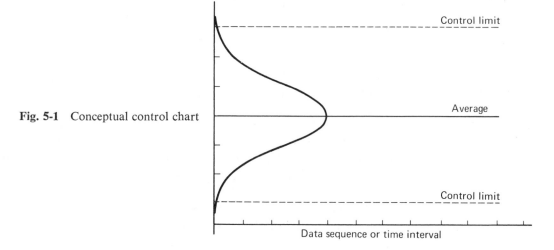

Fig. 5-1   Conceptual control chart

In use, sample statistic values plotted on a control chart are considered to be *in control* if the points fall within the control limits and show no signs of cycles, trends, or runs. Likewise, the operation under observation is considered to be subject to chance causes alone when the control chart indicates an *in-control* condition and to be subject to some assignable cause when the chart shows an *out-of-control* condition. When using control charts, the objective is to reduce excessive variation in an operation to the point that it corresponds to the required tolerance or other established goal.

If the control chart shows no points beyond the control limits and variation is at a desirable level, it cannot always be inferred that no assignable variation is present. The chart can show assignable factors such as tool wear, creating a drifting condition, or runs within the limits. The causes are often known and may be readily corrected by making a machine adjustment or replacing a tool.

Frequently in industry, informal record charts or tables are made to tabulate various data. Engineers, or industrial and research workers, often base important decisions on these records and are completely unaware that assignable variation is present. The control chart is a statistical tool which can aid in making valid decisions and placing them on a scientific basis.

Control charts in general can be classified as variable or attribute. The chart for variables is used when continuous data are collected, such as a dimension, a cost, a weight, a resistance, a sensitivity, a gain, a temperature, or a hardness. For this control, the average and range chart is used. The chart for attributes has application when either discrete data are obtained or when it is desired to classify continuous measurements as acceptable or unacceptable. The first category is exemplified by recording such items as work sampling observations, radiator leaks, or assembly defects, and the second category by recording the cars which fail to meet exhaust emission standards or fatigue failures. In these cases the percent defective chart or defect chart may be used.

PRELIMINARY DECISIONS BEFORE USING THE CONTROL CHART

After the decision has been made to utilize a control chart, certain preliminary questions must be answered:

1. What characteristic(s) is to be investigated?
2. What gages or testing devices will be needed?
3. What chart will accomplish the purpose?
4. What size sample should be taken?
5. How often should the sample be taken?
6. How should the sample be selected?

The answers to these questions may be based on practical engineering or economic considerations but are important to the overall usefulness and success of this statistical tool.

1. What characteristic(s) is to be investigated? It can usually be assumed that the desired characteristic is that which is the most critical in functional terms or that which has the tightest specification. If it is desired to investigate more than one characteristic with variable charts, a chart must be used for each characteristic studied. An attribute chart, however, permits studying one or more characteristics.

2. What gages or testing devices will be needed? Since the control chart is to be used to provide a basis for action, the chart data can be no better than the evaluation device employed. Consequently, these should be reviewed regularly for accuracy in measurement, repeatability, and calibration. (Refer to the appendix to Chapter 8.) For variable charts, the measurement increment must be considered (a dimension with tolerances in ten-thousandths of an inch cannot be controlled with a steel rule). In some instances the equipment available will determine the chart which can be used.

3. What chart will accomplish the purpose? Basically this answer is dictated by the measurement cost and the loss arising from the failure to detect important changes if they should occur. Since less information about a part is conveyed when it is classified as either good or bad, a variable chart, requiring measurements, is a more efficient device than an attribute chart. To compensate for this inefficiency, an attribute chart usually requires a larger sample size than a variable chart. Variable data, since measuring equipment is required, are often more costly to obtain than attribute data. In general, an attribute chart is used if

a. Measurements are not possible, as in visually inspecting a part.
b. Measurements are not practical because the gaging is too expensive or the time involved is excessive.
c. The part has many characteristics to evaluate.
d. The chart is to be based on 100 percent checking.

Use a variable chart if

a. A critical characteristic, such as a locating point, is involved.

b. More precise control than attribute control is desired.

4. What size sample should be taken? When using attribute charts, a constant percentage sample does not assure a constant risk that nonrandom variation will be detected. Thus the sample size should not be assigned in direct ratio to the lot size. No given size is appropriate for all applications. Generally, the size should be large enough so that there is a good chance that some defective items will appear in the sample and also that the lower control limit is above zero. The first requirement eliminates the situation in which one defective item in the sample might indicate an out-of-control condition. The second stipulation permits detecting laxity in the data collection or an improvement in the operation.

An essential precept in variables charting is to choose a sample size such that there is a minimum opportunity for within-sample variation. Therefore it is desirable that the sample be small. However, the smaller the size, the greater will be the variation between the successive sample averages. A compromise is needed. A five-piece sample will keep variation within the sample low and still be large enough to enable the averages to approach normality. Actually the sample size may be set at any convenient number such as 4, 5, 6, or 10, although the size 5 is in common use and provides a computational advantage. In any case, the sample size required to satisfy specified decision risks may be mathematically determined by methods which are beyond the scope of this material.

Another important consideration is obviously the cost associated with data acquisition and analysis. The latter is most often the primary factor in sample size determination.

5. How often should the sample be taken? This decision is again based essentially on economic considerations. Additionally to be considered are the savings derived from action taken with respect to out-of-control conditions. If past history which shows the time-to-time variation is available, this can be used to establish the sampling frequency. Whatever the decision, a definite checking moment (such as each hour on the hour) should be avoided. This will minimize the bias which can occur when the precise moment is known. For example, the person observed in a work sampling study is usually busy if he knows the time when he will be checked.

Normally, when a control chart is first applied, samples are taken more frequently. After the operation has been diagnosed and improved, the frequency tends to decrease, and only enough checks are made to assure maintaining the operation level desired.

6. How should the sample be selected? The important problem is eliminating any bias, for the sample selected must be random and represent the group from which it is drawn. If all the parts produced by a machine or process or tested on laboratory equipment are available as a lot, the sample may be randomly drawn from this lot and will adequately represent a specific time period. If successive parts comprise the sample, however, it represents that particular time only.

It is highly desirable that each sample be homogeneous. If assignable causes are present or could be introduced in an operation, the sample selection should be made so that any differences will show up between, rather than within, the sample.

For example, five parts taken sequentially from a single source might be expected to show only chance differences. Obviously, additional samples from this same source can be subject to assignable variation, such as a locking device coming loose, tool wear, or other changes in the man, measurement, machine, or material. For this reason, it is desirable to select sample parts from one machine, from only one machine, or from only one spindle of an automatic machine or to select materials from one source. Each sample should contain parts or material from one constant-cause system. The control chart will then reveal if successive samples are from essentially the same system.

THE CONTROL CHARTING PROCEDURE

Once the preliminary decisions just discussed have been made, the actual chart construction can begin. Standard graphical forms are usually available for this purpose. There are basically three different formats in use, one for variable charts and two for attribute charts. In addition to having a plotting area, the forms have a designated space in which to record the sample data.

If historical data are available for the operation to be charted, these data may be used for setting up the graphical scale on the control chart. When such data are not available, several samples must be taken and measured before constructing the scale. The initial chart scale should provide for approximately two to three times as much variation as that observed in the first several samples. The scales may be adjusted on subsequent charts.

Historical data can be used to calculate the control chart center line and the control limits. If no pertinent data are available, the information necessary for calculating these values will be obtained from the control chart as the sampling progresses. Following a "rule of thumb," the compiled data from the first 20 samples are used as a basis for calculations.

The decision lines on a control chart are the center line, the upper control limit (UCL), and the lower control limit (LCL). The center line is the overall average of the selected variable. Ordinarily the control limits are located three standard deviations above the average (UCL) and three below the average (LCL). When the LCL for an attribute chart is a negative value, it is set at zero. It is customary to draw the center line as a solid horizontal line across the chart and to construct the control limits as broken lines. The values for the center and control lines may be obtained from equations or other methods such as alignment charts or special slide rules.

When the three control values have been determined, lines are drawn on the chart. Sample values already plotted on the chart are checked for control. Any sample point beyond either limit is considered "out-of-control." At this time, the sample must be reevaluated and, whenever possible, the operation investigated to establish the reason for this behavior. Frequently this sample is deleted from the compiled data, and new control values are determined. The plotted points are then compared with the new control values. If necessary, this out-of-control point elimination and recalculation procedure is repeated until all remaining plotted points lie within the control limits. When many points are beyond the limits, the overall operation is judged to be too variable. Corrective measures to reduce the variation must be applied before a chart can be successfully used.

By contrast, when all sample plots are within control limits the operation is in control. The control lines are projected for the time period which the chart will display. Following this period, new control values should be determined from the data compiled to date and these new values projected. Control-value verification and projection should henceforth be done at approximately this interval.

The chart is ready for control purposes when at least 20 observed sample points are within the limits and the limits have been projected. Whenever an out-of-control condition is detected, an investigation should be made to find its cause and to reduce or eliminate it.

An out-of-control condition is defined to include

1. *A point outside.* A point beyond either control limit indicates that an external influence exists; that is, an assignable cause is present. Investigation should be made to incorporate desirable causes and eliminate those which are undesirable.

2. *A run.* At times, a change occurs even though no points fall outside the control limits. This change can be observed when successive plotted points are on one side with respect to the center line but are still within the limits. The run indicates a shift in average or a reduction in variation. For example, it is indicated when

    a. Eight successive points fall on the same side.

    b. Any 11 of 12 successive points fall on the same side.

    c. Any 13 of 15 successive points fall on the same side.

3. *A trend.* In some operations there is a steady progressive change in the plotted points. This is called a trend and may be caused by tool wear or machine deterioration. These factors may cause a trend in the average and also in the variability. When the variability is much less than the specifications permit, a trend can be used to control tool replacement by starting the operation near one limit and permitting a drift toward the other. Care must be taken to correct the trend before it goes too far. Special control limits are useful in this case.

4. *A cycle.* At times the operation is affected by cycles caused by psychological, chemical, or mechanical reasons or by daily, weekly, or seasonal effects. These make their appearance on the chart by a definite up and down pattern, with points possibly out of control at both limits, and can be construed as assignable variation.

These are typical rules developed to detect a change in operations. However, in all out-of-control conditions, the assignable cause must be determined before any effective control may be considered. When the control chart plot substantiates the conclusion that samples have been drawn from a constant-cause system, i.e., one where no assignable cause is evident, the operation can be continued with high (approximately 99 percent) assurance that an acceptable product is being made at the level designated.

CHAPTER SIX | ATTRIBUTE CONTROL CHARTS

When measuring a product or a part is not feasible or when the quality characteristic can be obtained only as an attribute—conforming or nonconforming to specifications—an attribute control chart can be used. The attribute technique analyzes characteristics which are either good or bad, with no reference to the degree; for example, go and no-go type of inspection. Either the product does or does not have a scratch; no attempt is made to measure the scratch length or size.

As statistical analysis tools, attribute charts are used to disclosed whether assignable variation is present or absent. Although not as sensitive as a variable chart, these charts play an important part in statistical quality control. For many processes, variable data are not economically obtainable. The attribute chart provides management with a quality history and can result in improved quality if management implements corrective action.

Prior to presenting attribute control charts, the following words must be defined:

1. *Defect:* any individual characteristic which is not in conformance with requirements.
2. *Defective:* any part possessing one or more defects.

The attribute control charts most commonly used are a chart for defectives, a p chart, and a chart for defects, a c chart. The p chart portrays the percent defective, and the c chart portrays the number of defects in a sample.

THE p CHART

One hundred times the fraction defective (the percent defective) in a sample is used as the basis for the p chart. If a sample, n, is taken from a source (assemblies, parts, raw materials) that contains a percent defective, p, some number of defectives, d, would be found in the sample. Then the percent defective in the sample would be $100d/n$. This would not necessarily be equal to the lot value. Other samples taken from the same source would show various percent defectives which will be both greater and less than p percent. The sample statistic, $100d/n$, plotted against time, with the appropriate control limits, forms a control chart for the percent defective.

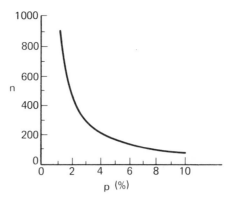

Fig. 6-1 Sample size vs estimated lot quality

SAMPLE SIZE

On some occasions, 100 percent inspection is performed for one or more part characteristics. In this situation, the sample size is a function of the plotting frequency. This may be 1 hour, 1 day, or 1 week and is dependent on the problems which may be encountered if a process change is not detected. At other times, the sample size for a *p* chart is determined by standard sampling plans. This is more apt to occur when material is segregated into lots or batches. It is recommended that samples should be large enough that when *no* defectives are found in the subgroup, a *significant improvement* over the standard is indicated. To attain this, it is necessary to have $n > (9 - 9\bar{p})/\bar{p}$.

The graph in Figure 6-1 gives *n* for $\bar{p}$ values up to 10 percent.

It should be reemphasized that these sample sizes are intended to reveal a significant improvement when *no* defectives are found in the sample. In most practical applications, much smaller sample sizes are used with a resulting sacrifice in the ability to detect shifts in the process average. Over some time interval (which may be long), shifts probably will be detected even with small samples by using the run analysis technique covered in Chapter 5.

DETERMINING THE CONTROL LIMITS

The *p* chart center line is $\bar{p}$ (pronounced "p bar"), which is the process average in percent and which may be calculated using the following equation:

$$\bar{p}\% = 100\left[\frac{\text{Sum } d \text{ for all samples}}{\text{Sum } n \text{ for all samples}}\right] = 100\left[\frac{\sum d}{\sum n}\right]$$

where $d =$ defectives in sample,
$n =$ sample size.

The *p* chart control limits are symmetrical about $\bar{p}$ percent and are obtained from

$$\bar{p}\% \pm 3\sqrt{\frac{\bar{p}\%(100 - \bar{p}\%)}{n}} \quad \text{or} \quad \bar{p}\% \pm 3\sigma_p\%$$

The lower limit is set at zero whenever it is negative. When the sample size is constant from sample to sample, a straight-line (constant) control limit results. Note from the *n* in the above equation that the control limits will change in width with each different sample size.

If this situation exists, alternative procedures which may be used are

1. Compute separate limits each time the sample size changes.
2. Compute limits based on the average sample size. This is practical if the range in sample size is as much as 40 percent from the average but is more acceptable if the range is less than 20 percent. If the 40 percent variation is exceeded a relatively few times, compute separate limits for the points involved.
3. Compute three different control limit sets if the range in sample size varies more than 40 percent from the average. One set would be for *n* close to the expected minimum,

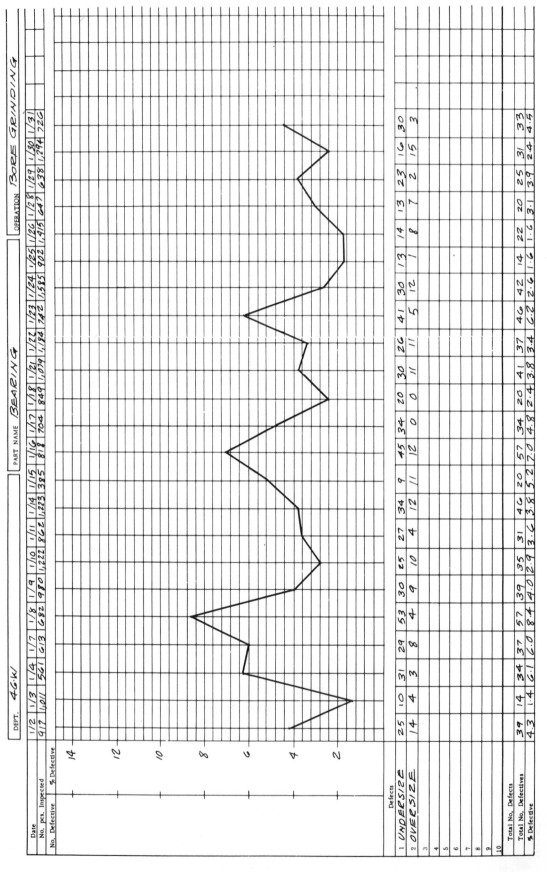

Fig. 6-2 Daily percent defective—bearing bores

76

one for the expected average, and one for the expected maximum. Sample size must be recorded on the chart along with the plotted point to properly evaluate whether a state of control exists.

4. Compute standardized limits. The normal table is an example using standardized values. Limits in this case are simply ± 3 units, and the statistic plotted is

$$\frac{p_i - \bar{p}}{\sqrt{\dfrac{\bar{p}(1-\bar{p})}{n}}}$$

where p_i = sample fraction defective (d/n),
$\bar{p}$ = average fraction defective $(\sum d / \sum n)$.

5. Binomial probability paper.

EXAMPLE

A p chart showing percent defective due to oversize and undersize grinding on bearing bores is shown in Figure 6-2. Since the sample size varies for each plotted point, the procedures outlined previously will be used to illustrate control limit computations.

1. Compute separate limits for each sample size.
   a. Calculate $\bar{p}$:

   $$\bar{p} = 100\left[\frac{\sum d}{\sum n}\right] = 100\left[\frac{39 + 14 + \cdots + 31 + 33}{917 + 1{,}011 + \cdots + 1{,}294 + 726}\right]$$
   $$= 100\left[\frac{774}{21{,}039}\right] = 100(0.0368) = 3.68 \text{ percent}$$

   b. Calculate σ_p:

   $$\sigma_p = \sqrt{\frac{\bar{p}\%(100 - \bar{p}\%)}{n}}$$

   For $n = 917$,

   $$\sigma_p = \sqrt{\frac{3.68(100 - 3.68)}{917}} = 0.62 \text{ percent}$$

   c. Calculate control limits:

   $$\bar{p}\% \pm 3\sigma_p\%$$
   $$\text{UCL} = 3.68 + 3(0.62)$$
   $$= 3.68 + 1.87 = 5.55 \text{ percent}$$
   $$\text{LCL} = 3.68 - 3(0.62)$$
   $$= 3.68 - 1.87 = 1.81 \text{ percent}$$

   These calculations have been done for each sample size, and the resulting control limits are tabulated in Figure 6-3 and plotted in Figure 6-4.

2. Compute limits based on average sample size. The average is

   $$\bar{n} = \frac{21{,}039}{23} = 915$$

n	$3\sigma_p\%$	UCL	LCL
917	1.87	5.55	1.81
1,011	1.78	5.46	1.90
561	2.39	6.07	1.29
613	2.28	5.96	1.40
682	2.16	5.84	1.52
980	1.80	5.48	1.88
1,222	1.62	5.30	2.06
862	1.92	5.60	1.76
1,223	1.62	5.30	2.06
385	2.88	6.56	0.80
818	1.97	5.65	1.71
704	2.13	5.81	1.55
849	1.94	5.62	1.74
1,079	1.72	5.40	1.96
1,184	1.64	5.32	2.04
742	2.07	5.75	1.61
1,585	1.42	5.10	2.26
902	1.88	5.56	1.80
1,415	1.50	5.18	2.18
647	2.72	6.40	0.96
638	2.24	5.92	1.44
1,294	1.57	5.25	2.11
726	2.10	5.78	1.58

Fig. 6-3 Control limit tabulations for varying n

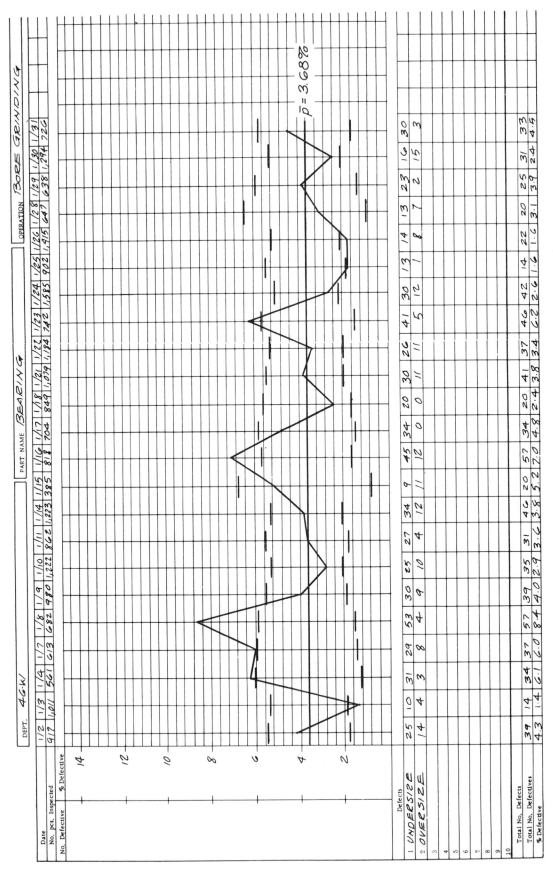

Fig. 6-4 Daily percent defective—bearing bores (varying control limits)

Using the 40 percent rule, the maximum $n = 915 + (0.40)(915) = 1,281$. The minimum $n = 915 - (0.4)(915) = 549$. Examining the data, there are three sample sizes above 1,281 (1,294, 1,415, 1,585) and one sample size that is below 549 (385). The control limits for the average sample size (915) are

$$\text{UCL} = 3.68 + 3\sqrt{\frac{3.68(100 - 3.68)}{915}}$$
$$= 3.68 + 1.88 = 5.56 \text{ percent}$$
$$\text{LCL} = 3.68 - 3\sqrt{\frac{3.68(100 - 3.68)}{915}}$$
$$= 3.68 - 1.88 = 1.80 \text{ percent}$$

These are shown plotted in Figure 6-5, with separate limits for the four points where the practical sample size variance was exceeded.

3. Compute three control limit sets: one for expected minimum n, one for expected average n, and one for expected maximum n. Examining the data, use as a minimum 350, an average 900, and a maximum 1,600. The control then would be

$$n = 350$$
$$\text{UCL} = 3.68 + 3\sqrt{\frac{3.68(100 - 3.68)}{350}}$$
$$= 3.68 + 3.02 = 6.70 \text{ percent}$$
$$\text{LCL} = 3.68 - 3.02 = 0.66 \text{ percent}$$
$$n = 900$$
$$\text{UCL} = 3.68 - 3\sqrt{\frac{3.68(100 - 3.68)}{900}}$$
$$= 3.68 + 1.88 = 5.56 \text{ percent}$$
$$\text{LCL} = 3.68 - 1.88 = 1.80 \text{ percent}$$
$$n = 1,600$$
$$\text{UCL} = 3.68 + 3\sqrt{\frac{3.68(100 - 3.68)}{1,600}}$$
$$= 3.68 + 1.41 = 5.09 \text{ percent}$$
$$\text{LCL} = 3.68 - 1.41 = 2.27 \text{ percent}$$

Figure 6-6 shows the limits which were plotted for the three n values selected.

4. Compute standardized limits.
    a. Set limits at ± 3 units.
    b. Calculate the following statistic for each sample:

$$\frac{p_i - \bar{p}}{\sqrt{\frac{\bar{p}(1 - \bar{p})}{n}}}$$

for $n = 917$,
    $p_i = 0.043$,
    $\bar{p} = 0.0368$.
Then,

$$\frac{0.043 - 0.0368}{\sqrt{\frac{0.0368(1 - 0.0368)}{917}}} = \frac{0.0062}{0.0062} = 1.0$$

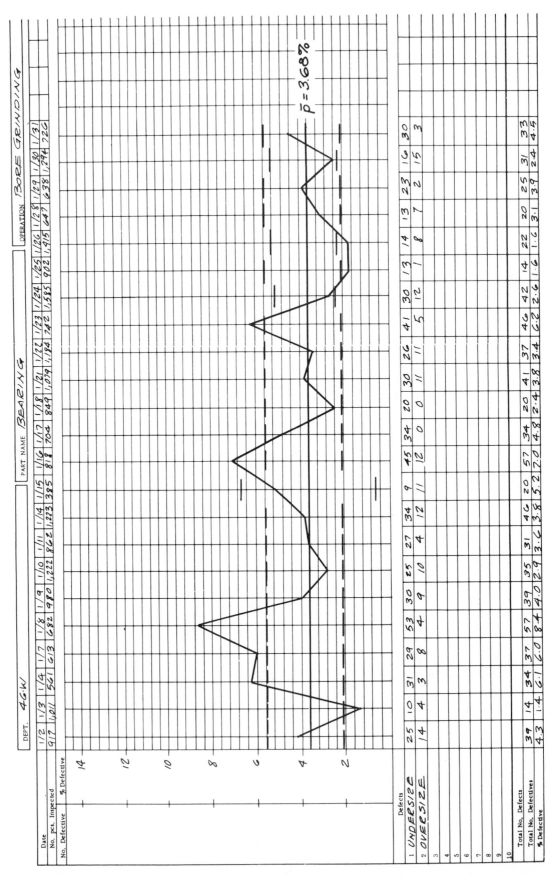

Fig. 6-5 Daily percent defective—bearing bores (control limits based on average n)

DEPT. 46-W   PART NAME BEARING   OPERATION BORE GRINDING

Date	1/2	1/3	1/4	1/7	1/8	1/9	1/10	1/11	1/14	1/15	1/16	1/17	1/18	1/21	1/22	1/23	1/24	1/25	1/26	1/28	1/29	1/30	1/31
No. pcs. Inspected	917	1,011	561	613	682	980	1,222	862	1,223	395	818	704	849	1,079	1,194	742	1,595	902	1,415	647	638	1,294	726

(chart axis labels — No. Defective / % Defective: 14, 12, 10, 8, 6, 4, 2)

Control limit labels: $n=350$, $n=900$, $n=1600$, $\bar{p}=3.68\%$, $n=1600$, $n=900$, $n=350$

Defects																							
1 UNDERSIZE	25	10	31	29	53	30	35	27	34	9	45	34	20	30	26	41	30	13	14	23	16	30	
2 OVERSIZE	14	4	3	8	4	9	10	4	12	11	12	0	0	11	11	5	12	1	8	7	2	15	3
3																							
4																							
5																							
6																							
7																							
8																							
9																							
10																							
Total No. Defects	39	14	34	37	57	39	35	31	46	20	57	34	20	41	37	46	42	14	22	20	25	31	33
Total No. Defectives	39	14	34	37	57	39	35	31	46	20	57	34	20	41	37	46	42	14	22	20	25	31	33
% Defective	4.3	1.4	6.1	6.0	8.4	4.0	2.9	3.6	3.8	5.2	7.0	4.8	2.4	3.8	3.1	6.2	2.6	1.6	3.1	3.1	3.9	2.4	4.5

Fig. 6-6 Daily percent defective—bearing bores (control limits based on minimum, average and maximum expected n)

81

Sample Size	Fraction Defective p_i	$\sqrt{\dfrac{\bar{p}(1-\bar{p})}{n}}$	$p_i - \bar{p}$	$\dfrac{p_i - \bar{p}}{\sqrt{\dfrac{\bar{p}(1-\bar{p})}{n}}}$
917	0.043	0.0062	0.0062	1.0
1,011	.014	0.0059	−0.0228	−3.86
561	.061	0.0079	0.0242	3.06
613	.060	0.0076	0.0232	3.05
682	.084	0.0072	0.0472	6.56
980	.040	0.0060	0.0032	0.53
1,222	.029	0.0054	−0.0078	−1.44
862	.036	0.0064	−0.0008	−0.13
1,223	.038	0.0054	0.0012	0.22
385	.052	0.0096	0.0152	1.58
818	.070	0.0066	0.0332	5.03
704	.048	0.0071	0.0112	1.58
849	.024	0.0065	−0.0128	−1.97
1,079	.038	0.0057	0.0012	0.21
1,184	.034	0.0055	0.0028	−0.51
742	.062	0.0069	0.0252	3.65
1,585	.026	0.0047	−0.0108	−2.30
902	.016	0.0063	−0.0208	−3.30
1,415	.016	0.0050	−0.0208	−4.16
647	.031	0.0074	−0.0058	−0.78
638	.039	0.0075	0.0022	0.29
1,294	.024	0.0052	−0.0128	−2.46
726	.045	0.0070	0.0082	1.17

Fig. 6-7 Standardized values for bearing bores

Fig. 6-8 Standardized percent defective—bearing bores

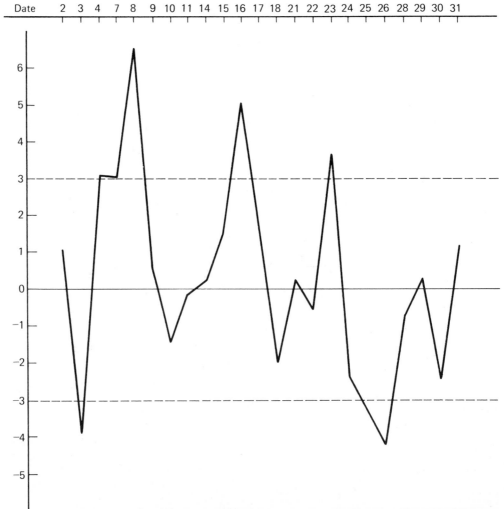

c. The standardized values for the bearing bore data are given in Figure 6-7 and plotted in chart form in Figure 6-8.

5. Binomial probability paper (BIPP). The procedure for plotting binomial probability paper is included in Appendix 1 to Chapter 4. To illustrate its application to the bearing bore data, refer to Figures 6-9 and 6-10. The first line plotted is the *split*, which is the average percent defective and which, as previously determined, is 3.68 percent. Since this represents 37 defectives and 963 nondefectives in 1,000, the average line is drawn through the origin, 963 on the horizontal axis, and 37 on the vertical axis. The parallel lines are constructed three standard deviations about this line using the individual standard errors scale. The sample points are then plotted as the coordinates of the number good vs. number bad in each sample. The numerical values are given in Figure 6-9 and plotted in Figure 6-10. If the sample points are identified by number sequence, it is possible to determine points out of control, runs, trends, and cycles—the four conditions discussed in Chapter 4. Results here are similar but not identical to previous analyses. Samples 2, 5, 11, 16, 18, and 19 fall outside the limits, and in all previous plotting samples 3 and 4 were out in addition to these.

Sample Number	Sample Size	Number Defective	Number Non-Defective
1	917	39	878
2	1,011	14	997
3	561	34	527
4	613	37	576
5	682	57	625
6	980	39	941
7	1,222	35	1,187
8	862	31	831
9	1,223	46	1,177
10	385	20	365
11	818	57	761
12	704	34	670
13	849	20	829
14	1,079	41	1,038
15	1,184	37	1,147
16	742	46	696
17	1,585	42	1,543
18	902	14	888
19	1,415	22	1,393
20	647	20	627
21	638	25	613
22	1,294	31	1,263
23	726	33	693

Fig. 6-9 Bearing bore data for plotting BIPP

Considering all these various procedures from a practical aspect, a final approach is recommended:

1. Calculate limits using the average sample size.

2. If a point is beyond the control limit, recalculate the limit when the sample size is less than the average.

3. If a point is inside but close to the control limit, recalculate the limit when the sample size is greater than the average.

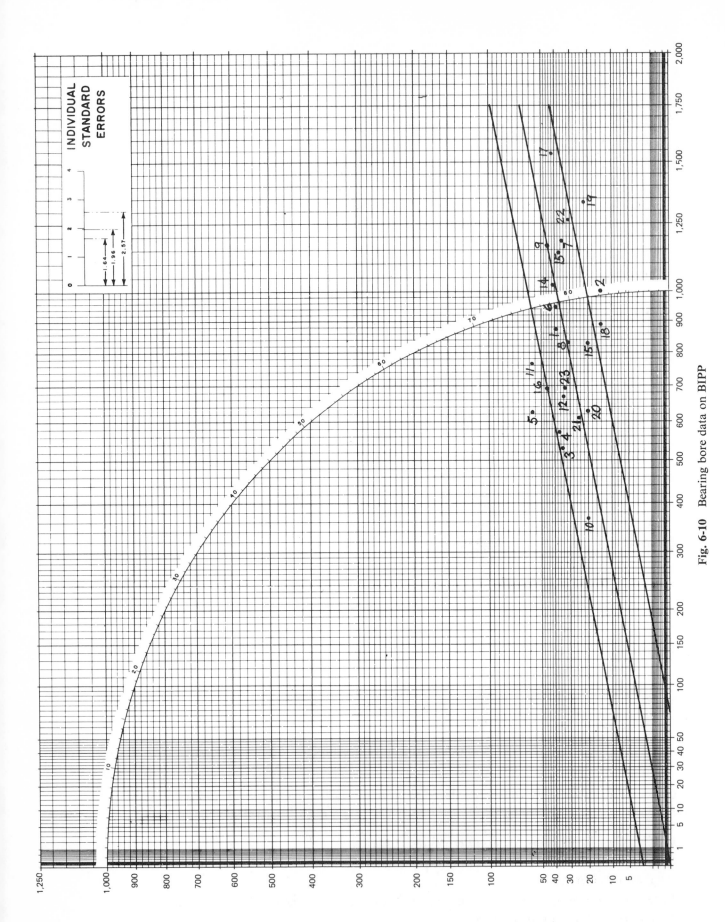

Fig. 6-10 Bearing bore data on BIPP

To illustrate this, refer to Figure 6-5. The first point beyond a limit is the second one plotted. However, since the sample size (1,011) is greater than 915, there is no need to recalculate the limit. The third plotted point is beyond the limit. In this case the sample size is 561, and since this is less than 915, the limit would be recalculated as shown in Figure 6-3. As shown in Figure 6-4, this point is still beyond the limit.

CHART ANALYSIS

It is interesting to note in Figure 6-2, when the bearing bore data were initially charted, that an apparently random variation pattern existed. However, in the subsequent control limit plotting, every method showed eight points beyond the limits which evidenced assignable causes.

When the points all lie within the calculated limits and no trends, runs, or cycles exist, it can be safely assumed that the operation is statistically in control. If the product is acceptable at the level demonstrated (process average percent defective), these limits are projected for subsequent charting. If the product is not acceptable at the level indicated, then an engineering investigation by product, process, and quality personnel must be conducted until the process is producing in control at a satisfactory level.

When the points are not all in control, such as the bearing bores, the simple approach is to discard such points and recalculate the limits. This results in discarding the eight points, and the new average and limits are

$$\bar{p} = 100\left[\frac{493}{14,295}\right] = 3.45 \text{ percent}$$

$$\text{Average } n = \frac{14,295}{15} = 953$$

$$3\sigma_p = 3\sqrt{\frac{(3.45)(100 - 3.45)}{953}} = 1.77 \text{ percent}$$

$$\text{UCL} = 3.45 + 1.77 = 5.22 \text{ percent}$$

$$\text{LCL} = 3.45 - 1.77 = 1.68 \text{ percent}$$

Figure 6-11 shows the revised chart. All points are within control, and if the percent defective is acceptable, these limits would be projected for the next time period.

THE SQC SLIDE RULE

To avoid the mathematics required to calculate control limits from the formulas previously given, a special slide rule (shown in Figure 6-12), has been used at General Motors Institute for many years. This slide rule is available from the Graphic Calculator Co., Barrington, Illinois. Directions for its use are included in Appendix 1 to this chapter.

THE DEFECTS CHART

Occasionally, product classification as merely good or bad is not enough, and yet variable measurements do not always apply. When the product is simple with relatively few specifications, such as a bearing race, classifying it as defective or nondefective may be adequate. However, when the end product is a complex assembly this is not done. For example, a new car could contain many defects, yet not be classified as a defective vehicle. In the first instance the defective races could be divided into scrap or rework. With the car, primarily due to the cost involved, the scrap category would not be appropriate.

DEPT. 46W   PART NAME BEARING   OPERATION BORE GRINDING

Date	1/2	1/3	1/4	1/7	1/8	1/9	1/10	1/11	1/14	1/15	1/16	1/17	1/18	1/21	1/22	1/23	1/24	1/25	1/26	1/28	1/29	1/30	1/31
No. pct. Inspected	917	1,011	561	613	682	980	1,222	862	1,223	385	818	704	849	1,079	1,194	742	1,585	902	1,415	647	638	1,294	726
No. Defective																							
% Defective																							

UCL = 5.22%

p̄ = 3.45%

LCL = 1.77%

⊙ POINTS DISCARDED FROM PREVIOUS CHARTS

Defects																							
1 UNDERSIZE	25	10	31	29	53	30	15	27	34	9	45	34	20	30	26	41	30	13	14	13	23	16	30
2 OVERSIZE	14	4	3	8	4	9	10	4	12	11	12	0	0	11	11	5	12	1	8	7	2	15	3
3																							
4																							
5																							
6																							
7																							
8																							
9																							
10																							
Total No. Defects	39	14	34	37	57	39	35	31	46	20	57	34	20	41	37	46	42	14	22	20	25	31	33
Total No. Defectives	39	14	34	37	57	39	35	31	46	20	57	34	20	41	37	46	42	14	22	20	25	31	33
% Defective	4.3	1.4	6.1	6.0	8.4	4.0	2.9	3.6	3.8	5.2	7.0	4.8	2.4	3.8	3.4	6.2	2.6	1.6	1.6	3.1	3.9	2.4	4.5

Fig. 6-11 Daily percent defective—bearing bores (revised chart with out-of-control points discarded)

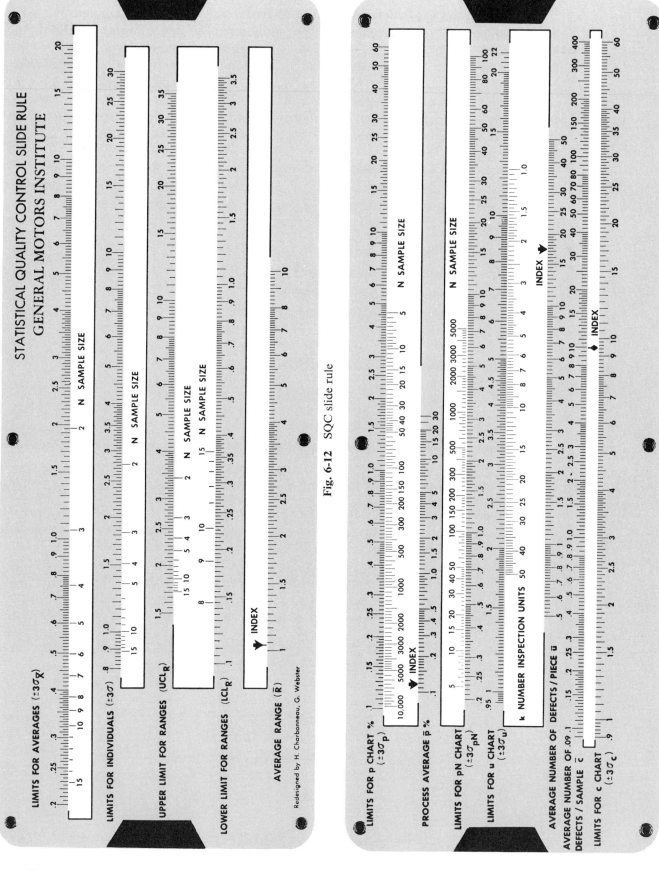

Fig. 6-12 SQC slide rule

87

It was stated in Chapter 4, in connection with the Poisson distribution, that it was essential to have a constant area of opportunity for a defect to occur. This can be further illustrated. Suppose steel is purchased for a punch press in coils 100 meters long. An inspector checks for visual defects as the coil is unrolled and recoiled. He finds four locations where lamination defects occur, so it may be said that the coil has four defects. A beginner might consider that it is 4 percent defective because there are four laminations in a 100-meter length, or that the steel is 0.4 percent defective because the lamination areas are small and there are 1,000 centimeters in the coil, or that the steel is 0.04 percent defective because there are four laminations in a 10,000-millimeter length.

Since the steel quality appeared to change when the measurement unit changed, it is obvious that a more logical approach must be used. This would be classifying the laminations as defects and fixing the length unit so that one coil could be compared to the next one.

When defects are the statistic recorded there are basically four types of charts to consider:

1. Number of defects (c chart).
2. Average number of defects (u chart).
3. Weighted number of defects (D chart).
4. Average weighted number of defects (U chart).

NUMBER OF DEFECTS (c CHART)

Theoretically, three conditions must be satisfied before a c chart can be employed:

1. The opportunities for defects to occur in each production unit are infinite.
2. The probability for a defect to occur at any place on the unit is relatively small and constant.
3. The area of opportunity for defects to occur is the same.

The statistic plotted (c) is the total number of defects found in an inspection unit where the unit, from one time interval to the next, is constant. It should be understood that this inspection unit (area of opportunity) could be 1 car, 10 cars, 1 liter, 10 liters, time, or length.

From a constant source, a varying number of defects (c) per unit is expected. For controlling such defects, the average, or process level, and the expected spread about this average must be found.

The center line is the average number of defects per unit, calculated as follows:

$$\bar{c} = \frac{\text{Sum } c \text{ for all inspection units}}{\text{Number of inspection units}} = \frac{\sum c}{K}$$

The control limits are

$$\bar{c} \pm 3\sigma_c = \bar{c} \pm 3\sqrt{c} \qquad \text{(in Chapter 4, } m \text{ was used instead of } \bar{c}\text{)}$$

EXAMPLE
Figure 6-13 shows a completed c chart. The steps to follow in constructing it are

1. Calculate $\bar{c}$:

$$\bar{c} = \frac{\sum c}{K} = \frac{21 + 23 + 18 + \cdots + 21}{20} = \frac{486}{20} = 24.3$$

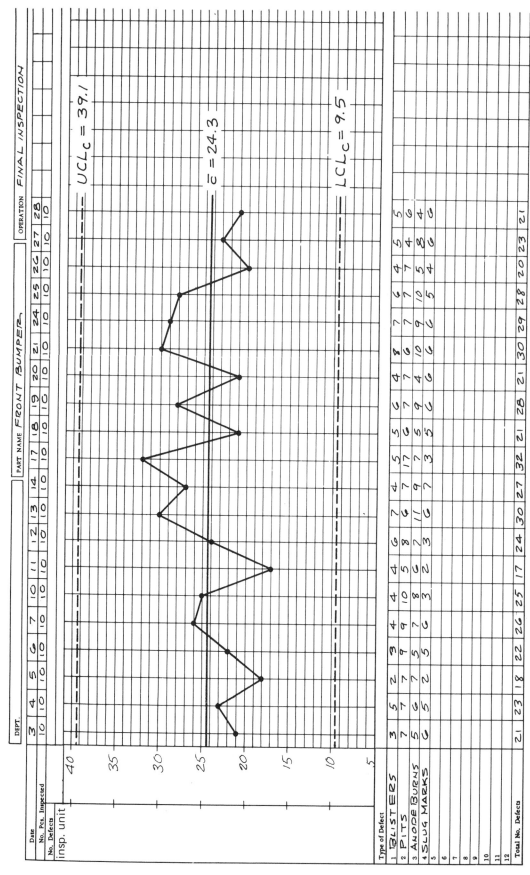

PART NAME FRONT BUMPER   OPERATION FINAL INSPECTION

DEPT.

$UCL_c = 39.1$

$\bar{c} = 24.3$

$LCL_c = 9.5$

Date	3	4	5	6	7	10	11	12	13	14	17	18	19	20	21	24	25	26	27	28
No. Pcs. Inspected	10	10	10	10	10	10	10	10	10	10	10	10	10	10	10	10	10	10	10	10
No. Defects	21	23	18	22	26	25	17	24	30	27	32	31	28	21	30	29	28	20	23	21

insp. unit

Type of Defect																				
1 BLISTERS	3	5	2	3	4	3	4	6	7	4	5	5	6	4	8	7	6	4	5	5
2 PITS	7	7	7	9	10	9	5	8	6	7	17	6	7	7	6	7	5	5	8	6
3 ANODE BURNS	5	6	7	5	8	6	7	11	9	9	4	5	10	4	10	9	6	6	4	4
4 SLUG MARKS	6	5	2	5	3	2	6	3	7	6	3	5	6	6	6	6	5	4	6	6
5																				
6																				
7																				
8																				
9																				
10																				
11																				
12																				
Total No. Defects	21	23	18	22	26	25	17	24	30	27	32	31	28	21	30	29	28	20	23	21

Fig. 6-13 Front bumper defects (c chart)

2. Calculate control limits:

$$\text{UCL} = 24.3 + 3\sqrt{24.3}$$
$$= 24.3 + 14.8 = 39.1$$
$$\text{LCL} = 24.3 - 3\sqrt{24.3}$$
$$= 24.3 - 14.8 = 9.5$$

In analyzing the chart, all points lie within the control limits, and no obvious trends, runs, or cycles exist, indicating adequate statistical control. Assuming that this defect level is operationally acceptable, these limits would be projected for the next time period.

AVERAGE NUMBER OF DEFECTS (*u* CHART)

Since the *u* chart again portrays defects similar to the *c* chart, the same conditions for its use, stated previously, apply. The basic difference between the two is that the *u* chart shows the average number of defects per *production unit*, i.e., per car, per liter. In contrast, the *c* chart shows the total number of defects per *inspection unit*, i.e., per 5 cars, per 10 liters. The *u* chart is generally more useful to supervisors because they are concerned with the average performance.

The appropriate inspection unit size in both the *c* and *u* charts is usually an arbitrary decision based on manpower available and other economic considerations. With the *c* chart, 5 production units are as effective in indicating product quality and the need for corrective action as 20 would be, assuming the Poisson conditions specified earlier are met. The *u* chart, however, is more sensitive to changes in quality level as the number of production units in the inspection unit increase. This is comparable to a fraction defective chart. The *u* chart has another advantage in that the scale values are smaller, which looks better from an employee and public relations viewpoint.

The statistic plotted ($u = c/n$) is the average number of defects per production unit. The center line is the grand average number of defects per production unit, calculated as follows:

$$\bar{u} = \frac{\text{Sum } c \text{ for all production units}}{\text{Total number of production units}} = \frac{\sum c}{nK}$$

or

$$\bar{u} = \frac{\text{Sum } u \text{ for all inspection units}}{\text{Number of inspection units}} = \frac{\sum u}{K}$$

The control limits are

$$\bar{u} \pm 3\sigma_u = \bar{u} \pm 3\sqrt{\frac{\bar{u}}{n}}$$

EXAMPLE

Figure 6-14 shows a completed *u* chart. The steps to follow in its construction are

1. Caclulate $\bar{u}$:

$$\bar{u} = \frac{\sum c}{nK} = \frac{21 + 23 + 18 + \cdots + 21}{10 \times 20} = \frac{486}{200} = 2.43$$

2. Calculate control limits:

$$\text{UCL} = 2.43 + 3\sqrt{\frac{2.43}{10}}$$
$$= 2.43 + 1.48 = 3.91$$
$$\text{LCL} = 2.43 - 3\sqrt{\frac{2.43}{10}}$$
$$= 2.43 - 1.48 = 0.95$$

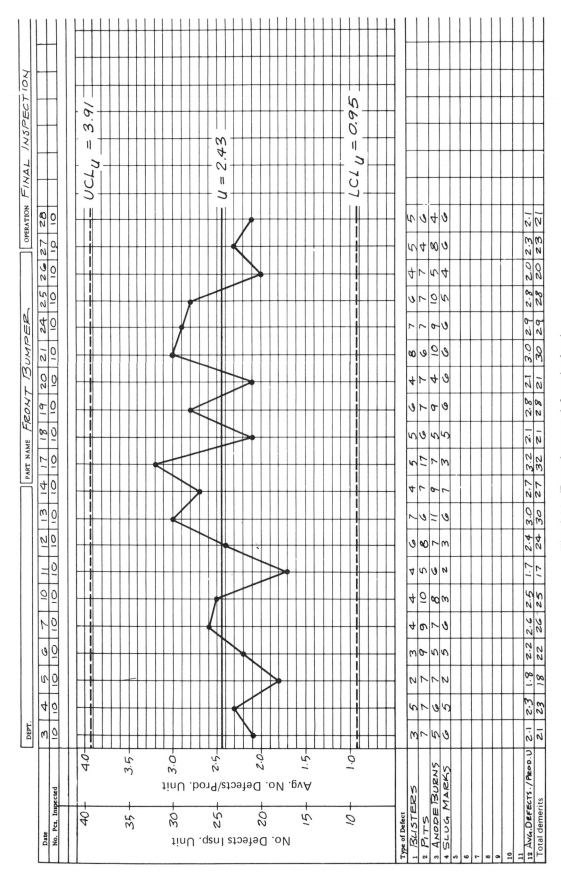

Fig. 6-14 Front bumper defects (*u* chart)

Note in Figure 6-14 that two scales are shown, one for the number of defects per inspection unit and one for the average number of defects per production unit. This has been done for illustration, since the appropriate scale would ordinarily be the only one shown.

As the data in Figure 6-14 are identical to those in Figure 6-13, the chart analysis would be the same.

WEIGHTED NUMBER OF DEFECTS (*D* CHART)

All attribute charts have a deficiency in that all defect types are considered to be equally important. In most applications this is obviously not true. Uniform car audits, for example, do not assign the same weight to a brake problem as they do to a paint defect. The procedure for assigning weights (demerits per unit) has been used for many years in receiving inspection plans. MIL-STD 105D has the classifications critical, major, and minor for assigning relative importance to various characteristics. H. F. Dodge described a more detailed plan in the *Bell System Technical Journal*, Vol. 7, April 1928. This was amplified in another article by Dodge and M. N. Torrey which appeared in *Industrial Quality Control*, Vol. 13, July 1956. These defect classes were

1. Class "A" defects—very serious (100 demerits):
    a. Will render unit totally unfit for service.
    b. Will surely cause operating failure in service which cannot be readily corrected on the job.
    c. Liable to cause personal injury or property damage.

2. Class "B" defects—serious (50 demerits):
    a. Will probably, but not surely, cause class "A" operating failure in service.
    b. Will surely cause trouble of a nature less serious than class "A" operating failure.
    c. Will surely cause increased maintenance or decreased life.

3. Class "C" defects—moderately serious (10 demerits):
    a. Will possibly cause operating failure in service.
    b. Likely to cause trouble of a nature less serious than operating failure.
    c. Likely to cause increased maintenance or decreased life.
    d. Major defects of appearance, finish, or workmanship.

4. Class "D" defects—not serious (1 demerit):
    a. Will not cause operating failure in service.
    b. Minor defects of appearance, finish, or workmanship.

Arbitrarily established weights should be agreed to by all parties concerned, i.e., quality control, inspection, and manufacturing. A more precise way to determine weights is to base them on rework cost. When this is done, chart interpretation is relatively easy. The fluctuation should be stable or down because any upward trend indicates increasing product cost. However, it should be pointed out that downward trends may reflect an uneconomic situation. For instance, a reduction in cost at final inspection could be attributed to excessive rework cost at some point earlier in the system.

The statistic plotted ($D = w_1c_1 + w_2c_2 + \cdots + w_dc_d$) is the total demerits per inspection unit. The center line is the average number of demerits per unit, calculated as follows:

$$\bar{D} = \frac{\text{Sum } D \text{ for all inspection units}}{\text{Number of inspection units}} = \frac{\sum D}{K}$$

The control limits are

$$\bar{D} \pm 3\sigma_D$$

where $\sigma_D = \sqrt{w_1^2 \bar{c}_1 + w_2^2 \bar{c}_2 + \cdots + w_d^2 \bar{c}_d}$,

$$\bar{c}_1 = \frac{\text{Sum } c \text{ (type 1 defect) for all inspection units}}{\text{Number of inspection units}} = \frac{\sum c_1}{K}.$$

EXAMPLE

Figure 6-15 shows a completed D chart for the front bumper defects. The weights assigned to the defects are

- Blisters (5)
- Pits (1)
- Anode burns (2)
- Slug marks (10)

Construction steps are as follows:

1. Calculate D by multiplying the individual defect quantity by its respective weight and sum for each inspection unit:

$$\bar{D}_1 = (5)(3) + (1)(7) + (2)(5) + (10)(6)$$
$$= 15 + 7 + 10 + 60 = 92$$

2. Calculate $\bar{D}$:

$$\bar{D} = \frac{\sum D}{K} = \frac{92 + 94 + 51 + \cdots + 99}{20} = \frac{1898}{20} = 94.9$$

3. Calculate control limits:

$$\text{UCL} = 94.9 + 3\sqrt{(5)^2(4.85) + (1)^2(7.45) + (2)^2(7.1) + (10)^2(4.9)}$$
$$= 94.9 + 3(25.44) = 92.9 + 76.32 = 171.22$$
$$\text{LCL} = 94.9 - 76.32 = 18.58$$

Comparison to the c chart previously plotted (Figure 6-13) shows a slightly different fluctuation, but again there are no obvious trends, runs, or cycles.

AVERAGE WEIGHTED NUMBER OF DEFECTS (U CHART)

This chart has the same relationship to the D chart that the u chart has to the c chart. Again the basic difference is that the u chart shows the average weighted number of defects per *production unit* (per car), while the D chart shows the weighted number of defects per *inspection unit* (per five cars). With quality costs receiving increasing attention, this information is not only useful in cost studies but permits higher management to become more effective in controlling these costs. It should be reemphasized that decreasing costs in one area may occur at the expense of increasing costs in another and that only a total system quality cost study would reveal the problem existing.

The statistic plotted ($U = D/n$) is the average weighted number of defects per production unit. The center line is the grand average weighted number of defects per production unit calculated:

$$\bar{U} = \frac{\text{Sum } D \text{ for all production units}}{\text{Total number of production units}} = \frac{\sum D}{nK}$$

or

$$\bar{U} = \frac{\text{Sum } U \text{ for all inspection units}}{\text{Number of inspection units}} = \frac{\sum U}{K}$$

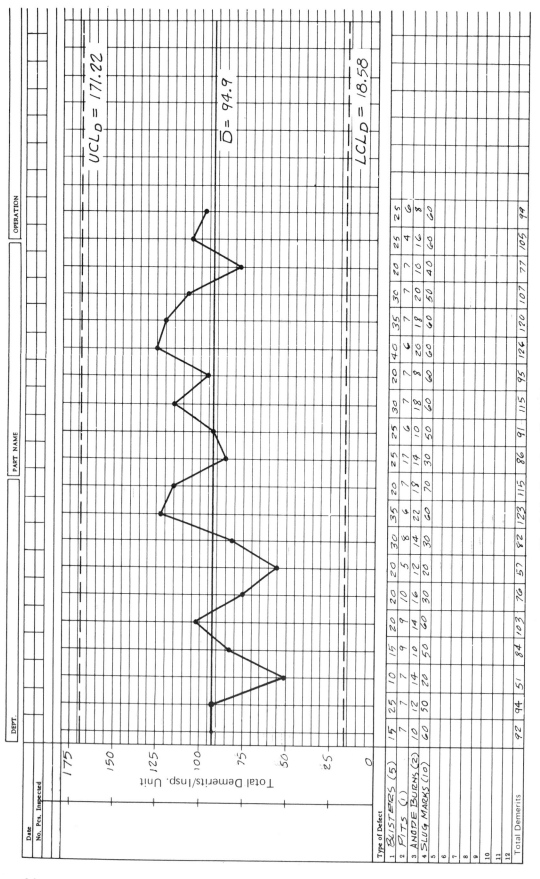

Fig. 6-15 Front bumper defects (*D* chart)

94

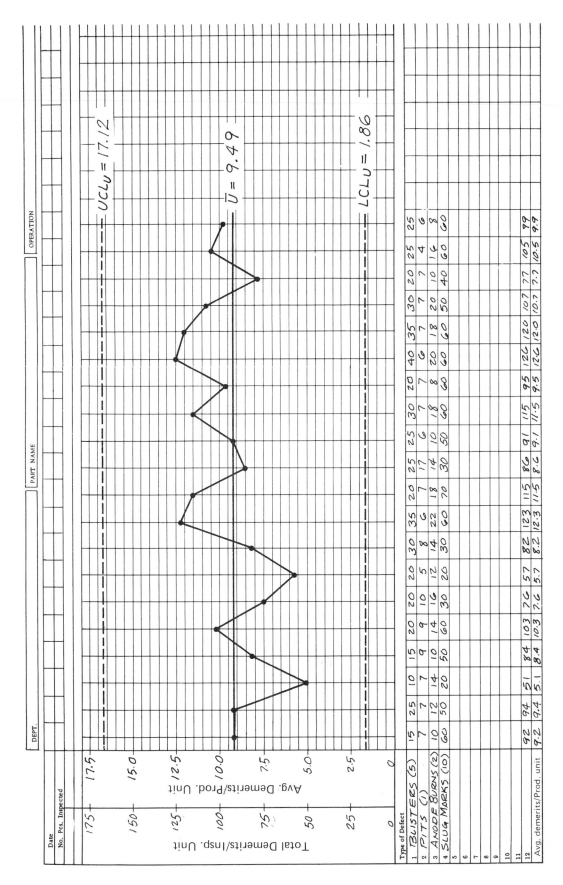

Fig. 6-16 Front bumper defects (*U* chart)

The control limits are

$$\bar{U} \pm 3\sigma_U$$

where

$$\sigma_U = \sqrt{\frac{w_1^2 \bar{c}_1 + w_2^2 \bar{c}_2 + \cdots + w_d^2 \bar{c}_d}{n^2}}$$

EXAMPLE

Figure 6-16 shows a completed U chart, using the same data shown in Figure 6-15. The construction steps are

1. Calculate : $\bar{U}$

$$U = \frac{\sum D}{nK} = \frac{1,898}{(10)(20)} = 9.49$$

2. Calculate control limits:

$$\text{UCL} = 9.49 + 3\sqrt{\frac{(5)^2(4.85) + (1)^2(7.45) + (2)^2(7.1) + (10)^2(4.9)}{(10)^2}}$$
$$= 9.49 + 3\sqrt{6.4710} = 9.29 + 7.63 = 17.12$$
$$\text{LCL} = 9.49 - 7.63 = 1.86$$

Note in Figure 6-16 that two scales are shown, one for weighted number of defects per inspection unit and one for average weighted defects per production unit. This has again been done for illustration, since the appropriate scale would ordinarily be the only one used.

ADDITIONAL ASPECTS

Achieving quality improvement by using attribute control charts can involve two factors, one psychological and one statistical. The former has probably been oversold in past years. Charts posted where they were readily visible were considered to motivate workers to reduce their errors, particularly those caused by carelessness, on the basis that everyone wanted his record to look good. Today, however, with the changing social climate, this assumption is questionable.

It is difficult to motivate a worker to improve quality when conditions which cause poor quality are beyond his control. If the material is substandard or if the process cannot meet specifications, then management action to correct these conditions is required. The internationally known consultant Dr. Joseph Juran aptly expressed this thought by stating that a pole vaulter does not clear 5 meters by mere exhortation to jump harder. The reasons that past vaulting records are exceeded so greatly result from a combination of factors: increased stature, improved training, and changing the pole from bamboo to resilient fiber glass.

The statistical factor involves achieving a controlled process at an economically acceptable level. An unacceptably high average may result from particular defects. To reduce these defects can require a different technique, such as precontrol or average and range charts.

In Chapter 5, out-of-control conditions were defined for charts in general. With attribute charts, points outside the control limits require special interpretation. A point above the upper control limit has a different meaning than one below the lower control limit. The point above could indicate either that some undesirable influence has entered the process or that the inspection standard has been tightened. The point below could indicate either that some desirable influence has affected the process or that the inspection standard has been relaxed. Whether the point is above or below and whatever the assignable cause, the influence which is desirable should be retained and that which is undesirable should be eliminated.

On occasion, an arbitrary standard (chart center line), such as budgeted scrap allowance, is selected and projected as a goal for production. In this case, points out of control cannot be interpreted the same as previously. For statistical purposes, another chart based on the actual process average should be maintained.

Attribute sampling plans, since they deal with defectives and defects, generate data which can be plotted on control charts. Frequently one can be used to supplement the other. A chart maintained on a process checked 100 percent which shows a consistent control and an acceptably low quality level may be replaced with an attribute sampling plan with consequent reduction in inspection costs. Also, although receiving inspection is the primary application for sampling plans, it is another area where charts may be effectively utilized. Data from sampling can be plotted on a control chart, making it possible to estimate the vendor's process average and state of control. This information is available to the purchasing department to aid in vendor evaluation and selection.

In summary, it should be reemphasized that charts only reflect conditions which exist and are absolutely worthless unless appropriate action is taken.

APPENDIX 1
CHAPTER SIX

DIRECTIONS FOR USE OF STATISTICAL QUALITY CONTROL SLIDE RULE

A. Directions for computing limits for averages, ranges, and individuals.

1. Set the index (red arrow) over the value for the average range (R) on the *average range* ($\bar{R}$) scale.
   a. If $\bar{R} = 0.015$, use 1.5 on the slide rule and code all other values accordingly.
   b. If $\bar{R} = 0.150$, use 1.5 on the slide rule and code all other values accordingly.
   c. If $\bar{R} = 0.0015$, use 1.5 on the slide rule and code all other values accordingly.

2. Directly above the sample size (size of each periodic sample on $\bar{X}$ and R charts) shown in red on the movable scale, read the upper control limit (UCL$_R$) for the ranges on the *upper limit for ranges (UCL$_R$)* scale. Directly beneath the same sample size in red, read the lower control limit (LCL$_R$) on the *lower limit for ranges (LCL$_R$)* scale. For sample sizes less than 8, LCL$_R$ = 0.

3. Directly above the sample size (in red), read the plus and minus limits for averages on the *limits for averages* ($\pm 3\sigma_{\bar{x}}$) scale. This value must be added to or subtracted from the grand average of the data for determining if averages are in natural control. This value must also be added to or subtracted from the nominal of the blueprint specification for future control if the process is to be operated on natural control limits.

4. Directly above the sample size (in red), read the plus and minus limits for individual pieces on the *limits for individuals* ($\pm 3\sigma$) scale. This value must be added to or subtracted from the grand average ($\bar{X}$) if the averages and ranges of the data are within the natural control limits. This will give a comparison of the process performance against the specification.

EXAMPLE

Specification = 0.500 inch ± 0.005 inch, and 0 = 0.500 inch.

Average range ($\bar{R}$) computed from 20 samples of 5 pieces each = 0.0043 inch (use 4.3 on the slide rule).

Grand average ($\bar{\bar{X}}$) = 0.5012 inch or ±1.2.

From the slide rule:

1. Upper control limit for ranges (UCL$_R$) = 9.1 or 0.0091 inch.
   Lower control limit for ranges (LCL$_R$) = 0.

2. Plus and minus limits for averages ($\pm 3\sigma_{\bar{x}}$) = ±2.48 or ±0.00248 inch. Variation of averages from grand average is

$$\text{UCL}_{\bar{x}} = \bar{\bar{X}} + 3\sigma_{\bar{x}} = +1.2 + 2.48 = +3.68 \text{ or } 0.50368 \text{ inch}$$
$$\text{LCL}_{\bar{x}} = \bar{\bar{X}} - 3\sigma_{\bar{x}} = +1.2 - 2.48 = -1.28 \text{ or } 0.49872 \text{ inch}$$

For process control from specification nominal (0 = 0.500 inch) to natural control limits,

$$\text{UCL}_{\bar{x}} = \text{Spec. nominal} + 3\sigma_{\bar{x}} = 0 + 2.48 = +2.48 \text{ or } 0.50248 \text{ inch}$$
$$\text{LCL}_{\bar{x}} = \text{Spec. nominal} - 3\sigma_{\bar{x}} = 0 - 2.48 = -2.48 \text{ or } 0.49752 \text{ inch}$$

3. Plus and minus limits for individuals ($\pm 3\sigma$) = ±5.5 or ±0.0055 inch. If averages and ranges are within natural control,

$$\text{Spread of individuals} = \bar{X} \pm 3\sigma = 0.5012 \pm 0.0055 \text{ inch}$$
$$\text{Process spread} = \pm 0.0055 \text{ or } 0.011 \text{ inch}$$
$$\text{Spec. spread} = \pm 0.005 \text{ or } 0.010 \text{ inch}$$
$$\text{Process capability} = 110\% \text{ of tolerance}$$

At $\bar{\bar{X}} = 0.5012$ inch and the individual spread at 0.5012 inch ±0.0055 inch, 1.7% will exceed specification limits.

B. Directions for percent (p) or number (pN) defective chart.

1. Set the index (in red) above the computed process average (expressed in percent) on the *process average ($\bar{p}\%$)* scale.

2. Limits for the percentage chart can be read on the *limits for p chart percent ($\pm 3\sigma_p$)* scale above the subgroup sample size in red.

3. Limits for the number defective chart can be read on the *limits for pN chart ($\pm 3\sigma_{pN}$)* scale beneath the subgroup sample size in red.

EXAMPLE

Thirty samples of 50 each have been taken. The total number of defectives found was 35.

$$\bar{p} = \frac{35}{30 \times 50} \times 100\% = \frac{35}{1,500} \times 100\% = 2.34\%$$

From the slide rule:

1. Plus/minus limits for p chart = 6.45%.

$$\text{UCL}_p = \bar{p} + 3\sigma_p = 2.34\% + 6.45\% = 8.79\%$$
$$\text{LCL}_p = \bar{p} - 3\sigma_p = 2.34\% - 6.45\% = 0$$

2. Plus/minus limits for pN chart $= 3.2$.

$$\bar{p}N = (0.0234)(50) = 1.17$$
$$UCL_{pN} = \bar{p}N + 3\sigma_{pN} = 1.17 + 3.2 = 4.37$$
$$LCL_{pN} = \bar{p}N - 3\sigma_{pN} = 1.17 - 3.2 = 0$$

C. Directions for chart for number of defects (c).

1. Set the red index under the average number of defects per sample ($\bar{c}$) shown on the *average number of defects per sample* ($\bar{c}$) scale. Read plus and minus limits directly beneath the index on the *limits for c chart* ($\pm 3\sigma_c$) scale.

EXAMPLE
Forty samples of 10 pieces each were taken from an assembly line. A total of 800 defects was found.

$$\bar{c} = \frac{800}{40} = 20 \text{ per sample (10 pieces)}$$

From the slide rule, limits $= \pm 13.4$.

$$UCL_c = \bar{c} + 3\sigma_c = 20 + 13.4 = 33.4$$
$$CLL_c = \bar{c} - 3\sigma_c = 20 - 13.4 = 6.6$$

Note: If $\bar{c}$ should exceed 400, divide $\bar{c}$ by 100 and set the index under $c \div 100$ on the *average number of defects per sample* ($\bar{c}$) scale. Read the answer below the index on the *limits for c chart* ($\pm 3\sigma_c$) scale and multiply this answer by 10. Thus, if $c = 600$, set the index at 6, and read 7.3. The plus and minus limits are 10×7.3 or 73.

D. Directions for chart for average number (u) of defects per piece or unit.

1. Set the red index over the average number of defects per piece or unit ($\bar{u}$) shown on the *average number of defects per piece* ($\bar{u}$) scale.

2. Plus and minus limits for the u chart can be read on the *limits for u chart* ($\pm 3\sigma_u$) scale above the number of pieces or units per sample (k) in red.

EXAMPLE
Twenty samples of 10 pieces each are taken, and 800 defects observed.

$$\bar{u} = \frac{800}{20 \times 10} = \frac{800}{200} = 4 \text{ (average number of defects per piece)}$$

From the slide rule:

$$\text{Limits} = \pm 1.9$$
$$UCL_u = \bar{u} + 3\sigma_u$$
$$= 4 + 1.9$$
$$= 5.9$$
$$LCL_u = \bar{u} - 3\sigma_u$$
$$= 4 - 1.9$$
$$= 2.1$$

APPENDIX 2
CHAPTER
SIX
CLASSIFICATION OF DISCREPANCIES FOR MOTOR VEHICLES

Class "A" (20 demerits): Discrepancies, failures, damage, or parts missing which could cause unexpected loss of vehicle control, driver visibility, or occupant jeopardy.

Class "B" (10 demerits): Items which could immobilize the car so that the car cannot be restarted or driven within a few minutes. Items which could cause great discomfort to owner or occupants. Items of high warranty cost.

Class "C" (4 demerits): Items which cause very annoying, substandard performance or which could cause increased maintenance or decreased life of vehicle components. Functional items not affecting the conveyance purposes of the vehicle. Appearance items that would generate warranty expense.

Class "D" (1 demerit): Items that could cause slight inconvenience or annoyance to an owner. This type of discrepancy will not keep the car from being used or affect service life, maintenance, or reliability to any great degree. This is the type of discrepancy that an owner might notice, but it would not cause him to rush to the dealer for immediate correction.

CHAPTER SEVEN | VARIABLES CONTROL CHARTS

For more precise control and when the measured data are continuous, a variables control chart is used. As previously explained, continuous data are those which express numerically a dimension, a weight, an output, a hardness, or a tensile strength. Any such characteristic which does not conform to specifications indicates the need for a variables control chart. In most applications the chart employed is the average and range chart ($\bar{X}$ and R), although other types have been devised (cumulative sum chart, midrange chart, moving average chart).

SAMPLE AVERAGES

Before presenting the average and range chart, an important concept relating to the manner in which sample means are distributed must be developed. In Chapter 3, the normal probability distribution was used in two examples to predict the percentages of shaft seals within specifications and the percentage of joint angles which exceeded the maximum permissible angle. These two cases were concerned with individual parts and their relation to specifications. While operations can be controlled by charting individual observations, greater sensitivity in detecting assignable variation is obtained by plotting sample averages.

Individual observations plotted in histogram or frequency distribution form often generate a normal distribution. Similarly, repeated samples from a given source will have averages which when plotted also tend to generate a normal distribution. This tendency is apparent regardless of the form the individual distributions possess and is based on a statistical concept known as the central limit theorem. Although the theorem refers specifically to random variable sums, division by a constant sample size merely extends the concept to include sample means. Increasing the sample size creates a distribution which is less variable and which more closely approaches the normal. To illustrate this, the data in Figure 7-1 have been plotted in three different distributions ($n = 1$, $n = 2$, $n = 5$), as shown in Figure 7-2.

Part No. __3780213__ Part Name __Transmission Output Shaft__ Plant __FMC__
Characteristic Measured __T.I.R.__ Recorded by _____ Unit of Measurement __0.0001 inch__
Zero Setting __0.0000__ Specification __0.0015 max.__

Sample No.	Date (and Hour)	Measurements of Each Item in Sample					Total	Average for Sample	Range for Sample
		X₁	X₂	X₃	X₄	X₅			
1		23	20	30	9	43	125	25.0	34
2		7	10	6	20	7	50	10.0	14
3		30	39	10	19	13	111	22.2	29
4		18	25	34	15	38	130	26.0	23
5		4	1	3	1	3	12	2.4	3
6		1	5	2	2	5	15	3.0	4
7		3	4	2	3	2	14	2.8	2
8		24	7	14	15	25	85	17.0	18
9		30	23	21	6	18	98	19.6	24
10		7	25	20	8	12	72	14.4	18
11		7	6	9	27	11	60	12.0	21
12		8	14	9	8	17	56	11.2	9
13		3	3	8	12	11	37	7.4	9
14		12	3	2	14	16	47	9.4	14
15		9	18	11	9	10	57	11.4	9
16		13	12	19	3	6	53	10.6	16
17		21	32	6	41	19	119	23.8	35
18		17	4	24	10	20	75	15.0	20
19		10	28	11	12	3	64	12.8	25
20		14	18	22	33	9	66	13.2	29
21		12	15	10	8	20	65	13.0	12
22		11	9	7	19	21	67	13.4	14
23		14	17	9	20	22	82	16.4	13
24		8	9	17	23	30	87	17.4	22
25		22	12	14	21	23	92	18.4	11
							Totals	347.8	418
							Average range		16.7
							Grand average	13.91	

Fig. 7-1 Data sheet—transmission output shaft T.I.R.

Fig. 7-2 Total indicator runout

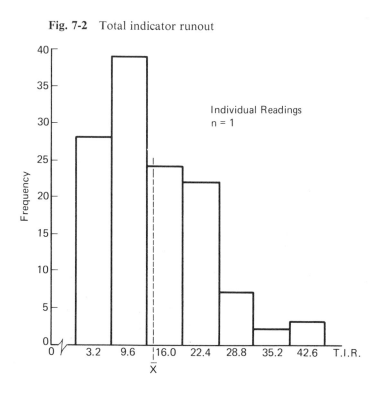

Individual Readings n = 1

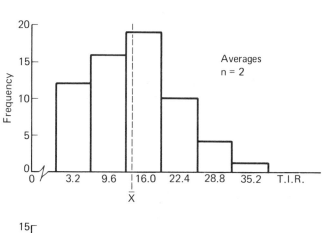

Averages n = 2

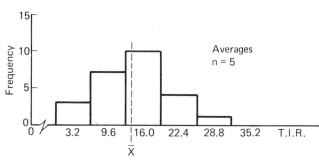

Averages n = 5

SAMPLE RANGES

The sample standard deviation measures variation, and in quality control work is designated by sigma (σ), although more recent statistical practice has conformed to a policy that uses Greek letters for population parameters and Roman letters for sample statistics. The range, the difference between the high and low values in a sample, is another way to express variability. The range is simpler to understand, is easier to calculate than the standard deviation, and for small samples (up to 15) provides a sufficiently accurate measure of variability. Figure 7-3 illustrates why the sample size 5 is commonly used with $\bar{X}$ and R charts. It can be observed that the histogram would be well approximated by the normal distribution.

Fig. 7-3 Range distribution—T.I.R.

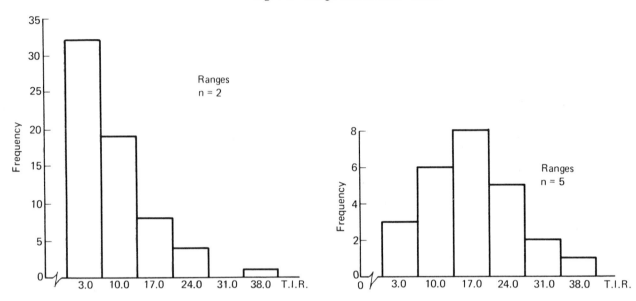

THE AVERAGE AND RANGE CHART

The average and range chart has probably received the most recognition accorded any statistical quality control tool. It is a graphical means for portraying the variability between samples ($\bar{X}$) and the variability within samples (R). Properly applied, this chart can answer several questions relating to an operations:

1. Is the variation due to chance or some assignable cause?
2. Is the operation in control at a desirable level?
   a. Is it properly centered?
   b. Is the spread satisfactory?
3. Can the operation be expected to continue in this manner?

The $\bar{X}$ and R chart differs from other control charts in that there usually are two separate charts on one form, averages ($\bar{X}$'s) at the top and ranges (R's) at the bottom. Consequently, after the sample parts are measured, two statistics are calculated and plotted. The first, $\bar{X}$, is determined by adding all the sample measurements and dividing by the sample size:

$$\bar{X} = \frac{X_1 + X_2 + \cdots + X_n}{n} = \frac{\sum X_i}{n}$$

where n = sample size.

The second, R, is calculated by subtracting the smallest measurement from the largest:

$$R = X_L - X_S$$

The center lines and control limits for this chart are determined from the following formulas:

1. *Average chart.*
   a. Center line:

$$\bar{\bar{X}} = \frac{\bar{X}_1 + \bar{X}_2 + \cdots + \bar{X}_K}{K} = \frac{\sum \bar{X}}{K}$$

   b. Control limits:

$$\bar{\bar{X}} \pm 3\sigma_{\bar{X}} = \bar{\bar{X}} \pm A_2 \bar{R}$$

2. *Range chart.*
   a. Center line:

$$\bar{R} = \frac{R_1 + R_2 + \cdots + R_K}{K} = \frac{\sum R}{K}$$

   b. Control limits:

$$\mathrm{UCL}_R = \bar{R} + 3\sigma_R = D_4 \bar{R}$$
$$\mathrm{LCL}_R = \bar{R} - 3\sigma_R = D_3 \bar{R}$$

where
$\bar{\bar{X}}$ = grand average,
K = number of samples (number of inspection units),
$\bar{R}$ = average range,
A_2, D_3, D_4 = constants found in Figure 7-6.

This is illustrated schematically in Figure 7-4.

Fig. 7-4 Sampling from a controlled process

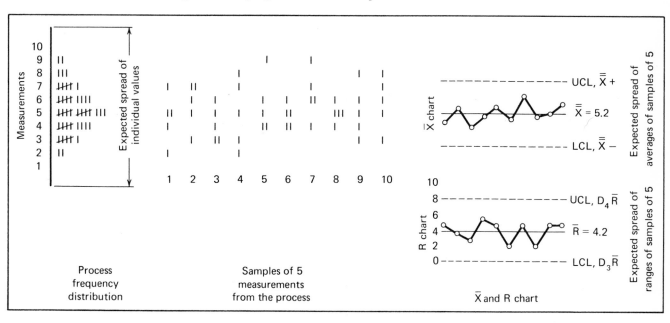

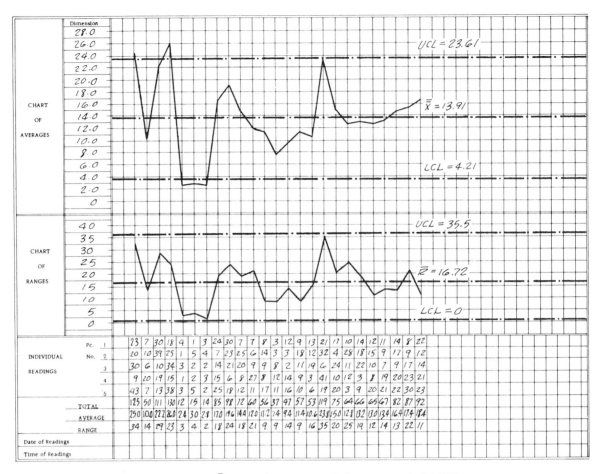

Fig. 7-5 $\bar{X}$ and R chart—transmission output shaft T.I.R.

Pc. 1	23	7	30	18	4	1	3	24	30	7	7	8	3	12	9	13	21	17	10	14	12	11	14	8	22
No. 2	20	10	39	25	1	5	4	7	23	25	6	14	3	3	18	12	32	4	28	18	15	9	17	9	12
3	30	6	10	34	3	2	2	14	21	20	9	9	8	2	11	19	6	24	11	22	10	7	9	17	14
4	9	20	19	15	1	2	3	15	6	8	27	8	12	14	9	3	41	10	12	3	8	19	20	23	21
5	43	7	13	38	3	5	2	25	18	12	11	17	11	16	10	6	19	20	3	9	20	21	22	30	23
TOTAL	125	50	111	130	12	15	14	85	98	72	60	56	37	47	57	53	119	75	64	66	65	67	82	87	92
AVERAGE	25.0	10.0	22.2	26.0	2.4	3.0	2.8	17.0	19.6	14.4	12.0	11.2	7.4	9.4	11.4	10.6	23.8	15.0	12.8	13.2	13.0	13.4	16.4	17.4	18.4
RANGE	34	14	29	23	3	4	2	18	24	18	21	9	9	14	9	16	35	20	25	19	12	14	13	22	11

EXAMPLE

The transmission output shaft data are shown in Figure 7-5 on an average and range chart. Steps in constructing it are

1.   Calculate $\bar{X}$'s:

$$\bar{X}_1 = \frac{23 + 20 + 30 + 9 + 43}{5} = \frac{125}{5} = 25.0$$

2.   Calculate R's:

$$R_1 = 43 - 9 = 34$$

3.   Calculate $\bar{\bar{X}}$:

$$\bar{\bar{X}} = \frac{25.0 + 10.0 + \cdots + 18.4}{25} = \frac{347.8}{25} = 13.91$$

4.   Calculate $\bar{R}$:

$$\bar{R} = \frac{34 + 14 + \cdots + 11}{25} = \frac{418}{25} = 16.7$$

5.   Calculate average chart control limits:

$$\text{UCL}_{\bar{x}} = 13.91 + (0.577)(16.7)$$
$$= 13.91 + 9.64 = 23.55$$

$$\text{LCL}_{\bar{x}} = 13.91 - (0.577)(16.7)$$
$$= 13.91 - 9.64 = 4.27$$

6. Calculate range chart control limits:

$$\text{UCL}_R = (2.114)(16.7)$$
$$= 35.3$$
$$\text{LCL}_R = (0.0)(16.7)$$
$$= 0$$

CHART ANALYSIS

Chart analysis will follow the general guidelines discussed in Chapter 5, in addition to the questions expressed earlier in this chapter.

1. Is the variation due to chance or assignable causes? Although all ranges are in control (two barely), the average chart shows six points out of control. The data, however, are for total indicator reading (runout) on the shaft. Thus the points above the upper limit have an interpretation different from those below the lower limit. In this case the latter indicate a highly desirable condition—assuming the data are valid. The abrupt change from the first four points plotted to the next three appears to indicate that an assignable cause exists.

2. Is the operation in control at a desirable level?
   a. Is it properly centered?
   b. Is the spread satisfactory?
   Referring to the data sheet (Figure 7-1), the specification is 0.0015 inch maximum runout. Since the grand average is 0.00139 inch with approximately half the values above this, it is obviously centered much too high. From the histograms plotted in Figure 7-2, it can be seen that individual measurements have a wider variation than sample averages. The estimated process limits for individuals are

$$\bar{X} \pm \frac{3\bar{R}}{d_2}$$

where d_2 is the constant found in Figure 7-6. For this process, then,

$$\text{UCL}_X = 13.91 + \frac{3(16.72)}{2.326}$$
$$= 13.91 + 21.57 = 35.48$$
$$\text{LCL}_X = 13.91 - \frac{3(16.72)}{2.326}$$
$$= 13.91 - 21.57 = -7.66 = 0$$

When the limits calculated for individual measurements do not lie within the process specifications, the process is not in control at a desirable level.

3. Can the operation be expected to continue in this manner? Due to the fact that the process is not meeting the specifications, an investigation to correct whatever problem exists should be made before control limits are projected into the future. This will be discussed more fully in Chapter 8.

Sample Size	Factor for			Factor for Estimated Standard Deviation (Sigma)	Sample Size
	Average	Range			
n	A_2	D_3	D_4	d_2	n
2	1.880	0.0	3.268	1.128	2
3	1.023	0.0	2.574	1.693	3
4	0.729	0.0	2.282	2.059	4
5	0.577	0.0	2.114	2.326	5
6	0.483	0.0	2.004	2.534	6
7	0.419	0.076	1.924	2.704	7
8	0.373	0.136	1.864	2.847	8
9	0.337	0.184	1.816	2.970	9
10	0.308	0.223	1.777	3.078	10
11	0.285	0.256	1.744	3.173	11
12	0.266	0.284	1.717	3.258	12
13	0.249	0.308	1.692	3.336	13
14	0.235	0.329	1.671	3.407	14
15	0.223	0.348	1.652	3.476	15

Formulas for Computing Control Limits

For Averages	For Range
$UCL_{\bar{X}} = \bar{\bar{X}} + A_2 \bar{R}$	$UCL_R = D_4 \bar{R}$
$LCL_{\bar{X}} = \bar{\bar{X}} - A_2 \bar{R}$	$LCL_R = D_3 \bar{R}$

Standard Deviation (Sigma)

$$Sigma = \frac{\bar{R}}{d_2}$$

Fig. 7-6 Factors for computing control limits on $\bar{X}$ and R charts

ADDITIONAL ASPECTS

Control limits may be computed after 20 or 25 samples have been taken. When the process is in control, the limits are projected for the subsequent time period but should be verified after another 10 to 15 samples have been taken.

It should be reemphasized that a state of control does not necessarily mean that the process is operating satisfactorily. The process might be stable at the wrong level or might have too much inherent variation.

The chart aids in producing quality products in the following ways:

- Determines if the process is capable
- Answers the operator's question "How am I doing?"
- Provides information as to when, and how much, to adjust the process
- Indicates when to leave a process alone
- Points out abnormal variations within or between samples
- Assists in defining problems such as tool wear, operator differences, or defective material

Finally, a word of caution should be given regarding chart application. It is a diagnostic tool and should be used where problems exist with respect to man, machine, material, or measurement.

CHAPTER EIGHT | CAPABILITY STUDIES

A quality product can be produced only when the machine or process involved can maintain the specified tolerances. When equipment cannot meet these tolerances, cost is added in the form of scrap, rework, or both. Prior to presenting the statistical techniques used, general definitions are in order.

Process capability: A processing method that includes man, machine, material, and measurement is studied to determine total variability and process stability. Time is an important factor to consider, since changes in quality level will occur as tools wear or are replaced, as the man makes corrective adjustments, when materials vary or are changed, when measuring equipment wears or drifts, or when any combination of these changes significantly.

Machine reliability: A concept that considers machine longevity and total maintenance expense during the machine life. This requires that extensive records be maintained along with close coordination between quality control, maintenance, and production. Properly applied, it would generate information valuable in making comparisons among different machine makes doing comparable work.

Machine capability: A machine or fabricating device is studied under controlled conditions to determine natural or inherent variation. The man is not permitted to make adjustments, the material quality is controlled, and the measuring equipment is accurately calibrated and repeatable. Tool wear and other influencing factors should also be considered.

Machine reliability will not be discussed further. Certain planning steps should precede actually collecting and analyzing the data for either the machine or process capability study.

These steps are

1. Become familiar with the part. Make a sketch, omitting all unnecessary dimensions.
   a. Study dimensional characteristics.
   b. Determine what measuring instruments are required and how the measurement will be made.
   c. Study part design and how it may affect results.
   d. Consider part material and its effect.
2. Review the processing method.
   a. Is it cut, grind, drill, ream, or pierce form?
   b. Is the work done on a single- or multiple-spindle operation?
   c. How is the part located—fixture, jigs?
   d. Are adjustments made manually or automatically?
   e. What is the operation time cycle?
   f. What coolants are used?
   g. Are speeds and feeds correctly specified?
3. Check the gage availability.
   a. Determine whether proper gages are used.
   b. Analyze gage repeatability and reproducibility. (See the appendix to this chapter.)
4. Check the part quality that will be coming to the machine.
   a. The roughing dimension must be acceptable.
   b. Don't use preselected parts.
   c. Use parts from normal material flow.
5. Investigate all information sources.
   a. Engineering.
   b. Inspection.
   c. Production.
   d. Processing.
   e. Any others concerned with the problem.

In addition to the preceding planning, the following information should be obtained:

1. Machine number.
2. Operation number.
3. Type or kind of tooling.
4. Feeds and speeds.
5. Coolant or lubricant type.
6. Amount of metal removal.
7. Other pertinent information.

When studying either a process or a machine, the capability is expressed as a number which can be compared to the specified tolerance. Since most industrial processes tend to follow the normal probability distribution, this number is defined as the *six standard deviation spread*. Another number which extends this idea is the capability ratio:

$$\text{Capability ratio } (\%) = \frac{6s}{\text{Total tolerance}}(100)$$

In general, new equipment is considered capable if this ratio is 67 percent or less, and existing equipment is considered capable if the ratio is 75 percent or less.

A process capability study, in its broadest sense, may involve a simple machine, a complex machine, a group of like machines, an entire production sequence, or a whole departmental activity. The study may be made with respect to a manufacturing process, an assembly process, or a testing process. In its simplest form, the process study involves a single measurable characteristic on a single machine. Since the broad study proceeds from the simpler, the single machine capability study will be developed first.

MACHINE CAPABILITY STUDY

The preferred point in time to conduct a machine capability study is when it is still at the machine tool vendor's plant. The reason is obvious, because if changes are required to meet the tolerances, they can be made more readily where it is built. The vendor should also be informed that the capability desired is not the tolerance but the ratio previously given. Regardless of where the study is performed, it should be conducted under normal operating conditions but holding as many variables constant as is possible. To elaborate on the earlier definition,

- Use raw material from one batch, one machine operator, and one inspector during the data collection.

- Calibrate the measuring instrument at the beginning and avoid further calibration unless this is a regularly scheduled event during the checking interval.

- Sequentially number the pieces as they are produced, recording the environmental conditions so that they may be reproduced if a recheck becomes necessary.

The simplest capability study concerns one part and one dimension. The objective is to determine the machine's inherent capability to meet the engineering tolerances for a particular dimension on a particular part. Since inadequate consideration is often given to any relationship between blueprint tolerances for a given dimension or characteristic and the machine's capability to produce what is required, this relationship's evaluation is essential.

The appropriate sample size to take in conducting the study is usually an arbitrary, not a statistical, decision. If it is done at the machine vendor's plant and prototype parts are used, the sample will be relatively small. An article entitled "Shortcuts for Machine Capability Studies," which appeared in *Quality Management and Engineering*, February 1972, suggested the following:

If a machine produces more than 200 pieces per hour, the sample should consist of 200 consecutive pieces. Should the production rate be less than 200 pieces per hour, the sample size should be equivalent to one hour's production, with a minimum of 50 pieces in the event the per hour rate may be less than 50. In the case of very high production equipment (2,000 pieces or more per hour), select samples of 200 consecutive pieces at random time intervals distributed over one hour's production. The important point is to avoid a constant time interval in selecting samples, as this may inadvertently coincide with a peculiarity in the machine cycle. Once designed, the same sequence may be used repeatedly.

There are four tests which should be applied to the data collected during the time the study is being made. These tests determine

1. The maximum allowable tolerance range for the sample subgroup size.
2. The control limits for maximum range to test for range stability.
3. The control limits for sample averages to determine the *state of control*.
4. The test for demonstrated machine capability.

The first is a quick test, made during the study, to roughly determine machine capability. For example, if 5 is the sample subgroup size, the range tolerance would be 0.82 of print tolerance. With a 10-piece subgroup size it would be (0.91) (total tolerance). This means that a machine which can continuously produce parts within the full print tolerance will produce a 5-piece sample within (0.82) (total tolerance) or a 10-piece sample within (0.91) (total tolerance). An additional 25 percent allowance is frequently made for other external factors, further narrowing the tolerance range. With a 5-piece sample, then, the tolerance range with a 0.010-inch print tolerance would be 0.006 [(0.010)(0.75)(0.82) = 0.006]. This test is not an absolute capability measure but can be used to anticipate the final outcome. If the value obtained indicates that the machine will not be qualified, the study can be terminated until corrections are made, thus avoiding further expenditure of time and parts.

The second test which is applied after the preceding trial run sets control limits for the maximum range to determine range stability. This would be done after the first few samples were acceptable under the range tolerance test. It assures that the machine was stable during the entire study and that it will remain stable under prolonged production conditions. The statistic involved is the same as that developed in Chapter 7:

$$\text{UCL}_R = D_4 \bar{R}$$

The third test determines machine stability by setting control limits for sample averages. It indicates whether the machine demonstrates a *state of control* or develops a trend away from the nominal print tolerance when it is operating under production conditions. These limits would again be established after the first few samples from the first test were acceptable. The control limit calculations utilize the average range and would preferably be established about the nominal print dimension:

$$\text{CL}_{\bar{x}} = \text{Print nominal} \pm A_2 \bar{R}$$

The last test for demonstrated machine capability is similar to the second. In this case the entire data collected are used to calculate the average range. Using this value and the d_2 factor from the table of constants (Figure 7-6), six standard deviations for individual pieces are calculated, the capability ratio is determined, and if this falls within the acceptability criteria, the machine is considered capable. That is,

$$\text{C.R.} = \text{Capability ratio} = \frac{6\sigma}{\text{Total tolerance}}$$

Accept as capable if:

New equipment: $\text{C.R.} \leq 0.67$ (total tolerance)

Existing equipment: $\text{C.R.} \leq 0.75$ (total tolerance)

EXAMPLE

The machine capability study will be illustrated using an operation which produces gear blanks. A diameter specification (1.6950–1.7000 inches) is the characteristic being studied. The procedure followed is that previously explained. Note that all data are coded. The measurement unit is 0.0001 inch, and readings are recorded from a 1.6900-inch zero setting.

1. Determine the maximum allowable tolerance range for the 5-piece subgroup.

Total print tolerance = 1.7000 inches − 1.6950 inches = 0.0050

or coded = 50

QUALITY CONTROL

PART NAME

Part No. _283G452I-GEAR BLANK_ Inspector _J. BLANK_ Date _____

Operation No. _47_ Machine No. _8622_ Shift _1ST_

B/P Specification _1.6950 - 1.7000 IN._ Characteristic Measured _DIAMETER_ Unit of Measurement _0.0001" ZERO SETTING 1.6950 IN._

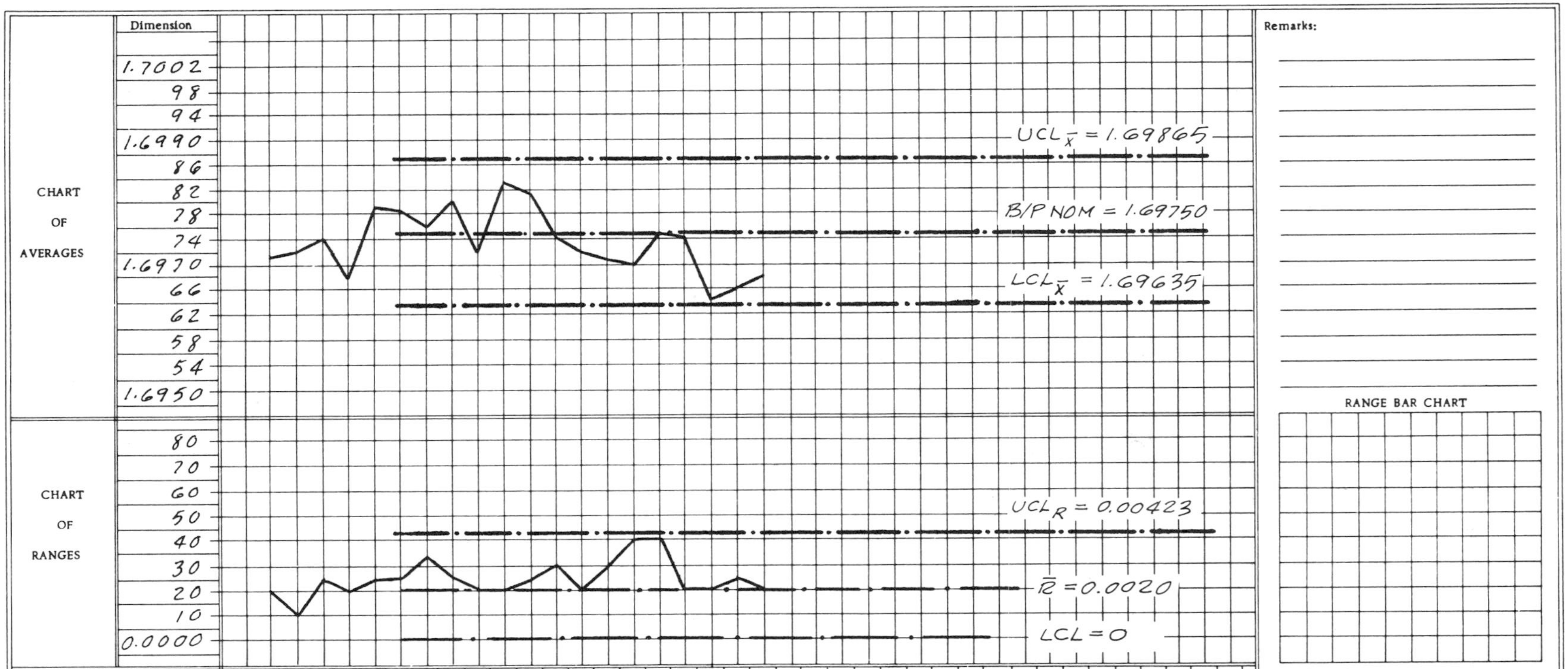

Remarks:

RANGE BAR CHART

Action Taken:

$UCL_{\bar{x}} = 1.69865$

$B/P\ NOM = 1.69750$

$LCL_{\bar{x}} = 1.69635$

$UCL_R = 0.00423$

$\bar{R} = 0.0020$

$LCL = 0$

Dimension		
1.7002		
98		
94		
1.6990		
86		
82		
78		
74		
1.6970		
66		
62		
58		
54		
1.6950		
0.0000		

CHART OF AVERAGES

80	
70	
60	
50	
40	
30	
20	
10	
0.0000	

CHART OF RANGES

	Pc. No.
INDIVIDUAL READINGS	1
	2
	3
	4
	5
TOTAL	
AVERAGE	
RANGE	

Date of Readings

Time of Readings

Fig. 8-1 Average and range chart—gear blank diameter

$$\text{Allowable tolerance range} = (0.82)(0.75)(\text{total tolerance})$$
$$= (0.82)(0.75)(50)$$
$$= 30.75$$

Check the ranges for the first five samples (see Figure 8-1):

$$R_1 = 20, \quad R_2 = 10, \quad R_3 = 25, \quad R_4 = 20, \quad R_5 = 25$$

Since these values are all less than 30.75, proceed to the next test.

2. Calculate the control limit for the maximum range to test for range stability:

$$\text{UCL}_R = D_4\bar{R}$$
$$\bar{R} = \frac{\sum R}{K} = \frac{20 + 10 + 25 + 20 + 25}{5} = \frac{100}{5} = 20$$
$$\text{UCL}_R = (2.155)(20) = 42.3$$

Project this value on the range chart to assess range stability for subsequent subgroups.

3. Calculate control limits for sample averages to determine the state of control:

$$\text{UCL}_{\bar{x}} = \text{Print nominal} + A_2\bar{R}$$
$$= 75 + (0.577)(20)$$
$$= 75 + 11.54 = 86.54 = 86.5$$
$$\text{LCL}_{\bar{x}} = \text{Print nominal} - A_2\bar{R}$$
$$= 75 - (0.577)(20)$$
$$= 75 - 11.54 = 63.46 = 63.5$$

Project these limits on the average chart to assess stability for subsequent subgroups.

4. Test for demonstrated machine capability. The 15 subsequent subgroups are within the limits projected for the averages and ranges. Therefore, the machine capability can be determined by calculating

$$3\sigma_X = \frac{3\bar{R}}{d_2}$$

where

$$\bar{R} = \frac{20 + 10 + \cdots + 20}{K} = \frac{495}{20} = 24.75$$

Then

$$3\sigma_X = \frac{3(24.75)}{2.326} = 31.92$$

and

$$6\sigma_X = 2(31.92) = 63.84$$

$$\text{Capability ratio} = \frac{6\sigma}{\text{Total tolerance}} = \frac{63.84}{50} = 1.28$$

Since $1.28 > 0.75$, the machine is not capable.

This study illustrates several interesting points. The first quick test for capability indicated that the study should be continued. After limits for ranges and averages were projected, subsequent samples indicated stability, since the points plotted were within the limits. It should be noted, however, that no subsequent ranges were below the estimated mean ($\bar{R}$) and that evidently some change occurred.

An alternative analysis method to determine machine capability is normal probability paper, presented in Chapter 3. The data from this study are shown on NOPP in Figure 8-2. The print limits reveal that approximately 2 percent are below 1.6950 and 1 percent above 1.700.

Fig. 8-2 Normal probability plot—gear blank diameter

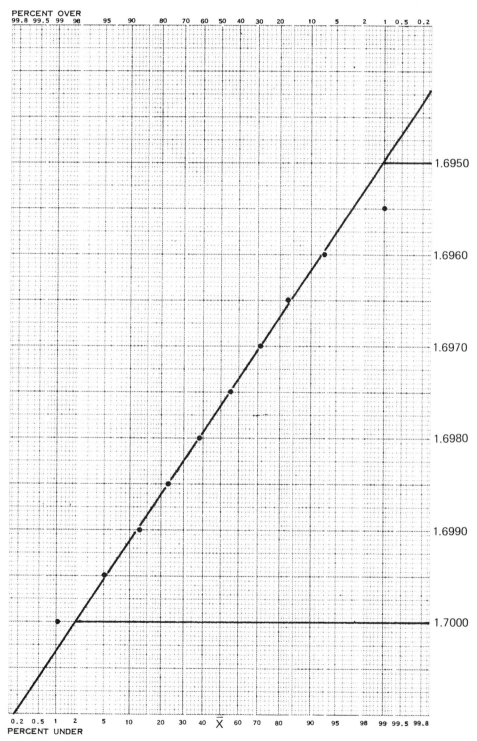

OTHER CONTROL LIMITS

Although this concept could have been covered in Chapter 7, it was important to develop machine capabilities first. Basically, there are three different types of limits which can be used with $\bar{X}$ and R charts. These types are

1. Natural.
2. Modified (temporary).
3. Modified-natural.

Natural limits are those established by the machine or process. The limits calculated in the previous example were *natural* since they were based on the data collected from the operation. When the natural limits are less than 75 percent of the print tolerance, it is frequently useful to combine them with print limits to permit maximum leeway on the average chart. These limits will be explained under modified-natural.

Modified or temporary limits are based entirely on the print specifications. These limits could be established prior to beginning a capability study as an alternative to the procedure previously outlined or used where temporary control is desired before data can be collected. There are also occasions where they might be used to permit more drift in the averages than would be permissible with natural limits. In determining these limits for the $\bar{X}$ and R chart, the sample size needs to be specified in advance. Their use also makes the assumption that the data which will be generated are normal, that the machine is centered on the print nominal dimension, and that six standard deviations for individuals are equal to the total tolerance. The concept will be explained using the specifications given previously for the gear blanks (1.6950–1.7000 inches).

EXAMPLE

1. Set

$$6\sigma_x = \text{Total tolerance}$$
$$= 1.7000 \text{ inches} - 1.6950 \text{ inches} = 0.0050$$
$$= 50 \text{ coded}$$

2. Calculate the average range. Specify $n = 5$.

$$\sigma_x = \frac{\bar{R}}{d_2}$$

or

$$6\sigma_x = \frac{6\bar{R}}{d_2}$$

$$\bar{R} = \frac{(d_2)(6\sigma_x)}{6}$$

$$= \frac{(2.326)(50)}{6} = 19.38$$

3. Calculate control limits for the range chart:

$$\text{UML}_R = D_4\bar{R}$$
$$= (2.115)(19.38) = 40.99$$
$$\text{LML}_R = D_3\bar{R}$$
$$= (0)(19.38) = 0$$

116

4. Calculate control limits for the average chart:

$$\text{UML}_{\bar{x}} = \text{Print nominal} + A_2\bar{R}$$
$$= 75 + (0.577)(19.38)$$
$$= 75 + 11.18 = 86.18 = 86.2$$
$$\text{LML}_{\bar{x}} = \text{Print nominal} - A_2\bar{R}$$
$$= 75 - (0.577)(19.38)$$
$$= 75 - 11.18 = 63.82 = 63.8$$

These limits may be obtained more readily with the SQC slide rule.

As a guideline in initially conducting a machine capability study, the $\bar{X}$ and R chart limits could be modified from 75 percent of the total tolerance. If the averages and ranges stayed within these limits, the machine would be acceptable.

Modified-natural limits, as the name implies, are a combination, i.e., modifying the print specifications and also using information concerning the machine's inherent capability. Under those conditions where the machine-demonstrated capability is less than 75 percent of the total tolerance, these limits permit the averages to drift a maximum amount without producing parts which exceed the specification limits. The limits for the range chart are still calculated using the constants D_3 and D_4, since $\bar{R}$ is known from the study. Control limits for the average chart are calculated as follows:

$$\text{UMNL}_{\bar{x}} = \text{Upper print limit} - 3\sigma_x + 3\sigma_{\bar{x}}$$
$$\text{LMNL}_{\bar{x}} = \text{Lower print limit} + 3\sigma_x - 3\sigma_{\bar{x}}$$

Fig. 8-3 Modified-natural limits

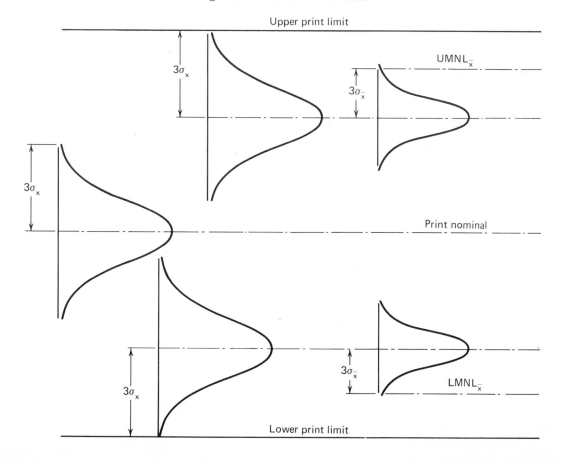

This is shown schematically in Figure 8-3. The technique is especially applicable where relatively rapid tool wear exists but the within-subgroup variability is small. By fitting a trend line to the averages plotted, it is possible to specify where the machine should be set initially, where it should be reset, and how many pieces can be produced between these points.

EXAMPLE

A machine capability study was made on a Brown and Sharpe single-spindle screw machine, cutting a small diameter. Specifications were 0.280 to 0.290 inch. A 50-piece sample was taken, with the data shown in Figure 8-4.

Subgroup	Measurement					Total	$\bar{x}$	R
1	0.281	0.282	0.282	0.283	0.282	1.410	0.2820	0.002
2	0.281	0.282	0.283	0.282	0.283	1.411	0.2822	0.002
3	0.284	0.283	0.284	0.283	0.284	1.418	0.2836	0.001
4	0.285	0.284	0.285	0.286	0.284	1.424	0.2848	0.002
5	0.283	0.284	0.286	0.287	0.285	1.425	0.2850	0.004
6	0.287	0.289	0.288	0.289	0.288	1.441	0.2882	0.002
7	0.287	0.289	0.291	0.289	0.290	1.446	0.2892	0.004
8	0.291	0.290	0.289	0.290	0.289	1.449	0.2898	0.002
9	0.288	0.287	0.286	0.287	0.288	1.436	0.2872	0.002
10	0.288	0.289	0.288	0.289	0.291	1.445	0.2890	0.002
					Totals		2.8610	0.023

Fig. 8-4   Diameter readings

1. Calculate $\bar{\bar{X}}$ and $\bar{R}$:

$$\bar{\bar{X}} = \frac{\sum \bar{X}}{K} = \frac{2.8610}{10} = 0.2861$$

$$\bar{R} = \frac{\sum R}{K} = \frac{0.023}{10} = 0.0023$$

2. Calculate $6\sigma_X$:

$$6\sigma_X = \frac{6\bar{R}}{d_2} = \frac{6(0.0023)}{2.326} = 0.0059$$

3. Determine the machine capability:

$$\text{Capability ratio} = \frac{6\sigma_X}{\text{Total tolerance}} = \frac{0.0059}{0.010} = 0.59$$

Since $0.59 < 0.75$, the machine is considered highly capable.

4. Calculate natural control limits:

$$\text{UCL}_R = D_4\bar{R} = (2.155)(0.0023) = 0.0049$$
$$\text{LCL}_R = D_3\bar{R} = (0)(0.0023) = 0$$
$$\text{UCL}_{\bar{x}} = \text{Print nominal} + A_2\bar{R} = 0.285 + (0.577)(0.0023) = 0.2863$$
$$\text{LCL}_{\bar{x}} = \text{Print nominal} - A_2\bar{R} = 0.285 - (0.577)(0.0023) = 0.2837$$

These limits for averages would unnecessarily restrict the averages; i.e., they could be allowed to drift without producing parts outside specifications. Modified-natural limits should be considered:

$$\text{UMNL}_{\bar{x}} = \text{Upper print limit} - 3\sigma_X + 3\sigma_{\bar{x}}$$

$$6\sigma_X = 0.0059$$

$$3\sigma_X = \frac{0.0059}{2} = 0.00285 = 0.0029$$

$$3\sigma_{\bar{x}} = A_2\bar{R} = (0.577)(0.0023) = 0.0013$$

Then

$$\text{UMNL}_{\bar{x}} = 0.290 - 0.0029 + 0.0013$$
$$= 0.2884$$

$$\text{LMNL}_{\bar{x}} = \text{Lower print limit} + 3\sigma_X - 3\sigma_{\bar{x}}$$
$$= 0.280 + 0.0029 - 0.0013$$
$$= 0.2816$$

To compare all three limits for averages (natural, modified-natural, and modified) the last type will be calculated for these data.

1. Set $3\sigma_X$ equal to one-half the total tolerance:

$$3\sigma_X = \frac{0.010}{2} = 0.005$$

2. Determine the average range:

$$3\sigma_X = \frac{3\bar{R}}{d_2}$$

or

$$\bar{R} = \frac{(d_2)(3\sigma_X)}{3} = \frac{(2.326)(0.005)}{3} = 0.0039$$

3. Calculate limits for averages:

$$\text{UML}_{\bar{x}} = \text{Print nominal} + A_2\bar{R}$$
$$= 0.285 + (0.577)(0.0039)$$
$$= 0.285 + 0.0023 = 0.2873$$

$$\text{LML}_{\bar{x}} = 0.285 - (0.577)(0.0039)$$
$$= 0.285 - 0.0023 = 0.2827$$

These limits are summarized in Figure 8-5.

Type Limit	Upper	Lower	Total Spread
Natural	0.2863	0.2837	0.0026
Modified	0.2873	0.2827	0.0046
Modified-natural	0.2884	0.2816	0.0068

Fig. 8-5 Comparison of limits

As can be observed, the modified-natural limits provide considerably more latitude for the averages and would be the preferred limits on this operation. However, a periodic check should be made on the standard deviation for individuals since, as the machine wears, this will become larger. At some point in time, unless preventive maintenance takes place, another type of limit may be preferable.

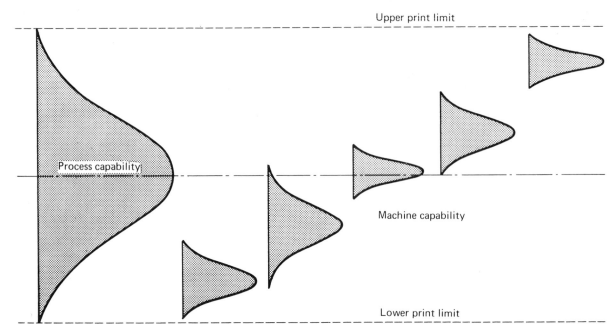

Upper print limit

Process capability

Machine capability

Lower print limit

Fig. 8-6 Process vs. machine capability

PROCESS CAPABILITY STUDY

The basic difference between the machine and process capability study is time. In the machine study the capability measure was calculated using the average range, which measured variation within small subgroups. When trends exist on the average chart and the data are plotted in histogram form or on NOPP, both the within- and between-subgroup variation is included in the standard deviation calculated. (See Figure 8-6.) This standard deviation is usually considered the better measure of process capability. When the two standard deviations (one based on $\bar{R}$ and one based on NOPP) differ substantially in magnitude, a decision as to whether the process is actually capable must be made. That is, the process may be made capable by frequent machine adjustments, tool changes, or redressing a wheel. If this must be done so often that it interferes with the production standard, then the process cannot be considered truly capable.

Many distinct factors or variables interact to create a single process output. With more complex processes it may become necessary, through separate analytical techniques, to break down the overall process output into its different variation sources. The capability study, however, is essentially the same as that previously developed.

To the basic graphic analysis tools, the $\bar{X}$ and R chart and normal probability paper, is added the Multi-Vari chart. The Multi-Vari chart is comparable to a three-dimensional individual measurement chart. By measuring the individual part dimensions at more than one location, an additional variation source is exposed. Lines are then drawn on the charts connecting the minimum and maximum within-part dimensions. This charting technique, actually an adaptation from a stock market analysis method, can show within-part variability, between-part variability, and time-to-time variability. The Multi-Vari chart analysis is thus a ready substitute for the $\bar{X}$ and R chart analysis, especially when the $\bar{X}$ and R chart shows an out-of-control condition.

A quite elaborately organized approach to a complex process analysis is called the *Span Plan*.† This technique follows the same basic approach as the simple machine analysis. However,

---

†L. Seder and D. Cowan, "The Span Plan Method of Process Capability Analysis," *American Society for Quality Control General Publication No. 3*, Milwaukee, Wisconsin, 1956.

when a complex process reveals excessive spread, the total variation must be subdivided into its more distinct factors. Generally the factors contributing to the variation encountered are

- Between machines or similar assembly lines
- Between times on production intervals
- Between successive parts
- Within a part
- Of measurement (or error)

The *Span Plan* uses a special work sheet to isolate and assess these different variation causes.

THE MINIMUM COST APPROACH

When a machine or process capability study demonstrates that it is impossible to obtain the desired tolerance, there are several courses of action:

1. Request that tolerances be widened.
2. Buy new equipment.
3. Repair or rebuild present equipment.
4. Completely inspect parts and sort as to good, scrap, or rework.
5. Set machine to minimize cost in action 4.

If the first three actions are rejected, the last two should be taken. Unfortunately, the fourth action is usually taken separately and not in conjunction with the fifth. Setting a machine to minimize total cost allows for a trade-off between scrap and rework. (See Figure 8-7.)

By moving the machine setting between the tolerance specified, it is obvious that the scrap and rework percentages can be varied. If the cost for each category is obtainable, a minimum cost point graph can be constructed and the optimum machine setting located. (See Figure 8-8.)

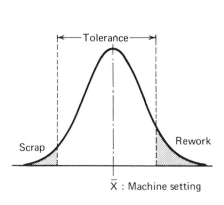

Fig. 8-7 Capability schematic

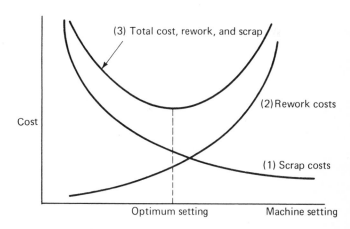

Fig. 8-8 Minimum cost point curve

The total cost curve (3) is determined by adding the ordinates of curves (1) and (2) for a given machine setting. Formulas used are

Rework cost/1,000 units = (Rework cost/unit)(1,000 units)(Rework probability)

Scrap cost/1,000 units = (Scrap cost/unit)(1,000 units)(Scrap probability)

The simplest way to calculate the rework and scrap probabilities is by plotting the capability study data on normal probability paper. Changes in machine setting are simulated by constructing lines parallel to the original line of best fit and then reading the percentages beyond the print limits.

A work sheet similar to that shown in Figure 8-9 provides a convenient means to tabulate the cost data prior to plotting the cost curves. *Note:* The illustration uses cost per thousand units. Analysis can be done on a per unit or any other desired basis.

Machine Setting	Percent Scrap	Scrap Cost Per 1,000 Units	Percent Rework	Rework Cost Per 1,000 Units	Total Cost Per 1,000 Units

Fig. 8-9 Cost work sheet

Although the preceding is a valid way to minimize operational costs, other factors may influence the ultimate decision. One factor is that any scrap will show on the budget, while rework costs can be hidden. The decision then is to move the machine setting to eliminate scrap and produce all rework.

OTHER CONSIDERATIONS

The best place to conduct capability studies is at the machine tool builder's facilities. However, since much equipment currently exists in plants, the studies should be undertaken on a regularly scheduled basis. The information developed not only can be used to correct existing problems but also becomes valuable to process engineers in assigning machines to particular jobs.

It should also be pointed out that if machines are qualified under given conditions, i.e., speeds, feeds, and coolants, they should be operated under these conditions.

If charts are maintained continually on a machine or process, it is generally possible to predict when preventive maintenance or rebuilding is required. The $\bar{X}$ and $\bar{R}$ chart shown in Figure 8-1 has a place for a range bar chart. If the average range is carried over from one chart to the next, a capability deterioration will be observable as the average range increases. If charts are not continually maintained, studies should be made at specified frequencies to ensure that the desired capability is maintained. The capability ratio is a function of the rate at which a machine, process, or tooling wears. If sufficient historical data are compiled, this would permit valid predictions.

APPENDIX 1

CHAPTER EIGHT

EVALUATING GAGE CAPABILITIES

To properly qualify gaging and/or test equipment requires the gage engineer to become familiar with statistical procedures which can be used to analyze the inherent variability contained in these instruments. Unfortunately, simply because a gaging device costs a large sum, people are prone to place implicit faith in the number generated. This general acceptance frequently results in misunderstanding and confusion and can have detrimental effects on the entire manufacturing operation and the products produced. While gage and test equipment manufacturers necessarily work to closer tolerances than may be required for some automotive components, they are also faced with product variability, since this factor cannot be economically eliminated. Knowledge concerning the procedures to follow in determining instrument capability is important for individuals who have this basic responsibility.

Prior to introducing the specific procedures which have been developed for assessing gage capability, it is essential to define the terms commonly employed:

Accuracy: The difference between the observed measurement average and the dimension or characteristic true value. The true value could be closely estimated by precision measurement at the Bureau of Standards or in a metrology laboratory.

Repeatability: Measurement variation obtained when one person measures the same dimension or characteristic several times with the same gage or test equipment.

Reproducibility: The variation in measurement averages when more than one person measures the same dimension or characteristic using the same measuring instrument.

Stability: The variation in the measurement averages when the measuring instrument values are recorded over a specified time interval.

Capability: Accuracy, repeatability, reproducibility, and stability combined in a single value.

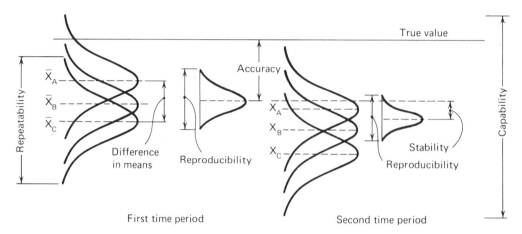

Fig. 8A1-1 Capability schematic

These capability elements are depicted graphically in Figure 8A1-1. At the left is shown the repeatability or the expected variation in one person's readings. The averages for three different people are shown as $\bar{X}_A$, $\bar{X}_B$, and $\bar{X}_C$, and the reproducibility distribution represents the average variation. Accuracy would be calculated by averaging $\bar{X}_A$, $\bar{X}_B$, and $\bar{X}_C$ and taking the difference between this figure and the true value. Stability appears as a distribution in the second time period and again is represented as a variation in average values. The capability is depicted as the difference between the extremes encountered over the time period.

To illustrate how these capability elements would appear in an actual study, refer to Figure 8A1-2. Five parts were selected and a single dimension specified for measurement. The parts are then numbered sequentially, 1 through 5. Three inspectors are selected, and each uses the same gaging instrument and measures the parts in a random order to assure that any drift or change will be spread randomly throughout the study. When the first set of readings is obtained, the inspectors again measure a second set in a random order. To eliminate the possibility that one inspector could bias another one's readings, the individual conducting the study should be certain that no information is exchanged. In Figure 8A1-2 the results are plotted on an average and range chart as a graphical illustration.

Fig. 8A1-2 Gage capability study

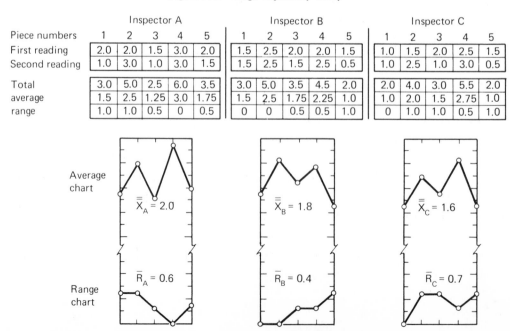

	Inspector A					Inspector B					Inspector C				
Piece numbers	1	2	3	4	5	1	2	3	4	5	1	2	3	4	5
First reading	2.0	2.0	1.5	3.0	2.0	1.5	2.5	2.0	2.0	1.5	1.0	1.5	2.0	2.5	1.5
Second reading	1.0	3.0	1.0	3.0	1.5	1.5	2.5	1.5	2.5	0.5	1.0	2.5	1.0	3.0	0.5
Total	3.0	5.0	2.5	6.0	3.5	3.0	5.0	3.5	4.5	2.0	2.0	4.0	3.0	5.5	2.0
average	1.5	2.5	1.25	3.0	1.75	1.5	2.5	1.75	2.25	1.0	1.0	2.0	1.5	2.75	1.0
range	1.0	1.0	0.5	0	0.5	0	0	0.5	0.5	1.0	0	1.0	1.0	0.5	1.0

Average chart

$\bar{\bar{X}}_A = 2.0$ $\bar{\bar{X}}_B = 1.8$ $\bar{\bar{X}}_C = 1.6$

$\bar{R}_A = 0.6$ $\bar{R}_B = 0.4$ $\bar{R}_C = 0.7$

Range chart

Inspector	Part Number	Individual Readings		Within Parts		Within Inspectors		Between Inspectors
				R_1	$\bar{X}_1$	R_2	$\bar{X}_2$	R_3
A	1	2.0	1.0	1.0	1.5	1.75	2.0	0.35
	2	2.0	3.0	1.0	2.5			
	3	1.5	1.0	0.5	1.25			
	4	3.0	3.0	0.0	3.0			
	5	2.0	1.5	0.5	1.75			
			$\bar{R}_A$	0.6				
B	1	1.5	1.5	0.0	1.5	1.5	1.8	
	2	2.5	2.5	0.0	2.5			
	3	2.0	1.5	0.5	1.75			
	4	2.0	2.5	0.5	2.25			
	5	1.5	0.5	1.0	1.0			
			$\bar{R}_B$	0.4				
C	1	1.0	1.0	0.0	1.0	1.75	1.65	
	2	1.5	2.5	1.0	2.0			
	3	2.0	1.0	1.0	1.5			
	4	2.5	3.0	0.5	2.75			
	5	1.5	0.5	1.0	1.0			
			$\bar{R}_C$	0.7				
Grand averages				0.567	1.817	1.67	1.817	

Fig. 8A1-3 Variance analysis

The element definitions described repeatability as the variation obtained when one person, using the same measuring instrument, measured the same dimension two or more times. In this example only two measurements were made on each piece, or a sample size of 2. The standard deviation for these values can be estimated using the average range. In control chart applications this is done using

$$\hat{\sigma}_x = \frac{1}{d_2} \cdot \bar{R}$$

The factor d_2 is essentially independent when the number of samples, k, is larger than 10 or 15. For smaller k values, Table 8A1-1 gives corrected $1/d_2$ factors.

To illustrate the analogy between control charts and the analysis of variance, using the range as an estimator, the data from Figure 8A1-2 is rearranged in Figure 8A1-3.

Table 8A1-1 Factors for Calculating Standard Deviation

Factors $1/d_2$† for Converting the Average Range, $\bar{R}$, into a Standard Deviation $\hat{\sigma}_x$

n \ k	1	2	3	4	5	8	10	∞
2	0.709	0.781	0.813	0.826	0.840	0.855	0.862	0.885
3	0.524	0.552	0.565	0.571	0.575	0.581	0.581	0.592
4	0.446	0.465	0.472	0.474	0.476	0.481	0.481	0.485
5	0.403	0.417	0.420	0.422	0.424	0.426	0.427	0.429
6	0.375	0.385	0.388	0.389	0.391	0.392	0.392	0.395
7	0.353	0.361	0.364	0.365	0.366	0.368	0.368	0.370
8	0.338	0.344	0.346	0.347	0.348	0.348	0.350	0.351
9	0.325	0.331	0.332	0.333	0.334	0.334	0.336	0.337
10	0.314	0.319	0.322	0.323	0.323	0.324	0.324	0.325

k = Number of samples

n = sample size

†Based on d_2 factors in A. J. Duncan, *Quality Control and Industrial Statistics*, 1965. Third Edition Richard D. Irwin, Homewood, Illinois Table D3, p. 910.

Calculating the estimated standard deviation within parts for each inspector in Figure 8A1-3 (repeatability) gives the following results:

$$Inspector\ A: \quad \bar{R} = 0.6$$

$$\frac{1^\dagger}{d_2} = 0.840$$

$$\hat{\sigma}_{\text{within parts}} = (0.840)(0.6) = 0.504$$

$$Inspector\ B: \quad \bar{R} = 0.4$$

$$\frac{1}{d_2} = 0.840$$

$$\hat{\sigma}_{\text{within parts}} = (0.840)(0.4) = 0.336$$

$$Inspector\ C: \quad \bar{R} = 0.7$$

$$\frac{1}{d_2} = 0.840$$

$$\hat{\sigma}_{\text{within parts}} = (0.840)(0.7) = 0.588$$

†Taken from Table 1: The sample size is 2, and five parts were measured.

Assessing these results individually, inspector B has the least variation and the best repeatability. Assuming, however, that all three inspectors normally perform this gaging operation, a standard deviation can be calculated using the average range for all three:

$$\bar{\bar{R}}_1 = \frac{0.6 + 0.4 + 0.7}{3} = 0.567$$

$$\hat{\sigma}_{\text{within parts}} = \frac{1^\dagger}{d_2} \cdot \bar{\bar{R}}_1 = (0.885)(0.567) = 0.5018 = 0.502$$

†*Note:* k has changed from 5 to 15, and from Table 8A1-1, $1/d_2 = 0.885$.

Although not germane to this analysis, the within-inspector variation (actually part variation) can be estimated using the average of the R_2 values:

$$\hat{\sigma}_{\text{within inspectors}} = \frac{1^\ddagger}{d_2} \cdot R_2 = (0.420)(1.67) = 0.7014$$

‡Taken from Table 8A1-1. The sample size is 5, and $k = 3$.

Reproducibility was defined as the variation in measurement averages (between-inspector variation), and this can be estimated using the R_3 value from Figure 8A1-3. The $1/d_2$ factor is based on one sample, with a sample size equal to 3. From Table 8A1-1, this value is 0.524. Then

$$\hat{\sigma}_{\text{between inspector}} = \frac{1}{d_2} \cdot R_3$$

$$= (0.524)(0.35) = 0.1834 = 0.183$$

Statistically, variances can be combined to give a single value according to the formula

$$\sigma_A^2 = \sigma_B^2 + \sigma_C^2$$

This resultant value would be used to measure the repeatability and reproducibility, or

$$\hat{\sigma}_{\text{repeatability and reproducibility}} = \sqrt{(0.502)^2 + (0.183)^2} = \underline{0.5343}$$

To find the spread which would include specified percentages of this data, Z factor multiples can be obtained from any "table of areas under the normal curve." For 99 percent, $Z = \pm 2.575$; for 95 percent, $Z = \pm 1.96$, and for 90 percent, $Z = \pm 1.645$. The results are

$$99\ percent:\quad 2 \times Z \times \hat{\sigma}_{R\,\&\,R} = (2)(2.575)(0.5343) = 2.752$$
$$95\ percent:\quad 2 \times Z \times \hat{\sigma}_{R\,\&\,R} = (2)(1.96)(0.5343) = 2.094$$
$$90\ percent:\quad 2 \times Z \times \hat{\sigma}_{R\,\&\,R} = (2)(1.645)(0.5343) = 1.758$$

These values can now be used to estimate the tolerance consumed by reproducibility and repeatability. Assume the total tolerance for the parts used in this study is 3.0; referring only to the 99 percent spread, the percent tolerance consumed is

$$(2.752 \div 3)(100) = 91.73 \text{ percent}$$

This percentage cannot be directly associated with the percent good parts rejected or the percent bad parts accepted, an aspect which is discussed later. Many gage engineers would consider this undesirable, however, since the accepted standard for gage capability is approximately 10 percent or less of the total tolerance.

The same information is shown in Figure 8A1-4 using a standardized form which simplifies the calculations required. The only value which may need clarification is the number 3.268, shown under "range evaluation." This is the D_4 factor for $n = 2$, taken from the standard table for control chart factors, which is used for calculating the upper control limit on a range chart. Any individual ranges beyond this limit should be discarded (assuming an assignable cause) and the average range recomputed along with a revised upper limit. This should be continued until all the range values are in control. If too many values have to be discarded, it would evidence a complete lack of control, and the experiment should be repeated. The appropriate $1/d_2$ factors can be obtained from Table 8A1-1 for the sample size and number of subgroups. As can be seen, the results tabulated in Figure 8A1-4 are the same as those obtained previously.

The two elements, accuracy and stability, were not determined in this study since the information needed was not available. It is immediately apparent that reduced variability could be attained by inspector training, which could minimize the differences in averages, or by obtaining a more precise gaging device.

Applications for these techniques are

1. Evaluating new measuring equipment (preferably at the vendor's plant).
2. Comparing one or more measuring instruments.
3. Checking equipment when there is a suspicion that it is in error.
4. Comparing measuring equipment before and after repair or adjustment.
5. Determining true process capability by remaining measurement variability.

The procedure for determining gage or test equipment reproducibility and repeatability is summarized in the following steps:

1. Select five or more parts and prepare them for gaging (wash, de-burr, and number).
2. Choose two or more appraisers (those who ordinarily use the equipment are preferable). Have each appraiser note any characteristics about the instrument which make reading difficult. The slightest defect should be corrected before conducting the study.
3. Each appraiser, using the same instrument, measures the parts in a random order and records the value obtained.
   a. Appraisers should not see each other's readings.

Gage Type _____ Date _____

B/P Spec. _____Characteristic _____ Machine No. _____

Part No. _____ Part Name _____ Gage No. _____

Col. No.	1	2	3	4	5	6	7	8	9
Inspector	A—			B—			C—		
Sample No.	1st Trial	2nd Trial	Diff.	1st Trial	2nd Trial	Diff.	1st Trial	2nd Trial	Diff.
1	2.0	1.0	1.0	1.5	1.5	0.0	1.0	1.0	0.0
2	2.0	3.0	1.0	2.5	2.5	0.0	1.5	2.5	1.0
3	1.5	1.0	0.5	2.0	1.5	0.5	2.0	1.0	1.0
4	3.0	3.0	0.0	2.0	2.5	0.5	2.5	3.0	0.5
5	2.0	1.5	0.5	1.5	0.5	1.0	1.5	0.5	1.0
6									
7									
8									
9									
10									
Totals	10.5	9.5	3.0	9.5	8.5	2.0	8.5	8.0	3.5
Averages	2.1	1.9	0.6	1.9	1.7	0.4	1.7	1.6	0.7

$\bar{R}_A$ 2.1   1.9   1.7

Sum. 4.0 $\bar{R}_A$ Sum. 3.6 $\bar{R}_B$ Sum. 3.3 $\bar{R}_C$

$\bar{X}_A$ 2.0 $\bar{X}_B$ 1.8 $\bar{X}_C$ 1.65

Range Evaluation

$\bar{R}_A$ (Col. 3)	0.6
$\bar{R}_B$ (Col. 6)	0.4
$\bar{R}_C$ (Col. 9)	0.7
Sum	1.7
$\bar{R}_1$	0.567

$UCL_R = (3.268)\,(\bar{R}_1)$

$= (3.268)\; \boxed{0.567}$

$= \boxed{1.85}$ ①

Reproducibility—Appraiser Variation

Difference in Means

$\bar{R}_3 = \bar{X}_L - \bar{X}_S = (\underline{2.0}) - (\underline{1.65}) = \boxed{0.35}$

Standard Deviation (SDM) $= (1/d_2)(\bar{R}_3)$

$= (\underline{0.524})\;(\underline{0.35}) = \boxed{0.183}$

Variance $= (SDM)^2 = \boxed{0.183}^2 = \underline{0.0335}$ ②

Repeatability—Equipment Variation

Difference in Readings

Standard Deviation (SDR) $= (1/d_2)(\bar{R}_1) =$

$(\underline{0.885})(\underline{0.567}) = \boxed{0.502}$

Variance $= (SDR)^2 = \boxed{0.502}^2 = \underline{0.252}$ ③

Reproducibility and Repeatability (Combined)

Standard Deviation (R & R) $= \sqrt{(SDM)^2 + (SDR)^2}$ $= \sqrt{\underline{0.0335} + \underline{0.252}}$

SDRR $= \boxed{0.5343}$ ④

Percent Tolerance Consumed by Reproducibility and Repeatability

P.T.C. $= [(5.15)(SDRR) \div \text{Drawing Tolerance}](100) =$

$[(5.15)(\underline{0.5343}) \div \underline{3}\,](100) = \boxed{91.73}\,\%$

Fig. 8A1-4   Calculation worksheet

b. Record readings to one more decimal place than the instrument's least count; i.e., if the least count is 0.001 inch, read to 0.0001 inch. This requires estimating, but in many cases is essential.

4. After the first set of measurements has been recorded, each appraiser repeats the measurements—without referring to his first results. (More than one repeat reading can be taken if deemed advisable.)

5. Record the readings in the appropriate columns on a form similar to Figure 8A1-4.

6. Calculate the range (difference between individual appraiser's readings) for each appraiser (columns 3, 6, and 9 in Figure 8A1-4). Fill in all totals, and calculate the averages indicated. Compute $\bar{R}_1$.

7. Calculate the upper control limit ① for the ranges, and compare individual ranges to this value. Discard points out of control, and recalculate $\bar{R}_1$. (Follow the procedure suggested previously.)

8. Determine the standard deviation to measure reproducibility. Calculate $\bar{R}_3$, the difference between the largest and smallest appraiser means ($\bar{R}_3 = \bar{X}_L - \bar{X}_S$); select the appropriate $1/d_2$ factor from Table 8A1-1. (For three appraisers, $n = 3$, $k = 1$.) Calculate the variance, and enter in ②.

9. Determine the standard deviation to measure repeatability. Select the appropriate $1/d_2$ factor from Table 8A1-1. (For three appraisers, each measuring five parts twice, $n = 2$ and $k = 15$, use $k = \infty$.) Calculate the standard deviation using $\bar{R}_1$, the variance, and enter in ③.

10. Combine the variances calculated in ② and ③, take the square root, and enter in ④ to determine the standard deviation for reproducibility and repeatability.

11. To find the percent tolerance consumed by repeatability and reproducibility, multiply the value in ④ by 5.15, divide by the drawing tolerance, and multiply by 100 to convert to a percent.

Example studies are shown at the end of this appendix.

MEASUREMENT ERROR EFFECT ON ACCEPTANCE DECISIONS

Previous mention was made concerning the effect that measurement error has on accepting defective material or rejecting good material. This aspect has been explored by Alan R. Eagle (see the references at the end of this appendix). The general concept is shown graphically in Figure 8A1-5. In this illustration, the gage or testing device is zeroed on the upper and lower specifications, and the measurement errors are distributed about these points.

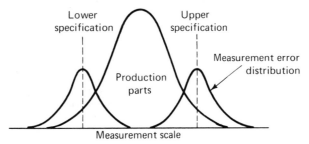

Fig. 8A1-5 Measurement error schematic

It becomes obvious that, due to these errors, a probability exists that a good part could be rejected or a bad part accepted. Mr. Eagle, using a numerical integration process, developed two sets of graphs for evaluating these probabilities (Figures 8A1-6 and 8A1-7).

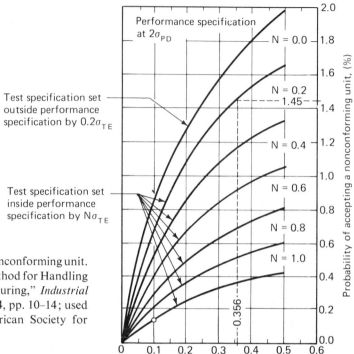

Test specification set outside performance specification by $0.2\sigma_{TE}$

Test specification set inside performance specification by $N\sigma_{TE}$

Fig. 8A1-6 Probability of accepting a nonconforming unit. Source: A. R. Eagle, "A Method for Handling Errors in Testing and Measuring," *Industrial Quality Control*, March 1954, pp. 10–14; used by permission of the American Society for Quality Control.

Several assumptions were made in calculating the probabilities involved (a normal practice in statistical analysis):

1. The distribution of production parts is normal.

2. The parts are centered on the blueprint nominal.

3. The specifications intersect the parts distribution at plus and minus two standard deviations.

4. The measurement error distribution is normal and distributed about the zero setting.

Fig. 8A1-7 Probability of rejecting an acceptable unit. Source: A. R. Eagle, "A Method for Handling Errors in Testing and Measuring," *Industrial Quality Control*, March 1954, pp. 10–14; used by permission of the American Society for Quality Control.

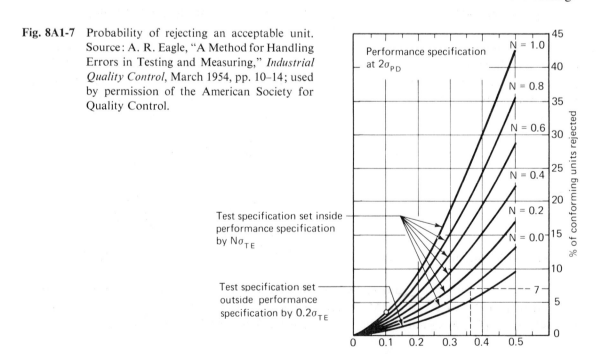

Test specification set inside performance specification by $N\sigma_{TE}$

Test specification set outside performance specification by $0.2\sigma_{TE}$

The graphs are designed to permit the zero setting to be placed inside the specification at 0, 0.2, 0.4, 0.6, 0.8, and 1.0 multiples of the standard deviation or at 0.2 times the standard deviation outside the specification.

The data in Figures 8A1-3 and 8A1-4 will be used to illustrate how the graphs are utilized. Gaging error attributed to reproducibility and repeatability equaled 0.5343. This is the σ_{TE} in Figures 8A1-6 and 8A1-7. The tolerance specified was 3.0, and the part standard deviation was estimated at 0.7014. Multiplying 0.7014 by 2 gives 1.4028, which is slightly less than one-half the tolerance (1.5) and complies with assumption 3. Refer now to Figure 8A1-6. σ_{TE}/one-half the tolerance $= 0.5343 \div 1.5 = 0.356$. Read this on the horizontal axis and intersect the $N = 0$ curve (the gage is set on the specification). Reading the probability scale indicates that approximately 1.45 percent defective parts would be accepted. Following the same procedure and referring to Figure 8A1-7, shows that approximately 7 percent good parts would be rejected. Obviously, the most serious error, accepting defective units, is relatively minimal, while the larger percentage (good parts rejected) would be reinspected prior to scrapping and be accepted. This with a gage which consumed 91 percent of the specified tolerance! In the text *Quality Planning and Analysis*, by J. M. Juran and Frank M. Gryna, Jr. (see the references), a rule of thumb is given:

If the ratio of three standard deviations of measurement error to product tolerance is less than about 25 percent, then the effect of measurement error on decisions can usually be ignored.

For situations where the specifications include more than plus and minus two standard deviations of the parts, the graphs overestimate the actual probabilities. For the converse situation, i.e., less than two standard deviations included in the specifications, the graphs underestimate, but the latter condition would indicate that the major problem exists in the machine or process, not the gaging.

If the process is not centered or not normal, errors will also exist, and the problem would have to be solved by other methods. Simulation is one technique which could be employed if the conditions warranted such an approach. Also, if the gage is used to obtain data for control chart purposes, the fact that the process mean fluctuates could produce results that would have to be individually analyzed.

This method was presented primarily to reveal that the percent tolerance consumed by repeatability, and reproducibility should not be judged solely by its magnitude but must be further evaluated to determine its effect on potential decision errors.

REFERENCES

BASS, L., "Diagnosis, for a Common Gage Ailment," *Industrial Quality Control*, July 1957.

EAGLE, A. R., "A Method for Handling Errors in Testing and Measuring," *Industrial Quality Control*, March 1954.

JURAN, J. M., and F. M. GRYNA, JR., *Quality Planning and Analysis*, McGraw-Hill Book Company, New York, 1970.

TRAVER, R. W., "Measuring Equipment Repeatability—The Rubber Ruler," *ASQC Transactions*, 1962.

Gage Type _INDICATOR — READINGS IN 0.001 IN._ Date _5-28-71_

B/P Spec. _±0.005_ Characteristic _ANCHOR SLOT LOC._ Machine No. _____

Part No. _37884_ Part Name _230 ROD CAP_ Gage No. _G-16020_

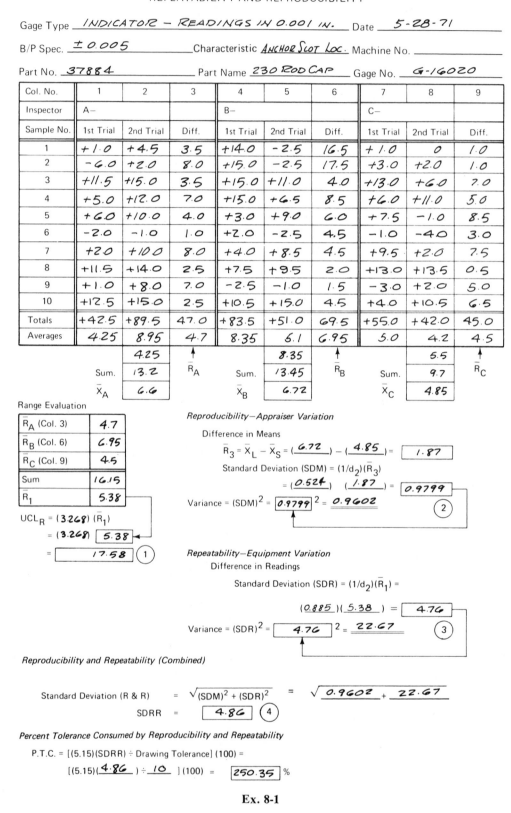

Col. No.	1	2	3	4	5	6	7	8	9
Inspector	A—			B—			C—		
Sample No.	1st Trial	2nd Trial	Diff.	1st Trial	2nd Trial	Diff.	1st Trial	2nd Trial	Diff.
1	+1.0	+4.5	3.5	+14.0	−2.5	16.5	+1.0	0	1.0
2	−6.0	+2.0	8.0	+15.0	−2.5	17.5	+3.0	+2.0	1.0
3	+11.5	+15.0	3.5	+15.0	+11.0	4.0	+13.0	+6.0	7.0
4	+5.0	+12.0	7.0	+15.0	+6.5	8.5	+6.0	+11.0	5.0
5	+6.0	+10.0	4.0	+3.0	+9.0	6.0	+7.5	−1.0	8.5
6	−2.0	−1.0	1.0	+2.0	−2.5	4.5	−1.0	−4.0	3.0
7	+2.0	+10.0	8.0	+4.0	+8.5	4.5	+9.5	+2.0	7.5
8	+11.5	+14.0	2.5	+7.5	+9.5	2.0	+13.0	+13.5	0.5
9	+1.0	+8.0	7.0	−2.5	−1.0	1.5	−3.0	+2.0	5.0
10	+12.5	+15.0	2.5	+10.5	+15.0	4.5	+4.0	+10.5	6.5
Totals	+42.5	+89.5	47.0	+83.5	+51.0	69.5	+55.0	+42.0	45.0
Averages	4.25	8.95	4.7	8.35	5.1	6.95	5.0	4.2	4.5

	4.25	$\bar{R}_A$	8.35	$\bar{R}_B$	5.5	$\bar{R}_C$
Sum.	13.2		Sum. 13.45		Sum. 9.7	
$\bar{X}_A$	6.6		$\bar{X}_B$ 6.72		$\bar{X}_C$ 4.85	

Range Evaluation

$\bar{R}_A$ (Col. 3)	4.7
$\bar{R}_B$ (Col. 6)	6.95
$\bar{R}_C$ (Col. 9)	4.5
Sum	16.15
$\bar{R}_1$	5.38

$UCL_R = (3.268)(\bar{R}_1)$

$= (3.268)\boxed{5.38}$

$= \boxed{17.58} \;(1)$

Reproducibility—Appraiser Variation

Difference in Means

$\bar{R}_3 = \bar{X}_L - \bar{X}_S = (\underline{6.72}) - (\underline{4.85}) = \boxed{1.87}$

Standard Deviation (SDM) $= (1/d_2)(\bar{R}_3)$

$= (\underline{0.524})(\underline{1.87}) = \boxed{0.9799}$

Variance $= (SDM)^2 \boxed{0.9799}^2 = 0.9602$ $\boxed{0.9799}$ (2)

Repeatability—Equipment Variation

Difference in Readings

Standard Deviation (SDR) $= (1/d_2)(\bar{R}_1) =$

$(\underline{0.885})(\underline{5.38}) = \boxed{4.76}$

Variance $= (SDR)^2 \boxed{4.76}^2 = 22.67$ (3)

Reproducibility and Repeatability (Combined)

Standard Deviation (R & R) $= \sqrt{(SDM)^2 + (SDR)^2} = \sqrt{\underline{0.9602} + \underline{22.67}}$

SDRR $= \boxed{4.86}$ (4)

Percent Tolerance Consumed by Reproducibility and Repeatability

P.T.C. $= [(5.15)(SDRR) \div \text{Drawing Tolerance}](100) =$

$[(5.15)(\underline{4.86}) \div \underline{10}](100) = \boxed{250.35}$ %

Ex. 8-1

REPEATABILITY AND REPRODUCIBILITY

Gage Type _INDICATOR - READINGS IN 0.001 IN._ Date _6-1-71_

B/P Spec. _± 0.005_ Characteristic _ANCHOR SLOT LOC._ Machine No. _____

Part No. _____ Part Name _ROD CAP 230_ Gage No. _G-16020_

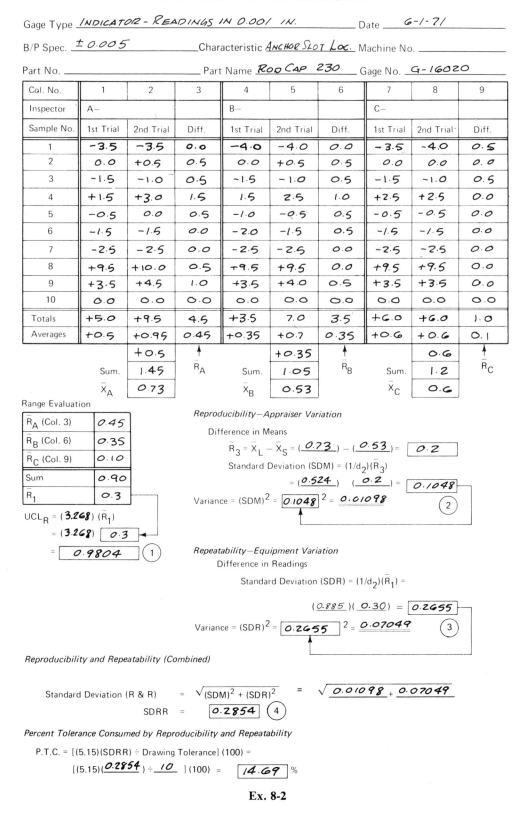

Col. No.	1	2	3	4	5	6	7	8	9
Inspector	A—			B—			C—		
Sample No.	1st Trial	2nd Trial	Diff.	1st Trial	2nd Trial	Diff.	1st Trial	2nd Trial	Diff.
1	−3.5	−3.5	0.0	−4.0	−4.0	0.0	−3.5	−4.0	0.5
2	0.0	+0.5	0.5	0.0	+0.5	0.5	0.0	0.0	0.0
3	−1.5	−1.0	0.5	−1.5	−1.0	0.5	−1.5	−1.0	0.5
4	+1.5	+3.0	1.5	1.5	2.5	1.0	+2.5	+2.5	0.0
5	−0.5	0.0	0.5	−1.0	−0.5	0.5	−0.5	−0.5	0.0
6	−1.5	−1.5	0.0	−2.0	−1.5	0.5	−1.5	−1.5	0.0
7	−2.5	−2.5	0.0	−2.5	−2.5	0.0	−2.5	−2.5	0.0
8	+9.5	+10.0	0.5	+9.5	+9.5	0.0	+9.5	+9.5	0.0
9	+3.5	+4.5	1.0	+3.5	+4.0	0.5	+3.5	+3.5	0.0
10	0.0	0.0	0.0	0.0	0.0	0.0	0.0	0.0	0.0
Totals	+5.0	+9.5	4.5	+3.5	7.0	3.5	+6.0	+6.0	1.0
Averages	+0.5	+0.95	0.45	+0.35	+0.7	0.35	+0.6	+0.6	0.1

	+0.5	↑ $\bar{R}_A$		+0.35	↑ $\bar{R}_B$		0.6	↑ $\bar{R}_C$
Sum.	1.45		Sum.	1.05		Sum.	1.2	
$\bar{X}_A$	0.73		$\bar{X}_B$	0.53		$\bar{X}_C$	0.6	

Range Evaluation

$\bar{R}_A$ (Col. 3)	0.45
$\bar{R}_B$ (Col. 6)	0.35
$\bar{R}_C$ (Col. 9)	0.10
Sum	0.90
$\bar{R}_1$	0.3

$UCL_R = (3.268)(\bar{R}_1)$

$= (3.268)$ [0.3]

$=$ [0.9804] ①

Reproducibility—Appraiser Variation

Difference in Means

$\bar{R}_3 = \bar{X}_L - \bar{X}_S = ($ _0.73_ $) - ($ _0.53_ $) =$ [0.2]

Standard Deviation (SDM) = $(1/d_2)(\bar{R}_3)$

$= ($ _0.524_ $)($ _0.2_ $) =$ [0.1048]

Variance = $(SDM)^2 =$ [0.1048]$^2 = 0.01098$ ②

Repeatability—Equipment Variation

Difference in Readings

Standard Deviation (SDR) = $(1/d_2)(\bar{R}_1) =$

$($ _0.885_ $)($ _0.30_ $) =$ [0.2655]

Variance = $(SDR)^2 =$ [0.2655]$^2 = 0.07049$ ③

Reproducibility and Repeatability (Combined)

Standard Deviation (R & R) $= \sqrt{(SDM)^2 + (SDR)^2} = \sqrt{0.01098 + 0.07049}$

SDRR $=$ [0.2854] ④

Percent Tolerance Consumed by Reproducibility and Repeatability

P.T.C. = [(5.15)(SDRR) ÷ Drawing Tolerance] (100) =

[(5.15)(_0.2854_) ÷ _10_] (100) = [14.69] %

Ex. 8-2

Gage Type _INDICATOR – READINGS IN 0.001 IN._ Date _5-27-71_

B/P Spec. _0.497 – 0.507_ Characteristic _ANCHOR SLOT DEPTH_ Machine No. _____

Part No. _37843_ Part Name _230 ROD_ Gage No. _G-16837_

Col. No.	1	2	3	4	5	6	7	8	9
Inspector	A– KING			B– WILT			C– SMITH		
Sample No.	1st Trial	2nd Trial	Diff.	1st Trial	2nd Trial	Diff.	1st Trial	2nd Trial	Diff.
1	–3.0	–3.0	0.0	–3.0	–3.0	0.0	–3.0	–3.0	0.0
2	–3.0	–4.0	1.0	–3.0	–4.0	1.0	–3.0	–4.0	1.0
3	–5.0	–5.0	0.0	–5.5	–5.0	0.5	–5.0	–5.0	0.0
4	–6.0	–6.5	0.5	–6.5	–6.5	0.0	–6.5	–6.5	0.0
5	–1.0	–1.5	0.5	–1.0	–1.5	0.5	–1.0	–1.0	0.0
6	–3.0	–3.0	0.0	–3.0	–3.0	0.0	–2.5	–2.5	0.0
7	–4.0	–5.0	1.0	–4.5	–4.5	0.0	–4.5	–4.5	0.0
8	–3.5	–4.0	0.5	–4.0	–4.5	0.5	–4.0	–4.0	0.0
9	–3.0	–4.0	1.0	–3.5	–4.0	0.5	–4.0	–4.0	0.0
10	–2.5	–2.5	0.0	–2.5	–2.0	0.5	–3.0	–3.0	0.0
Totals	–34.0	–38.5	4.5	–36.5	–39.0	3.5	–36.5	–37.5	1.0
Averages	–3.4	–3.85	+0.45	–3.65	–3.90	+0.35	–3.65	–3.75	+0.1

	–3.4	$\bar{R}_A$		–3.65	$\bar{R}_B$		–3.65	$\bar{R}_C$
Sum.	–7.25		Sum.	–7.55		Sum.	–7.40	
$\bar{X}_A$	–3.63		$\bar{X}_B$	–3.78		$\bar{X}_C$	–3.70	

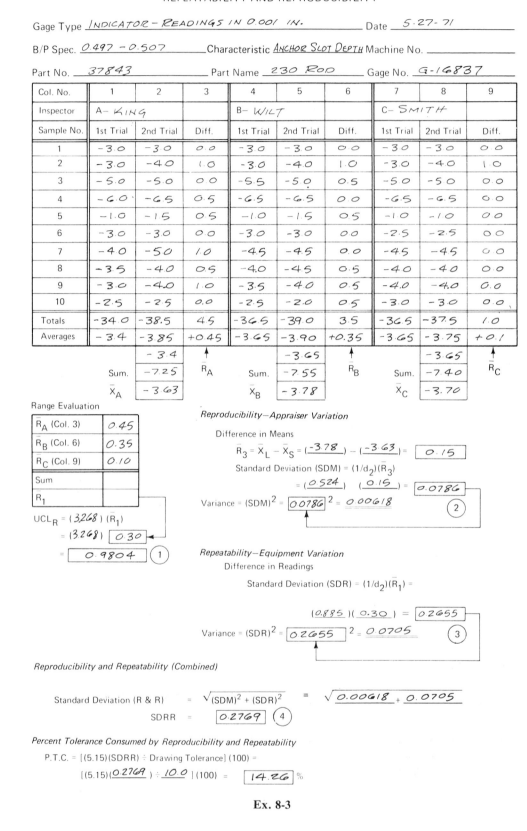

Range Evaluation

$\bar{R}_A$ (Col. 3)	0.45
$\bar{R}_B$ (Col. 6)	0.35
$\bar{R}_C$ (Col. 9)	0.10
Sum	
$\bar{R}_1$	

$UCL_R = (3.268)(\bar{R}_1)$

$= (3.268)\boxed{0.30}$

$= \boxed{0.9804}$ ①

Reproducibility—Appraiser Variation

Difference in Means

$\bar{R}_3 = \bar{X}_L - \bar{X}_S = (\underline{-3.78}) - (\underline{-3.63}) = \boxed{0.15}$

Standard Deviation (SDM) = $(1/d_2)(\bar{R}_3)$

$= (\underline{0.524})\ (\underline{0.15}) = \boxed{0.0786}$

Variance = $(SDM)^2 = \boxed{0.0786}^2 = 0.00618$ ②

Repeatability—Equipment Variation

Difference in Readings

Standard Deviation (SDR) = $(1/d_2)(\bar{R}_1)$ =

$(\underline{0.885})(\underline{0.30}) = \boxed{0.2655}$

Variance = $(SDR)^2 = \boxed{0.2655}^2 = 0.0705$ ③

Reproducibility and Repeatability (Combined)

Standard Deviation (R & R) = $\sqrt{(SDM)^2 + (SDR)^2}$ = $\sqrt{0.00618 + 0.0705}$

SDRR = $\boxed{0.2769}$ ④

Percent Tolerance Consumed by Reproducibility and Repeatability

P.T.C. = [(5.15)(SDRR) ÷ Drawing Tolerance] (100) =

[(5.15)(_0.2769_) ÷ _10.0_] (100) = $\boxed{14.26}$ %

Ex. 8-3

REPEATABILITY AND REPRODUCIBILITY

Gage Type _INDICATOR - READINGS IN 0.001 IN._ Date _5-27-71_

B/P Spec. _±0.005_ Characteristic _BOLT HOLE TO SIDE_ **LOCATION -** Machine No. _____

Part No. _38836_ Part Name _230 ROD & CAP_ Gage No. _0316309_

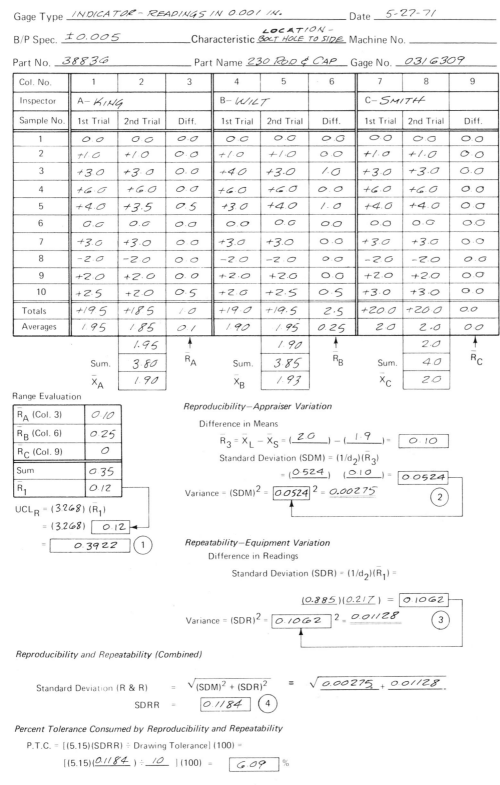

Col. No.	1	2	3	4	5	6	7	8	9
Inspector	A- KING			B- WILT			C- SMITH		
Sample No.	1st Trial	2nd Trial	Diff.	1st Trial	2nd Trial	Diff.	1st Trial	2nd Trial	Diff.
1	0.0	0.0	0.0	0.0	0.0	0.0	0.0	0.0	0.0
2	+1.0	+1.0	0.0	+1.0	+1.0	0.0	+1.0	+1.0	0.0
3	+3.0	+3.0	0.0	+4.0	+3.0	1.0	+3.0	+3.0	0.0
4	+6.0	+6.0	0.0	+6.0	+6.0	0.0	+6.0	+6.0	0.0
5	+4.0	+3.5	0.5	+3.0	+4.0	1.0	+4.0	+4.0	0.0
6	0.0	0.0	0.0	0.0	0.0	0.0	0.0	0.0	0.0
7	+3.0	+3.0	0.0	+3.0	+3.0	0.0	+3.0	+3.0	0.0
8	-2.0	-2.0	0.0	-2.0	-2.0	0.0	-2.0	-2.0	0.0
9	+2.0	+2.0	0.0	+2.0	+2.0	0.0	+2.0	+2.0	0.0
10	+2.5	+2.0	0.5	+2.0	+2.5	0.5	+3.0	+3.0	0.0
Totals	+19.5	+18.5	1.0	+19.0	+19.5	2.5	+20.0	+20.0	0.0
Averages	1.95	1.85	0.1	1.90	1.95	0.25	2.0	2.0	0.0

	1.95	↑ $\bar{R}_A$
Sum.	3.80	
$\bar{X}_A$	1.90	

	1.90	↑ $\bar{R}_B$
Sum.	3.85	
$\bar{X}_B$	1.93	

	2.0	↑ $\bar{R}_C$
Sum.	4.0	
$\bar{X}_C$	2.0	

Range Evaluation

$\bar{R}_A$ (Col. 3)	0.10
$\bar{R}_B$ (Col. 6)	0.25
$\bar{R}_C$ (Col. 9)	0
Sum	0.35
$\bar{R}_1$	0.12

$UCL_R = (3.268)(\bar{R}_1)$

$= (3.268) \boxed{0.12}$

$= \boxed{0.3922}$ (1)

Reproducibility—Appraiser Variation

Difference in Means

$\bar{R}_3 = \bar{X}_L - \bar{X}_S = (\underline{2.0}) - (\underline{1.9}) = \boxed{0.10}$

Standard Deviation (SDM) = $(1/d_2)(\bar{R}_3)$

$= (\underline{0.524}) \ (\underline{0.10}) = \boxed{0.0524}$

Variance = $(SDM)^2 = \boxed{0.0524}^2 = \underline{0.00275}$ (2)

Repeatability—Equipment Variation

Difference in Readings

Standard Deviation (SDR) = $(1/d_2)(\bar{R}_1)$ =

$(\underline{0.885})(\underline{0.217}) = \boxed{0.1062}$

Variance = $(SDR)^2 = \boxed{0.1062}^2 = \underline{0.01128}$ (3)

Reproducibility and Repeatability (Combined)

Standard Deviation (R & R) = $\sqrt{(SDM)^2 + (SDR)^2}$ = $\sqrt{\underline{0.00275} + \underline{0.01128}}$

SDRR = $\boxed{0.1184}$ (4)

Percent Tolerance Consumed by Reproducibility and Repeatability

P.T.C. = [(5.15)(SDRR) ÷ Drawing Tolerance] (100) =

[(5.15)(\underline{0.1184}) ÷ \underline{10}] (100) = $\boxed{6.09}$ %

Ex. 8-4

REPEATABILITY AND REPRODUCIBILITY

Gage Type *INDICATOR - READINGS IN 0.001* _____ Date *6-1-71* _____

B/P Spec. *±0.005* _____ Characteristic *CONT. FACE FROM PIN* Machine No. _____

Part No. _____ Part Name *ROD 230* _____ Gage No. *0316363* _____

Col. No.	1	2	3	4	5	6	7	8	9
Inspector	A−			B−			C−		
Sample No.	1st Trial	2nd Trial	Diff.	1st Trial	2nd Trial	Diff.	1st Trial	2nd Trial	Diff.
1	-2.5	-2.5	0.0	-3.0	-2.5	0.5	-2.5	-2.5	0.0
2	-3.5	-3.0	0.5	-3.0	-3.0	0.0	-3.0	-3.0	0.0
3	-1.0	0.0	1.0	-1.0	0.0	1.0	0.0	0.0	0.0
4	-3.0	-2.5	0.5	-2.5	-2.0	0.5	-2.0	-2.0	0.0
5	-2.0	-2.0	0.0	-1.0	-1.0	0.0	-1.0	-1.0	0.0
6	-1.5	-1.0	0.5	-0.5	-0.5	0.0	-0.5	-0.5	0.0
7	-2.5	-2.0	0.5	-1.5	-1.0	0.5	-2.0	-2.0	0.0
8	-2.0	-2.0	0.0	-1.5	-1.5	0.0	-1.5	-2.0	0.5
9	-4.5	-4.0	0.5	-4.0	-4.0	0.0	-4.0	-4.0	0.0
10	-3.5	-3.5	0.0	-3.0	-3.0	0.0	-3.0	-3.0	0.0
Totals	-26.0	-22.5	3.5	-21.0	-19.0	2.5	-19.5	-20.0	0.5
Averages	-2.6	-2.25	0.35	-2.1	-1.9	0.25	-1.95	-2.0	0.05

	-2.6	↑ $\bar{R}_A$		-2.1	↑ $\bar{R}_B$		-1.95	↑ $\bar{R}_C$
Sum.	-4.85		Sum.	-4.0		Sum.	-3.95	
$\bar{X}_A$	-2.43		X_B	-2.0		$\bar{X}_C$	-1.98	

Range Evaluation

$\bar{R}_A$ (Col. 3)	0.35
$\bar{R}_B$ (Col. 6)	0.25
$\bar{R}_C$ (Col. 9)	0.05
Sum	0.65
$\bar{R}_1$	0.217

$UCL_R = (3.268)(\bar{R}_1)$

$= (3.268) \boxed{0.21}$

$= \boxed{0.7092}$ ①

Reproducibility—Appraiser Variation

  Difference in Means

$$\bar{R}_3 = \bar{X}_L - \bar{X}_S = (\underline{-2.43}) - (\underline{-1.98}) = \boxed{0.45}$$

  Standard Deviation (SDM) = $(1/d_2)(\bar{R}_3)$

$$= (\underline{0.524})(\underline{0.45}) = \boxed{0.2358}$$

  Variance = $(SDM)^2 = \boxed{0.2358}^2 = 0.0556$ ②

Repeatability—Equipment Variation

  Difference in Readings

  Standard Deviation (SDR) = $(1/d_2)(\bar{R}_1) =$

$$(\underline{0.885})(\underline{0.217}) = \boxed{0.1920}$$

  Variance = $(SDR)^2 = \boxed{0.1920}^2 = 0.0369$ ③

Reproducibility and Repeatability (Combined)

  Standard Deviation (R & R) $= \sqrt{(SDM)^2 + (SDR)^2} = \sqrt{\underline{0.0556} + \underline{0.0369}}$

  SDRR $= \boxed{0.3041}$ ④

Percent Tolerance Consumed by Reproducibility and Repeatability

  P.T.C. = [(5.15)(SDRR) ÷ Drawing Tolerance](100) =

  [(5.15)(<u>0.3041</u>) ÷ <u>.010</u>](100) = $\boxed{15.66}$ %

Ex. 8-5

CHAPTER NINE | ACCEPTANCE SAMPLING

Historically, sampling to judge quality is probably the oldest technique in existence. Cooks have always sampled to judge flavor, the brewmaster or wine taster has sampled to determine quality, and when grain is taken to a mill the miller samples to determine impurities. Cheese makers provide samples for their customers. From this it can be inferred that acceptance sampling is not used to control quality but rather to ascertain whether a desired quality exists. It should be obvious that the quality is already inherent in the product by the time sampling occurs. The statistician's contribution to sampling has basically been establishing sample sizes and defining risks to aid the sampler in making more intelligent decisions regarding product acceptability.

Acceptance sampling plans are divided into two categories, attribute sampling and variables sampling plans. Attribute plans are simpler in that they involve only counting the defective units in a sample and comparing this number to an acceptance number. Variables plans are more complex in that measurements are needed along with calculating the mean and standard deviation for the sample. The formal tables available for each category are the following: for attribute plans,

- Sampling Inspection Tables (H. F. Dodge and H. G. Romig)
- MIL-STD-105D
- Phillips Standard Sampling System

and for variables plans,

- Simon's Grand Lot Scheme
- Hamilton Standard Lot Plot Method of Acceptance Sampling by Variables (D. Shainin)
- Sampling Inspection by Variables (A. H. Bowker and H. P. Goode)
- MIL-STD-414
- Sampling Procedures and Charts for Inspection by Variables, Defense Standard, Great Britain

Primary emphasis in this chapter will be placed on MIL-STD-105D and MIL-STD-414.

PRELIMINARY CONSIDERATIONS

Several misconceptions exist in respect to acceptance sampling, and they should be clarified prior to explaining the specific plans.

Nothing but perfect lots can be used. In some situations perfect lots may be necessary. In many industrial processes, however, the concept that no defective parts can be tolerated or that 100 percent inspection is a must is economically impractical. Such ideas are usually conceived by those far removed from the actual operation. Practically, the inspection cost required to obtain a perfect product should be balanced against the scrap and/or rework cost created by an occasional defective part in the assembly area.

A lot can be judged by looking at a few pieces. This concept is fallacious, since the sampling risks are not normally evaluated. Usually the decision to accept or reject is not based on the sample alone but on past experience with the supplier, which requires an astute memory. Whenever a decision is based on examining part of a lot, an error in judging lot quality is possible. This error is related to sample size. With a formal sampling plan, the decision risks can be specified in advance, something not achievable with arbitrary sample sizes.

Ten percent inspection is adequate sampling. When the sample size is a constant proportion of the lot size, the inspection cost per unit remains constant; however, the risks of wrong decisions are not constant but increase with decreasing lot size. In formal sampling plans, the sample size does not vary proportionally with the lot size. Ten percent sampling actually gives highly variable protection. For example, with small lots (sampling 5 from 50) the risk of wrong decisions is great; with large lots (sampling 1,000 from 10,000) the risk is low but sampling costs are high. Any constant percentage sampling does not balance risks and costs.

A strong sampling plan is one that rejects a lot when a single defect is found in the sample. A sample does not depict exactly the lot from which it is drawn, although this error decreases with an increase in sample size. Suppose a 50-piece lot contained one defective piece. If this were divided into five 10-piece samples, one sample would contain 9 good pieces and 1 defective piece, while the other four samples would contain all good ones. The actual lot quality percent defective (2 percent), however, would not be correctly estimated by any sample. From this it is evident that the no-defect-in-a-sample restriction will not guarantee defect-free lots, although many bad lots will be rejected. More importantly, many good lots, those with low defective rates which might be economically acceptable, will also be rejected. If rejected lots are screened (100 percent inspected), the total inspection cost obviously increases.

Random sampling is not necessary. Random sampling is as important in selecting a sample for acceptance procedures as it is in selecting pieces for control charting. An effort must be made to select a sample which will represent the lot. Random selection implies that each item in the lot has an equal probability of being selected for the sample. Individual laziness or indifference does more to hinder random sampling than anything else. It is easy to assume that pieces from the top of a heavy container, or pieces from one of several boxes, represent the entire shipment. The random sample should contain parts from each box or each layer in the container. Failure to sample randomly can increase the risk of making wrong decisions.

One hundred percent inspection is the only way to assure good quality. Acceptance sampling procedures, properly applied, are designed to limit risks to a predetermined degree. These risks are undefined and unknown with ordinary inspection practices. Even 100 percent inspection has an associated risk since it is seldom, if ever, 100 percent effective. One reason is the monotony and fatigue associated with it; another is familiarity with what is being done. Studies conducted in the past have revealed that even 300 percent inspection is only 97 percent effective. In many cases, an effectively administered sampling program is more practical and economical.

138

DEFINITIONS AND SYMBOLS FOR ATTRIBUTE ACCEPTANCE SAMPLING

Term	Symbol or Abbreviation	Definition†
Lot size	N	The number of units in the lot
Sample size	n	The number of units in the sample
Fraction defective	p'	The fraction defective of the lot
Probability of acceptance	P_a	The probability that a lot or process will be accepted
Operating characteristic curve	OC curve	A curve showing the relation between the probability of acceptance and either lot quality or process quality, whichever is applicable
Acceptance number	Ac or c	The largest number of defectives (or defects) in the sample or samples under consideration that will permit the acceptance of the sample lot
Rejection number	Re	The smallest number of defectives (or defects) in the sample or samples under consideration that will require the rejection of the inspection lot
Acceptable quality level	AQL or p'_1	The maximum percent defective which can be considered satisfactory as a process average, or the percent defective whose probability of rejection is designated by α
Producers' risk	PR or α	The probability or risk of rejecting a lot for a given lot quality (usually applied to AQL quality)
Lot tolerance percent defective	LTPD or p'_t or p'_2	The percent defective which is to be accepted a minimum or arbitrary fraction of the time, or that percent defective whose probability of rejection is designated by β
Consumers' risk	CR or β	The probability or risk of accepting a lot for a given lot quality (usually applied to LTPD quality)
Average outgoing quality	AOQ	The average quality of outgoing product after 100% inspection of rejected lot, with replacement by good units of all defective units found in inspection
Average outgoing quality limit	AOQL	The maximum average outgoing quality (AOQ) for a sampling plan
Indifference quality	$p_{0.50}$	The percent defective whose probability of acceptance equals 50%
Average sample number	ASN	The average number of sample units inspected per lot in reaching a decision to accept or reject
Average total inspection	ATI	The average number of units inspected per lot including all units in rejected lots (applicable when the procedure calls for 100% inspection of rejected lots)
Process average	$\bar{p}$	The average fraction defective in observed samples (calculated from first samples only)

†These definitions in general are those proposed by the ASQC Standards Committee.

Fig. 9-1 Symbols and definitions

There are many sampling plans and many reasons for choosing one plan in preference to another. In some situations, physical limitations or budget restrictions may dictate the sample size. Before adopting a particular sampling scheme, consideration should be given to the following questions:

1. Is 100 percent inspection necessary?
2. Can some nonconforming pieces be tolerated?
3. Can the total pieces proposed for sampling be divided into lots produced under essentially the same conditions, i.e., the same machine type, the same procedure, the same shift, or the same vendor?
4. Is attribute or variable sampling to be used? Factors influencing this decision are
    a. Attribute sampling requires a larger sample than variable sampling to obtain equivalent discrimination between good and bad lots. Variable sampling is preferable if pieces are costly or if inspection is destructive.
    b. Variable sampling requires measurements and relatively involved computations. This may be more costly than the counting needed for attribute plans.
    c. Less training for inspection personnel is required with attribute sampling.
    d. The information generated with variable sampling is valuable in diagnosing production problems.

BASIC DEFINITIONS AND CONCEPTS

An understanding of acceptance sampling concepts requires defining various terms and symbols, which are shown in Figure 9-1. They will be introduced as needed in developing the more relevant concepts. In either attribute or variable sampling, the most important statistical tool is the operating characteristic curve (OC curve).

The OC curve depicts the risks inherent in a particular sampling plan. For a lot having a specified percent defective, the curve gives the probability that it will be accepted by the sampling plan. Each plan has its particular OC curve, so familiarity with this curve is a prerequisite to understanding what protection a sampling plan provides.

Figure 9-2 shows a typical OC curve. Some general aspects should be noted prior to illustrating how the curves are constructed. Each curve starts with 100 percent acceptance at 0 percent defective. The acceptance rate decreases as the percent defective increases. The curve's relative steepness measures the plan's power to discriminate between various quality levels and is thus related to the cost and amount of inspection.

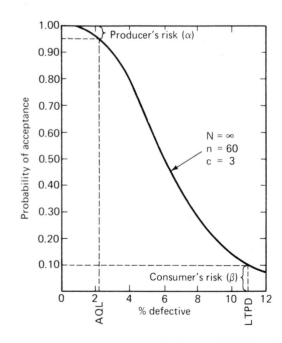

Fig. 9-2 Typical OC curve

The calculation of the probabilities shown on the ordinate in Figure 9-2 necessitates using either the binomial or Poisson distribution since the statistic (percent defective) is derived from discrete data. These distributions were discussed in Chapter 4. For convenience, the Poisson distribution is usually used to approximate the binomial in constructing most OC curves.

EXAMPLE

Refer again to Figure 9-2. The lot size (N) is ∞, the sample size (n) is 60, and the acceptance number (c) is 3. To determine the probabilities only the sample size and acceptance number are needed. Since $c = 3$, any sample containing 0, 1, 2, or 3 defective units would result in accepting the lot. The percent defective values range from zero to whatever value might be anticipated for lot quality percent defective. In this case, it ranges from 0 to 12. To enter the Poisson tables, values for np' are needed. (Refer to the Poisson tables in Appendix 2 in Chapter 4.) It is convenient to arrange the data in tabular form, as shown in Figure 9-3.

p'	np'	p_a
0.00	0.00	1.00
0.01	0.60	0.997
0.02	1.20	0.966
0.03	1.80	0.891
0.04	2.40	0.779
0.05	3.00	0.647
0.06	3.60	0.515
0.07	4.20	0.395
0.08	4.80	0.294
0.09	5.40	0.213
0.10	6.00	0.151
0.11	6.60	0.105
0.12	7.20	0.072

Fig. 9-3 Calculations for OC curve

There are certain sampling situations where the binomial distribution should be used or where a distribution called the hypergeometric is more appropriate. Since this is intended as a basic text, however, only the Poisson distribution has been illustrated.

OC curves are defined by referring to the two quality levels shown in Figure 9-2. The first is the AQL (acceptable quality level) and the second is the LTPD (lot tolerance percent defective). The AQL may be considered as a desirable quality level and the LTPD an undesirable quality level. More specifically,

The AQL is defined as the material grade considered "good." Consequently, when lots containing this percent defective are submitted for inspection, a relatively "high" acceptance is desired. This "high" acceptance is nominally about 95 percent, although it may vary between 90 and 99 percent, depending on the plan. Since the AQL value is supposedly acceptable to the consumer, the producer is interested in the probability that lots containing this percent defective will be rejected. This is also illustrated in Figure 9-2, by reference to the *producer's risk* (α). The producer's risk is obviously the complement of the consumer's acceptance at the AQL. All sampling plans in MIL-STD-105D are defined by an AQL value.

The LTPD is defined as the material grade considered "bad." Consequently, when lots containing this percent defective are submitted for inspection, a relatively "low" acceptance is desired. This "low acceptance" is defined as 10 percent, since the consumer wants to minimize the risk that lots which are "bad" will be accepted. The consumer's risk (β) is also illustrated in Figure 9-2 in connection with the LTPD. LTPD plans are one of two categories included in Dodge and Romig's Sampling Inspection Tables.

Selecting the correct AQL or LTPD value is often an arbitrary decision made by a quality control engineer or someone in receiving inspection. However, various areas such as engineering, purchasing, manufacturing, reliability, quality control, and inspection should be in a position to contribute information and participate in specifying what percent defective is appropriate for a specific application.

Actually the two quality levels AQL and LTPD divide the area under the OC curve into three zones, or divide the lots submitted for inspection into three quality classes:

1. Good lots (AQL or less percent defective), which will have approximately 95 percent or more acceptance.

2. Intermediate lots (percent defective between the AQL and LTPD), which will have various chances of acceptance.

3. Bad lots (LTPD or greater percent defective), which will have approximately 10 percent or less acceptance.

The intermediate zone width measures the sampling plan discriminating power. A wide zone results in small samples and economical inspection but increases the overall risk. A narrow zone results in large samples, increased inspection, and decreased risk. Good judgment, statistical knowledge, and specialized information are needed to balance inspection cost against risk.

Specifying the quality levels, AQL and LTPD, and their associated risks, α and β, restricts the sampling plan selection, since only one plan can satisfy both criteria. (This will be explained later under Designing a Sampling Plan.) Designating only one point on an OC curve (AQL and α or LTPD and β) broadens the sampling plan selection, since there are many plans that can satisfy a single criterion. Figure 9-4 illustrates what occurs when the AQL and α specify the point on the OC curve. As the sample size decreases, protection against accepting poor-quality lots decreases significantly. Figure 9-5 illustrates what occurs when the LTPD and β specify the point on the OC curve. As the sample size decreases, fewer good lots are accepted, which may reduce sampling costs but which will create problems with the vendor due to the fact that more good lots will be rejected. This is the reason that knowledge concerning OC curves is so essential for quality and reliability engineers.

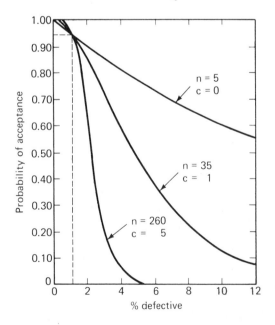

Fig. 9-4 OC curves for sampling plans with the same AQL and α

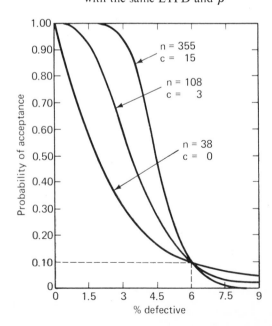

Fig. 9-5 OC curves for sampling plans with the same LTPD and β

A few further examples will help to reinforce some concepts which were mentioned previously. Ten percent sampling was described as a poor approach because the protection varied so much with changes in the lot size. Figure 9-6 shows this with lots ranging from 50 to 1,000 pieces and the acceptance number held constant at zero. To obtain higher acceptance at any quality level, all a vendor needs to do is reduce his lot size.

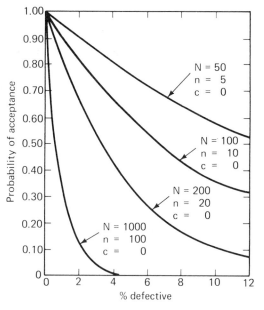

Fig. 9-6 OC curves comparing 10 percent sampling plans

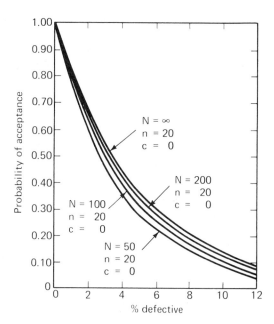

Fig. 9-7 OC curves for constant *n* and *c* with varying lot size

Many people unfamiliar with statistics believe that the protection afforded by a sampling plan should improve drastically as the sample size becomes proportionally larger with respect to the lot size. Figure 9-7 refutes this idea, using a constant 20-piece sample with lots that vary from 50 to infinity. This is the reason that OC curves, in most cases, are determined using only the sample size (*n*) and the acceptance number (*c*).

The effect that changing the acceptance number and holding the sample size constant has on the probability of acceptance is seen in Figure 9-8. The sample size is held constant at 50, while the acceptance number equals 0, 1, 2, and 3. It should be intuitively obvious that as more defective units are permitted for acceptance, the probability of accepting a lot at a given percent defective will increase.

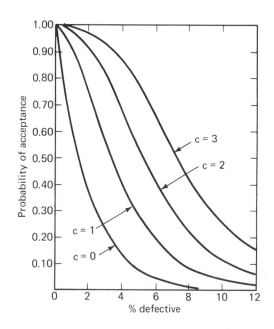

Fig. 9-8 OC curves for constant *n* and varying *c*

The concepts presented up to this point have primarily illustrated how sampling plans are intended to operate over the long run. A given size sample is taken from a lot, and if the acceptance number is not exceeded, the lot is accepted for use. When a lot is rejected, however, two alternative actions may be taken:

1. Return material to the vendor.

2. Keep the material and 100 percent inspect.

The first action is costly since excess transportation will be required and, due to limited inventory floats, may result in stopping production. When parts are required, sorting may be the only feasible option. This leads into another sampling concept, termed AOQ (average outgoing quality). This concept is depicted in Figure 9-9.

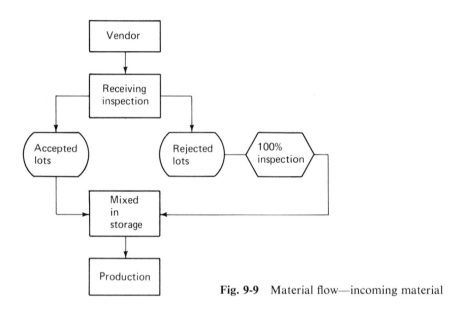

Fig. 9-9 Material flow—incoming material

What occurs when this concept is used is best illustrated with an example. Given:

- One hundred material lots are received, each containing 1,000 pieces.
- Each lot is exactly 3 percent defective.
- A sampling plan is selected with $n = 100$, $c = 2$.

Solution:

$$np' = (100)(0.03) = 3.00$$

From the Poisson tables with this np' and $c = 2$, $P_a = 0.423$; with 100 lots submitted, then, approximately 42 would be accepted and 58 rejected. Assuming that all defective parts are discovered and replaced, the average outgoing quality (AOQ) would be

$$\text{AOQ} = \frac{(58)(1,000)(0.0) + (42)(1,000)(0.03)}{(100)(1,000)} = \frac{1,260}{100,000}$$
$$= 0.0126 \text{ or } 1.26 \text{ percent}$$

This is under the premise that rejected lots, which are 100 percent sorted, are mixed with the accepted lots, which are still 3 percent defective going into the storage area. If the lots go directly to production as accepted, this concept does not apply. A general approximation formula for the AOQ is

$$AOQ \doteq (P_a)(p')$$

Substituting values from the preceding problem gives

$$AOQ \doteq (0.423)(0.03) = 0.01269 = 1.269 \text{ percent}$$

The p' values used in the above expression are the same as those used in constructing an OC curve. For any OC curve, then, AOQ values may be calculated which result in an average outgoing quality curve. This is shown in Figure 9-10 for $n = 100$, $c = 2$.

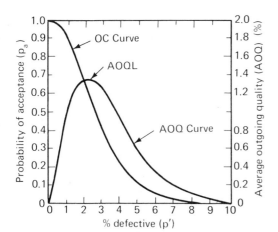

p'	np'	p_a	AOQ%
0.00	0	1.000	0.0
0.01	1.0	0.920	0.92
0.02	2.0	0.677	1.354
0.03	3.0	0.423	1.268
0.04	4.0	0.238	0.952
0.05	5.0	0.125	0.625
0.06	6.0	0.062	0.372
0.07	7.0	0.030	0.210
0.08	8.0	0.014	0.112
0.09	9.0	0.006	0.054
0.10	10.0	0.003	0.030

← AOQL (average outgoing quality limit)

Fig. 9-10   OC and AOQ curves for $n = 100$, $c = 2$

The AOQ curve reveals that a peak (the AOQL) is reached at some incoming quality level; then the outgoing quality improves. This can be attributed to the fact that more lots are rejected and 100 percent inspected, but it does allow inspection to assure production that quality will never exceed some maximum percent defective. In this example the AOQL is approximately 1.35 percent regardless of the quality submitted by the vendor. Again it should be emphasized that this requires the ability to hold and mix incoming material shipments. The Dodge-Romig sampling tables contain plans based on specific AOQL values, and MIL-STD-105D has a table which gives the AOQL values for the sampling plans.

The AOQL plans in Dodge-Romig were also selected to minimize the average total inspection required when the rejected lots are sorted. For the example used, i.e., $N = 1,000$, $n = 100$, and $c = 2$,

$$ATI = n + (1 - p_a)(N - n)$$
$$= 100 + (1 - 0.423)(1,000 - 100)$$
$$= 100 + 519.3 = 619.3 \text{ or } 619 \text{ pieces}$$

On the average, then, if all lots were to come in at 3 percent defective, 619 pieces would be inspected per lot. Information such as this can be used in conjunction with any sampling plan utilizing sorting to estimate manpower requirements and cost.

In general, acceptance sampling plans force the producer, whether another department or another company, to submit lots whose quality is such that only a small percentage will be rejected. Choosing a desirable sampling plan is preferably based on analyzing the OC curve rather than blindly following the procedure which may be indicated in a manual.

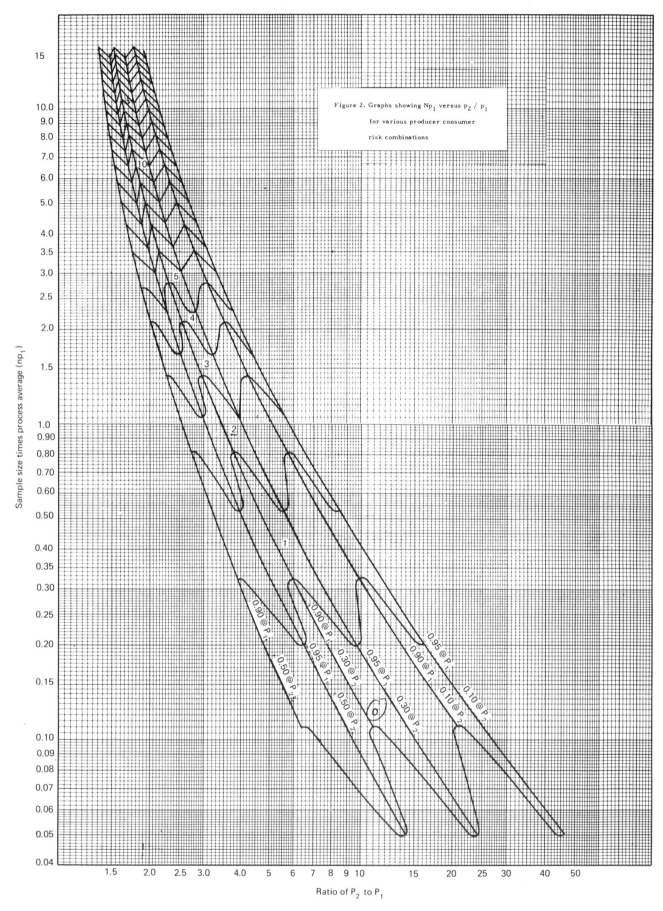

Fig. 9-11 Graphs showing np_1 vs. p_2/p_1 for various producer consumer risk combinations

DESIGNING A SAMPLING PLAN

Although many standard sampling tables are readily available, there are occasions when it may be necessary to devise a sampling plan to meet some specific conditions. Somewhat involved approximation methods may be found in statistical textbooks. A relatively simple approach was developed at General Motors Institute in the early 1950's which uses the graphs shown in Figure 9-11.

Earlier it was stated that a sampling plan could be completely defined by specifying two points for the OC curve. These points are the AQL-α and LTPD-β values. In Figure 9-11, p_1 is used to designate the AQL and p_2 to designate the LTPD. Rather than specifying α, $1 - \alpha$ (or the acceptance value) is shown at p_1. The β value is given at p_2. Figure 9-12 illustrates this.

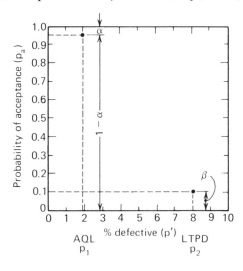

Fig. 9-12 Schematic showing AQL-α and LTPD-β

The graphs offer a limited flexibility in designing a plan in that two acceptance values (0.90 and 0.95) are given at p_1 in combination with three acceptance values (0.10, 0.30, and 0.50) at p_2. The large variation in risk at p_2 will provide for smaller sample sizes when appropriate and larger sample sizes when needed for adequate protection. For example, if the vendor process average adheres closely to the AQL, the probability that an individual lot quality will be near the LTPD may be small. In that case a 0.50 risk at p_2 might be selected. However, if the LTPD were close to the AQL, then a 0.10 risk at p_2 would be required.

The procedure for using Figure 9-11 is

1. Specify values for AQL (p_1) and LTPD (p_2).
2. Specify the acceptance desired at p_1 and p_2 ($1 - \alpha$, β).
3. Calculate the ratio p_2 to p_1.
4. Locate this value on the horizontal axis.
5. Project vertically from this value to intersect the curve defined by step 2.
6. From this intersection point, project horizontally to intersect the vertical axis.
7. Read the value on this axis as np.
8. Using the p_1 value, solve for n.
9. Read the plan acceptance number as the values shown between the wavy and diagonal lines.
10. Using the n and c values, construct an OC curve to determine if the conditions specified are met.

147

Example

1. AQL (p_1) = 2.0 percent, LTPD (p_2) = 6.0 percent.
2. $1 - \alpha = 0.95$, $\beta = 0.10$.
3. $p_2/p_1 = 6.0/2.0 = 3.0$.
4. See Figure 9-11.
5. See Figure 9-11.
6. See Figure 9-11.
7. $np_1 \doteq 3.8$.
8. $n \doteq 3.8/0.02 = 190$.
9. $c = 7$.
10. See Figure 9-13.

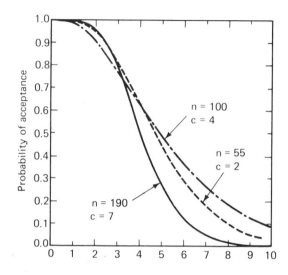

Fig. 9-13   OC curves

Curves are also shown in Figure 9-13 for β risks set at 0.30 and 0.10 with $1 - \alpha$ remaining at 0.95. The reason that the specified points are not exactly satisfied is that whole integers must be used for sample sizes and acceptance numbers. If greater accuracy is required, either n, c, or both can be adjusted slightly to determine if the points can be met more precisely. Since the probabilities pertain only to the "long run," however, the need for such precision would be questionable.

TYPES OF ATTRIBUTE SAMPLING PLANS

In selecting a sampling plan there are three different types to consider. These are described by the number of samples which may be drawn from the lot before a decision to accept or reject can be made.

- *Single sampling.* A sample (n) is selected at random from a lot (N) and inspected. The nonconforming units (d) are counted and compared to the plan's acceptance number (c). If d is less than or equal to c, the lot is accepted. If d is greater than c, the lot is rejected.

- *Double sampling.* A sample (n_1) is selected at random from a lot (N) and inspected. The nonconforming units (d_1) are counted and compared to n_1's acceptance number (c_1) and n_2's acceptance number (c_2). If d_1 is less than or equal to c_1, the lot is accepted. If d_1 is greater than c_2, the lot is rejected. If d_1 is greater than c_1 but less than or equal to c_2 numbers, a second sample (n_2) is drawn. The nonconforming units in this sample are counted and added to those from the first sample. If d_1 plus d_2 are less than or equal to n_2's acceptance number (c_2), the lot is accepted. If d_1 plus d_2 is greater than c_2, the lot is rejected.

- *Multiple sampling.* This plan extends the concept described in double sampling to possibly as many as nine samples before a decision is reached. At each stage (sample), nonconforming units are cumulatively counted and compared to the acceptance number for that sample. Any of three decisions are possible at each stage, i.e., accept, continue, or reject. An accept or reject decision must be made, however, on the last sample.

When these plans are found in formal sampling tables, they are usually designed to have essentially the same OC curve. This implies that basically the same protection can be obtained with either single, double, or multiple sampling and that choosing a particular type is dependent on other factors. Among these factors are

- Teaching the plan to inspectors and vendors
- Supervising the plan
- Drawing the sample
- Storage space
- Inventory float

It should be pointed out that the average sample number required to arrive at a decision is usually less for both double and multiple sampling than it is for single. While this advantage should result in lower inspection cost, the disadvantage usually cited is the difficulties encountered in teaching the plans to inspection personnel.

Following this somewhat condensed introduction to acceptance sampling, the plans in more general use will be discussed.

ATTRIBUTE SAMPLING PLANS

Attribute sampling plans are the most commonly used sampling techniques, primarily because they are easy to administer and the printed tables are readily available.

The two major sources for attribute sampling plans are

1. Sampling Inspection Tables, Single and Double Sampling,† by H. F. Dodge and H. G. Romig (commonly referred to as the Dodge-Romig tables). The Dodge-Romig tables list single and double sampling plans by two classifications:
   a. LTPD plans: LTPD's vary from 0.5 to 10.0 percent. Process averages vary from zero to one-half the specified LTPD values. β is fixed at 10 percent. Minimum inspection is proposed.
   b. AOQL plans: AOQL's vary from 0.1 percent to 10.0 percent. Process averages vary from zero to the AOQL value. β is fixed at 10 percent. Minimum inspection is proposed.

2. Military Standard Sampling Procedures and Tables for Inspection by Attribute‡ (commonly known as MIL-STD-105D).
   a. MIL-STD-105D lists single, double, and multiple sampling plans characterized by AQL values and several inspection levels and degrees.
   b. AQL's vary from 0.015 to 10.0 percent. α varies from 20 percent (small sample) to 0.2 percent (large sample).
   c. Small-sample inspection has four inspection levels.
   d. Ordinary inspection has three inspection levels.
   e. Degrees of inspection: normal, tightened, and reduced.

Since MIL-STD-105D is the most widely used sampling table for attribute inspection, this is the only table which will be explained in detail.

---

†Available from John Wiley & Sons, Inc., 440 Fourth Avenue, New York, New York.
‡Available from Superintendent of Documents, U.S. Government Printing Office, Washington, D.C. 20402.

USING MIL-STD-105D

MIL-STD-105D tables are used when directed by the government or when maximum acceptance is desired at a predetermined quality level (the AQL). These tables have provisions for classifying defects as critical, major, or minor and using different AQL values for each classification. Complete instructions for applying the standard are given in the first eight pages. The following will summarize the information required for their use:

1. Select the AQL to be used from the preferred values given. AQL's less than or equal to 10.0 may be expressed either in percent defective or defects per hundred units. Those greater than 10.0 are expressed only in defects per hundred units. *Example:* 2.5 percent AQL is specified.

2. Determine the lot size. Refer to Table I to find sample size code letter. General inspection level II is usually specified. Level I is less discriminating, and level III is more discriminating. The special inspection levels are used when small samples are necessary and large risks can be tolerated. *Example:* The lot size is 1,000 pieces. The inspection level II is specified. The code letter from Table I is J.

3. Select the appropriate sampling plan.
   a. Use Table II-A for single sample. *Example:* Code letter J, sample size 80. With 2.5 percent AQL, accept on five or less, and reject on six or more.
   b. Use Table III-A for double sampling. *Example:* Code letter J, 2.5 percent AQL.

   $n_1 = 50$; accept on 2 or less, reject on 5 or more

   $n_2 = 50$; accept on 6 or less, reject on 7 or more

   Note: Defectives are cumulative from n_1 to n_2.
   c. Use Table IV-A for multiple sample. *Example:* Code letter J, 2.5 percent AQL.

   $n_1 = 20$; no acceptance (number), reject on 4 or more

   $n_2 = 20$; accept on 1 or less, reject on 5 or more

   $n_3 = 20$; accept on 2 or less, reject on 6 or more

   $n_4 = 20$; accept on 3 or less, reject on 7 or more

   $n_5 = 20$; accept on 5 or less, reject on 8 or more

   $n_6 = 20$; accept on 7 or less, reject on 9 or more

   $n_7 = 20$; accept on 9 or less, reject on 10 or more

The preceding sampling plans are referred to as normal inspection plans. MIL-STD-105D has provisions for switching from normal to tightened inspection, from tightened to normal inspection, from normal to reduced inspection, and from reduced to normal inspection. Tightened inspection essentially reduces the sampling risks when the process average is at an unacceptable level. This is indicated when two out of five lots have been rejected on original inspection. Specific plans for tightened inspection are

1. Use Table II-B for single sampling. *Example:* Code letter J, 2.5 percent AQL.

   $n = 80$; accept on 3 or less, reject on 4 or more

2. Use Table III-B for double sampling. *Example:* Code letter J, 2.5 percent AQL.

   $n_1 = 50$; accept on 1 or less, reject on 3 or more

   $n_2 = 50$; accept on 4 or less, reject on 5 or more

Table I Sample Size Code Letters

Lot or batch size	Special inspection levels				General inspection levels		
	S-1	S-2	S-3	S-4	I	II	III
2 to 8	A	A	A	A	A	A	B
9 to 15	A	A	A	A	A	B	C
16 to 25	A	A	B	B	B	C	D
26 to 50	A	B	B	C	C	D	E
51 to 90	B	B	C	C	C	E	F
91 to 150	B	B	C	D	D	F	G
151 to 280	B	C	D	E	E	G	H
281 to 500	B	C	D	E	F	H	J
501 to 1200	C	C	E	F	G	J	K
1201 to 3200	C	D	E	G	H	K	L
3201 to 10000	C	D	F	G	J	L	M
10001 to 35000	C	D	F	H	K	M	N
35001 to 150000	D	E	G	J	L	N	P
150001 to 500000	D	E	G	J	M	P	Q
500001 and over	D	E	H	K	N	Q	R

Table II-A Single Sampling Plans for Normal Inspection (Master Table)

Acceptable Quality Levels (normal inspection)

Each cell below shows "Ac Re" (Acceptance number, Rejection number). ↓ = Use first sampling plan below arrow. ↑ = Use first sampling plan above arrow.

Sample size code letter	Sample size	0.010	0.015	0.025	0.040	0.065	0.10	0.15	0.25	0.40	0.65	1.0	1.5	2.5	4.0	6.5	10	15	25	40	65	100	150	250	400	650	1000
A	2	↓	↓	↓	↓	↓	↓	↓	↓	↓	↓	↓	↓	↓	↓	↓	↓	0 1	1 2	2 3	3 4	5 6	7 8	10 11	14 15	21 22	30 31
B	3	↓	↓	↓	↓	↓	↓	↓	↓	↓	↓	↓	↓	↓	↓	↓	0 1	1 2	2 3	3 4	5 6	7 8	10 11	14 15	21 22	30 31	44 45
C	5	↓	↓	↓	↓	↓	↓	↓	↓	↓	↓	↓	↓	↓	↓	0 1	1 2	2 3	3 4	5 6	7 8	10 11	14 15	21 22	30 31	44 45	↑
D	8	↓	↓	↓	↓	↓	↓	↓	↓	↓	↓	↓	↓	↓	0 1	1 2	2 3	3 4	5 6	7 8	10 11	14 15	21 22	30 31	44 45	↑	↑
E	13	↓	↓	↓	↓	↓	↓	↓	↓	↓	↓	↓	↓	0 1	1 2	2 3	3 4	5 6	7 8	10 11	14 15	21 22	30 31	44 45	↑	↑	↑
F	20	↓	↓	↓	↓	↓	↓	↓	↓	↓	↓	↓	0 1	1 2	2 3	3 4	5 6	7 8	10 11	14 15	21 22	30 31	44 45	↑	↑	↑	↑
G	32	↓	↓	↓	↓	↓	↓	↓	↓	↓	↓	0 1	1 2	2 3	3 4	5 6	7 8	10 11	14 15	21 22	30 31	44 45	↑	↑	↑	↑	↑
H	50	↓	↓	↓	↓	↓	↓	↓	↓	↓	0 1	1 2	2 3	3 4	5 6	7 8	10 11	14 15	21 22	30 31	44 45	↑	↑	↑	↑	↑	↑
J	80	↓	↓	↓	↓	↓	↓	↓	↓	0 1	1 2	2 3	3 4	5 6	7 8	10 11	14 15	21 22	30 31	44 45	↑	↑	↑	↑	↑	↑	↑
K	125	↓	↓	↓	↓	↓	↓	↓	0 1	1 2	2 3	3 4	5 6	7 8	10 11	14 15	21 22	30 31	44 45	↑	↑	↑	↑	↑	↑	↑	↑
L	200	↓	↓	↓	↓	↓	↓	0 1	1 2	2 3	3 4	5 6	7 8	10 11	14 15	21 22	30 31	44 45	↑	↑	↑	↑	↑	↑	↑	↑	↑
M	315	↓	↓	↓	↓	↓	0 1	1 2	2 3	3 4	5 6	7 8	10 11	14 15	21 22	30 31	44 45	↑	↑	↑	↑	↑	↑	↑	↑	↑	↑
N	500	↓	↓	↓	↓	0 1	1 2	2 3	3 4	5 6	7 8	10 11	14 15	21 22	30 31	44 45	↑	↑	↑	↑	↑	↑	↑	↑	↑	↑	↑
P	800	↓	↓	↓	0 1	1 2	2 3	3 4	5 6	7 8	10 11	14 15	21 22	30 31	44 45	↑	↑	↑	↑	↑	↑	↑	↑	↑	↑	↑	↑
Q	1250	↓	↓	0 1	1 2	2 3	3 4	5 6	7 8	10 11	14 15	21 22	30 31	44 45	↑	↑	↑	↑	↑	↑	↑	↑	↑	↑	↑	↑	↑
R	2000	↓	0 1	1 2	2 3	3 4	5 6	7 8	10 11	14 15	21 22	30 31	44 45	↑	↑	↑	↑	↑	↑	↑	↑	↑	↑	↑	↑	↑	↑

⇩ = Use first sampling plan below arrow. If sample size equals, or exceeds, lot or batch size, do 100 percent inspection.

⇧ = Use first sampling plan above arrow.

Ac = Acceptance number.

Re = Rejection number.

Table III-A   Double Sampling Plans for Normal Inspection (Master Table)

Acceptable Quality Levels (normal inspection)

Each AQL cell below gives the plan as "Ac Re" (Acceptance number / Rejection number). ↓ = use first sampling plan below arrow; ↑ = use first sampling plan above arrow; • = use corresponding single sampling plan.

Code	Sample	Sample size	Cumulative sample size	0.010	0.015	0.025	0.040	0.065	0.10	0.15	0.25	0.40	0.65	1.0	1.5	2.5	4.0	6.5	10	15	25	40	65	100	150	250	400	650	1000
A	—			↓	↓	↓	↓	↓	↓	↓	↓	↓	↓	↓	↓	↓	↓	↓	↓	•	•	•	•	•	•	•	•	•	•
B	First	2	2	↓	↓	↓	↓	↓	↓	↓	↓	↓	↓	↓	↓	↓	↓	↓	•	0 2	0 3	1 4	2 5	3 7	5 9	7 11	11 16	17 22	25 31
B	Second	2	4	↓	↓	↓	↓	↓	↓	↓	↓	↓	↓	↓	↓	↓	↓	↓	•	1 2	3 4	4 5	6 7	8 9	12 13	18 19	26 27	37 38	56 57
C	First	3	3	↓	↓	↓	↓	↓	↓	↓	↓	↓	↓	↓	↓	↓	↓	•	0 2	0 3	1 4	2 5	3 7	5 9	7 11	11 16	17 22	25 31	↑
C	Second	3	6	↓	↓	↓	↓	↓	↓	↓	↓	↓	↓	↓	↓	↓	↓	•	1 2	3 4	4 5	6 7	8 9	12 13	18 19	26 27	37 38	56 57	↑
D	First	5	5	↓	↓	↓	↓	↓	↓	↓	↓	↓	↓	↓	↓	↓	•	0 2	0 3	1 4	2 5	3 7	5 9	7 11	11 16	17 22	25 31	↑	↑
D	Second	5	10	↓	↓	↓	↓	↓	↓	↓	↓	↓	↓	↓	↓	↓	•	1 2	3 4	4 5	6 7	8 9	12 13	18 19	26 27	37 38	56 57	↑	↑
E	First	8	8	↓	↓	↓	↓	↓	↓	↓	↓	↓	↓	↓	↓	•	0 2	0 3	1 4	2 5	3 7	5 9	7 11	11 16	17 22	25 31	↑	↑	↑
E	Second	8	16	↓	↓	↓	↓	↓	↓	↓	↓	↓	↓	↓	↓	•	1 2	3 4	4 5	6 7	8 9	12 13	18 19	26 27	37 38	56 57	↑	↑	↑
F	First	13	13	↓	↓	↓	↓	↓	↓	↓	↓	↓	↓	↓	•	0 2	0 3	1 4	2 5	3 7	5 9	7 11	11 16	17 22	25 31	↑	↑	↑	↑
F	Second	13	26	↓	↓	↓	↓	↓	↓	↓	↓	↓	↓	↓	•	1 2	3 4	4 5	6 7	8 9	12 13	18 19	26 27	37 38	56 57	↑	↑	↑	↑
G	First	20	20	↓	↓	↓	↓	↓	↓	↓	↓	↓	↓	•	0 2	0 3	1 4	2 5	3 7	5 9	7 11	11 16	17 22	25 31	↑	↑	↑	↑	↑
G	Second	20	40	↓	↓	↓	↓	↓	↓	↓	↓	↓	↓	•	1 2	3 4	4 5	6 7	8 9	12 13	18 19	26 27	37 38	56 57	↑	↑	↑	↑	↑
H	First	32	32	↓	↓	↓	↓	↓	↓	↓	↓	↓	•	0 2	0 3	1 4	2 5	3 7	5 9	7 11	11 16	17 22	25 31	↑	↑	↑	↑	↑	↑
H	Second	32	64	↓	↓	↓	↓	↓	↓	↓	↓	↓	•	1 2	3 4	4 5	6 7	8 9	12 13	18 19	26 27	37 38	56 57	↑	↑	↑	↑	↑	↑
J	First	50	50	↓	↓	↓	↓	↓	↓	↓	↓	•	0 2	0 3	1 4	2 5	3 7	5 9	7 11	11 16	17 22	25 31	↑	↑	↑	↑	↑	↑	↑
J	Second	50	100	↓	↓	↓	↓	↓	↓	↓	↓	•	1 2	3 4	4 5	6 7	8 9	12 13	18 19	26 27	37 38	56 57	↑	↑	↑	↑	↑	↑	↑
K	First	80	80	↓	↓	↓	↓	↓	↓	↓	•	0 2	0 3	1 4	2 5	3 7	5 9	7 11	11 16	17 22	25 31	↑	↑	↑	↑	↑	↑	↑	↑
K	Second	80	160	↓	↓	↓	↓	↓	↓	↓	•	1 2	3 4	4 5	6 7	8 9	12 13	18 19	26 27	37 38	56 57	↑	↑	↑	↑	↑	↑	↑	↑
L	First	125	125	↓	↓	↓	↓	↓	↓	•	0 2	0 3	1 4	2 5	3 7	5 9	7 11	11 16	17 22	25 31	↑	↑	↑	↑	↑	↑	↑	↑	↑
L	Second	125	250	↓	↓	↓	↓	↓	↓	•	1 2	3 4	4 5	6 7	8 9	12 13	18 19	26 27	37 38	56 57	↑	↑	↑	↑	↑	↑	↑	↑	↑
M	First	200	200	↓	↓	↓	↓	↓	•	0 2	0 3	1 4	2 5	3 7	5 9	7 11	11 16	17 22	25 31	↑	↑	↑	↑	↑	↑	↑	↑	↑	↑
M	Second	200	400	↓	↓	↓	↓	↓	•	1 2	3 4	4 5	6 7	8 9	12 13	18 19	26 27	37 38	56 57	↑	↑	↑	↑	↑	↑	↑	↑	↑	↑
N	First	315	315	↓	↓	↓	↓	•	0 2	0 3	1 4	2 5	3 7	5 9	7 11	11 16	17 22	25 31	↑	↑	↑	↑	↑	↑	↑	↑	↑	↑	↑
N	Second	315	630	↓	↓	↓	↓	•	1 2	3 4	4 5	6 7	8 9	12 13	18 19	26 27	37 38	56 57	↑	↑	↑	↑	↑	↑	↑	↑	↑	↑	↑
P	First	500	500	↓	↓	↓	•	0 2	0 3	1 4	2 5	3 7	5 9	7 11	11 16	17 22	25 31	↑	↑	↑	↑	↑	↑	↑	↑	↑	↑	↑	↑
P	Second	500	1000	↓	↓	↓	•	1 2	3 4	4 5	6 7	8 9	12 13	18 19	26 27	37 38	56 57	↑	↑	↑	↑	↑	↑	↑	↑	↑	↑	↑	↑
Q	First	800	800	↓	↓	•	0 2	0 3	1 4	2 5	3 7	5 9	7 11	11 16	17 22	25 31	↑	↑	↑	↑	↑	↑	↑	↑	↑	↑	↑	↑	↑
Q	Second	800	1600	↓	↓	•	1 2	3 4	4 5	6 7	8 9	12 13	18 19	26 27	37 38	56 57	↑	↑	↑	↑	↑	↑	↑	↑	↑	↑	↑	↑	↑
R	First	1250	1250	↓	•	0 2	0 3	1 4	2 5	3 7	5 9	7 11	11 16	17 22	25 31	↑	↑	↑	↑	↑	↑	↑	↑	↑	↑	↑	↑	↑	↑
R	Second	1250	2500	↓	•	1 2	3 4	4 5	6 7	8 9	12 13	18 19	26 27	37 38	56 57	↑	↑	↑	↑	↑	↑	↑	↑	↑	↑	↑	↑	↑	↑

⇩ = Use first sampling plan below arrow. If sample size equals or exceeds lot or batch size, do 100 percent inspection.

⇧ = Use first sampling plan above arrow.

Ac = Acceptance number

Re = Rejection number

• = Use corresponding single sampling plan (or alternatively, use double sampling plan below, where available).

Table IV-A Multiple Sampling Plans for Normal Inspection (Master Table)

Acceptable Quality Levels (normal inspection)

Sample size code letter	Sample	Sample size	Cumulative sample size
A			
B			
C			
D	First	2	2
	Second	2	4
	Third	2	6
	Fourth	2	8
	Fifth	2	10
	Sixth	2	12
	Seventh	2	14
E	First	3	3
	Second	3	6
	Third	3	9
	Fourth	3	12
	Fifth	3	15
	Sixth	3	18
	Seventh	3	21
F	First	5	5
	Second	5	10
	Third	5	15
	Fourth	5	20
	Fifth	5	25
	Sixth	5	30
	Seventh	5	35
G	First	8	8
	Second	8	16
	Third	8	24
	Fourth	8	32
	Fifth	8	40
	Sixth	8	48
	Seventh	8	56
H	First	13	13
	Second	13	26
	Third	13	39
	Fourth	13	52
	Fifth	13	65
	Sixth	13	78
	Seventh	13	91
J	First	20	20
	Second	20	40
	Third	20	60
	Fourth	20	80
	Fifth	20	100
	Sixth	20	120
	Seventh	20	140

Legend:

⇩ = Use first sampling plan below arrow (refer to continuation of table on following page, when necessary). If sample size equals or exceeds lot or batch size, do 100 percent inspection.

⇧ = Use first sampling plan above arrow.

Ac = Acceptance number.

Re = Rejection number.

• = Use corresponding single sampling plan (or alternatively, use multiple sampling plan below, where available).

‡ = Use corresponding double sampling plan (or alternatively, use multiple sampling plan below, where available).

* = Acceptance not permitted at this sample size.

154

Table IV-A Multiple Sampling Plans for Normal Inspection (Master Table) (Continued)

Acceptable Quality Levels (normal inspection)

= Use first sampling plan below arrow. If sample size equals or exceeds lot or batch size, do 100 percent inspection.

= Use first sampling plan above arrow (refer to preceding page, when necessary).

Ac = Acceptance number.

Re = Rejection number.

= Use corresponding single sampling plan (or alternatively, use multiple plan below, where available)

* = Acceptance not permitted at this sample size.

155

Table II-B Single Sampling Plans for Tightened Inspection (Master Table)

Acceptable Quality Levels (tightened inspection)

In each cell the value shown is the acceptance/rejection plan "Ac Re". ↓ = down arrow (use first sampling plan below arrow); ↑ = up arrow (use first sampling plan above arrow).

Sample size code letter	Sample size	0.010	0.015	0.025	0.040	0.065	0.10	0.15	0.25	0.40	0.65	1.0	1.5	2.5	4.0	6.5	10	15	25	40	65	100	150	250	400	650	1000
A	2	↓	↓	↓	↓	↓	↓	↓	↓	↓	↓	↓	↓	↓	↓	↓	↓	↓	0 1	1 2	2 3	3 4	5 6	8 9	12 13	18 19	27 28
B	3	↓	↓	↓	↓	↓	↓	↓	↓	↓	↓	↓	↓	↓	↓	↓	↓	0 1	1 2	2 3	3 4	5 6	8 9	12 13	18 19	27 28	41 42
C	5	↓	↓	↓	↓	↓	↓	↓	↓	↓	↓	↓	↓	↓	↓	↓	0 1	1 2	2 3	3 4	5 6	8 9	12 13	18 19	27 28	41 42	↑
D	8	↓	↓	↓	↓	↓	↓	↓	↓	↓	↓	↓	↓	↓	↓	0 1	1 2	2 3	3 4	5 6	8 9	12 13	18 19	27 28	41 42	↑	↑
E	13	↓	↓	↓	↓	↓	↓	↓	↓	↓	↓	↓	↓	↓	0 1	1 2	2 3	3 4	5 6	8 9	12 13	18 19	27 28	41 42	↑	↑	↑
F	20	↓	↓	↓	↓	↓	↓	↓	↓	↓	↓	↓	↓	0 1	1 2	2 3	3 4	5 6	8 9	12 13	18 19	27 28	41 42	↑	↑	↑	↑
G	32	↓	↓	↓	↓	↓	↓	↓	↓	↓	↓	↓	0 1	1 2	2 3	3 4	5 6	8 9	12 13	18 19	27 28	41 42	↑	↑	↑	↑	↑
H	50	↓	↓	↓	↓	↓	↓	↓	↓	↓	↓	0 1	1 2	2 3	3 4	5 6	8 9	12 13	18 19	27 28	41 42	↑	↑	↑	↑	↑	↑
J	80	↓	↓	↓	↓	↓	↓	↓	↓	↓	0 1	1 2	2 3	3 4	5 6	8 9	12 13	18 19	27 28	41 42	↑	↑	↑	↑	↑	↑	↑
K	125	↓	↓	↓	↓	↓	↓	↓	↓	0 1	1 2	2 3	3 4	5 6	8 9	12 13	18 19	27 28	41 42	↑	↑	↑	↑	↑	↑	↑	↑
L	200	↓	↓	↓	↓	↓	↓	↓	0 1	1 2	2 3	3 4	5 6	8 9	12 13	18 19	27 28	41 42	↑	↑	↑	↑	↑	↑	↑	↑	↑
M	315	↓	↓	↓	↓	↓	↓	0 1	1 2	2 3	3 4	5 6	8 9	12 13	18 19	27 28	41 42	↑	↑	↑	↑	↑	↑	↑	↑	↑	↑
N	500	↓	↓	↓	↓	↓	0 1	1 2	2 3	3 4	5 6	8 9	12 13	18 19	27 28	41 42	↑	↑	↑	↑	↑	↑	↑	↑	↑	↑	↑
P	800	↓	↓	↓	↓	0 1	1 2	2 3	3 4	5 6	8 9	12 13	18 19	27 28	41 42	↑	↑	↑	↑	↑	↑	↑	↑	↑	↑	↑	↑
Q	1250	↓	↓	↓	0 1	1 2	2 3	3 4	5 6	8 9	12 13	18 19	27 28	41 42	↑	↑	↑	↑	↑	↑	↑	↑	↑	↑	↑	↑	↑
R	2000	↓	↓	0 1	1 2	2 3	3 4	5 6	8 9	12 13	18 19	27 28	41 42	↑	↑	↑	↑	↑	↑	↑	↑	↑	↑	↑	↑	↑	↑
S	3150	↓	0 1	1 2	2 3	3 4	5 6	8 9	12 13	18 19	27 28	41 42	↑	↑	↑	↑	↑	↑	↑	↑	↑	↑	↑	↑	↑	↑	↑

⇩ = Use first sampling plan below arrow. If sample size equals or exceeds lot or batch size, do 100 percent inspection.

⇧ = Use first sampling plan above arrow.

Ac = Acceptance number.

Re = Rejection number.

Table III-B Double Sampling Plans for Tightened Inspection (Master Table)

Acceptable Quality Levels (tightened inspection)

Each cell shows "Ac Re" (Acceptance number, Rejection number). Each code letter has a First and Second (cumulative) sample row.

Sample size code letter	Sample	Sample size	Cumulative sample size	0.010	0.015	0.025	0.040	0.065	0.10	0.15	0.25	0.40	0.65	1.0	1.5	2.5	4.0	6.5	10	15	25	40	65	100	150	250	400	650	1000
A				↓	↓	↓	↓	↓	↓	↓	↓	↓	↓	↓	↓	↓	↓	↓	↓	↓	↓	•	↓	↓	↓	↓	↓	↓	↓
B	First	2	2	↓	↓	↓	↓	↓	↓	↓	↓	↓	↓	↓	↓	↓	↓	↓	↓	•	0 2	0 3	1 4	2 5	3 7	6 10	9 14	15 20	23 29
	Second	2	4																		1 2	3 4	4 5	6 7	11 12	15 16	23 24	31 32	52 53
C	First	3	3	↓	↓	↓	↓	↓	↓	↓	↓	↓	↓	↓	↓	↓	↓	↓	•	0 2	0 3	1 4	2 5	3 7	6 10	9 14	15 20	23 29	↑
	Second	3	6																	1 2	3 4	4 5	6 7	11 12	15 16	23 24	31 32	52 53	
D	First	5	5	↓	↓	↓	↓	↓	↓	↓	↓	↓	↓	↓	↓	↓	↓	•	0 2	0 3	1 4	2 5	3 7	6 10	9 14	15 20	23 29	↑	↑
	Second	5	10																1 2	3 4	4 5	6 7	11 12	15 16	23 24	31 32	52 53		
E	First	8	8	↓	↓	↓	↓	↓	↓	↓	↓	↓	↓	↓	↓	↓	•	0 2	0 3	1 4	2 5	3 7	6 10	9 14	15 20	23 29	↑	↑	↑
	Second	8	16															1 2	3 4	4 5	6 7	11 12	15 16	23 24	31 32	52 53			
F	First	13	13	↓	↓	↓	↓	↓	↓	↓	↓	↓	↓	↓	↓	•	0 2	0 3	1 4	2 5	3 7	6 10	9 14	15 20	23 29	↑	↑	↑	↑
	Second	13	26														1 2	3 4	4 5	6 7	11 12	15 16	23 24	31 32	52 53				
G	First	20	20	↓	↓	↓	↓	↓	↓	↓	↓	↓	↓	↓	•	0 2	0 3	1 4	2 5	3 7	6 10	9 14	15 20	23 29	↑	↑	↑	↑	↑
	Second	20	40													1 2	3 4	4 5	6 7	11 12	15 16	23 24	31 32	52 53					
H	First	32	32	↓	↓	↓	↓	↓	↓	↓	↓	↓	↓	•	0 2	0 3	1 4	2 5	3 7	6 10	9 14	15 20	23 29	↑	↑	↑	↑	↑	↑
	Second	32	64												1 2	3 4	4 5	6 7	11 12	15 16	23 24	31 32	52 53						
J	First	50	50	↓	↓	↓	↓	↓	↓	↓	↓	↓	•	0 2	0 3	1 4	2 5	3 7	6 10	9 14	15 20	23 29	↑	↑	↑	↑	↑	↑	↑
	Second	50	100											1 2	3 4	4 5	6 7	11 12	15 16	23 24	31 32	52 53							
K	First	80	80	↓	↓	↓	↓	↓	↓	↓	↓	•	0 2	0 3	1 4	2 5	3 7	6 10	9 14	15 20	23 29	↑	↑	↑	↑	↑	↑	↑	↑
	Second	80	160										1 2	3 4	4 5	6 7	11 12	15 16	23 24	31 32	52 53								
L	First	125	125	↓	↓	↓	↓	↓	↓	↓	•	0 2	0 3	1 4	2 5	3 7	6 10	9 14	15 20	23 29	↑	↑	↑	↑	↑	↑	↑	↑	↑
	Second	125	250									1 2	3 4	4 5	6 7	11 12	15 16	23 24	31 32	52 53									
M	First	200	200	↓	↓	↓	↓	↓	↓	•	0 2	0 3	1 4	2 5	3 7	6 10	9 14	15 20	23 29	↑	↑	↑	↑	↑	↑	↑	↑	↑	↑
	Second	200	400								1 2	3 4	4 5	6 7	11 12	15 16	23 24	31 32	52 53										
N	First	315	315	↓	↓	↓	↓	↓	•	0 2	0 3	1 4	2 5	3 7	6 10	9 14	15 20	23 29	↑	↑	↑	↑	↑	↑	↑	↑	↑	↑	↑
	Second	315	630							1 2	3 4	4 5	6 7	11 12	15 16	23 24	31 32	52 53											
P	First	500	500	↓	↓	↓	↓	•	0 2	0 3	1 4	2 5	3 7	6 10	9 14	15 20	23 29	↑	↑	↑	↑	↑	↑	↑	↑	↑	↑	↑	↑
	Second	500	1000						1 2	3 4	4 5	6 7	11 12	15 16	23 24	31 32	52 53												
Q	First	800	800	↓	↓	↓	•	0 2	0 3	1 4	2 5	3 7	6 10	9 14	15 20	23 29	↑	↑	↑	↑	↑	↑	↑	↑	↑	↑	↑	↑	↑
	Second	800	1600					1 2	3 4	4 5	6 7	11 12	15 16	23 24	31 32	52 53													
R	First	1250	1250	↓	↓	•	0 2	0 3	1 4	2 5	3 7	6 10	9 14	15 20	23 29	↑	↑	↑	↑	↑	↑	↑	↑	↑	↑	↑	↑	↑	↑
	Second	1250	2500				1 2	3 4	4 5	6 7	11 12	15 16	23 24	31 32	52 53														
S	First	2000	2000	↓	•	0 2	0 3	1 4	2 5	3 7	6 10	9 14	15 20	23 29	↑	↑	↑	↑	↑	↑	↑	↑	↑	↑	↑	↑	↑	↑	↑
	Second	2000	4000			1 2	3 4	4 5	6 7	11 12	15 16	23 24	31 32	52 53															

↓ = Use first sampling plan below arrow. If sample size equals or exceeds lot or batch size, do 100 percent inspection.

↑ = Use first sampling plan above arrow.

Ac = Acceptance number

Re = Rejection number

• = Use corresponding single sampling plan (or, alternatively, use double sampling plan below, where available).

157

3. Use Table IV-B for multiple sampling. *Example:* Code letter J, 2.5 percent AQL.

$n_1 = 20$; no acceptance (number), reject on 3 or more

$n_2 = 20$; accept on 0, reject on 3 or more

$n_3 = 20$; accept on 1 or less, reject on 3 or more

$n_4 = 20$; accept on 2 or less, reject on 5 or more

$n_5 = 20$; accept on 3 or less, reject on 6 or more

$n_6 = 20$; accept on 4 or less, reject on 6 or more

$n_7 = 20$; accept on 6 or less, reject on 7 or more

When its use is permitted, reduced inspection decreases sampling costs due to the smaller sample size specified. All of the following conditions have to be satisfied to switch from normal to reduced inspection:

- The preceding 10 lots have been on normal inspection, and none have been rejected on original inspection.
- The total number of defectives in the samples from the preceding 10 lots is equal to or less than the applicable number in Table VIII. If double or multiple sampling is in use, all samples inspected must be included—not "first" samples only.
- Production is at a steady rate.

Example: Code letter J, 2.5 percent AQL. Single sampling with $n = 80$ has been in effect. No lot in the last 10 has been rejected. Total sample units inspected would be $(80)(10) = 800$. From Table VIII, the limit number would be 14. If the total number of defectives in 800 units inspected were less than or equal to 14, reduced inspection could be instituted. (The indicated quality with 14 would be 14/800 equals 0.0175 or 1.75 percent.)

Specific plans for reduced inspection are

1. Use Table II-C for single sampling. *Example:* Code letter J, 2.5 percent AQL.

$n = 32$; accept on 2 or less, reject on 5 or more†

2. Use Table III-C for double sampling. *Example:* Code letter J, 2.5 percent AQL.

$n_1 = 20$; accept on 0, reject on 4 or more†

$n_2 = 20$; accept on 3 or less, reject on 6 or more

3. Use Table IV-C for multiple sampling. *Example:* Code letter J, 2.5 percent AQL.

$n_1 = 8$; no acceptance (number), reject on 3 or more†

$n_2 = 8$; accept on 0, reject on 4 or more

$n_3 = 8$; accept on 0, reject on 5 or more

$n_4 = 8$; accept on 1 or less, reject on 6 or more

$n_5 = 8$; accept on 2 or less, reject on 7 or more

$n_6 = 8$; accept on 3 or less, reject on 7 or more

$n_7 = 8$; accept on 4 or less, reject on 8 or more

†See note † under tables.

Table IV-B Multiple Sampling Plans for Tightened Inspection (Master Table)

Acceptable Quality Levels (tightened inspection)

The master table cross-references Sample size code letters (A, B, C, D, E, F, G, H, J) and their seven cumulative samples against Acceptable Quality Levels from 0.010 to 1000, giving Acceptance (Ac) and Rejection (Re) numbers.

Sample size code letter	Sample	Sample size	Cumulative sample size
C	First / Second / Third / Fourth / Fifth / Sixth / Seventh	2 / 2 / 2 / 2 / 2 / 2 / 2	2 / 4 / 6 / 8 / 10 / 12 / 14
D	First / Second / Third / Fourth / Fifth / Sixth / Seventh	3 / 3 / 3 / 3 / 3 / 3 / 3	3 / 6 / 9 / 12 / 15 / 18 / 21
E	First / Second / Third / Fourth / Fifth / Sixth / Seventh	5 / 5 / 5 / 5 / 5 / 5 / 5	5 / 10 / 15 / 20 / 25 / 30 / 35
F	First / Second / Third / Fourth / Fifth / Sixth / Seventh	8 / 8 / 8 / 8 / 8 / 8 / 8	8 / 16 / 24 / 32 / 40 / 48 / 56
G	First / Second / Third / Fourth / Fifth / Sixth / Seventh	13 / 13 / 13 / 13 / 13 / 13 / 13	13 / 26 / 39 / 52 / 65 / 78 / 91
H	First / Second / Third / Fourth / Fifth / Sixth / Seventh	20 / 20 / 20 / 20 / 20 / 20 / 20	20 / 40 / 60 / 80 / 100 / 120 / 140

↓ = Use first sampling plan below arrow (refer to continuation of table on following page, when necessary). If sample size equals or exceeds lot or batch size, do 100 percent inspection.

↑ = Use first sampling plan above arrow

Ac = Acceptance number

Re = Rejection number

■ = Use corresponding single sampling plan (or alternatively, use multiple sampling plan below, where available).

■ = Use corresponding double sampling plan (or alternatively, use multiple sampling plan below, where available).

⇩⇩ Ac Re • ‡

* = Acceptance not permitted at this sample size.

159

Table IV-B Multiple Sampling Plans for Tightened Inspection (Master Table) (Continued)

Acceptable Quality Levels (tightened inspection)

The table is organized with the following left‑hand reference columns and AQL data columns (each AQL has an **Ac** (Acceptance number) and **Re** (Rejection number) sub‑column): 0.010, 0.015, 0.025, 0.040, 0.065, 0.10, 0.15, 0.25, 0.40, 0.65, 1.0, 1.5, 2.5, 4.0, 6.5, 10, 15, 25, 40, 65, 100, 150, 250, 400, 650, 1000.

Sample size code letter	Sample	Sample size	Cumulative sample size
K	First	32	32
	Second	32	64
	Third	32	96
	Fourth	32	128
	Fifth	32	160
	Sixth	32	192
	Seventh	32	224
L	First	50	50
	Second	50	100
	Third	50	150
	Fourth	50	200
	Fifth	50	250
	Sixth	50	300
	Seventh	50	350
M	First	80	80
	Second	80	160
	Third	80	240
	Fourth	80	320
	Fifth	80	400
	Sixth	80	480
	Seventh	80	560
N	First	125	125
	Second	125	250
	Third	125	375
	Fourth	125	500
	Fifth	125	625
	Sixth	125	750
	Seventh	125	875
P	First	200	200
	Second	200	400
	Third	200	600
	Fourth	200	800
	Fifth	200	1000
	Sixth	200	1200
	Seventh	200	1400
Q	First	315	315
	Second	315	630
	Third	315	945
	Fourth	315	1260
	Fifth	315	1575
	Sixth	315	1890
	Seventh	315	2205
R	First	500	500
	Second	500	1000
	Third	500	1500
	Fourth	500	2000
	Fifth	500	2500
	Sixth	500	3000
	Seventh	500	3500
S	First	800	800
	Second	800	1600
	Third	800	2400
	Fourth	800	3200
	Fifth	800	4000
	Sixth	800	4800
	Seventh	800	5600

The central portion of the table consists of the Ac/Re data band running diagonally across the AQL columns, bounded by up‑arrows (↑) on the upper/right side and down‑arrows (↓) on the lower/left side, with "•" symbols marking where the corresponding single sampling plan is to be used.

Legend:

↓ = Use first sampling plan below arrow. If sample size equals or exceeds lot or batch size, do 100 percent inspection.

↑ = Use first sampling plan above arrow (refer to preceding page, when necessary).

Ac = Acceptance number

Re = Rejection number

• = Use corresponding single sampling plan (or alternatively, use multiple sampling plan below, where available).

▪ = Acceptance not permitted at this sample size.

160

Table VIII Limit Numbers for Reduced Inspection

Acceptable Quality Level

Number of sample units from last 10 lots or batches	0.010	0.015	0.025	0.040	0.065	0.10	0.15	0.25	0.40	0.65	1.0	1.5	2.5	4.0	6.5	10	15	25	40	65	100	150	250	400	650	1000
20 - 29	•	•	•	•	•	•	•	•	•	•	•	•	•	•	•	0	0	2	4	8	14	22	40	68	115	181
30 - 49	•	•	•	•	•	•	•	•	•	•	•	•	•	•	0	0	1	3	7	13	22	36	63	105	178	277
50 - 79	•	•	•	•	•	•	•	•	•	•	•	•	•	0	0	2	3	7	14	25	40	63	110	181	301	
80 - 129	•	•	•	•	•	•	•	•	•	•	•	•	0	0	2	4	7	14	24	42	68	105	181	297		
130 - 199	•	•	•	•	•	•	•	•	•	•	•	0	0	2	4	7	13	25	42	72	115	177	301	490		
200 - 319	•	•	•	•	•	•	•	•	•	•	0	0	2	4	8	14	22	40	68	115	181	277	471			
320 - 499	•	•	•	•	•	•	•	•	•	0	0	1	4	8	14	24	39	68	113	169						
500 - 799	•	•	•	•	•	•	•	•	0	0	2	3	7	14	25	40	63	110	181							
800 - 1249	•	•	•	•	•	•	•	0	0	2	4	7	14	24	42	68	105	181								
1250 - 1999	•	•	•	•	•	•	0	0	2	4	7	13	24	40	69	110	169									
2000 - 3149	•	•	•	•	•	0	0	2	4	8	14	22	40	68	115	181										
3150 - 4999	•	•	•	•	0	0	1	4	8	14	24	38	67	111	186											
5000 - 7999	•	•	•	0	0	2	3	7	14	25	40	63	110	181												
8000 - 12499	•	•	0	0	2	4	7	14	24	42	68	105	181													
12500 - 19999	•	0	0	2	4	7	13	24	40	69	110	169														
20000 - 31499	0	0	2	4	8	14	22	40	68	115	181															
31500 - 49999	0	1	4	8	14	24	38	67	111	186																
50000 & Over	2	3	7	14	25	40	63	110	181	301																

*Denotes that the number of sample units from the last ten lots or batches is not sufficient for reduced inspection for this AQL. In this instance more than ten lots or batches may be used for the calculation, provided that the lots or batches used are the most recent ones in sequence, that they have all been on normal inspection, and that none has been rejected while on original inspection.

161

Table II-C Single Sampling Plans for Reduced Inspection (Master Table)

Ac = Acceptance number. Re = Rejection number. Values are given below as Ac/Re.
↓ = Use first sampling plan below arrow. ↑ = Use first sampling plan above arrow. ⇳ = Use first sampling plan above or below arrow.

Acceptable Quality Levels (reduced inspection)†

Sample size code letter	Sample size	0.010	0.015	0.025	0.040	0.065	0.10	0.15	0.25	0.40	0.65	1.0	1.5	2.5	4.0	6.5	10	15	25	40	65	100	150	250	400	650	1000
A	2	↓	↓	↓	↓	↓	↓	↓	↓	↓	↓	↓	↓	↓	↓	↓	0/1	⇳	1/2	2/3	3/4	5/6	7/8	10/11	14/15	21/22	30/31
B	2	↓	↓	↓	↓	↓	↓	↓	↓	↓	↓	↓	↓	↓	↓	0/1	⇳	0/2	1/3	2/4	3/5	5/6	7/8	10/11	14/15	21/22	30/31
C	2	↓	↓	↓	↓	↓	↓	↓	↓	↓	↓	↓	↓	↓	0/1	⇳	0/2	1/3	1/4	2/5	3/6	5/8	7/10	10/13	14/17	21/24	↑
D	3	↓	↓	↓	↓	↓	↓	↓	↓	↓	↓	↓	↓	0/1	⇳	0/2	1/3	1/4	2/5	3/6	5/8	7/10	10/13	14/17	21/24	↑	↑
E	5	↓	↓	↓	↓	↓	↓	↓	↓	↓	↓	↓	0/1	⇳	0/2	1/3	1/4	2/5	3/6	5/8	7/10	10/13	14/17	21/24	↑	↑	↑
F	8	↓	↓	↓	↓	↓	↓	↓	↓	↓	↓	0/1	⇳	0/2	1/3	1/4	2/5	3/6	5/8	7/10	10/13	↑	↑	↑	↑	↑	↑
G	13	↓	↓	↓	↓	↓	↓	↓	↓	↓	0/1	⇳	0/2	1/3	1/4	2/5	3/6	5/8	7/10	10/13	↑	↑	↑	↑	↑	↑	↑
H	20	↓	↓	↓	↓	↓	↓	↓	↓	0/1	⇳	0/2	1/3	1/4	2/5	3/6	5/8	7/10	10/13	↑	↑	↑	↑	↑	↑	↑	↑
J	32	↓	↓	↓	↓	↓	↓	↓	0/1	⇳	0/2	1/3	1/4	2/5	3/6	5/8	7/10	10/13	↑	↑	↑	↑	↑	↑	↑	↑	↑
K	50	↓	↓	↓	↓	↓	↓	0/1	⇳	0/2	1/3	1/4	2/5	3/6	5/8	7/10	10/13	↑	↑	↑	↑	↑	↑	↑	↑	↑	↑
L	80	↓	↓	↓	↓	↓	0/1	⇳	0/2	1/3	1/4	2/5	3/6	5/8	7/10	10/13	↑	↑	↑	↑	↑	↑	↑	↑	↑	↑	↑
M	125	↓	↓	↓	↓	0/1	⇳	0/2	1/3	1/4	2/5	3/6	5/8	7/10	10/13	↑	↑	↑	↑	↑	↑	↑	↑	↑	↑	↑	↑
N	200	↓	↓	↓	0/1	⇳	0/2	1/3	1/4	2/5	3/6	5/8	7/10	10/13	↑	↑	↑	↑	↑	↑	↑	↑	↑	↑	↑	↑	↑
P	315	↓	↓	0/1	⇳	0/2	1/3	1/4	2/5	3/6	5/8	7/10	10/13	↑	↑	↑	↑	↑	↑	↑	↑	↑	↑	↑	↑	↑	↑
Q	500	↓	0/1	⇳	0/2	1/3	1/4	2/5	3/6	5/8	7/10	10/13	↑	↑	↑	↑	↑	↑	↑	↑	↑	↑	↑	↑	↑	↑	↑
R	800	0/1	⇳	0/2	1/3	1/4	2/5	3/6	5/8	7/10	10/13	↑	↑	↑	↑	↑	↑	↑	↑	↑	↑	↑	↑	↑	↑	↑	↑

↓ = Use first sampling plan below arrow. If sample size equals or exceeds lot or batch size, do 100 percent inspection.
↑ = Use first sampling plan above arrow.
Ac = Acceptance number.
Re = Rejection number.
⇳ = If the acceptance number has been exceeded, but the rejection number has not been reached, accept the lot, but reinstate normal inspection (see 10.1.4).
† = (see 10.1.4).

162

Table III-C Double Sampling Plans for Reduced Inspection (Master Table)

Acceptable Quality Levels (reduced inspection)†

Legend: each AQL column is divided into Ac (acceptance number) and Re (rejection number); in the cells below, values are shown as the pair "Ac Re". ↓ = use first sampling plan below arrow (if sample size equals or exceeds lot or batch size, do 100 percent inspection); ↑ = use first sampling plan above arrow; • = use corresponding single sampling plan (or alternatively, use double sampling plan below, when available).

Code	Sample	Sample size	Cum. sample size	0.010	0.015	0.025	0.040	0.065	0.10	0.15	0.25	0.40	0.65	1.0	1.5	2.5	4.0	6.5	10	15	25	40	65	100	150	250	400	650	1000
A				↓	↓	↓	↓	↓	↓	↓	↓	↓	↓	↓	↓	↓	↓	↓	↓	↓	↓	↓	↓	↓	↓	↓	↓	↓	↓
B				↓	↓	↓	↓	↓	↓	↓	↓	↓	↓	↓	↓	↓	↓	↓	↓	↓	↓	↓	↓	↓	↓	↓	↓	↓	↓
C				↓	↓	↓	↓	↓	↓	↓	↓	↓	↓	↓	↓	↓	↓	↓	↓	↓	↓	↓	↓	↓	↓	↓	↓	↓	↓
D	First	2	2	↓	↓	↓	↓	↓	↓	↓	↓	↓	↓	↓	↓	↓	•	0 2	0 3	0 4	0 4	1 5	2 7	3 8	5 10	7 12	11 17	↑	↑
	Second	2	4	↓	↓	↓	↓	↓	↓	↓	↓	↓	↓	↓	↓	↓	•	0 2	0 4	1 5	3 6	4 7	6 9	8 12	12 16	18 22	26 30	↑	↑
E	First	3	3	↓	↓	↓	↓	↓	↓	↓	↓	↓	↓	↓	↓	•	0 2	0 3	0 4	0 4	1 5	2 7	3 8	5 10	7 12	11 17	↑	↑	↑
	Second	3	6	↓	↓	↓	↓	↓	↓	↓	↓	↓	↓	↓	↓	•	0 2	0 4	1 5	3 6	4 7	6 9	8 12	12 16	18 22	26 30	↑	↑	↑
F	First	5	5	↓	↓	↓	↓	↓	↓	↓	↓	↓	↓	↓	•	0 2	0 3	0 4	0 4	1 5	2 7	3 8	5 10	7 12	11 17	↑	↑	↑	↑
	Second	5	10	↓	↓	↓	↓	↓	↓	↓	↓	↓	↓	↓	•	0 2	0 4	1 5	3 6	4 7	6 9	8 12	12 16	18 22	26 30	↑	↑	↑	↑
G	First	8	8	↓	↓	↓	↓	↓	↓	↓	↓	↓	↓	•	0 2	0 3	0 4	0 4	1 5	2 7	3 8	5 10	7 12	11 17	↑	↑	↑	↑	↑
	Second	8	16	↓	↓	↓	↓	↓	↓	↓	↓	↓	↓	•	0 2	0 4	1 5	3 6	4 7	6 9	8 12	12 16	18 22	26 30	↑	↑	↑	↑	↑
H	First	13	13	↓	↓	↓	↓	↓	↓	↓	↓	↓	•	0 2	0 3	0 4	0 4	1 5	2 7	3 8	5 10	7 12	11 17	↑	↑	↑	↑	↑	↑
	Second	13	26	↓	↓	↓	↓	↓	↓	↓	↓	↓	•	0 2	0 4	1 5	3 6	4 7	6 9	8 12	12 16	18 22	26 30	↑	↑	↑	↑	↑	↑
J	First	20	20	↓	↓	↓	↓	↓	↓	↓	↓	•	0 2	0 3	0 4	0 4	1 5	2 7	3 8	5 10	7 12	11 17	↑	↑	↑	↑	↑	↑	↑
	Second	20	40	↓	↓	↓	↓	↓	↓	↓	↓	•	0 2	0 4	1 5	3 6	4 7	6 9	8 12	12 16	18 22	26 30	↑	↑	↑	↑	↑	↑	↑
K	First	32	32	↓	↓	↓	↓	↓	↓	↓	•	0 2	0 3	0 4	0 4	1 5	2 7	3 8	5 10	7 12	11 17	↑	↑	↑	↑	↑	↑	↑	↑
	Second	32	64	↓	↓	↓	↓	↓	↓	↓	•	0 2	0 4	1 5	3 6	4 7	6 9	8 12	12 16	18 22	26 30	↑	↑	↑	↑	↑	↑	↑	↑
L	First	50	50	↓	↓	↓	↓	↓	↓	•	0 2	0 3	0 4	0 4	1 5	2 7	3 8	5 10	7 12	11 17	↑	↑	↑	↑	↑	↑	↑	↑	↑
	Second	50	100	↓	↓	↓	↓	↓	↓	•	0 2	0 4	1 5	3 6	4 7	6 9	8 12	12 16	18 22	26 30	↑	↑	↑	↑	↑	↑	↑	↑	↑
M	First	80	80	↓	↓	↓	↓	↓	•	0 2	0 3	0 4	0 4	1 5	2 7	3 8	5 10	7 12	11 17	↑	↑	↑	↑	↑	↑	↑	↑	↑	↑
	Second	80	160	↓	↓	↓	↓	↓	•	0 2	0 4	1 5	3 6	4 7	6 9	8 12	12 16	18 22	26 30	↑	↑	↑	↑	↑	↑	↑	↑	↑	↑
N	First	125	125	↓	↓	↓	↓	•	0 2	0 3	0 4	0 4	1 5	2 7	3 8	5 10	7 12	11 17	↑	↑	↑	↑	↑	↑	↑	↑	↑	↑	↑
	Second	125	250	↓	↓	↓	↓	•	0 2	0 4	1 5	3 6	4 7	6 9	8 12	12 16	18 22	26 30	↑	↑	↑	↑	↑	↑	↑	↑	↑	↑	↑
P	First	200	200	↓	↓	↓	•	0 2	0 3	0 4	0 4	1 5	2 7	3 8	5 10	7 12	11 17	↑	↑	↑	↑	↑	↑	↑	↑	↑	↑	↑	↑
	Second	200	400	↓	↓	↓	•	0 2	0 4	1 5	3 6	4 7	6 9	8 12	12 16	18 22	26 30	↑	↑	↑	↑	↑	↑	↑	↑	↑	↑	↑	↑
Q	First	315	315	↓	↓	•	0 2	0 3	0 4	0 4	1 5	2 7	3 8	5 10	7 12	11 17	↑	↑	↑	↑	↑	↑	↑	↑	↑	↑	↑	↑	↑
	Second	315	630	↓	↓	•	0 2	0 4	1 5	3 6	4 7	6 9	8 12	12 16	18 22	26 30	↑	↑	↑	↑	↑	↑	↑	↑	↑	↑	↑	↑	↑
R	First	500	500	↓	•	0 2	0 3	0 4	0 4	1 5	2 7	3 8	5 10	7 12	11 17	↑	↑	↑	↑	↑	↑	↑	↑	↑	↑	↑	↑	↑	↑
	Second	500	1000	↓	•	0 2	0 4	1 5	3 6	4 7	6 9	8 12	12 16	18 22	26 30	↑	↑	↑	↑	↑	↑	↑	↑	↑	↑	↑	↑	↑	↑

↓ = Use first sampling plan below arrow. If sample size equals or exceeds lot or batch size, do 100 percent inspection.

↑ = Use first sampling plan above arrow.

Ac = Acceptance number.

Re = Rejection number.

• = Use corresponding single sampling plan (or alternatively, use double sampling plan below, when available.)

† = If, after the second sample, the acceptance number has been exceeded, but the rejection number has not been reached, accept the lot, but reinstate normal inspection (see 10.14).

163

Table IV-C Multiple Sampling Plans for Reduced Inspection (Master Table)

Acceptable Quality Levels (reduced inspection) †

Sample size code letter	Sample	Sample size	Cumulative sample size
A			
B			
C, D			
E			
F	First	2	2
	Second	2	4
	Third	2	6
	Fourth	2	8
	Fifth	2	10
	Sixth	2	12
	Seventh	2	14
G	First	3	3
	Second	3	6
	Third	3	9
	Fourth	3	12
	Fifth	3	15
	Sixth	3	18
	Seventh	3	21
H	First	5	5
	Second	5	10
	Third	5	15
	Fourth	5	20
	Fifth	5	25
	Sixth	5	30
	Seventh	5	35
J	First	8	8
	Second	8	16
	Third	8	24
	Fourth	8	32
	Fifth	8	40
	Sixth	8	48
	Seventh	8	56
K	First	13	13
	Second	13	26
	Third	13	39
	Fourth	13	52
	Fifth	13	65
	Sixth	13	78
	Seventh	13	91

AQL column headers (each with Ac and Re): 0.010, 0.015, 0.025, 0.040, 0.065, 0.10, 0.15, 0.25, 0.40, 0.65, 1.0, 1.5, 2.5, 4.0, 6.5, 10, 15, 25, 40, 65, 100, 150, 250, 400, 650, 1000.

Legend:

⇩ = Use first sampling plan below arrow (refer to continuation of table on following page, when necessary). If sample size equals, or exceeds lot or batch size, do 100 percent inspection.

⇧ = Use first sampling plan above arrow.

Ac = Acceptance number

Re = Rejection number

• = Use corresponding single sampling plan (or alternatively, use multiple sampling plan below, where available).

‡ = Use corresponding double sampling plan (or alternatively, use multiple sampling plan below, where available).

■ = Acceptance not permitted at this sample size.

† = If, after the final sample, the acceptance number has been exceeded, but the rejection number has not been reached, accept the lot but reinstate normal inspection (see 10 1.4).

164

Table IV-C Multiple Sampling Plans for Reduced Inspection (Master Table) (Continued)

Acceptable Quality Levels (reduced inspection) †

Legend (Ac = Acceptance number, Re = Rejection number):

↓ = Use first sampling plan below arrow. If sample size equals, or exceeds, lot or batch size, do 100 percent inspection.
↑ = Use first sampling plan above arrow (refer to preceding page when necessary).
Ac = Acceptance number
Re = Rejection number
* = Acceptance not permitted at this sample size.
† = If, after the final sample, the acceptance number has been exceeded, but the rejection number has not been reached, accept the lot, but reinstate normal inspection (see 10.1.4).

The left structural columns read: Sample size code letter | Sample | Sample size | Cumulative sample size.

Code letter L — Sample size 20

Sample	Cum. size	AQL 0.25 (Ac/Re)	0.40	0.65	1.0	1.5	2.5	4.0	6.5
First	20	*/2	*/2	*/3	*/3	*/4	*/4	*/5	0/6
Second	40	*/2	*/3	*/3	0/4	0/5	*/6	1/7	3/9
Third	60	0/3	0/3	0/4	0/5	1/6	0/8	3/9	6/12
Fourth	80	0/3	0/4	0/5	1/6	2/7	1/10	5/12	8/15
Fifth	100	0/3	1/5	1/6	2/7	3/8	3/11	7/13	11/17
Sixth	120	1/5	1/6	1/7	3/7	4/9	5/12	10/15	14/20
Seventh	140	1/5	2/7	2/7	4/8	6/10	7/14	13/17	18/22

(AQL ≤ 0.15: ↓ ; AQL ≥ 10: ↑)

Code letter M — Sample size 32

Sample	Cum. size	AQL 0.15	0.25	0.40	0.65	1.0	1.5	2.5	4.0
First	32	*/2	*/2	*/3	*/3	*/4	*/4	*/5	0/6
Second	64	*/2	*/3	*/3	0/4	0/5	*/6	1/7	3/9
Third	96	0/3	0/3	0/4	0/5	1/6	0/8	3/9	6/12
Fourth	128	0/3	0/4	0/5	1/6	2/7	1/10	5/12	8/15
Fifth	160	0/3	1/5	1/6	2/7	3/8	3/11	7/13	11/17
Sixth	192	1/5	1/6	1/7	3/7	4/9	5/12	10/15	14/20
Seventh	224	1/5	2/7	2/7	4/8	6/10	7/14	13/17	18/22

(AQL ≤ 0.10: ↓ ; AQL ≥ 6.5: ↑)

Code letter N — Sample size 50

Sample	Cum. size	AQL 0.10	0.15	0.25	0.40	0.65	1.0	1.5	2.5
First	50	*/2	*/2	*/3	*/3	*/4	*/4	*/5	0/6
Second	100	*/2	*/3	*/3	0/4	0/5	*/6	1/7	3/9
Third	150	0/3	0/3	0/4	0/5	1/6	0/8	3/9	6/12
Fourth	200	0/3	0/4	0/5	1/6	2/7	1/10	5/12	8/15
Fifth	250	0/3	1/5	1/6	2/7	3/8	3/11	7/13	11/17
Sixth	300	1/5	1/6	1/7	3/7	4/9	5/12	10/15	14/20
Seventh	350	1/5	2/7	2/7	4/8	6/10	7/14	13/17	18/22

(AQL ≤ 0.065: ↓ ; AQL ≥ 4.0: ↑)

Code letter P — Sample size 80

Sample	Cum. size	AQL 0.065	0.10	0.15	0.25	0.40	0.65	1.0	1.5
First	80	*/2	*/2	*/3	*/3	*/4	*/4	*/5	0/6
Second	160	*/2	*/3	*/3	0/4	0/5	*/6	1/7	3/9
Third	240	0/3	0/3	0/4	0/5	1/6	0/8	3/9	6/12
Fourth	320	0/3	0/4	0/5	1/6	2/7	1/10	5/12	8/15
Fifth	400	0/3	1/5	1/6	2/7	3/8	3/11	7/13	11/17
Sixth	480	1/5	1/6	1/7	3/7	4/9	5/12	10/15	14/20
Seventh	560	1/5	2/7	2/7	4/8	6/10	7/14	13/17	18/22

(AQL ≤ 0.040: ↓ ; AQL ≥ 2.5: ↑)

Code letter Q — Sample size 125

Sample	Cum. size	AQL 0.040	0.065	0.10	0.15	0.25	0.40	0.65	1.0
First	125	*/2	*/2	*/3	*/3	*/4	*/4	*/5	0/6
Second	250	*/2	*/3	*/3	0/4	0/5	*/6	1/7	3/9
Third	375	0/3	0/3	0/4	0/5	1/6	0/8	3/9	6/12
Fourth	500	0/3	0/4	0/5	1/6	2/7	1/10	5/12	8/15
Fifth	625	0/3	1/5	1/6	2/7	3/8	3/11	7/13	11/17
Sixth	750	1/5	1/6	1/7	3/7	4/9	5/12	10/15	14/20
Seventh	875	1/5	2/7	2/7	4/8	6/10	7/14	13/17	18/22

(AQL ≤ 0.025: ↓ ; AQL ≥ 1.5: ↑)

Code letter R — Sample size 200

Sample	Cum. size	AQL 0.025	0.040	0.065	0.10	0.15	0.25	0.40	0.65
First	200	*/2	*/2	*/3	*/3	*/4	*/4	*/5	0/6
Second	400	*/2	*/3	*/3	0/4	0/5	*/6	1/7	3/9
Third	600	0/3	0/3	0/4	0/5	1/6	0/8	3/9	6/12
Fourth	800	0/3	0/4	0/5	1/6	2/7	1/10	5/12	8/15
Fifth	1000	0/3	1/5	1/6	2/7	3/8	3/11	7/13	11/17
Sixth	1200	1/5	1/6	1/7	3/7	4/9	5/12	10/15	14/20
Seventh	1400	1/5	2/7	2/7	4/8	6/10	7/14	13/17	18/22

(AQL ≤ 0.015: ↓ ; AQL ≥ 1.0: ↑)

In the event that the user would like to employ MIL-STD-105D sampling plans using the average outgoing quality concept, the AOQL values for single sampling, both normal and tightened inspection, are shown in Table V-A and Table V-B.

Example: Code letter J, 2.5 percent AQL. Normal inspection, $n = 80$, AOQL $= 4.0$ percent (Table V-A). Tightened inspection, $n = 80$, AOQL $= 2.4$ percent (Table V-B).

The preceding sampling plans and procedures were designed to be used where the production units are produced in a continuing series of lots over a given time period. However, if the lot is an isolated one, it is desirable to limit the sampling plan selection to those plans associated with a designated AQL value that provide not less than a specified limiting quality protection. These plans are comparable to the LTPD concept discussed previously.

Limiting quality values are shown in Table VI-A, Table VI-B, Table VII-A, and Table VII-B.

A feature which did not appear in any MIL-STD sampling plan table until MIL-STD-105D is shown in Table IX. This gives the average sample size curves for double and multiple sampling plans and permits comparing them to the single sampling plans. The n on the vertical axis is the size of the single sampling plan, with fractional n values down to zero. The horizontal axis is n times the proportion defective. Individual boxes are identified by the acceptance number for the particular sampling plan. The arrow shown indicates the AQL value as a number defective, not percent.

Example: Code letter J, 2.5 percent AQL, $n = 80$, accept on 5. $c = 5$ is the fourth box from the left on the top row. $(0.0025)(80) = 2.0$. (The arrow is located at this value.) The top line represents $n = 80$. If lots were to come in at the AQL, the average sample size would be determined by projecting a line from the AQL up to the double and multiple curves and then projecting to the vertical axis. For double sampling this is approximately $(\frac{11}{16})(n)$ or $(\frac{11}{16})(80) = 55$. For multiple sampling this is approximately $(\frac{5}{8})(n)$ or $(\frac{5}{8})(80) = 50$.

It should be noticed that the average sample size required to reach a decision using double or multiple sampling will never exceed the single sample size. In most cases it will be substantially less, regardless of what the incoming quality level is.

Table X-J, Table X-J-1, and Table X-J-2 are for code letter J. Each code letter has similar tables which show the operating characteristic curves for the single sampling plan (double and multiple curves are essentially the same), tabulated values for the OC curves, and single, double, and multiple plans for both normal and tightened inspection.

Table V-A Average Outgoing Quality Limit Factors for Normal Inspection (Single Sampling)

Code Letter	Sample Size	0.010	0.015	0.025	0.040	0.065	0.10	0.15	0.25	0.40	0.65	1.0	1.5	2.5	4.0	6.5	10	15	25	40	65	100	150	250	400	650	1000
A	2															18			42	69	97	160	220	330	470	730	1100
B	3														12			28	46	65	110	150	220	310	490	720	1100
C	5													7.4			17	27	39	63	90	130	190	290	430	660	
D	8												4.6			11	17	24	40	56	82	120	180	270	410		
E	13											2.8			6.5	11	15	24	34	50	72	110	170	250			
F	20										1.8			4.2	6.9	9.7	16	22	33	47	73						
G	32									1.2			2.6	4.3	6.1	9.9	14	21	29	46							
H	50								0.74			1.7	2.7	3.9	6.3	9.0	13	19	29								
J	80							0.46			1.1	1.7	2.4	4.0	5.6	8.2	12	18									
K	125						0.29			0.67	1.1	1.6	2.5	3.6	5.2	7.5	12										
L	200					0.18			0.42	0.69	0.97	1.6	2.2	3.3	4.7	7.3											
M	315				0.12			0.27	0.44	0.62	1.00	1.4	2.1	3.0	4.7												
N	500			0.074			0.17	0.27	0.39	0.63	0.90	1.3	1.9	2.9													
P	800		0.046			0.11	0.17	0.24	0.40	0.56	0.82	1.2	1.8														
Q	1250	0.029			0.067	0.11	0.16	0.25	0.36	0.52	0.75	1.2															
R	2000			0.042	0.069	0.097	0.16	0.22	0.33	0.47	0.73																

Acceptable Quality Level

Note: For the exact AOQL, the above values must be multiplied by (1 − Sample size / Lot or Batch size)   (see 11.4)

167

Table V-B Average Outgoing Quality Limit Factors for Tightened Inspection (Single Sampling)

Code letter	Sample size	— Acceptable Quality Level																									
		0.010	0.015	0.025	0.040	0.065	0.10	0.15	0.25	0.40	0.65	1.0	1.5	2.5	4.0	6.5	10	15	25	40	65	100	150	250	400	650	1000
A	2																			42	69	97	160	260	400	620	970
B	3																		28	46	55	110	170	270	410	650	1100
C	5																	17	27	39	63	100	160	250	390	610	
D	8																11	17	24	40	64	99	160	240	380		
E	13															12	11	15	24	40	61	95	150	240			
F	20														7.4	6.5	9.7	16	26	40	62						
G	32													4.6	4.2	6.9	9.9	16	25	39							
H	50												2.8	2.6	4.3	6.1	10	16	25								
J	80											1.8	1.7	2.7	3.9	6.3	9.9	16									
K	125										1.2	1.1	1.7	2.4	4.0	6.4	9.9										
L	200									0.74	0.67	1.1	1.6	2.5	4.1	6.4											
M	315								0.46	0.42	0.69	0.97	1.6	2.6	4.0	6.2											
N	500							0.29	0.27	0.44	0.62	1.0	1.6	2.5	3.9												
P	800						0.18	0.17	0.27	0.39	0.63	1.0	1.6	2.5													
Q	1250					0.12	0.11	0.17	0.24	0.40	0.64	0.99	1.6														
R	2000			0.046	0.074	0.067	0.11	0.16	0.25	0.41	0.64	0.99															
S	3150	0.018	0.029	0.027	0.042	0.069	0.097	0.16	0.26	0.40	0.62																

Notes: For the exact AOQL, the above values must be multiplied by $\left(1 - \dfrac{\text{Sample size}}{\text{Lot or Batch size}}\right)$ (see 11.4)

Table VI-A Limiting Quality (in Percent Defective) for Which $P_a = 10\%$
(for Normal Inspection, Single Sampling)

Code letter	Sample size	*Acceptable Quality Level — 0.010	0.015	0.025	0.040	0.065	0.10	0.15	0.25	0.40	0.65	1.0	1.5	2.5	4.0	6.5	10
A	2															68	
B	3														54		
C	5													37		41	58
D	8												25		27	36	54
E	13											16		18	25	30	44
F	20										11		12	16	20	27	42
G	32									6.9		7.6	10	13	18	22	34
H	50								4.5			6.5	8.2	11	14	19	29
J	80							2.8			4.8	5.4	7.4	9.4	12	16	24
K	125						1.8			3.1	4.3	4.6	5.9	7.7	10	14	23
L	200					1.2			2.0	2.7	3.3	3.7	4.9	6.4	9.0		
M	315				0.73			1.2	1.7	2.1	2.9	3.1	4.0	5.6			
N	500			0.46			0.78	1.1	1.3	1.9	2.4	2.5	3.5				
P	800		0.29			0.49	0.67	0.84	1.2	1.5	1.9	2.3					
Q	1250	0.18			0.31	0.43	0.53	0.74	0.94	1.2	1.6						
R	2000			0.20	0.27	0.33	0.46	0.59	0.77	1.0	1.4						

169

Table VI-B Limiting Quality (in Defects Per 100 Units) for Which $P_a = 10\%$ (for Normal Inspection, Single Sampling)

Acceptable Quality Level

Code letter	Sample size	0.010	0.015	0.025	0.040	0.065	0.10	0.15	0.25	0.40	0.65	1.0	1.5	2.5	4.0	6.5	10	15	25	40	65	100	150	250	400	650	1000
A	2															120			200	270	330	460	590	770	1000	1400	1900
B	3														77			130	180	220	310	390	510	670	940	1300	1800
C	5													46			78	110	130	190	240	310	400	560	770	1100	
D	8												29			49	67	84	120	150	190	250	350	480	670		
E	13											18			30	41	51	71	91	120	160	220	300	410			
F	20										12			20	27	33	46	59	77	100	140						
G	32									7.2			12	17	21	29	37	48	63	88							
H	50								4.6			7.8	11	13	19	24	31	40	56								
J	80							2.9			4.9	6.7	8.4	12	15	19	25	35									
K	125						1.8			3.1	4.3	5.4	7.4	9.4	12	16	23										
L	200					1.2			2.0	2.7	3.3	4.6	5.9	7.7	10	14											
M	315				0.73			1.2	1.7	2.1	2.9	3.7	4.9	6.4	9.0												
N	500			0.46			0.78	1.1	1.3	1.9	2.4	3.1	4.0	5.6													
P	800		0.29			0.49	0.67	0.84	1.2	1.5	1.9	2.5	3.5														
Q	1250	0.18			0.31	0.43	0.53	0.74	0.94	1.2	1.6	2.3															
R	2000			0.20	0.27	0.33	0.46	0.59	0.77	1.0	1.4																

170

Table VII-A Limiting Quality (in Percent Defective) for Which P_a = 5% (for Normal Inspection, Single Sampling)

Code letter	Sample size	0.010	0.015	0.025	0.040	0.065	0.10	0.15	0.25	0.40	0.65	1.0	1.5	2.5	4.0	6.5	10
																Acceptable Quality Level	
A	2															78	
B	3														63		
C	5													45			66
D	8												31			47	60
E	13											21			32	41	50
F	20										14			22	28	34	46
G	32									8.9			14	18	23	30	37
H	50								5.8			9.1	12	15	20	25	32
J	80							3.7			5.8	7.7	9.4	13	16	20	26
K	125						2.4			3.8	5.0	6.2	8.4	11	14	18	24
L	200					1.5			2.4	3.2	3.9	5.3	6.6	8.5	11	15	
M	315				0.95			1.5	2.0	2.5	3.3	4.2	5.4	7.0	9.6		
N	500			0.60			0.95	1.3	1.6	2.1	2.6	3.4	4.4	6.1			
P	800		0.38			0.59	0.79	0.97	1.3	1.6	2.1	2.7	3.8				
Q	1250	0.24			0.38	0.50	0.62	0.84	1.1	1.4	1.8	2.4					
R	2000			0.24	0.32	0.39	0.53	0.66	0.85	1.1	1.5						

Table VII-B Limiting Quality (in Defects Per 100 Units) for Which $P_a = 5\%$ (for Normal Inspection, Single Sampling)

Acceptable Quality Level

Code letter	Sample size	0.010	0.015	0.025	0.040	0.065	0.10	0.15	0.25	0.40	0.65	1.0	1.5	2.5	4.0	6.5	10	15	25	40	65	100	150	250	400	650	1000
A	2															150			240	320	390	530	660	850	1100	1500	2000
B	3														100			160	210	260	350	440	570	730	1000	1400	1900
C	5													60			95	130	160	210	260	340	440	610	810	1100	
D	8												38			59	79	97	130	160	210	270	380	510	710		
E	13											23			37	48	60	81	100	130	170	230	310	440			
F	20										15			24	32	39	53	66	85	110	150						
G	32									9.4			15	20	24	33	41	53	68	95							
H	50								6.0			9.5	13	16	21	26	34	44	61								
J	80							3.8			5.9	7.9	9.7	13	16	21	27	38									
K	125						2.4			3.8	5.0	6.2	8.4	11	14	18	24										
L	200					1.5			2.4	3.2	3.9	5.3	6.6	8.5	11	15											
M	315				0.95			1.5	2.0	2.5	3.3	4.2	5.4	7.0	9.6												
N	500			0.60			0.95	1.3	1.6	2.1	2.6	3.4	4.4	6.1													
P	800		0.38			0.59	0.79	0.97	1.1	1.6	2.1	2.7	3.8														
Q	1250	0.24			0.38	0.50	0.62	0.84	1.1	1.4	1.8	2.4															
R	2000			0.24	0.32	0.39	0.53	0.66	0.85	1.1	1.5																

172

Table IX Average Sample Size Curves for Double and Multiple Sampling
(Normal and Tightened Inspection)

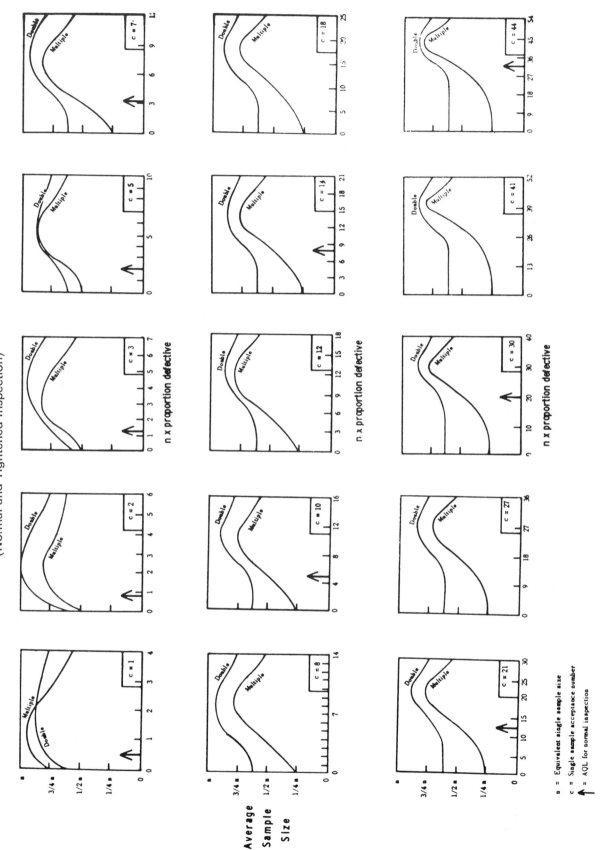

a = Equivalent single sample size

c = Single sample acceptance number

↑ = AQL for normal inspection

Table X-J   Tables for Sample Size Code Letter: J

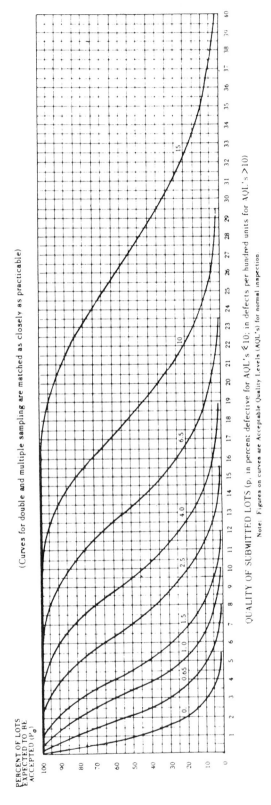

(Curves for double and multiple sampling are matched as closely as practicable)

PERCENT OF LOTS EXPECTED TO BE ACCEPTED (P_a)

QUALITY OF SUBMITTED LOTS (p, in percent defective for AQL's ≤ 10; in defects per hundred units for AQL's > 10)

Note: Figures on curves are Acceptable Quality Levels (AQL's) for normal inspection

Table X-J-1   Tabulated Values for Operating Characteristic Curves for Single Sampling Plans

Acceptable Quality Levels (normal inspection)

P_a	0.15	0.65	1.0	1.5	2.5	4.0	X	6.5	X	10	X	15
	_	_	_	_	_	p (in defects per hundred units)						
99.0	0.013	0.186	0.545	1.03	2.23	3.63	4.38	5.96	7.62	9.35	12.9	15.7
95.0	0.064	0.444	1.02	1.71	3.27	4.98	5.87	7.71	9.61	11.6	15.6	18.6
90.0	0.131	0.665	1.38	2.18	3.94	5.82	6.79	8.78	10.8	12.9	17.1	20.3
75.0	0.360	1.20	2.16	3.17	5.27	7.45	8.55	10.8	13.0	15.3	19.9	23.4
50.0	0.866	2.10	3.34	4.59	7.09	9.59	10.8	13.3	15.8	18.3	23.3	27.1
25.0	1.73	3.37	4.90	6.39	9.28	12.1	13.5	16.3	19.0	21.8	27.2	31.2
10.0	2.88	4.86	6.65	8.35	11.6	14.7	16.2	19.3	22.2	25.2	30.9	35.2
5.0	3.75	5.93	7.87	9.69	13.1	16.4	18.0	21.2	24.3	27.4	33.4	37.8
1.0	5.76	8.30	10.5	12.6	16.4	20.0	21.8	25.2	28.5	31.8	38.2	42.9
	0.25	1.0	1.5	2.5	4.0	6.5	X	10	X	15		

Acceptable Quality Levels (tightened inspection)

P_a	0.15	0.65	1.0	1.5	2.5	4.0	X	6.5	10	X
						p (in percent defective)				
99.0	0.013	0.188	0.550	1.05	2.30	3.72	4.50	6.13	7.88	9.75
95.0	0.064	0.444	1.03	1.73	3.32	5.06	5.98	7.91	9.89	11.9
90.0	0.132	0.666	1.38	2.20	3.98	5.91	6.91	8.95	11.0	13.2
75.0	0.359	1.202	2.16	3.18	5.30	7.50	8.62	10.9	13.2	15.5
50.0	0.863	2.09	3.33	4.57	7.06	9.55	10.8	13.3	15.8	18.3
25.0	1.72	3.33	4.84	6.31	9.14	11.9	13.3	16.0	18.6	21.3
10.0	2.84	4.78	6.52	8.16	11.3	14.2	15.7	18.6	21.4	24.2
5.0	3.68	5.80	7.66	9.39	12.7	15.8	17.3	20.3	23.2	26.0
1.0	5.59	8.00	10.1	12.0	15.6	18.9	20.5	23.6	26.5	29.5
	0.25	1.0	1.5	2.5	4.0	6.5	X	10	X	

Note: All values given in above table based on Poisson distribution as an approximation to the Binomial.

174

Table X-J-2 Sampling Plans for Sample Size Code Letter: J

Acceptable Quality Levels (normal inspection) — values given as "Ac Re"

Type of sampling plan	Cumulative sample size	<0.15	0.15	0.25	0.40	0.65	1.0	1.5	2.5	4.0	6.5	10	15	>15
Single	80	▽	0 1	Use Letter H		1 2	2 3	3 4	5 6	7 8	10 11	14 15	21 22	△
Double	50	▽	•	Use Letter L		0 2	0 3	1 4	2 5	3 7	5 9	7 11	11 16	△
Double	100					1 2	3 4	4 5	6 7	8 9	12 13	18 19	26 27	
Multiple	20	▽	•	Use Letter K		# 2	# 2	# 3	# 4	0 4	0 5	1 7	2 9	△
Multiple	40					# 2	0 3	0 3	1 5	1 6	3 8	4 10	7 14	
Multiple	60					0 2	0 3	1 4	2 6	3 8	6 10	8 13	13 19	
Multiple	80					0 3	1 4	2 5	3 7	5 10	8 13	12 17	19 25	
Multiple	100					1 3	2 4	3 6	5 8	7 11	11 15	17 20	25 29	
Multiple	120					1 3	3 5	4 6	7 9	10 12	14 17	21 23	31 33	
Multiple	140					2 3	4 5	6 7	9 10	13 14	18 19	25 26	37 38	

Acceptable Quality Levels (tightened inspection) — the columns above correspond, from left to right, to tightened AQLs:

	Less than 0.25	0.25	0.40	0.65	1.0	1.5	2.5	4.0	6.5	10	15	Higher than 15

Legend:

- △ = Use next preceding sample size code letter for which acceptance and rejection numbers are available.
- ▽ = Use next subsequent sample size code letter for which acceptance and rejection numbers are available.
- Ac = Acceptance number
- Re = Rejection number
- • = Use single sampling plan above (or alternatively use letter M)
- # = Acceptance not permitted at this sample size.

VARIABLES ACCEPTANCE SAMPLING

Sampling by variables is a technique wherein individual part characteristics are measured and recorded. From the data so obtained and after some mathematical calculations, decisions are made as to the lot disposition.

The choice between attribute and variables sampling plans is largely an economic one. Variables sampling requires smaller sample sizes, provides useful information, and presents no inspection problems as to accepting borderline pieces. At the same time it requires greater record keeping, demands more inspection skill and training, and necessitates stringent distributional assumptions of normality. When choosing between the two modes of inspection, the plan which results in the lowest total cost—inspection, clerical, and administrative—is the plan that should be selected. Variables plans can be designed to provide cost-risk functions comparable to attribute plans.

The following are variables sampling plan sources:

1. Simon's Grand Lot Scheme from *An Engineer's Manual of Statistical Methods*, L. E. Simon, published about 1941. These plans are particularly useful when a product is received in several boxes. The boxes are considered as sublots from a single grand lot, and statistical tests (usually $\bar{X}$ and R control charts) are applied to confirm or refute this assumption. If these charts show good control, it is evidence that the lots had the same origin, production time, or similar manufacturing conditions. Final acceptance depends on determining the percent beyond specifications and deciding whether this meets the individual requirements. Mathematical formulas for selecting sample sizes and control limits to use can be found in most statistical texts.

2. *Hamilton Standard Lot Plot Method of Acceptance Sampling by Variables*, Dorian Shainin, (Article, Oct. 12, 1950 issue The Iron Age). The lot plot plan considers each received lot separately and accepts or rejects the lot on its own merits. This plan requires one random sample from the whole lot, treating the lot as the universe from which to sample. A frequency tabulation of the measurements from the random sample is also required. If material is not produced under statistical control, when 100 percent sorting chops off the tails, or when physical limitations cause lack of symmetry (eccentricity measurements), a nonnormal distribution is created. Experience has shown that as shipments are analyzed and the plots submitted to the producers these distributions tend to become normal and stay within specifications. Lot plot should not be used for any in-process control procedures since the control chart is far superior for this analysis.

3. *Sampling Inspection by Variables*, Albert H. Bowker and Henry P. Goode, Mc-Graw-Hill Book Company, Inc., New York, 1952. Administering and installing these plans is more costly than the previous plans. These plans cover conditions where the standard deviation is known or unknown. Operating characteristic curves are included for all plans, both single and double. Selecting a sample size letter and an AQL class determines the degree of protection for a plan regardless of the type of plan selected or the number of pieces in the sample. The primary drawback of these plans is the calculations required.

4. *Military Standard Sampling Procedures and Tables for Inspection by Variables for Percent Defective, MIL-STD-414*. These plans are similar in many respects to the Bowker and Goode plans, although only single sampling plans are listed. The variables plans apply to a single quality characteristic which can be measured on a continuous

scale and for which quality is expressed in terms of percent defective. The standard is divided into four sections:

a. General description of sampling plans.

b. Specific procedures and applications of sampling plans when the variability is unknown using the standard deviation.

c. Specific procedures and applications (as above) using the range.

d. Specific procedures and sampling plans when the standard deviation is known.

The last three sections give plans for both single specification limits and for double specification limits. OC curves are shown for all sampling plans, showing the relationship between quality and the percent of lots expected to be accepted. The assumption that measurements are selected at random from a normal distribution is the basis for these plans and the OC curves. Tightened and reduced sampling provisions are also provided. MIL-STD-414 sampling plans were once designed to correspond closely with MIL-STD-105 sampling plans. That is, the OC curves from both standards were comparable for the same sample size code letter. With modification D to MIL-STD-105, this is no longer true, and the plans must be matched by comparing OC curves.

USING MIL-STD-414

These plans are superior to attribute inspection plans due to the decrease in sample size required for comparable protection and the information which is generated. To illustrate the complete coverage provided, the table of contents is shown in Figure 9-14.

In most applications, plans outlined in either Section B or Section C are used. Single and double specification limit plans are included under each section. Examples taken from the standard will illustrate using the double specification limit plans only.

Included in the standard is an AQL conversion table (Table A-1) from which a specific AQL is selected. For example, if a 2 percent AQL were specified, a 2.5 percent AQL plan would be used.

Table A-2 gives the sample size code letter, which is determined by the lot size and inspection level. Inspection level IV is generally specified. Levels, I, II, and III increase the sampling risk, while inspection level V decreases the risk. If the lot size were 1,000 pieces, with level IV specified, code letter K would be used.

Similar to the recommendation made for using MIL-STD-105D, the OC curve for the AQL and code letter selected should be evaluated to determine if it provides adequate protection. Table A-3 shows the OC curves for code letter K. The 2.5 percent AQL curve has about a 6 percent α risk, and the percent defective with a 10 percent β risk is close to 11 percent. These OC curves provide essentially the same protection given by the code letter J curves in MIL-STD-105D. Refer to Table X-J for comparison.

Table B-3 is the master table for normal and tightened inspection, variability unknown—standard deviation method. Table C-3 is the master table for normal and tightened inspection, variability unknown—range method. From Table B-3 note that the sample size required for code letter K is 35 and that from Table C-3 it is 40. This compares to an 80-piece sample specified for code letter J in MIL-STD-105D. In the first case this is a 56.25 percent reduction in sample size and in the second case a 50.0 percent reduction. Cost reduction is obvious, although these labor savings may be offset by the computations required to make the final accept or reject decisions.

Example B-3, taken from the standard, indicates how completely each application is illustrated. Data are given, and the calculations required are demonstrated in a step-by-step procedure. Note that this example is for the double specification limit, variability unknown—standard deviation method.

Fig. 9-14

CONTENTS

Fig. 9-14 (Cont.)

CONTENTS—Continued

Fig. 9-14 (Cont.)

CONTENTS—Continued

Table A-1 (Below)   AQL Conversion Table

For specified AQL values falling within these ranges	Use this AQL value
—— to 0.049	0.04
0.050 to 0.069	0.065
0.070 to 0.109	0.10
0.110 to 0.164	0.15
0.165 to 0.279	0.25
0.280 to 0.439	0.40
0.440 to 0.699	0.65
0.700 to 1.09	1.0
1.10 to 1.64	1.5
1.65 to 2.79	2.5
2.80 to 4.39	4.0
4.40 to 6.99	6.5
7.00 to 10.9	10.0
11.00 to 16.4	15.0

Table A-2 (Right)   Sample Size Code Letters[1]

Lot Size	Inspection Levels				
	I	II	III	IV	V
3 to 8	B	B	B	B	C
9 to 15	B	B	B	B	D
16 to 25	B	B	B	C	E
26 to 40	B	B	B	D	F
41 to 65	B	B	C	E	G
66 to 110	B	B	D	F	H
111 to 180	B	C	E	G	I
181 to 300	B	D	F	H	J
301 to 500	C	E	G	I	K
501 to 800	D	F	H	J	L
801 to 1,300	E	G	I	K	L
1,301 to 3,200	F	H	J	L	M
3,201 to 8,000	G	I	L	M	N
8,001 to 22,000	H	J	M	N	O
22,001 to 110,000	I	K	N	O	P
110,001 to 550,000	I	K	O	P	Q
550,001 and over	I	K	P	Q	Q

[1]Sample size code letters given in body of table are applicable when the indicated inspection levels are to be used.

Table A-3 Operating Characteristic Curves for Sampling Plans Based
on Standard Deviation Method: Sample Size Code Letter K

(Curves for sampling plans based on range method and known variability are essentially equivalent)

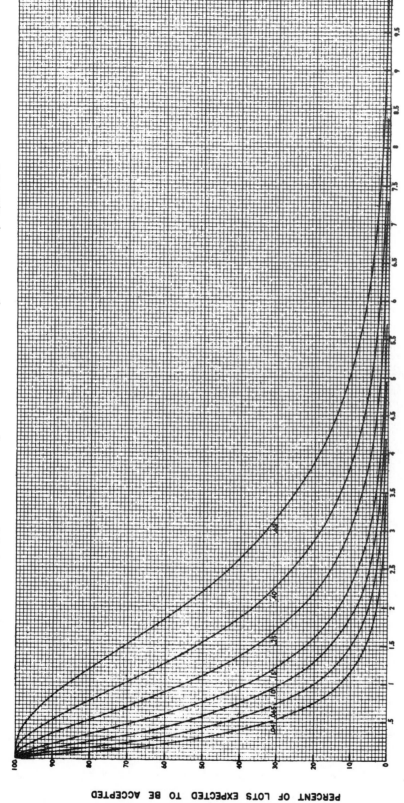

PERCENT OF LOTS EXPECTED TO BE ACCEPTED

QUALITY OF SUBMITTED LOTS   (In percent defective)

Note: Figures on curves are Acceptable Quality Levels for normal inspection.

The values of the percent of lots expected to be
accepted are valid only when measurements are
selected at random from a normal distribution.

181

Table A-3 (Cont.) Operating Characteristic Curves for Sampling Plans Based
on Standard Deviation Method : Sample Size Code Letter K

(Curves for sampling plans based on range method and known variability are essentially equivalent)

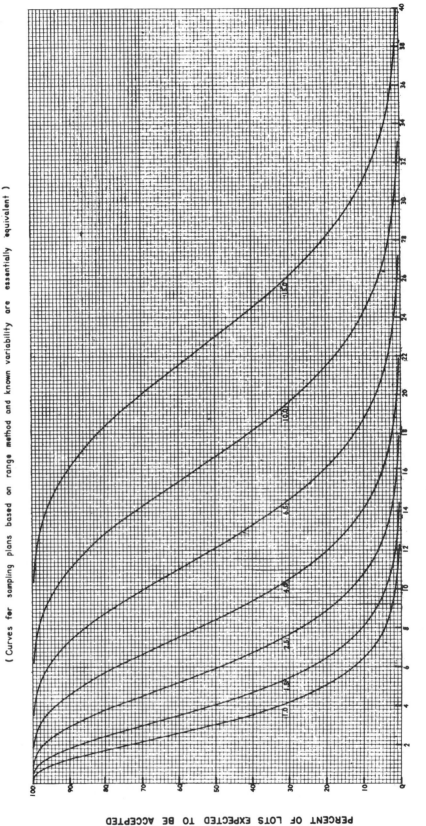

The values of the percent of lots expected to be
accepted are valid only when measurements are
selected at random from a normal distribution.

QUALITY OF SUBMITTED LOTS (In percent defective)

Note: Figures on curves are Acceptable Quality Levels for normal inspection.

182

Table B-3 Master Table for Normal and Tightened Inspection for Plans Based on Variability Unknown (Double Specification Limit and Form 2—Single Specification Limit)—Standard Deviation Method

Sample size code letter	Sample size	.04 M	.065 M	.10 M	.15 M	.25 M	.40 M	.65 M	1.00 M	1.50 M	2.50 M	4.00 M	6.50 M	10.00 M	15.00 M
B	3	→	→	→	→	→	→	→	▼	▼	7.59	18.86	26.94	33.69	40.47
C	4	→	→	→	→	→	→	→	1.53	5.50	10.92	16.45	22.86	29.45	36.90
D	5	→	→	→	→	→	→	1.33	3.32	5.83	9.80	14.39	20.19	26.56	33.99
E	7	→	→	→	→	0.422	1.06	2.14	3.55	5.35	8.40	12.20	17.35	23.29	30.50
F	10	→	→	→	0.349	0.716	1.30	2.17	3.26	4.77	7.29	10.54	15.17	20.74	27.57
G	15	0.099	0.186	0.312	0.503	0.818	1.31	2.11	3.05	4.31	6.56	9.46	13.71	18.94	25.61
H	20	0.135	0.228	0.365	0.544	0.846	1.29	2.05	2.95	4.09	6.17	8.92	12.99	18.03	24.53
I	25	0.155	0.250	0.380	0.551	0.877	1.29	2.00	2.86	3.97	5.97	8.63	12.57	17.51	23.97
J	30	0.179	0.280	0.413	0.581	0.879	1.29	1.98	2.83	3.91	5.86	8.47	12.36	17.24	23.58
K	35	0.170	0.264	0.388	0.535	0.847	1.23	1.87	2.68	3.70	5.57	8.10	11.87	16.65	22.91
L	40	0.179	0.275	0.401	0.566	0.873	1.26	1.88	2.71	3.72	5.58	8.09	11.85	16.61	22.86
M	50	0.163	0.250	0.363	0.503	0.789	1.17	1.71	2.49	3.45	5.20	7.61	11.23	15.87	22.00
N	75	0.147	0.228	0.330	0.467	0.720	1.07	1.60	2.29	3.20	4.87	7.15	10.63	15.13	21.11
O	100	0.145	0.220	0.317	0.447	0.689	1.02	1.53	2.20	3.07	4.69	6.91	10.32	14.75	20.66
P	150	0.134	0.203	0.293	0.413	0.638	0.949	1.43	2.05	2.89	4.43	6.57	9.88	14.20	20.02
Q	200	0.135	0.204	0.294	0.414	0.637	0.945	1.42	2.04	2.87	4.40	6.53	9.81	14.12	19.92
		.065	.10	.15	.25	.40	.65	1.00	1.50	2.50	4.00	6.50	10.00	15.00	

Acceptable Quality Levels (normal inspection)

Acceptability Quality Levels (tightened inspection)

All AQL and table values are in percent defective.

↓ Use first sampling plan below arrow, that is, both sample size as well as M value. When sample size equals or exceeds lot size, every item in the lot must be inspected.

Table C-3 Master Table for Normal and Tightened Inspection for Plans Based on Variability Unknown (Double Specification Limit and for Form 2—Single Specification Limit)—Range Method

Sample size code letter	Sample size	c factor	Acceptable Quality Levels (normal inspection)													
			.04	.065	.10	.15	.25	.40	.65	1.00	1.50	2.50	4.00	6.50	10.00	15.00
			M	M	M	M	M	M	M	M	M	M	M	M	M	M
B	3	1.910	↓	↓	↓	↓	↓	↓	↓	▼	▼	7.59	18.86	26.94	33.69	40.47
C	4	2.234	↓	↓	↓	↓	↓	↓	↓	1.53	5.50	10.92	16.45	22.86	29.45	36.90
D	5	2.474	↓	↓	↓	↓	↓	↓	1.42	3.44	5.93	9.90	14.47	20.27	26.59	33.95
E	7	2.830	↓	↓	↓	↓	.28	.89	1.99	3.46	5.32	8.47	12.35	17.54	23.50	30.66
F	10	2.405	↓	↓	↓	.23	.58	1.14	2.05	3.23	4.77	7.42	10.79	15.49	21.06	27.90
G	15	2.379	.061	.136	.253	.430	.786	1.30	2.10	3.11	4.44	6.76	9.76	14.09	19.30	25.92
H	25	2.358	.125	.214	.336	.506	.827	1.27	1.95	2.82	3.96	5.98	8.65	12.59	17.48	23.79
I	30	2.353	.147	.240	.366	.537	.856	1.29	1.96	2.81	3.92	5.88	8.50	12.36	17.19	23.42
J	35	2.349	.165	.261	.391	.564	.883	1.33	1.98	2.82	3.90	5.85	8.42	12.24	17.03	23.21
K	40	2.346	.160	.252	.375	.539	.842	1.25	1.88	2.69	3.73	5.61	8.11	11.84	16.55	22.38
L	50	2.342	.169	.261	.381	.542	.838	1.25	1.60	2.63	3.64	5.47	7.91	11.57	16.20	22.26
M	60	2.339	.158	.244	.356	.504	.781	1.16	1.74	2.47	3.44	5.17	7.54	11.10	15.64	21.63
N	85	2.335	.156	.242	.350	.493	.755	1.12	1.67	2.37	3.30	4.97	7.27	10.73	15.17	21.05
O	115	2.333	.153	.230	.333	.468	.718	1.06	1.58	2.25	3.14	4.76	6.99	10.37	14.74	20.57
P	175	2.331	.139	.210	.303	.427	.655	.972	1.46	2.08	2.93	4.47	6.60	9.89	14.15	19.88
Q	230	2.330	.142	.215	.308	.432	.661	.976	1.47	2.08	2.92	4.46	6.57	9.84	14.10	19.82
			.065	.10	.15	.25	.40	.65	1.00	1.50	2.50	4.00	6.50	10.00	15.00	
			Acceptable Quality Levels (tightened inspection)													

All AQL and table values are in percent defective.
↓ Use first sampling plan below arrow, that is, both sample size as well as M value. When sample size equals or exceeds lot size, every item in the lot must be inspected.

184

Lines 13 and 14 refer to Table B-5, a portion of which is shown. Essentially this is an area table, corrected for the sample size employed, and is used to estimate the lot percent defective beyond the specification limit(s). The estimated percent defective above and below the specification limits are added together on line 15, and the total is compared to the maximum allowable percent defective on line 16. The latter value (3.32 percent) is obtained from Table B-3 under the AQL specified for the example (1 percent) and opposite the code letter (D). If the estimated total percent defective is greater than the maximum allowable, the lot is rejected. If it is less, the lot is accepted.

Example B-3 Example of Calculations, Double Specification Limit,
Variability Unknown—Standard Deviation Method,
One AQL Value for both Upper and Lower Specification Limit Combined

Example   The minimum temperature of operation for a certain device is specified as 180° F. The maximum temperature is 209° F. A lot of 40 items is submitted for inspection. Inspection Level IV, normal inspection, with AQL = 1% is to be used. From Tables A-2 and B-3 it is seen that a sample of size 5 is required. Suppose the measurements obtained are as follows: 197°, 188°, 184°, 205°, and 201°; and compliance with the acceptability criterion is to be determined.

Line	Information Needed	Value Obtained	Explanation
1	Sample Size: n	5	
2	Sum of Measurements: ΣX	975	
3	Sum of Squared Measurements: ΣX^2	190,435	
4	Correction Factor (CF): $(\Sigma X)^2/n$	190,125	$(975)^2/5$
5	Corrected Sum of Squares (SS): $\Sigma X^2 - CF$	310	190,435-190,125
6	Variance (V): $SS/(n-1)$	77.5	310/4
7	Estimate of Lot Standard Deviation s: $\sqrt{V}$	8.81	$\sqrt{77.5}$
8	Sample Mean $\overline{X}$: $\Sigma X/n$	195	975/5
9	Upper Specification Limit: U	209	
10	Lower Specification Limit: L	180	
11	Quality Index: $Q_U = (U-\overline{X})/s$	1.59	(209-195)/8.81
12	Quality Index: $Q_L = (\overline{X}-L)/s$	1.70	(195-180)/8.81
13	Est. of Lot Percent Def. above U: p_U	2.19%	See Table B-5
14	Est. of Lot Percent Def. below L: p_L	.66%	See Table B-5
15	Total Est. Percent Def. in Lot: $p = p_U + p_L$	2.85%	2.19% + .66%
16	Max. Allowable Percent Def.: M	3.32%	See Table B-3
17	Acceptability Criterion: Compare $p = p_U + p_L$ with M	2.85% < 3.32%	See Para. B12.1.2 (7)

The lot meets the acceptability criterion, since $p = p_U + p_L$ is less than M.

Table B-5 Table for Estimating the Lot Percent Defective Using Standard Deviation Method

Sample Size

Q_U or Q_L	3	4	5	7	10	15	20	25	30	35	40	50	75	100	150	200
1.50	0.00	0.00	3.80	5.28	5.87	6.20	6.34	6.41	6.46	6.50	6.52	6.55	6.60	6.62	6.64	6.65
1.51	0.00	0.00	3.61	5.13	5.73	6.06	6.20	6.28	6.33	6.36	6.39	6.42	6.47	6.49	6.51	6.52
1.52	0.00	0.00	3.42	4.97	5.59	5.93	6.07	6.15	6.20	6.23	6.26	6.29	6.34	6.36	6.38	6.39
1.53	0.00	0.00	3.23	4.82	5.45	5.80	5.94	6.02	6.07	6.11	6.13	6.17	6.21	6.24	6.26	6.27
1.54	0.00	0.00	3.05	4.67	5.31	5.67	5.81	5.89	5.95	5.98	6.01	6.04	6.09	6.11	6.13	6.15
1.55	0.00	0.00	2.87	4.52	5.18	5.54	5.69	5.77	5.82	5.86	5.88	5.92	5.97	5.99	6.01	6.02
1.56	0.00	0.00	2.69	4.38	5.05	5.41	5.56	5.65	5.70	5.74	5.76	5.80	5.85	5.87	5.89	5.90
1.57	0.00	0.00	2.52	4.24	4.92	5.29	5.44	5.53	5.58	5.62	5.64	5.68	5.73	5.75	5.78	5.79
1.58	0.00	0.00	2.35	4.10	4.79	5.16	5.32	5.41	5.46	5.50	5.53	5.56	5.61	5.64	5.66	5.67
1.59	0.00	0.00	2.19	3.96	4.66	5.04	5.20	5.29	5.34	5.38	5.41	5.45	5.50	5.52	5.54	5.56
1.60	0.00	0.00	2.03	3.83	4.54	4.92	5.09	5.17	5.23	5.27	5.30	5.33	5.38	5.41	5.43	5.44
1.61	0.00	0.00	1.87	3.69	4.41	4.81	4.97	5.06	5.12	5.16	5.18	5.22	5.27	5.30	5.32	5.33
1.62	0.00	0.00	1.72	3.57	4.30	4.69	4.86	4.95	5.01	5.04	5.07	5.11	5.16	5.19	5.21	5.23
1.63	0.00	0.00	1.57	3.44	4.18	4.58	4.75	4.84	4.90	4.94	4.97	5.01	5.06	5.08	5.11	5.12
1.64	0.00	0.00	1.42	3.31	4.06	4.47	4.64	4.73	4.79	4.83	4.86	4.90	4.95	4.98	5.00	5.01
1.65	0.00	0.00	1.28	3.19	3.95	4.36	4.53	4.62	4.68	4.72	4.75	4.79	4.85	4.87	4.90	4.91
1.66	0.00	0.00	1.15	3.07	3.84	4.25	4.43	4.52	4.58	4.62	4.65	4.69	4.74	4.77	4.79	4.81
1.67	0.00	0.00	1.02	2.95	3.73	4.15	4.32	4.42	4.48	4.52	4.55	4.59	4.64	4.67	4.70	4.71
1.68	0.00	0.00	0.89	2.84	3.62	4.05	4.22	4.32	4.38	4.42	4.45	4.49	4.55	4.57	4.60	4.61
1.69	0.00	0.00	0.77	2.73	3.52	3.94	4.12	4.22	4.28	4.32	4.35	4.39	4.45	4.47	4.50	4.51
1.70	0.00	0.00	0.66	2.62	3.41	3.84	4.02	4.12	4.18	4.22	4.25	4.30	4.35	4.38	4.41	4.42
1.71	0.00	0.00	0.55	2.51	3.31	3.75	3.93	4.02	4.09	4.13	4.16	4.20	4.26	4.29	4.31	4.32
1.72	0.00	0.00	0.45	2.41	3.21	3.65	3.83	3.93	3.99	4.04	4.07	4.11	4.17	4.19	4.22	4.23
1.73	0.00	0.00	0.36	2.30	3.11	3.56	3.74	3.84	3.90	3.94	3.98	4.02	4.08	4.10	4.13	4.14
1.74	0.00	0.00	0.27	2.20	3.02	3.46	3.65	3.75	3.81	3.85	3.89	3.93	3.99	4.01	4.04	4.05
1.75	0.00	0.00	0.19	2.11	2.93	3.37	3.56	3.66	3.72	3.77	3.80	3.84	3.90	3.93	3.95	3.97
1.76	0.00	0.00	0.12	2.01	2.83	3.28	3.47	3.57	3.63	3.68	3.72	3.76	3.81	3.84	3.87	3.88
1.77	0.00	0.00	0.06	1.92	2.74	3.20	3.38	3.48	3.55	3.59	3.63	3.67	3.73	3.76	3.78	3.80
1.78	0.00	0.00	0.02	1.83	2.66	3.11	3.30	3.40	3.47	3.51	3.54	3.59	3.64	3.67	3.70	3.71
1.79	0.00	0.00	0.00	1.74	2.57	3.03	3.21	3.32	3.38	3.43	3.46	3.51	3.56	3.59	3.63	3.63
1.80	0.00	0.00	0.00	1.65	2.49	2.94	3.13	3.24	3.30	3.35	3.38	3.43	3.48	3.51	3.54	3.55
1.81	0.00	0.00	0.00	1.57	2.40	2.86	3.05	3.16	3.22	3.27	3.30	3.35	3.40	3.43	3.46	3.47
1.82	0.00	0.00	0.00	1.49	2.32	2.79	2.98	3.08	3.15	3.19	3.22	3.27	3.33	3.36	3.38	3.40
1.83	0.00	0.00	0.00	1.41	2.25	2.71	2.90	3.00	3.07	3.11	3.15	3.19	3.25	3.28	3.31	3.32
1.84	0.00	0.00	0.00	1.34	2.17	2.63	2.82	2.93	2.99	3.04	3.07	3.12	3.18	3.21	3.23	3.25
1.85	0.00	0.00	0.00	1.26	2.09	2.56	2.75	2.85	2.92	2.97	3.00	3.05	3.10	3.13	3.16	3.17
1.86	0.00	0.00	0.00	1.19	2.02	2.48	2.68	2.78	2.85	2.89	2.93	2.97	3.03	3.06	3.09	3.10
1.87	0.00	0.00	0.00	1.12	1.95	2.41	2.61	2.71	2.78	2.82	2.86	2.90	2.96	2.99	3.02	3.03
1.88	0.00	0.00	0.00	1.06	1.88	2.34	2.54	2.64	2.71	2.75	2.79	2.83	2.89	2.92	2.95	2.96
1.89	0.00	0.00	0.00	0.99	1.81	2.28	2.47	2.57	2.64	2.69	2.72	2.77	2.83	2.85	2.88	2.90

Sample Size

Q_U or Q_L	3	4	5	7	10	15	20	25	30	35	40	50	75	100	150	200
1.90	0.00	0.00	0.00	0.93	1.75	2.21	2.40	2.51	2.57	2.62	2.65	2.70	2.76	2.79	2.82	2.83
1.91	0.00	0.00	0.00	0.87	1.68	2.14	2.34	2.44	2.51	2.55	2.59	2.63	2.69	2.72	2.75	2.77
1.92	0.00	0.00	0.00	0.81	1.62	2.08	2.27	2.38	2.45	2.49	2.52	2.57	2.63	2.66	2.69	2.70
1.93	0.00	0.00	0.00	0.76	1.56	2.02	2.21	2.32	2.39	2.43	2.46	2.51	2.57	2.60	2.62	2.64
1.94	0.00	0.00	0.00	0.70	1.50	1.96	2.15	2.25	2.32	2.37	2.40	2.45	2.51	2.54	2.56	2.58
1.95	0.00	0.00	0.00	0.65	1.44	1.90	2.09	2.19	2.26	2.31	2.34	2.39	2.45	2.48	2.50	2.52
1.96	0.00	0.00	0.00	0.60	1.38	1.84	2.03	2.14	2.20	2.25	2.28	2.33	2.39	2.42	2.44	2.46
1.97	0.00	0.00	0.00	0.56	1.33	1.78	1.97	2.08	2.14	2.19	2.22	2.27	2.33	2.36	2.39	2.40
1.98	0.00	0.00	0.00	0.51	1.27	1.73	1.92	2.02	2.09	2.13	2.17	2.21	2.27	2.30	2.33	2.34
1.99	0.00	0.00	0.00	0.47	1.22	1.67	1.86	1.97	2.03	2.08	2.11	2.16	2.22	2.25	2.27	2.29
2.00	0.00	0.00	0.00	0.43	1.17	1.62	1.81	1.91	1.98	2.03	2.06	2.10	2.16	2.19	2.22	2.23
2.01	0.00	0.00	0.00	0.39	1.12	1.57	1.76	1.86	1.93	1.97	2.01	2.05	2.11	2.14	2.17	2.18
2.02	0.00	0.00	0.00	0.36	1.07	1.52	1.71	1.81	1.87	1.92	1.95	2.00	2.06	2.09	2.11	2.13
2.03	0.00	0.00	0.00	0.32	1.03	1.47	1.66	1.76	1.82	1.87	1.90	1.95	2.01	2.04	2.06	2.08
2.04	0.00	0.00	0.00	0.29	0.98	1.42	1.61	1.71	1.77	1.82	1.85	1.90	1.96	1.99	2.01	2.03
2.05	0.00	0.00	0.00	0.26	0.94	1.37	1.56	1.66	1.73	1.77	1.80	1.85	1.91	1.94	1.96	1.98
2.06	0.00	0.00	0.00	0.23	0.90	1.33	1.51	1.61	1.68	1.72	1.76	1.80	1.86	1.89	1.92	1.93
2.07	0.00	0.00	0.00	0.21	0.86	1.28	1.47	1.57	1.63	1.68	1.71	1.76	1.81	1.84	1.87	1.88
2.08	0.00	0.00	0.00	0.18	0.82	1.24	1.42	1.52	1.59	1.63	1.66	1.71	1.77	1.79	1.82	1.84
2.09	0.00	0.00	0.00	0.16	0.78	1.20	1.38	1.48	1.54	1.59	1.62	1.66	1.72	1.75	1.78	1.79
2.10	0.00	0.00	0.00	0.14	0.74	1.16	1.34	1.44	1.50	1.54	1.58	1.62	1.68	1.71	1.73	1.75
2.11	0.00	0.00	0.00	0.12	0.71	1.12	1.30	1.39	1.46	1.50	1.53	1.58	1.63	1.66	1.69	1.70
2.12	0.00	0.00	0.00	0.10	0.67	1.08	1.26	1.35	1.42	1.46	1.49	1.54	1.59	1.62	1.65	1.66
2.13	0.00	0.00	0.00	0.08	0.64	1.04	1.22	1.31	1.38	1.42	1.45	1.50	1.55	1.58	1.61	1.62
2.14	0.00	0.00	0.00	0.07	0.61	1.00	1.18	1.28	1.34	1.38	1.41	1.46	1.51	1.54	1.57	1.58
2.15	0.00	0.00	0.00	0.06	0.58	0.97	1.14	1.24	1.30	1.34	1.37	1.42	1.47	1.50	1.53	1.54
2.16	0.00	0.00	0.00	0.05	0.55	0.93	1.10	1.20	1.26	1.30	1.34	1.38	1.43	1.46	1.49	1.50
2.17	0.00	0.00	0.00	0.04	0.52	0.90	1.07	1.16	1.22	1.27	1.30	1.34	1.40	1.42	1.45	1.46
2.18	0.00	0.00	0.00	0.03	0.49	0.87	1.03	1.13	1.19	1.23	1.26	1.30	1.36	1.39	1.41	1.42
2.19	0.00	0.00	0.00	0.02	0.46	0.83	1.00	1.09	1.15	1.20	1.23	1.27	1.32	1.35	1.38	1.39
2.20	0.000	0.000	0.000	0.015	0.437	0.803	0.968	1.061	1.120	1.161	1.192	1.233	1.287	1.314	1.340	1.352
2.21	0.000	0.000	0.000	0.010	0.413	0.772	0.936	1.028	1.087	1.128	1.158	1.199	1.253	1.279	1.305	1.318
2.22	0.000	0.000	0.000	0.006	0.389	0.743	0.905	0.996	1.054	1.095	1.125	1.166	1.219	1.245	1.271	1.283
2.23	0.000	0.000	0.000	0.003	0.366	0.715	0.875	0.965	1.023	1.063	1.093	1.134	1.186	1.212	1.238	1.250
2.24	0.000	0.000	0.000	0.002	0.345	0.687	0.845	0.935	0.992	1.032	1.061	1.102	1.154	1.180	1.205	1.218
2.25	0.000	0.000	0.000	0.001	0.324	0.660	0.816	0.905	0.962	1.002	1.031	1.071	1.123	1.148	1.173	1.186
2.26	0.000	0.000	0.000	0.000	0.304	0.634	0.789	0.876	0.933	0.972	1.001	1.041	1.092	1.117	1.142	1.155
2.27	0.000	0.000	0.000	0.000	0.285	0.609	0.762	0.848	0.904	0.943	0.972	1.011	1.062	1.087	1.112	1.124
2.28	0.000	0.000	0.000	0.000	0.267	0.585	0.735	0.821	0.876	0.915	0.943	0.982	1.033	1.058	1.082	1.094
2.29	0.000	0.000	0.000	0.000	0.250	0.561	0.710	0.794	0.849	0.887	0.915	0.954	1.004	1.029	1.053	1.065

Table B-5 (Cont.)

$\hat{\sigma}/\sigma$	Sample Size															
	3	4	5	7	10	15	20	25	30	35	40	50	75	100	150	200
2.30	0.000	0.000	0.000	0.000	0.233	0.538	0.685	0.769	0.823	0.861	0.888	0.927	0.977	1.001	1.025	1.037
2.31	0.000	0.000	0.000	0.000	0.218	0.516	0.661	0.743	0.797	0.834	0.862	0.900	0.949	0.974	0.997	1.009
2.32	0.000	0.000	0.000	0.000	0.203	0.495	0.637	0.719	0.772	0.809	0.836	0.874	0.923	0.947	0.971	0.982
2.33	0.000	0.000	0.000	0.002	0.189	0.474	0.614	0.695	0.748	0.784	0.811	0.848	0.897	0.921	0.944	0.956
2.34	0.000	0.000	0.000	0.002	0.175	0.454	0.592	0.672	0.724	0.760	0.787	0.824	0.872	0.895	0.915	0.930
2.35	0.000	0.000	0.000	0.000	0.163	0.435	0.571	0.650	0.701	0.736	0.763	0.799	0.847	0.870	0.893	0.903
2.36	0.000	0.000	0.000	0.000	0.151	0.416	0.550	0.628	0.678	0.714	0.740	0.776	0.823	0.846	0.869	0.880
2.37	0.000	0.000	0.000	0.000	0.139	0.398	0.530	0.606	0.656	0.691	0.717	0.753	0.799	0.822	0.845	0.856
2.38	0.000	0.000	0.000	0.000	0.128	0.381	0.510	0.586	0.635	0.670	0.695	0.730	0.777	0.799	0.822	0.833
2.39	0.000	0.000	0.000	0.000	0.118	0.364	0.491	0.566	0.614	0.648	0.674	0.709	0.754	0.777	0.799	0.810
2.40	0.000	0.000	0.000	0.000	0.109	0.348	0.473	0.546	0.594	0.628	0.653	0.687	0.732	0.755	0.777	0.787
2.41	0.000	0.000	0.000	0.000	0.100	0.332	0.455	0.527	0.575	0.608	0.633	0.667	0.711	0.733	0.755	0.766
2.42	0.000	0.000	0.000	0.000	0.091	0.317	0.437	0.509	0.555	0.588	0.613	0.646	0.691	0.712	0.734	0.744
2.43	0.000	0.000	0.000	0.000	0.083	0.302	0.421	0.491	0.537	0.569	0.593	0.627	0.670	0.692	0.713	0.724
2.44	0.000	0.000	0.000	0.000	0.076	0.288	0.404	0.474	0.519	0.551	0.575	0.608	0.651	0.672	0.693	0.703
2.45	0.000	0.000	0.000	0.000	0.069	0.275	0.389	0.457	0.501	0.533	0.556	0.589	0.632	0.653	0.673	0.684
2.46	0.000	0.000	0.000	0.000	0.063	0.262	0.373	0.440	0.484	0.516	0.539	0.571	0.613	0.634	0.654	0.664
2.47	0.000	0.000	0.000	0.000	0.057	0.249	0.359	0.425	0.468	0.499	0.521	0.553	0.595	0.615	0.635	0.646
2.48	0.000	0.000	0.000	0.000	0.051	0.237	0.344	0.409	0.452	0.482	0.505	0.536	0.577	0.597	0.617	0.627
2.49	0.000	0.000	0.000	0.000	0.046	0.225	0.331	0.394	0.436	0.466	0.488	0.519	0.560	0.580	0.600	0.609
2.50	0.000	0.000	0.000	0.000	0.041	0.214	0.317	0.380	0.421	0.451	0.473	0.503	0.543	0.563	0.582	0.592
2.51	0.000	0.000	0.000	0.000	0.037	0.204	0.304	0.366	0.407	0.436	0.457	0.487	0.527	0.546	0.565	0.575
2.52	0.000	0.000	0.000	0.000	0.033	0.193	0.292	0.352	0.392	0.421	0.442	0.472	0.511	0.530	0.549	0.558
2.53	0.000	0.000	0.000	0.000	0.029	0.184	0.280	0.339	0.379	0.407	0.428	0.457	0.495	0.514	0.533	0.542
2.54	0.000	0.000	0.000	0.000	0.026	0.174	0.268	0.326	0.365	0.393	0.413	0.442	0.480	0.499	0.517	0.527
2.55	0.000	0.000	0.000	0.000	0.023	0.165	0.257	0.314	0.352	0.379	0.400	0.428	0.465	0.484	0.502	0.511
2.56	0.000	0.000	0.000	0.000	0.020	0.156	0.246	0.302	0.340	0.366	0.386	0.414	0.451	0.469	0.487	0.496
2.57	0.000	0.000	0.000	0.000	0.017	0.148	0.236	0.291	0.327	0.354	0.373	0.401	0.437	0.455	0.473	0.482
2.58	0.000	0.000	0.000	0.000	0.015	0.140	0.226	0.279	0.316	0.341	0.361	0.388	0.424	0.441	0.459	0.468
2.59	0.000	0.000	0.000	0.000	0.013	0.133	0.216	0.269	0.304	0.330	0.349	0.375	0.410	0.428	0.445	0.454
2.60	0.000	0.000	0.000	0.000	0.011	0.125	0.207	0.258	0.293	0.318	0.337	0.363	0.398	0.415	0.432	0.441
2.61	0.000	0.000	0.000	0.000	0.009	0.118	0.198	0.248	0.282	0.307	0.325	0.351	0.385	0.402	0.419	0.428
2.62	0.000	0.000	0.000	0.000	0.007	0.112	0.189	0.238	0.272	0.296	0.314	0.339	0.373	0.390	0.406	0.415
2.63	0.000	0.000	0.000	0.000	0.007	0.105	0.181	0.229	0.262	0.285	0.303	0.328	0.361	0.378	0.394	0.402
2.64	0.000	0.000	0.000	0.000	0.005	0.099	0.172	0.220	0.252	0.275	0.293	0.317	0.350	0.366	0.382	0.390
2.65	0.000	0.000	0.000	0.000	0.005	0.094	0.165	0.211	0.243	0.265	0.282	0.307	0.339	0.355	0.371	0.379
2.66	0.000	0.000	0.000	0.000	0.004	0.088	0.157	0.202	0.233	0.256	0.273	0.296	0.328	0.344	0.359	0.367
2.67	0.000	0.000	0.000	0.000	0.003	0.083	0.150	0.194	0.224	0.246	0.263	0.286	0.317	0.333	0.348	0.356
2.68	0.000	0.000	0.000	0.000	0.002	0.078	0.143	0.186	0.216	0.237	0.254	0.277	0.307	0.322	0.338	0.345
2.69	0.000	0.000	0.000	0.000	0.002	0.073	0.136	0.179	0.208	0.229	0.245	0.267	0.297	0.312	0.327	0.335

$\hat{\sigma}/\sigma$	Sample Size															
	3	4	5	7	10	15	20	25	30	35	40	50	75	100	150	200
2.70	0.000	0.000	0.000	0.000	0.001	0.069	0.130	0.171	0.200	0.220	0.236	0.258	0.288	0.302	0.317	0.325
2.71	0.000	0.000	0.000	0.000	0.001	0.064	0.124	0.164	0.192	0.212	0.227	0.249	0.278	0.293	0.307	0.315
2.72	0.000	0.000	0.000	0.000	0.000	0.060	0.118	0.157	0.184	0.204	0.219	0.241	0.269	0.283	0.298	0.305
2.73	0.000	0.000	0.000	0.000	0.000	0.057	0.112	0.151	0.177	0.197	0.211	0.232	0.260	0.274	0.288	0.296
2.74	0.000	0.000	0.000	0.000	0.000	0.053	0.107	0.144	0.170	0.189	0.204	0.224	0.252	0.266	0.279	0.286
2.75	0.000	0.000	0.000	0.000	0.000	0.049	0.102	0.138	0.163	0.182	0.196	0.216	0.243	0.257	0.271	0.277
2.76	0.000	0.000	0.000	0.000	0.000	0.046	0.097	0.132	0.157	0.175	0.189	0.209	0.235	0.249	0.262	0.269
2.77	0.000	0.000	0.000	0.000	0.000	0.043	0.092	0.126	0.151	0.168	0.182	0.201	0.227	0.241	0.254	0.260
2.78	0.000	0.000	0.000	0.000	0.000	0.040	0.087	0.121	0.145	0.162	0.175	0.194	0.220	0.233	0.246	0.252
2.79	0.000	0.000	0.000	0.000	0.000	0.037	0.083	0.115	0.139	0.156	0.169	0.187	0.212	0.225	0.238	0.244
2.80	0.000	0.000	0.000	0.000	0.000	0.035	0.079	0.110	0.133	0.150	0.162	0.181	0.205	0.218	0.230	0.237
2.81	0.000	0.000	0.000	0.000	0.000	0.032	0.075	0.105	0.128	0.144	0.156	0.174	0.198	0.211	0.223	0.229
2.82	0.000	0.000	0.000	0.000	0.000	0.030	0.071	0.101	0.122	0.138	0.150	0.168	0.192	0.204	0.216	0.222
2.83	0.000	0.000	0.000	0.000	0.000	0.028	0.067	0.096	0.117	0.133	0.145	0.162	0.185	0.197	0.209	0.215
2.84	0.000	0.000	0.000	0.000	0.000	0.026	0.064	0.092	0.112	0.128	0.139	0.156	0.179	0.190	0.202	0.208
2.85	0.000	0.000	0.000	0.000	0.000	0.024	0.060	0.088	0.108	0.122	0.134	0.150	0.173	0.184	0.195	0.201
2.86	0.000	0.000	0.000	0.000	0.000	0.022	0.057	0.084	0.103	0.118	0.129	0.145	0.167	0.178	0.189	0.195
2.87	0.000	0.000	0.000	0.000	0.000	0.020	0.054	0.080	0.099	0.113	0.124	0.139	0.161	0.172	0.183	0.188
2.88	0.000	0.000	0.000	0.000	0.000	0.019	0.051	0.076	0.094	0.108	0.119	0.134	0.155	0.166	0.177	0.182
2.89	0.000	0.000	0.000	0.000	0.000	0.017	0.048	0.073	0.090	0.104	0.114	0.129	0.150	0.160	0.171	0.176
2.90	0.000	0.000	0.000	0.000	0.000	0.016	0.046	0.069	0.087	0.100	0.110	0.125	0.145	0.155	0.165	0.171
2.91	0.000	0.000	0.000	0.000	0.000	0.015	0.043	0.066	0.083	0.096	0.106	0.120	0.140	0.150	0.160	0.165
2.92	0.000	0.000	0.000	0.000	0.000	0.013	0.041	0.063	0.079	0.092	0.101	0.115	0.135	0.145	0.155	0.160
2.93	0.000	0.000	0.000	0.000	0.000	0.012	0.038	0.060	0.076	0.088	0.097	0.111	0.130	0.140	0.149	0.154
2.94	0.000	0.000	0.000	0.000	0.000	0.011	0.036	0.057	0.072	0.084	0.093	0.107	0.125	0.135	0.144	0.149
2.95	0.000	0.000	0.000	0.000	0.000	0.010	0.034	0.054	0.069	0.081	0.090	0.103	0.121	0.130	0.140	0.144
2.96	0.000	0.000	0.000	0.000	0.000	0.009	0.032	0.051	0.066	0.077	0.086	0.099	0.117	0.126	0.135	0.140
2.97	0.000	0.000	0.000	0.000	0.000	0.009	0.030	0.049	0.063	0.074	0.083	0.095	0.112	0.121	0.130	0.135
2.98	0.000	0.000	0.000	0.000	0.000	0.008	0.028	0.046	0.060	0.071	0.079	0.091	0.108	0.117	0.126	0.130
2.99	0.000	0.000	0.000	0.000	0.000	0.007	0.027	0.044	0.057	0.068	0.076	0.088	0.104	0.113	0.122	0.126
3.00	0.000	0.000	0.000	0.000	0.000	0.006	0.025	0.042	0.055	0.065	0.073	0.084	0.101	0.109	0.118	0.122
3.01	0.000	0.000	0.000	0.000	0.000	0.006	0.024	0.040	0.052	0.062	0.070	0.081	0.097	0.105	0.114	0.118
3.02	0.000	0.000	0.000	0.000	0.000	0.005	0.022	0.038	0.050	0.059	0.067	0.078	0.093	0.101	0.110	0.114
3.03	0.000	0.000	0.000	0.000	0.000	0.005	0.021	0.036	0.048	0.057	0.064	0.075	0.090	0.098	0.106	0.110
3.04	0.000	0.000	0.000	0.000	0.000	0.004	0.019	0.034	0.045	0.054	0.061	0.072	0.087	0.094	0.102	0.106
3.05	0.000	0.000	0.000	0.000	0.000	0.004	0.018	0.032	0.043	0.052	0.059	0.069	0.083	0.091	0.099	0.103
3.06	0.000	0.000	0.000	0.000	0.000	0.003	0.017	0.030	0.041	0.050	0.056	0.066	0.080	0.088	0.095	0.099
3.07	0.000	0.000	0.000	0.000	0.000	0.003	0.015	0.029	0.039	0.047	0.054	0.064	0.077	0.085	0.092	0.096
3.08	0.000	0.000	0.000	0.000	0.000	0.003	0.015	0.027	0.037	0.045	0.052	0.061	0.074	0.081	0.089	0.092
3.09	0.000	0.000	0.000	0.000	0.000	0.002	0.014	0.026	0.036	0.043	0.049	0.059	0.072	0.079	0.086	0.089

Table B-5 (Cont.) Table for Estimating the Lot Percent Defective Using Standard Deviation Method

Q_U or Q_L	3	4	5	7	10	15	20	25	30	35	40	50	75	100	150	200
												Sample Size				
3.10	0.000	0.000	0.000	0.000	0.000	0.002	0.013	0.024	0.034	0.041	0.047	0.056	0.069	0.076	0.083	0.086
3.11	0.000	0.000	0.000	0.000	0.000	0.002	0.012	0.023	0.032	0.039	0.045	0.054	0.066	0.073	0.080	0.083
3.12	0.000	0.000	0.000	0.000	0.000	0.002	0.011	0.022	0.031	0.038	0.043	0.052	0.064	0.070	0.077	0.080
3.13	0.000	0.000	0.000	0.000	0.000	0.002	0.011	0.021	0.029	0.036	0.041	0.050	0.061	0.068	0.074	0.077
3.14	0.000	0.000	0.000	0.000	0.000	0.001	0.010	0.019	0.028	0.034	0.040	0.048	0.059	0.065	0.071	0.075
3.15	0.000	0.000	0.000	0.000	0.000	0.001	0.009	0.018	0.026	0.033	0.038	0.046	0.057	0.063	0.069	0.072
3.16	0.000	0.000	0.000	0.000	0.000	0.001	0.009	0.017	0.025	0.031	0.036	0.044	0.055	0.060	0.066	0.069
3.17	0.000	0.000	0.000	0.000	0.000	0.001	0.008	0.016	0.024	0.030	0.035	0.042	0.053	0.058	0.064	0.067
3.18	0.000	0.000	0.000	0.000	0.000	0.001	0.007	0.015	0.022	0.028	0.033	0.040	0.050	0.056	0.062	0.065
3.19	0.000	0.000	0.000	0.000	0.000	0.001	0.007	0.015	0.021	0.027	0.032	0.038	0.049	0.054	0.059	0.062
3.20	0.000	0.000	0.000	0.000	0.000	0.001	0.006	0.014	0.020	0.026	0.030	0.037	0.047	0.052	0.057	0.060
3.21	0.000	0.000	0.000	0.000	0.000	0.001	0.006	0.013	0.019	0.024	0.029	0.035	0.045	0.050	0.055	0.058
3.22	0.000	0.000	0.000	0.000	0.000	0.001	0.005	0.012	0.018	0.023	0.027	0.034	0.043	0.048	0.053	0.056
3.23	0.000	0.000	0.000	0.000	0.000	0.001	0.005	0.011	0.017	0.022	0.026	0.032	0.041	0.046	0.051	0.054
3.24	0.000	0.000	0.000	0.000	0.000	0.001	0.005	0.011	0.016	0.021	0.025	0.031	0.040	0.044	0.049	0.052
3.25	0.000	0.000	0.000	0.000	0.000	0.001	0.004	0.010	0.015	0.020	0.024	0.030	0.038	0.043	0.048	0.050
3.26	0.000	0.000	0.000	0.000	0.000	0.000	0.004	0.009	0.015	0.019	0.023	0.028	0.037	0.041	0.046	0.048
3.27	0.000	0.000	0.000	0.000	0.000	0.000	0.004	0.009	0.014	0.018	0.022	0.027	0.035	0.040	0.044	0.046
3.28	0.000	0.000	0.000	0.000	0.000	0.000	0.003	0.008	0.013	0.017	0.021	0.026	0.034	0.038	0.042	0.045
3.29	0.000	0.000	0.000	0.000	0.000	0.000	0.003	0.008	0.012	0.016	0.020	0.025	0.032	0.037	0.041	0.043
3.30	0.000	0.000	0.000	0.000	0.000	0.000	0.003	0.007	0.012	0.015	0.019	0.024	0.031	0.035	0.039	0.042
3.31	0.000	0.000	0.000	0.000	0.000	0.000	0.003	0.007	0.011	0.015	0.018	0.023	0.030	0.034	0.038	0.040
3.32	0.000	0.000	0.000	0.000	0.000	0.000	0.002	0.006	0.010	0.014	0.017	0.022	0.029	0.032	0.036	0.039
3.33	0.000	0.000	0.000	0.000	0.000	0.000	0.002	0.006	0.010	0.013	0.016	0.021	0.027	0.031	0.035	0.037
3.34	0.000	0.000	0.000	0.000	0.000	0.000	0.002	0.006	0.009	0.013	0.015	0.020	0.026	0.030	0.034	0.036
3.35	0.000	0.000	0.000	0.000	0.000	0.000	0.002	0.005	0.009	0.012	0.015	0.019	0.025	0.029	0.032	0.034
3.36	0.000	0.000	0.000	0.000	0.000	0.000	0.002	0.005	0.008	0.011	0.014	0.018	0.024	0.028	0.031	0.033
3.37	0.000	0.000	0.000	0.000	0.000	0.000	0.002	0.005	0.008	0.011	0.013	0.017	0.023	0.026	0.030	0.032
3.38	0.000	0.000	0.000	0.000	0.000	0.000	0.001	0.004	0.007	0.010	0.013	0.016	0.022	0.025	0.029	0.031
3.39	0.000	0.000	0.000	0.000	0.000	0.000	0.001	0.004	0.007	0.010	0.012	0.016	0.021	0.024	0.028	0.029
3.40	0.000	0.000	0.000	0.000	0.000	0.000	0.001	0.004	0.007	0.009	0.011	0.015	0.020	0.023	0.027	0.028
3.41	0.000	0.000	0.000	0.000	0.000	0.000	0.001	0.003	0.006	0.009	0.011	0.014	0.020	0.022	0.026	0.027
3.42	0.000	0.000	0.000	0.000	0.000	0.000	0.001	0.003	0.005	0.008	0.010	0.014	0.019	0.022	0.025	0.026
3.43	0.000	0.000	0.000	0.000	0.000	0.000	0.001	0.003	0.005	0.008	0.010	0.013	0.018	0.021	0.024	0.025
3.44	0.000	0.000	0.000	0.000	0.000	0.000	0.001	0.003	0.005	0.007	0.009	0.012	0.017	0.020	0.023	0.024
3.45	0.000	0.000	0.000	0.000	0.000	0.000	0.001	0.003	0.005	0.007	0.008	0.012	0.016	0.019	0.022	0.023
3.46	0.000	0.000	0.000	0.000	0.000	0.000	0.001	0.002	0.004	0.006	0.008	0.011	0.016	0.018	0.021	0.022
3.47	0.000	0.000	0.000	0.000	0.000	0.000	0.001	0.002	0.004	0.006	0.007	0.011	0.015	0.017	0.020	0.022
3.48	0.000	0.000	0.000	0.000	0.000	0.000	0.001	0.002	0.004	0.005	0.007	0.010	0.014	0.017	0.019	0.021
3.49	0.000	0.000	0.000	0.000	0.000	0.000	0.000	0.002	0.004	0.005	0.007	0.010	0.014	0.016	0.019	0.020

Q_U or Q_L	3	4	5	7	10	15	20	25	30	35	40	50	75	100	150	200
												Sample Size				
3.50	0.000	0.000	0.000	0.000	0.000	0.000	0.000	0.002	0.003	0.005	0.007	0.009	0.013	0.015	0.018	0.019
3.51	0.000	0.000	0.000	0.000	0.000	0.000	0.000	0.002	0.003	0.005	0.006	0.009	0.013	0.015	0.017	0.018
3.52	0.000	0.000	0.000	0.000	0.000	0.000	0.000	0.002	0.003	0.005	0.006	0.008	0.012	0.014	0.017	0.018
3.53	0.000	0.000	0.000	0.000	0.000	0.000	0.000	0.001	0.003	0.004	0.006	0.008	0.012	0.014	0.016	0.017
3.54	0.000	0.000	0.000	0.000	0.000	0.000	0.000	0.001	0.003	0.004	0.005	0.008	0.011	0.013	0.015	0.016
3.55	0.000	0.000	0.000	0.000	0.000	0.000	0.000	0.001	0.003	0.004	0.005	0.007	0.011	0.012	0.015	0.016
3.56	0.000	0.000	0.000	0.000	0.000	0.000	0.000	0.001	0.002	0.004	0.005	0.007	0.010	0.012	0.014	0.015
3.57	0.000	0.000	0.000	0.000	0.000	0.000	0.000	0.001	0.002	0.004	0.005	0.007	0.010	0.012	0.013	0.014
3.58	0.000	0.000	0.000	0.000	0.000	0.000	0.000	0.001	0.002	0.003	0.004	0.006	0.010	0.011	0.013	0.014
3.59	0.000	0.000	0.000	0.000	0.000	0.000	0.000	0.000	0.002	0.003	0.004	0.006	0.009	0.010	0.012	0.013
3.60	0.000	0.000	0.000	0.000	0.000	0.000	0.000	0.001	0.002	0.003	0.004	0.006	0.008	0.010	0.012	0.013
3.61	0.000	0.000	0.000	0.000	0.000	0.000	0.000	0.001	0.002	0.003	0.004	0.005	0.008	0.010	0.011	0.012
3.62	0.000	0.000	0.000	0.000	0.000	0.000	0.000	0.001	0.002	0.003	0.003	0.005	0.008	0.009	0.011	0.012
3.63	0.000	0.000	0.000	0.000	0.000	0.000	0.000	0.001	0.001	0.002	0.003	0.005	0.007	0.009	0.010	0.011
3.64	0.000	0.000	0.000	0.000	0.000	0.000	0.000	0.001	0.001	0.002	0.003	0.004	0.007	0.008	0.010	0.011
3.65	0.000	0.000	0.000	0.000	0.000	0.000	0.000	0.001	0.001	0.002	0.003	0.004	0.007	0.008	0.010	0.011
3.66	0.000	0.000	0.000	0.000	0.000	0.000	0.000	0.000	0.001	0.002	0.003	0.004	0.006	0.008	0.009	0.010
3.67	0.000	0.000	0.000	0.000	0.000	0.000	0.000	0.000	0.001	0.002	0.002	0.004	0.006	0.007	0.009	0.010
3.68	0.000	0.000	0.000	0.000	0.000	0.000	0.000	0.000	0.001	0.002	0.002	0.003	0.006	0.007	0.008	0.009
3.69	0.000	0.000	0.000	0.000	0.000	0.000	0.000	0.000	0.001	0.002	0.002	0.003	0.005	0.007	0.008	0.009

Q_U or Q_L	3	4	5	7	10	15	20	25	30	35	40	50	75	100	150	200
												Sample Size				
3.70	0.000	0.000	0.000	0.000	0.000	0.000	0.000	0.000	0.001	0.002	0.002	0.003	0.005	0.006	0.008	0.008
3.71	0.000	0.000	0.000	0.000	0.000	0.000	0.000	0.000	0.001	0.001	0.002	0.003	0.005	0.006	0.007	0.008
3.72	0.000	0.000	0.000	0.000	0.000	0.000	0.000	0.000	0.001	0.001	0.002	0.003	0.005	0.006	0.007	0.008
3.73	0.000	0.000	0.000	0.000	0.000	0.000	0.000	0.000	0.001	0.001	0.002	0.003	0.004	0.006	0.007	0.007
3.74	0.000	0.000	0.000	0.000	0.000	0.000	0.000	0.000	0.001	0.001	0.002	0.002	0.004	0.005	0.007	0.007
3.75	0.000	0.000	0.000	0.000	0.000	0.000	0.000	0.000	0.001	0.001	0.001	0.002	0.004	0.005	0.006	0.007
3.76	0.000	0.000	0.000	0.000	0.000	0.000	0.000	0.000	0.001	0.001	0.001	0.002	0.004	0.005	0.006	0.007
3.77	0.000	0.000	0.000	0.000	0.000	0.000	0.000	0.000	0.000	0.001	0.001	0.002	0.003	0.005	0.006	0.007
3.78	0.000	0.000	0.000	0.000	0.000	0.000	0.000	0.000	0.000	0.001	0.001	0.002	0.003	0.004	0.005	0.006
3.79	0.000	0.000	0.000	0.000	0.000	0.000	0.000	0.000	0.000	0.001	0.001	0.002	0.003	0.004	0.005	0.006
3.80	0.000	0.000	0.000	0.000	0.000	0.000	0.000	0.000	0.000	0.001	0.001	0.002	0.003	0.004	0.005	0.006
3.81	0.000	0.000	0.000	0.000	0.000	0.000	0.000	0.000	0.000	0.001	0.001	0.001	0.003	0.004	0.005	0.005
3.82	0.000	0.000	0.000	0.000	0.000	0.000	0.000	0.000	0.000	0.001	0.001	0.001	0.002	0.003	0.005	0.005
3.83	0.000	0.000	0.000	0.000	0.000	0.000	0.000	0.000	0.000	0.000	0.001	0.001	0.002	0.003	0.004	0.005
3.84	0.000	0.000	0.000	0.000	0.000	0.000	0.000	0.000	0.000	0.000	0.001	0.001	0.002	0.003	0.004	0.005
3.85	0.000	0.000	0.000	0.000	0.000	0.000	0.000	0.000	0.000	0.000	0.001	0.001	0.002	0.003	0.004	0.004
3.86	0.000	0.000	0.000	0.000	0.000	0.000	0.000	0.000	0.000	0.000	0.001	0.001	0.002	0.003	0.004	0.004
3.87	0.000	0.000	0.000	0.000	0.000	0.000	0.000	0.000	0.000	0.000	0.001	0.001	0.002	0.003	0.004	0.004
3.88	0.000	0.000	0.000	0.000	0.000	0.000	0.000	0.000	0.000	0.000	0.001	0.001	0.002	0.003	0.003	0.004
3.89	0.000	0.000	0.000	0.000	0.000	0.000	0.000	0.000	0.000	0.000	0.001	0.001	0.002	0.003	0.003	0.004
3.90	0.000	0.000	0.000	0.000	0.000	0.000	0.000	0.000	0.000	0.000	0.001	0.001	0.002	0.003	0.003	0.004

188

Example C-3 Example of Calculations, Double Specification Limit,
Variability Unknown—Average Method,
One AQL Value for Both Upper and Lower Specification Limit Combined

Example The specifications for electrical resistance of a certain electrical component is 650.0 ± 30 ohms. A lot of 100 items is submitted for inspection. Inspection Level IV, normal inspection, with AQL = .4% is to be used. From Tables A-2 and C-3 it is seen that a sample of size 10 is required. Suppose the values of the sample resistance in the order reading from left to right are as follows:

$$643, 651, 619, 627, 658, (R_1 = 658 - 619 = 39)$$
$$670, 673, 641, 638, 650, (R_2 = 673 - 638 = 35)$$

and compliance with the acceptability criterion is to be determined.

Line	Information Needed	Value Obtained	Explanation
1	Sample Size: n	10	
2	Sum of Measurements: ΣX	6470	
3	Sample Mean $\overline{X}$: $\Sigma X/n$	647	6470/10
4	Average Range $\overline{R}$: ΣR/no. of subgroups	37	(39 + 35)/2
5	Factor c	2.405	See Table C-3
6	Upper Specification Limit: U	680	
7	Lower Specification Limit: L	620	
8	Quality Index: $Q_U = (U-\overline{X})c/\overline{R}$	2.15	(680-647)2.405/37
9	Quality Index: $Q_L = (\overline{X}-L)c/\overline{R}$	1.76	(647-620)2.405/37
10	Est. of Lot Percent Def. above U: p_U	.35%	See Table C-5
11	Est. of Lot Percent Def. below L: p_L	2.54%	See Table C-5
12	Total Est. Percent Def. in Lot: $p = p_U + p_L$	2.89%	.35% + 2.54%
13	Max. Allowable Percent Def.: M	1.14%	See Table C-3
14	Acceptability Criterion: Compare p = $p_U + p_L$ with M	2.89% > 1.14%	See Para. C12.1.2(7)

The lot does not meet the acceptability criterion, since $p = p_U + p_L$ is greater than M.

Example C-3, also taken from the standard, shows another application. This again uses a double specification limit but is for variability unknown—range method, which means that the average range is being used to estimate the standard deviation, similar to the technique used with average and range charts.

Line 5 refers to a factor *c*, found in Table C-3. This is similar to d_2 found in the table of constants for control charts but is again corrected for sample size. Lines 10 and 11 refer to Table C-5, portions of which are shown. The procedure followed from lines 11 through 14 is identical to Example B-3.

As stated previously, the major objection to using MIL-STD-414 involves the complex calculations. Considered step by step they are not actually difficult, but they do take time. This time can be readily reduced by using computer terminals or desk calculators programmed for calculating the mean and standard deviation.

Table C-5 Table for Estimating the Lot Percent Defective Using Range Method

Upper table:

Q_U or Q_L	Sample Size															
	3	4	5	7	10	15	25	30	35	40	50	60	85	115	175	230
1.90	0.00	0.00	0.00	0.67	1.45	1.99	2.38	2.47	2.53	2.57	2.64	2.68	2.74	2.77	2.81	2.83
1.91	0.00	0.00	0.00	0.62	1.38	1.93	2.32	2.41	2.47	2.51	2.58	2.61	2.67	2.70	2.74	2.76
1.92	0.00	0.00	0.00	0.56	1.32	1.86	2.25	2.34	2.41	2.45	2.51	2.55	2.61	2.64	2.68	2.70
1.93	0.00	0.00	0.00	0.51	1.26	1.80	2.19	2.28	2.34	2.38	2.45	2.49	2.55	2.58	2.61	2.63
1.94	0.00	0.00	0.00	0.46	1.20	1.74	2.13	2.22	2.28	2.32	2.39	2.43	2.49	2.52	2.55	2.57
1.95	0.00	0.00	0.00	0.42	1.15	1.68	2.07	2.16	2.22	2.26	2.33	2.37	2.43	2.46	2.49	2.51
1.96	0.00	0.00	0.00	0.37	1.09	1.62	2.01	2.10	2.16	2.20	2.27	2.31	2.37	2.40	2.43	2.45
1.97	0.00	0.00	0.00	0.33	1.04	1.57	1.95	2.04	2.10	2.14	2.21	2.25	2.31	2.34	2.38	2.40
1.98	0.00	0.00	0.00	0.30	0.99	1.51	1.90	1.99	2.05	2.09	2.15	2.19	2.25	2.28	2.32	2.34
1.99	0.00	0.00	0.00	0.26	0.94	1.46	1.84	1.93	1.99	2.03	2.10	2.14	2.20	2.23	2.26	2.28
2.00	0.00	0.00	0.00	0.23	0.89	1.41	1.79	1.88	1.94	1.98	2.05	2.08	2.14	2.17	2.21	2.23
2.01	0.00	0.00	0.00	0.20	0.84	1.36	1.74	1.83	1.89	1.93	1.99	2.03	2.09	2.12	2.16	2.18
2.02	0.00	0.00	0.00	0.17	0.80	1.31	1.69	1.78	1.83	1.87	1.94	1.98	2.04	2.07	2.10	2.12
2.03	0.00	0.00	0.00	0.14	0.75	1.26	1.64	1.73	1.78	1.82	1.89	1.93	1.99	2.02	2.05	2.07
2.04	0.00	0.00	0.00	0.12	0.71	1.21	1.59	1.68	1.73	1.77	1.84	1.88	1.94	1.97	2.00	2.02
2.05	0.00	0.00	0.00	0.10	0.67	1.17	1.54	1.63	1.69	1.73	1.79	1.83	1.89	1.92	1.95	1.97
2.06	0.00	0.00	0.00	0.08	0.63	1.12	1.49	1.58	1.64	1.68	1.74	1.78	1.84	1.87	1.91	1.93
2.07	0.00	0.00	0.00	0.06	0.60	1.08	1.45	1.54	1.58	1.63	1.70	1.74	1.79	1.82	1.86	1.88
2.08	0.00	0.00	0.00	0.05	0.56	1.04	1.40	1.49	1.55	1.59	1.65	1.69	1.75	1.78	1.81	1.83
2.09	0.00	0.00	0.00	0.03	0.53	1.00	1.36	1.45	1.50	1.54	1.61	1.64	1.70	1.73	1.77	1.79
2.10	0.00	0.00	0.00	0.02	0.49	0.96	1.32	1.41	1.46	1.50	1.56	1.60	1.66	1.69	1.72	1.74
2.11	0.00	0.00	0.00	0.01	0.46	0.92	1.28	1.36	1.42	1.46	1.52	1.56	1.61	1.64	1.68	1.70
2.12	0.00	0.00	0.00	0.00	0.43	0.88	1.24	1.32	1.38	1.42	1.48	1.52	1.57	1.60	1.64	1.66
2.13	0.00	0.00	0.00	0.00	0.40	0.85	1.20	1.28	1.34	1.38	1.44	1.48	1.53	1.56	1.60	1.62
2.14	0.00	0.00	0.00	0.00	0.38	0.81	1.16	1.25	1.30	1.34	1.40	1.44	1.49	1.52	1.56	1.58
2.15	0.00	0.00	0.00	0.00	0.35	0.78	1.13	1.21	1.26	1.30	1.36	1.40	1.45	1.48	1.52	1.54
2.16	0.00	0.00	0.00	0.00	0.32	0.75	1.09	1.17	1.22	1.26	1.32	1.36	1.41	1.44	1.48	1.50
2.17	0.00	0.00	0.00	0.00	0.30	0.71	1.06	1.13	1.18	1.22	1.29	1.32	1.38	1.41	1.44	1.46
2.18	0.00	0.00	0.00	0.00	0.28	0.68	1.02	1.10	1.15	1.19	1.25	1.28	1.34	1.37	1.40	1.41
2.19	0.00	0.00	0.00	0.00	0.26	0.65	0.99	1.06	1.11	1.15	1.22	1.25	1.30	1.33	1.37	1.39
2.20	0.000	0.000	0.000	0.000	0.236	0.625	0.954	1.030	1.083	1.122	1.178	1.214	1.267	1.299	1.330	1.346
2.21	0.000	0.000	0.000	0.000	0.217	0.597	0.922	0.997	1.050	1.089	1.144	1.180	1.233	1.265	1.295	1.311
2.22	0.000	0.000	0.000	0.000	0.199	0.570	0.891	0.966	1.018	1.056	1.111	1.147	1.199	1.231	1.261	1.277
2.23	0.000	0.000	0.000	0.000	0.182	0.544	0.861	0.935	0.986	1.025	1.079	1.115	1.167	1.197	1.228	1.244
2.24	0.000	0.000	0.000	0.000	0.166	0.519	0.831	0.905	0.956	0.994	1.048	1.083	1.135	1.165	1.195	1.211
2.25	0.000	0.000	0.000	0.000	0.150	0.495	0.802	0.875	0.926	0.964	1.018	1.052	1.104	1.134	1.163	1.179
2.26	0.000	0.000	0.000	0.000	0.136	0.471	0.775	0.847	0.897	0.935	0.987	1.022	1.073	1.103	1.132	1.148
2.27	0.000	0.000	0.000	0.000	0.123	0.449	0.748	0.819	0.869	0.906	0.958	0.993	1.043	1.073	1.103	1.118
2.28	0.000	0.000	0.000	0.000	0.111	0.427	0.722	0.792	0.841	0.878	0.930	0.964	1.014	1.044	1.073	1.088
2.29	0.000	0.000	0.000	0.000	0.099	0.406	0.697	0.766	0.814	0.851	0.902	0.936	0.986	1.015	1.044	1.059

Lower table:

Q_U or Q_L	Sample Size									
	3	4	5	7	10	15	25	30	35	40
1.50	0.00	0.00	3.80	5.08	5.66	6.05	6.33	6.39	6.43	6.46
1.51	0.00	0.00	3.61	4.92	5.51	5.91	6.19	6.25	6.30	6.33
1.52	0.00	0.00	3.42	4.76	5.37	5.77	6.06	6.12	6.17	6.20
1.53	0.00	0.00	3.23	4.60	5.22	5.64	5.93	5.99	6.04	6.07
1.54	0.00	0.00	3.05	4.45	5.08	5.50	5.80	5.86	5.91	5.95
1.55	0.00	0.00	2.87	4.30	4.94	5.37	5.68	5.74	5.79	5.82
1.56	0.00	0.00	2.69	4.15	4.81	5.24	5.55	5.62	5.67	5.70
1.57	0.00	0.00	2.52	4.01	4.67	5.11	5.43	5.50	5.55	5.58
1.58	0.00	0.00	2.35	3.86	4.54	4.99	5.31	5.38	5.43	5.46
1.59	0.00	0.00	2.19	3.72	4.41	4.86	5.19	5.26	5.31	5.34
1.60	0.00	0.00	2.03	3.58	4.28	4.74	5.08	5.14	5.19	5.23
1.61	0.00	0.00	1.87	3.45	4.16	4.62	4.96	5.03	5.08	5.12
1.62	0.00	0.00	1.72	3.31	4.03	4.51	4.85	4.92	4.97	5.01
1.63	0.00	0.00	1.57	3.18	3.91	4.39	4.74	4.81	4.86	4.90
1.64	0.00	0.00	1.42	3.06	3.79	4.28	4.63	4.70	4.75	4.79
1.65	0.00	0.00	1.28	2.93	3.68	4.17	4.52	4.59	4.64	4.68
1.66	0.00	0.00	1.15	2.81	3.56	4.06	4.41	4.49	4.54	4.58
1.67	0.00	0.00	1.02	2.69	3.45	3.95	4.31	4.39	4.44	4.48
1.68	0.00	0.00	0.89	2.57	3.34	3.85	4.21	4.29	4.34	4.38
1.69	0.00	0.00	0.77	2.46	3.23	3.74	4.10	4.19	4.24	4.28
1.70	0.00	0.00	0.66	2.35	3.13	3.64	4.00	4.09	4.14	4.18
1.71	0.00	0.00	0.55	2.24	3.02	3.54	3.92	3.99	4.05	4.09
1.72	0.00	0.00	0.45	2.13	2.92	3.45	3.82	3.90	3.95	3.99
1.73	0.00	0.00	0.36	2.03	2.82	3.35	3.73	3.81	3.86	3.90
1.74	0.00	0.00	0.27	1.93	2.73	3.26	3.63	3.72	3.77	3.81
1.75	0.00	0.00	0.19	1.83	2.63	3.16	3.54	3.63	3.68	3.72
1.76	0.00	0.00	0.12	1.73	2.54	3.07	3.45	3.54	3.59	3.63
1.77	0.00	0.00	0.06	1.64	2.45	2.99	3.37	3.45	3.51	3.55
1.78	0.00	0.00	0.02	1.55	2.36	2.90	3.28	3.37	3.43	3.47
1.79	0.00	0.00	0.00	1.46	2.27	2.81	3.20	3.28	3.34	3.38
1.80	0.00	0.00	0.00	1.38	2.19	2.73	3.11	3.20	3.26	3.30
1.81	0.00	0.00	0.00	1.29	2.10	2.65	3.03	3.12	3.18	3.22
1.82	0.00	0.00	0.00	1.21	2.02	2.57	2.96	3.05	3.11	3.15
1.83	0.00	0.00	0.00	1.14	1.94	2.49	2.88	2.97	3.03	3.07
1.84	0.00	0.00	0.00	1.06	1.87	2.42	2.80	2.89	2.95	2.99
1.85	0.00	0.00	0.00	0.99	1.79	2.34	2.73	2.82	2.88	2.92
1.86	0.00	0.00	0.00	0.92	1.72	2.27	2.66	2.75	2.81	2.85
1.87	0.00	0.00	0.00	0.86	1.65	2.20	2.59	2.68	2.74	2.78
1.88	0.00	0.00	0.00	0.79	1.58	2.13	2.52	2.61	2.67	2.71
1.89	0.00	0.00	0.00	0.73	1.51	2.06	2.45	2.54	2.60	2.64

Table C-5 (Cont.)

Sample Size

σ̂/σ	3	4	5	7	10	15	25	30	35	40	50	60	85	115	175	230
2.70	0.000	0.000	0.000	0.000	0.000	0.023	0.123	0.156	0.182	0.201	0.228	0.248	0.277	0.295	0.311	0.321
2.71	0.000	0.000	0.000	0.000	0.000	0.021	0.117	0.150	0.174	0.193	0.220	0.239	0.267	0.285	0.302	0.311
2.72	0.000	0.000	0.000	0.000	0.000	0.019	0.111	0.143	0.167	0.185	0.212	0.231	0.259	0.275	0.292	0.301
2.73	0.000	0.000	0.000	0.000	0.000	0.017	0.106	0.137	0.160	0.178	0.205	0.222	0.250	0.266	0.283	0.292
2.74	0.000	0.000	0.000	0.000	0.000	0.015	0.101	0.131	0.153	0.171	0.197	0.215	0.241	0.258	0.274	0.282
2.75	0.000	0.000	0.000	0.000	0.000	0.014	0.096	0.125	0.147	0.164	0.189	0.207	0.233	0.248	0.266	0.274
2.76	0.000	0.000	0.000	0.000	0.000	0.012	0.091	0.120	0.141	0.158	0.182	0.200	0.225	0.241	0.257	0.265
2.77	0.000	0.000	0.000	0.000	0.000	0.011	0.086	0.114	0.135	0.152	0.175	0.192	0.217	0.232	0.249	0.257
2.78	0.000	0.000	0.000	0.000	0.000	0.010	0.081	0.109	0.130	0.146	0.169	0.185	0.210	0.226	0.241	0.249
2.79	0.000	0.000	0.000	0.000	0.000	0.008	0.077	0.103	0.124	0.140	0.163	0.179	0.202	0.218	0.233	0.241
2.80	0.000	0.000	0.000	0.000	0.000	0.007	0.074	0.099	0.118	0.134	0.156	0.172	0.196	0.210	0.225	0.233
2.81	0.000	0.000	0.000	0.000	0.000	0.007	0.070	0.094	0.113	0.129	0.150	0.165	0.189	0.204	0.218	0.226
2.82	0.000	0.000	0.000	0.000	0.000	0.006	0.066	0.090	0.109	0.123	0.144	0.159	0.183	0.194	0.211	0.219
2.83	0.000	0.000	0.000	0.000	0.000	0.005	0.062	0.085	0.103	0.118	0.139	0.154	0.176	0.190	0.204	0.212
2.84	0.000	0.000	0.000	0.000	0.000	0.004	0.059	0.082	0.099	0.113	0.134	0.148	0.170	0.184	0.197	0.205
2.85	0.000	0.000	0.000	0.000	0.000	0.004	0.055	0.078	0.095	0.109	0.128	0.143	0.164	0.178	0.191	0.198
2.86	0.000	0.000	0.000	0.000	0.000	0.003	0.053	0.074	0.091	0.104	0.124	0.137	0.159	0.172	0.185	0.192
2.87	0.000	0.000	0.000	0.000	0.000	0.003	0.050	0.070	0.087	0.100	0.119	0.132	0.152	0.166	0.179	0.185
2.88	0.000	0.000	0.000	0.000	0.000	0.002	0.047	0.067	0.082	0.095	0.114	0.127	0.147	0.160	0.173	0.179
2.89	0.000	0.000	0.000	0.000	0.000	0.002	0.044	0.064	0.079	0.091	0.109	0.122	0.142	0.155	0.167	0.173
2.90	0.000	0.000	0.000	0.000	0.000	0.002	0.042	0.061	0.075	0.088	0.105	0.117	0.138	0.149	0.161	0.168
2.91	0.000	0.000	0.000	0.000	0.000	0.001	0.039	0.057	0.072	0.084	0.101	0.112	0.132	0.143	0.156	0.162
2.92	0.000	0.000	0.000	0.000	0.000	0.001	0.037	0.055	0.069	0.080	0.097	0.107	0.127	0.140	0.151	0.157
2.93	0.000	0.000	0.000	0.000	0.000	0.001	0.035	0.052	0.066	0.077	0.093	0.104	0.123	0.134	0.146	0.151
2.94	0.000	0.000	0.000	0.000	0.000	0.001	0.033	0.049	0.062	0.073	0.089	0.100	0.118	0.129	0.141	0.146
2.95	0.000	0.000	0.000	0.000	0.000	0.001	0.031	0.047	0.059	0.070	0.086	0.096	0.114	0.125	0.136	0.142
2.96	0.000	0.000	0.000	0.000	0.000	0.001	0.029	0.044	0.056	0.067	0.082	0.092	0.110	0.121	0.132	0.137
2.97	0.000	0.000	0.000	0.000	0.000	0.000	0.027	0.042	0.054	0.064	0.079	0.088	0.105	0.116	0.127	0.132
2.98	0.000	0.000	0.000	0.000	0.000	0.000	0.025	0.039	0.051	0.061	0.075	0.085	0.101	0.112	0.123	0.128
2.99	0.000	0.000	0.000	0.000	0.000	0.000	0.024	0.038	0.049	0.058	0.072	0.082	0.098	0.108	0.119	0.124
3.00	0.000	0.000	0.000	0.000	0.000	0.000	0.022	0.036	0.047	0.056	0.069	0.078	0.094	0.105	0.115	0.120
3.01	0.000	0.000	0.000	0.000	0.000	0.000	0.021	0.034	0.044	0.053	0.066	0.075	0.091	0.101	0.111	0.116
3.02	0.000	0.000	0.000	0.000	0.000	0.000	0.020	0.032	0.042	0.050	0.063	0.072	0.087	0.097	0.107	0.112
3.03	0.000	0.000	0.000	0.000	0.000	0.000	0.019	0.030	0.040	0.048	0.061	0.069	0.084	0.094	0.103	0.108
3.04	0.000	0.000	0.000	0.000	0.000	0.000	0.017	0.028	0.038	0.045	0.058	0.066	0.081	0.090	0.099	0.104
3.05	0.000	0.000	0.000	0.000	0.000	0.000	0.016	0.027	0.036	0.043	0.056	0.064	0.078	0.086	0.096	0.101
3.06	0.000	0.000	0.000	0.000	0.000	0.000	0.015	0.025	0.034	0.041	0.053	0.061	0.075	0.083	0.092	0.097
3.07	0.000	0.000	0.000	0.000	0.000	0.000	0.014	0.024	0.032	0.039	0.051	0.059	0.072	0.080	0.089	0.094
3.08	0.000	0.000	0.000	0.000	0.000	0.000	0.013	0.022	0.030	0.037	0.049	0.056	0.069	0.077	0.086	0.091
3.09	0.000	0.000	0.000	0.000	0.000	0.000	0.012	0.021	0.029	0.036	0.046	0.054	0.067	0.075	0.083	0.088

Sample Size

σ̂/σ	3	4	5	7	10	15	25	30	35	40	50	60	85	115	175	230
2.30	0.000	0.000	0.000	0.000	0.089	0.386	0.672	0.741	0.789	0.825	0.875	0.909	0.959	0.988	1.016	1.031
2.31	0.000	0.000	0.000	0.000	0.079	0.367	0.648	0.716	0.763	0.799	0.849	0.882	0.931	0.960	0.988	1.003
2.32	0.000	0.000	0.000	0.000	0.070	0.348	0.624	0.691	0.739	0.774	0.823	0.856	0.905	0.934	0.962	0.976
2.33	0.000	0.000	0.000	0.000	0.061	0.330	0.601	0.668	0.715	0.750	0.798	0.831	0.879	0.908	0.935	0.950
2.34	0.000	0.000	0.000	0.000	0.054	0.313	0.579	0.645	0.691	0.726	0.774	0.807	0.854	0.882	0.909	0.924
2.35	0.000	0.000	0.000	0.000	0.047	0.296	0.558	0.623	0.669	0.703	0.750	0.782	0.829	0.857	0.884	0.899
2.36	0.000	0.000	0.000	0.000	0.040	0.280	0.538	0.602	0.646	0.680	0.728	0.759	0.806	0.833	0.860	0.874
2.37	0.000	0.000	0.000	0.000	0.035	0.265	0.518	0.580	0.624	0.658	0.705	0.736	0.782	0.809	0.836	0.850
2.38	0.000	0.000	0.000	0.000	0.029	0.250	0.498	0.560	0.604	0.637	0.683	0.714	0.759	0.787	0.813	0.827
2.39	0.000	0.000	0.000	0.000	0.025	0.236	0.479	0.541	0.584	0.616	0.662	0.693	0.737	0.764	0.791	0.804
2.40	0.000	0.000	0.000	0.000	0.021	0.223	0.461	0.521	0.564	0.596	0.641	0.671	0.715	0.742	0.769	0.782
2.41	0.000	0.000	0.000	0.000	0.017	0.210	0.443	0.503	0.545	0.577	0.621	0.651	0.695	0.721	0.747	0.760
2.42	0.000	0.000	0.000	0.000	0.014	0.198	0.426	0.485	0.526	0.557	0.601	0.631	0.674	0.701	0.726	0.739
2.43	0.000	0.000	0.000	0.000	0.011	0.186	0.410	0.467	0.508	0.539	0.582	0.611	0.654	0.679	0.705	0.718
2.44	0.000	0.000	0.000	0.000	0.009	0.175	0.393	0.450	0.491	0.521	0.564	0.593	0.635	0.660	0.685	0.698
2.45	0.000	0.000	0.000	0.000	0.007	0.165	0.378	0.434	0.473	0.503	0.545	0.573	0.616	0.641	0.665	0.678
2.46	0.000	0.000	0.000	0.000	0.005	0.154	0.362	0.417	0.456	0.486	0.528	0.556	0.597	0.622	0.646	0.659
2.47	0.000	0.000	0.000	0.000	0.004	0.145	0.348	0.403	0.441	0.470	0.511	0.538	0.579	0.604	0.627	0.640
2.48	0.000	0.000	0.000	0.000	0.003	0.136	0.333	0.387	0.425	0.454	0.494	0.522	0.562	0.586	0.609	0.622
2.49	0.000	0.000	0.000	0.000	0.002	0.127	0.321	0.372	0.409	0.438	0.478	0.504	0.545	0.569	0.593	0.605
2.50	0.000	0.000	0.000	0.000	0.001	0.118	0.307	0.358	0.395	0.423	0.463	0.489	0.528	0.552	0.575	0.587
2.51	0.000	0.000	0.000	0.000	0.001	0.111	0.294	0.345	0.381	0.409	0.447	0.473	0.512	0.536	0.558	0.570
2.52	0.000	0.000	0.000	0.000	0.001	0.103	0.282	0.331	0.367	0.394	0.432	0.458	0.497	0.519	0.542	0.553
2.53	0.000	0.000	0.000	0.000	0.001	0.096	0.270	0.319	0.354	0.381	0.418	0.444	0.481	0.503	0.526	0.537
2.54	0.000	0.000	0.000	0.000	0.000	0.089	0.258	0.306	0.340	0.367	0.404	0.428	0.466	0.488	0.510	0.522
2.55	0.000	0.000	0.000	0.000	0.000	0.083	0.247	0.294	0.328	0.354	0.390	0.415	0.451	0.473	0.495	0.506
2.56	0.000	0.000	0.000	0.000	0.000	0.077	0.237	0.283	0.316	0.341	0.377	0.401	0.437	0.459	0.480	0.491
2.57	0.000	0.000	0.000	0.000	0.000	0.071	0.227	0.272	0.304	0.328	0.364	0.388	0.424	0.445	0.466	0.477
2.58	0.000	0.000	0.000	0.000	0.000	0.066	0.217	0.261	0.292	0.317	0.352	0.376	0.411	0.432	0.452	0.463
2.59	0.000	0.000	0.000	0.000	0.000	0.061	0.207	0.251	0.282	0.305	0.340	0.363	0.397	0.418	0.439	0.449
2.60	0.000	0.000	0.000	0.000	0.000	0.056	0.198	0.240	0.271	0.294	0.328	0.351	0.385	0.406	0.426	0.436
2.61	0.000	0.000	0.000	0.000	0.000	0.052	0.189	0.231	0.260	0.283	0.317	0.339	0.372	0.393	0.413	0.423
2.62	0.000	0.000	0.000	0.000	0.000	0.048	0.181	0.221	0.250	0.273	0.306	0.327	0.360	0.381	0.400	0.410
2.63	0.000	0.000	0.000	0.000	0.000	0.044	0.173	0.212	0.241	0.263	0.295	0.316	0.349	0.369	0.388	0.398
2.64	0.000	0.000	0.000	0.000	0.000	0.040	0.164	0.203	0.232	0.253	0.285	0.306	0.338	0.357	0.376	0.386
2.65	0.000	0.000	0.000	0.000	0.000	0.037	0.157	0.195	0.223	0.244	0.274	0.295	0.327	0.346	0.365	0.375
2.66	0.000	0.000	0.000	0.000	0.000	0.034	0.149	0.186	0.213	0.234	0.265	0.285	0.316	0.335	0.353	0.363
2.67	0.000	0.000	0.000	0.000	0.000	0.031	0.143	0.179	0.205	0.225	0.255	0.275	0.305	0.324	0.342	0.352
2.68	0.000	0.000	0.000	0.000	0.000	0.028	0.136	0.171	0.197	0.217	0.246	0.266	0.296	0.314	0.332	0.342
2.69	0.000	0.000	0.000	0.000	0.000	0.025	0.129	0.164	0.190	0.209	0.238	0.257	0.286	0.304	0.321	0.331

Table C-5 (Cont.) Table for Estimating the Lot Percent
Defective Using Range Method

Q_U or Q_L	Sample Size															
	3	4	5	7	10	15	25	30	35	40	50	60	85	115	175	230
3.10	0.000	0.000	0.000	0.000	0.000	0.000	0.011	0.020	0.027	0.034	0.044	0.051	0.064	0.072	0.080	0.085
3.11	0.000	0.000	0.000	0.000	0.000	0.000	0.011	0.019	0.026	0.032	0.042	0.050	0.061	0.069	0.077	0.082
3.12	0.000	0.000	0.000	0.000	0.000	0.000	0.010	0.018	0.025	0.031	0.041	0.048	0.060	0.067	0.074	0.079
3.13	0.000	0.000	0.000	0.000	0.000	0.000	0.010	0.017	0.024	0.029	0.039	0.046	0.057	0.064	0.072	0.075
3.14	0.000	0.000	0.000	0.000	0.000	0.000	0.009	0.015	0.022	0.028	0.037	0.044	0.055	0.062	0.069	0.073
3.15	0.000	0.000	0.000	0.000	0.000	0.000	0.008	0.014	0.021	0.026	0.036	0.042	0.053	0.060	0.067	0.070
3.16	0.000	0.000	0.000	0.000	0.000	0.000	0.008	0.014	0.020	0.025	0.034	0.040	0.051	0.057	0.064	0.067
3.17	0.000	0.000	0.000	0.000	0.000	0.000	0.007	0.013	0.019	0.024	0.033	0.038	0.049	0.056	0.062	0.065
3.18	0.000	0.000	0.000	0.000	0.000	0.000	0.006	0.012	0.017	0.022	0.031	0.036	0.046	0.053	0.060	0.063
3.19	0.000	0.000	0.000	0.000	0.000	0.000	0.006	0.012	0.017	0.021	0.030	0.034	0.044	0.052	0.057	0.060
3.20	0.000	0.000	0.000	0.000	0.000	0.000	0.005	0.011	0.016	0.020	0.028	0.033	0.043	0.049	0.055	0.058
3.21	0.000	0.000	0.000	0.000	0.000	0.000	0.005	0.010	0.015	0.019	0.027	0.032	0.041	0.047	0.053	0.056
3.22	0.000	0.000	0.000	0.000	0.000	0.000	0.004	0.009	0.014	0.018	0.025	0.031	0.040	0.045	0.051	0.054
3.23	0.000	0.000	0.000	0.000	0.000	0.000	0.004	0.009	0.013	0.017	0.024	0.029	0.037	0.043	0.049	0.052
3.24	0.000	0.000	0.000	0.000	0.000	0.000	0.004	0.009	0.013	0.016	0.023	0.028	0.037	0.042	0.047	0.050
3.25	0.000	0.000	0.000	0.000	0.000	0.000	0.003	0.008	0.012	0.015	0.022	0.027	0.035	0.040	0.046	0.049
3.26	0.000	0.000	0.000	0.000	0.000	0.000	0.003	0.007	0.011	0.015	0.021	0.025	0.033	0.039	0.044	0.047
3.27	0.000	0.000	0.000	0.000	0.000	0.000	0.003	0.007	0.011	0.014	0.021	0.024	0.032	0.037	0.042	0.045
3.28	0.000	0.000	0.000	0.000	0.000	0.000	0.003	0.006	0.010	0.013	0.019	0.023	0.031	0.036	0.040	0.043
3.29	0.000	0.000	0.000	0.000	0.000	0.000	0.003	0.006	0.009	0.012	0.018	0.023	0.029	0.034	0.039	0.042
3.30	0.000	0.000	0.000	0.000	0.000	0.000	0.003	0.005	0.009	0.012	0.017	0.021	0.028	0.033	0.037	0.040
3.31	0.000	0.000	0.000	0.000	0.000	0.000	0.003	0.005	0.008	0.011	0.017	0.021	0.027	0.032	0.036	0.039
3.32	0.000	0.000	0.000	0.000	0.000	0.000	0.002	0.004	0.007	0.010	0.016	0.020	0.026	0.030	0.034	0.037
3.33	0.000	0.000	0.000	0.000	0.000	0.000	0.002	0.004	0.007	0.010	0.015	0.019	0.025	0.029	0.033	0.036
3.34	0.000	0.000	0.000	0.000	0.000	0.000	0.002	0.004	0.007	0.009	0.014	0.018	0.024	0.028	0.032	0.035
3.35	0.000	0.000	0.000	0.000	0.000	0.000	0.002	0.004	0.006	0.009	0.014	0.017	0.023	0.027	0.031	0.033
3.36	0.000	0.000	0.000	0.000	0.000	0.000	0.002	0.004	0.006	0.008	0.013	0.016	0.022	0.026	0.030	0.032
3.37	0.000	0.000	0.000	0.000	0.000	0.000	0.002	0.004	0.006	0.008	0.012	0.015	0.021	0.024	0.028	0.031
3.38	0.000	0.000	0.000	0.000	0.000	0.000	0.001	0.003	0.005	0.007	0.012	0.014	0.019	0.024	0.027	0.030
3.39	0.000	0.000	0.000	0.000	0.000	0.000	0.001	0.003	0.005	0.007	0.011	0.014	0.019	0.022	0.027	0.029
3.40	0.000	0.000	0.000	0.000	0.000	0.000	0.001	0.003	0.005	0.007	0.010	0.013	0.018	0.021	0.026	0.028
3.41	0.000	0.000	0.000	0.000	0.000	0.000	0.001	0.002	0.004	0.006	0.010	0.012	0.018	0.021	0.025	0.027
3.42	0.000	0.000	0.000	0.000	0.000	0.000	0.001	0.002	0.004	0.006	0.009	0.012	0.017	0.020	0.024	0.026
3.43	0.000	0.000	0.000	0.000	0.000	0.000	0.001	0.002	0.004	0.005	0.009	0.011	0.016	0.019	0.023	0.025
3.44	0.000	0.000	0.000	0.000	0.000	0.000	0.001	0.002	0.004	0.005	0.008	0.011	0.015	0.018	0.022	0.024
3.45	0.000	0.000	0.000	0.000	0.000	0.000	0.001	0.002	0.004	0.005	0.008	0.011	0.014	0.017	0.021	0.023
3.46	0.000	0.000	0.000	0.000	0.000	0.000	0.001	0.002	0.003	0.005	0.008	0.010	0.014	0.017	0.020	0.022
3.47	0.000	0.000	0.000	0.000	0.000	0.000	0.001	0.002	0.003	0.004	0.007	0.010	0.014	0.016	0.019	0.021
3.48	0.000	0.000	0.000	0.000	0.000	0.000	0.001	0.002	0.003	0.004	0.007	0.009	0.013	0.015	0.018	0.020
3.49	0.000	0.000	0.000	0.000	0.000	0.000	0.000	0.001	0.003	0.004	0.006	0.009	0.012	0.015	0.018	0.020

A GRAPHICAL TECHNIQUE

The April 1963 issue of *Industrial Quality Control* contained an article titled "A Graphical Application of Military Standard 414," written by Thomas E. Diviney and Nasim A. David. They presented a simple graphical technique which can be used to reduce the calculations required when using MIL-STD-414 by determining what sample means ($\bar{X}$) and what average ranges ($\bar{R}$) can be accepted.

The specific sampling plan illustrated was the Double Specification Limit, Variability Unknown—Average Range Method with One AQL Value for Both Upper and Lower Specification Limit Combined. The technique could also be used if single specification limits were involved or if separate AQL's were specified on double limit plans.

The procedure developed is as follows:

Step 1. For the code letter and AQL specified, find the appropriate C and M values from Table C-3. From Table C-5, determine the Q_U or Q_L value which corresponds to the sample size (n) and the M value found in Table C-3.

Step 2. Using the quality index equations, solve for the average ($\bar{X}$).

$$Q_U = \frac{(U - \bar{X})C}{\bar{R}}$$

Then

$$\bar{X} = U - \frac{Q_U}{C}\bar{R} \tag{1}$$

$$Q_L = \frac{(\bar{X} - L)C}{\bar{R}}$$

Then

$$\bar{X} = L + \frac{Q_L}{C}\bar{R} \tag{2}$$

The values obtained in step 1 for C, Q_U, and Q_L (using the same value for Q_U and Q_L) are substituted into Equations (1) and (2). For U and L the specification limits are used. When plotted on graph paper this results in two intersecting straight lines, as shown in Figure 9-15. Selected increments of the specification tolerance are used as ordinates and appropriate average range values as abscissas. As noted, this defines both an acceptance and rejection region. This is reasonably accurate for all values of $\bar{X}$ and $\bar{R}$ associated with a given lot but may be somewhat inaccurate when $\bar{R}$ is close to the triangle's vertex. While it is possible to simultaneously solve Equations (1) and (2) for $\bar{R}$ and find a slightly different $\bar{R}$ for the vertex, arbitrarily truncating slightly to the left of the vertex will, in most cases, be adequate.

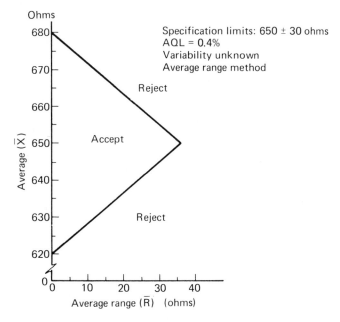

Fig. 9-15 Graph for variable sampling

EXAMPLE

The data shown in Example C-3 will be used. Given: Specification limits: 650 ± 30 ohms.

$$AQL = 0.4 \text{ percent}$$
$$n = 10$$

Step 1. From Table C-3,

$$C = 2.405$$
$$M = 1.14 \text{ percent}$$

For this M value and $n = 10$, obtain, from Table C-5, Q_U or $Q_L = 1.95$.

Step 2. Using Equations (1) and (2),

$$\bar{X} = U - \frac{Q_U}{C}\bar{R}$$
$$= 680 - \frac{1.95}{2.405}\bar{R} = 680 - 0.81\bar{R}$$

and

$$\bar{X} = L + \frac{Q_L}{C}\bar{R}$$
$$= 620 + \frac{1.95}{2.405}\bar{R} = 620 + 0.81\bar{R}$$

Appropriate $\bar{R}$ values are substituted into these equations, and the two lines are constructed as shown in Figure 9-15.

Graphs such as these may be constructed by the quality control engineer and used in receiving inspection areas. All that is required is to calculate the mean and average range and determine whether to accept or reject the lot.

If different AQL's are specified for the two limits, such graphs can still be designed, but it involves more of a trial-and-error procedure. It should also be obvious that a similar graphical approach can be used with standard deviation plans, but the range statistic is much simpler to calculate and the difference in sample size is not that much greater.

In summary, when the data collected are a measurement rather than a discrete value, variables sampling plans should be seriously considered.

CHAPTER TEN | ORGANIZING FOR QUALITY

THE QUALITY CONTROL FUNCTION

The quality control function exists primarily as a service organization, interpreting specifications established by product engineering and assisting the manufacturing department in producing to meet these specifications. As such, the function is responsible for collecting and analyzing vast quantities of data and then presenting the findings to various other departments for appropriate corrective action.

To properly understand such a function requires an awareness of the quality concept. Product quality is a somewhat intangible characteristic in many aspects. Essentially, quality is established by the customer, and the product designed and manufactured for sale is intended to meet these customer requirements. Inferior quality, as indicated by appearance or performance, is ultimately reflected in a declining sales picture, and if not corrected, the particular business may be forced to terminate its activity.

These customer quality requirements are interpreted by the product engineer who establishes the specifications and sets tolerances. Process engineering is responsible for specifying the operations as well as designing and/or procuring equipment which will meet the product specifications. Manufacturing utilizes this equipment to produce, and the quality control function ensures that the manufactured product conforms to the specifications.

It is well to reemphasize the need for conformance to specifications and why the product, including components, must be produced within the allowable tolerances. Product uniformity is attained by adhering to specifications. Uniformity permits the interchangeability of parts, which is a basic principle in modern manufacturing and without which mass production would be impossible.

Uniformity does not imply absolute identity. It is a well-known fact that no two objects are ever identical in all respects. In view of this, the product designer must decide what variation can be tolerated in each characteristic and then set up specifications indicating this. The total permissible variation will depend on the following factors:

195

1. The variation permissible without destroying the product usefulness or the customer acceptance.
2. The variation generated by the unavoidable deviations in the performance of the machines which will do the work and the persons who will operate the machines.
3. The variation generated by the characteristics of the material which enters the plant either for processing or to be used in processing.

Thus quality is a relative measure of product goodness, and quality standards may fluctuate depending on customer requirements and on product availability. If the product is better than the standards, manufacturing costs may be prohibitive. If the product is below the standards, then performance may be impaired, and customer acceptance may decline.

The Quality Control Organization

Over the years, the status of the quality control organization changed from a function merely responsible for detecting inferior or substandard material to a function that establishes what are termed *preventive programs*. These programs are designed to detect quality problems in the design stage or at any point in the manufacturing process and to follow up on corrective action. Immediate responsibility for quality products rests, of course, with the manufacturing departments, but all activities concerning product quality are usually brought together in one organization which may be known as inspection, quality control, quality assurance, or another similar name.

This organization is normally a part of the manufacturing department but is preferably not under its control. The reason for this is obvious. Since the quality control function has authority delegated by management to evaluate material produced by the manufacturing department, the department should not be in a position to control or dictate to the quality activity. Quality control is, therefore, a staff activity since it serves the line or production departments by assisting them in maintaining quality.

Some typical quality control organization subdivisions might be

1. An inspection activity which includes all inspectors who conduct all line inspection in receiving, processing, and final assembly.
2. A salvage inspection activity to determine rejected-part and assembly disposition.
3. A records-and-reports activity to maintain records on accepted and rejected material. Such records might be used in reporting inspection information to manufacturing or to management.
4. A statistical activity to design tests and quality control programs, to analyze and evaluate collected information, and to establish sampling plans and procedures.
5. A gage activity for the inspection, storage, and maintenance of gages used in the plant.
6. A design activity to design the various special gages needed.

Multiproduct, multidivision, and multiplant corporations sponsor various committee activities as an aid in encouraging and assisting in quality control improvement. Committee members are selected by their management because of their knowledge, experience, and interest in improving the quality of products and equipment. Their interest as members is not limited to benefits for their particular division or plant but is also expected to contribute to the objective of improved quality control operations throughout the entire corporation.

Meetings and conferences provide a medium for idea exchange, the elimination of duplicate research and experimental work, mutual-problem discussion, increased cooperation between divisions, and a broader knowledge of all subjects related to quality control activities. Figure 10-1 shows how the committees and task groups might be structured. Task-group assignments are to explore and study specific applications and to organize and publish their findings as recommended practices in quality control and inspection operation manuals. Task-group formation and assignments are frequently changed in order to keep abreast of current operating problems.

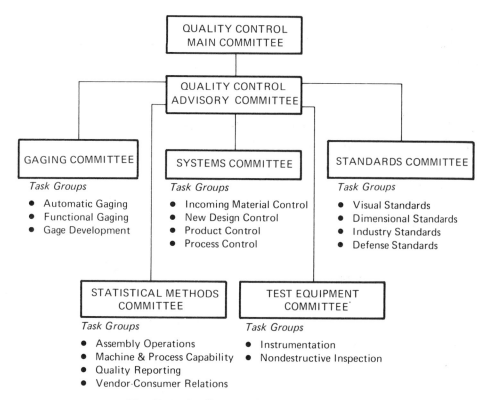

Fig. 10-1 Quality committees and task groups

Total Quality Control

Nowadays, many organizations have given thought, and in some cases substance, to what might be considered as an ideal quality control organization. The "total quality control" concept was originated by Dr. A. V. Feigenbaum in the 1950's. At the time, he was Manager of Manufacturing Operations and Quality Control at General Electric staff headquarters in New York City. The philosophy and techniques for implementing it are expressed in the book published in 1961 (see the references at the end of the chapter).

Actually, it is difficult to train people in this approach since it is as much a "state of mind" as it is a "course of action." It involves inculcating all organization members—from top management to hourly workers—with the concept that product quality should be first and foremost in everyone's mind. Product quality is defined as "the composite product characteristics of engineering and manufacture that determine the degree to which the product in use will meet the expectations of the customer." Terms such as reliability, serviceability, and maintainability are defined as characteristics which contribute to the composite product quality. While this may be tacitly accepted, there is frequently a tendency to consider them as separate entities, with small subgroups specifically responsible to assure they receive attention.

The book presents quality control as a body of technical, analytical, and managerial knowledge which Dr. Feigenbaum perceived could be applied to any stage in the industrial cycle. Within each cycle, applicable quality control techniques were delineated. This was undoubtedly one reason for the misconceptions which developed in respect to implementing the total-quality-control philosophy. Indeed, a person reading the book, particularly Chapter 3, can get the impression that total quality control superimposes an elaborate system on the already existing system. The reaction from other departments is that quality control is infringing on the autonomy of their operations, and thus expected resentment occurs.

Quality control activities during the production cycle are described in three main categories: new design control, incoming material control, and product control. The specific activities in the cycle are

1. New design control.
    a. Selling quality products.
    b. Engineering quality products.
    c. Planning quality processes.
2. Incoming material control.
    a. Buying quality material.
    b. Receiving and inspecting quality material.
3. Product control.
    a. Manufacturing quality parts and products.
    b. Inspecting and testing quality products.
    c. Shipping quality products.
    d. Installing and servicing quality products.

Control, by definition, means (1) the act or power of directing; authority; superintendence; (2) a check, restraint; a means of comparison, as for verifying. Therefore, appending the word to the quality activity reinforces opposition to the concept. Although everyone is subjected to some controls on the job, most people strenuously object to the imposition of added controls. As can be noted from the categorical list, practically everything associated with the product is included in some control activity—sales, product and process engineering, purchasing, material control, manufacturing, inspection, shipping, and servicing. The implication is that people in these various activities are not performing adequately—at least from the quality-objective viewpoint—and that controls are necessary to assure adherence to quality and reliability standards. The astute individual is aware that quality and reliability standards frequently fluctuate and are influenced by factors such as production volume and cost. While the factors are critical in enterprise success, they are no more important in the long run than quality and reliability standards, and nothing is more demoralizing to industrial personnel than fluctuating standards.

To avoid any misconceptions concerning total quality control as advocated by Dr. Feigenbaum, the following statements regarding organization are given†:

Total-quality-control programs thus require, as an initial step, top management's re-emphasis of the respective quality responsibilities and accountabilities of all company employees in new-design control, in incoming-material control, in product control, and in special-process studies.
The second principle of total-quality-control organization is a corollary to this first one: because quality is everybody's job in a business, it may become nobody's job. Thus the second step required in total-quality programs becomes clear. Top management must

†*Total Quality Control*, p. 49 (see the references).

recognize that the many individual responsibilities for quality will be exercised most effectively when they are buttressed and serviced by a well-organized, genuinely modern management function whose only area of specialization is product quality, whose only area of operation is in the quality-control jobs, and whose only "responsibilities" are to be sure that the products shipped are right—and at the right quality cost.

The need for top management support is evident and is emphasized by Dr. Feigenbaum. This is obviously nothing new, since management support is required for any activity to be successful, but it is too frequently used as an excuse for inaction. Management is never quoted as opposing quality efforts—in fact, quite the contrary—but if items such as production, cost, and quality are ranked by importance, they often occur precisely in that order. A quality attitude survey, conducted in 1969 by Quality Research Management Consultants, Ann Arbor, Michigan, reported on the quality attitudes of presidents and general managers in the metal-working industry. One question asked them to rate, by organization level, what they felt was the attitude toward achieving good product quality. The results are shown in Figure 10-2.

Level	Strong	Adequate	Weak	Total
Upper management	57%	36%	7%	100%
Middle management	21%	61%	18%	100%
First-line supervision	14%	46%	40%	100%
Salaried nonsupervision	—	37%	63%	100%
Hourly personnel	—	25%	75%	100%

Fig. 10-2 Quality attitude survey

The figures indicate that upper management feels that even when they themselves place strong emphasis on product quality that this attitude diminishes rapidly further down in the organization. If this is true, it is an indictment of top management, since they are evidently not communicating effectively with the organization or else they are actually placing greater emphasis on other aspects of the operation. In other words, they communicate instead the attitude "Don't do as I do, do as I say," while those below think to themselves, "What you are speaks so loudly that I can't hear what you say."

An editorial comment in *Quality Management and Engineering*, July 1971, stated that if the United States is to be reestablished as the unquestionable leader in product quality, U.S. management must shake the cobwebs loose and apply a few basic, yet positive, uncomplicated rules:

- Establish a clear and understandable quality policy without deviating.
- Require that intended end use of the product is thoroughly determined.
- Demand that specifications reflect intended use.
- Ascertain that the product looks and performs like the specifications.
- Insist that advertising accurately and briefly describes product use and performance.

Undoubtedly, the most succinct quality policy is that advocated by Phillip B. Crosby, Vice-President and Director of Reliability and Quality Control, International Telephone and Telegraph. This policy states: "Perform exactly like the requirement or cause the requirement to be changed officially to what we and the customer really need." ITT has a formal 14-step quality implementation program which was described in detail on page 25 in *Quality Management and Engineering*, January 1975.

THE QUALITY CONTROL ENGINEERING FUNCTION

The ultimate objective of the quality control endeavor is to provide quality assurance for the finished product and to assure optimum quality costs. To accomplish this objective, a manufacturer needs an integrated program for product quality control, including its reliability elements. The activity in totality will be subsequently described under work elements, but these should not be construed to imply that all this is expected of any single quality control engineer or any particular quality control organization. It should be emphasized that a quality control engineer may engage or specialize in only one or a few elements and still be performing an adequate job. In essence, quality control engineering encompasses the planning and execution of the analysis, the control, the evaluation, and the reporting for all quality aspects from product conception through manufacture, processing, storage, delivery, installation, maintenance, and repair to the end of its service life.

Obviously all industrial organization functions have specific responsibilities for a quality product. It should not be a quality control engineer's intention to usurp or conflict in any way with these responsibilities. The quality control activity, does, however, provide an effective way to acquaint each supervisor and engineer with specific and overall quality costs, thus enabling him to make decisions leading to optimum product cost and quality.

The activity which coordinates and directs the planning, control, evaluation, and reporting for all the quality aspects of the production task is definitely engineering and is characterized by creative work. Statistics, technical process and product knowledge, and practical shop experience are combined in attaining the goal—optimum-quality products at the lowest possible cost.

The quality control engineering work elements are in six broad categories:

1. General engineering.
2. New design engineering.
3. Incoming material engineering.
4. Process engineering.
5. Product evaluation engineering.
6. Special activities engineering.

Within each category there are certain specific work elements which further clarify the full extent of the quality control engineer's task. These will be dealt with individually, with an explanation and examples for clarification wherever pertinent.

General Engineering

Training and Promotion Programs

Educational material should be prepared for conducting training programs in all the various quality control aspects. It is also essential that training be conducted at all levels of the organization, the material presented being in accordance with the desired end results.

Quality Standards

Where required, develop quality standards on quantitative characteristics, such as dimensional and functional variables, and on qualitative characteristics, such as visual, audio, and tactile variables.

Measurement and Analytical Facilities

Responsibilities may entail determining, recommending, and/or designing, procuring, and qualifying measuring equipment essential for product quality evaluation. Equipment surveillance should include developing an economic program for periodic precision and accuracy checks on all measurement and analytical facilities.

Methods and Procedures

Forms and instructions for collecting, analyzing, and reporting quality data should be developed. In addition, procedures for identifying responsibility and implementing actions should be instituted.

Discrepant Material

The procedure for the disposition of material which does not conform to quality and functional requirements should be clearly established, along with the responsibility for such material and the proper extra-cost allocation.

Program Audit

To properly evaluate the effectiveness of instituted control measures, methods should be established for auditing which will reflect the quality control program costs and savings.

New Design Engineering

Since the quality engineering function is normally cognizant of field problems, this information as it relates to product design can often prove invaluable to the product engineer. Some specific work element areas follow.

Product and Process Research

This should involve designing and analyzing experiments and tests to determine what variables affect component product and process quality. Means should also be devised to analyze and evaluate products and product designs from suppliers.

Specifications

Collect and present data obtained from the field, manufacturing, and vendors concerning previous design deficiencies. Recommend suggested solutions to the design engineer which will minimize or eliminate these problems.

Tolerances

Acquaint product engineering with the statistical concepts of tolerancing and utilize, where available, process capability studies to predict overall product tolerances. Conversely, the product tolerance may be used to determine specific component tolerances. On complex systems, investigate computer use and Monte-Carlo simulation techniques as predictive devices.

Initial Samples

Develop statistical approaches to adequately evaluate the limited quantity usually available on initial product samples. Compare to design objectives, realizing that 100 percent conformance is rarely obtained and is often unnecessary. The statistical-tolerance-limits technique will enable predicting with specified confidence and specified population proportion when as few as two items (two-sided limits) are tested or as few as three (one-sided limits).

Methods of Achieving Quality Production

Assist production engineering in attaining process improvements on fixtures, tools, jigs, inspection and testing devices, where such improvements are required to achieve process control and maintain desired quality.

Trial Runs

Determine which trial lot characteristics are to be measured and controlled. Collect and use data to predict future production lot performance.

Incoming Material Engineering

Since finished product quality is critically influenced by the purchased material quality, the quality control engineer has an indirect responsibility regarding supplier selection and a direct responsibility for incoming material economic control. Accordingly, the following work elements are required to accomplish this objective.

Supplier Capability

Determine suppliers' ability to meet quality requirements and develop a performance rating system. Use this information to assist purchasing in selecting those suppliers capable of meeting established quality levels.

Quality Requirements

Through purchasing, provide suppliers with what is desired in quality requirements. Provide adequate follow-up to determine that the supplier fully understands and adheres to these specifications.

Inspection Methods

Thoroughly understand inspection equipment and methods used by a supplier. Coordinate and correlate these with equipment and methods employed by the consuming plant to avoid mistakes and misunderstandings.

Documentation and Feedback

Develop systems which provide information relating to supplier conformance and channel this information to the proper authorities.

Process Engineering

Capability Studies

Make capability studies on new and current production equipment and processes. Determine the measurements to be taken, the analysis of data, and the action required to correct undesirable conditions.

Process Controls

Adequate process controls should be established wherever required to maintain an economic control. To some extent, computers are now being used for this purpose. Written procedures and instructions should be available for personnel performing this activity to avoid confusion and permit uniformity in results.

Periodic Review

All continuous-type process controls should be reviewed on a periodic basis to eliminate those no longer required, to evaluate the effectiveness of those which will be continued, and to determine new areas which might require additional effort.

Troubleshooting

When evidence exists on out-of-control conditions, the quality control engineer should assist manufacturing and/or engineering personnel in identifying and interpreting contributing causes.

Designed Experiments

To avoid effort duplication, it is essential that a planned and formalized approach be employed in problem solution involving either process or product. Such study results should be communicated to those responsible for instituting corrective measures.

Product Evaluation Engineering

This portion is concerned with the development, installation, and maintenance of inspection practices and product evaluation procedures to ensure that only those products which meet rigid quality requirements are shipped. It is, in essence, the auditing function and has the work elements discussed below.

Inspection Methods

Employ whatever methods are essential to adequately evaluate the product quality level. This should involve determining the compatibility between process and product acceptance.

Sampling Plans

Formal and/or informal sampling plans using lot-by-lot or continuous procedures should be developed and applied.

Feedback

Information generated at the end of the production line should be fed back into the system so that corrective action can be taken with minimum delay.

Quality Levels and Defect Classifications

Establish desirable quality-level defect classification systems and defect weighting factors for a complete quality rating on all components of the completed product.

Auditing

It is essential that an outgoing quality audit be performed on all products. Accordingly, those procedures required to implement the activity must be developed.

Complaints

Analyze customer complaints, defective material notices, and field reports. Identify causes and responsibility, and initiate corrective action.

Inventory Evaluation

Material which is subject to deterioration in storage should be periodically sampled to ensure that the quality level remains acceptable. In addition, institute policies which will optimize quality and minimize cost.

Special Activities Engineering

These work elements are general in nature and are not in the engineer's everyday activity.

New Techniques

Do not be content with the old method or technique. Develop and search for new approaches and techniques in problem solving.

Special Studies

Assist personnel in management functions such as safety, finance, and production control in developing statistical approaches to their problems.

The Cost Approach to Quality

Since cost is inextricably woven all through an industrial activity, the quality control engineer must be aware of cost factors, how they relate to the function, and how these factors may be utilized to promote and evaluate the function effectiveness. It should be obvious that inspection and quality control activities are, by their nature, intangible and, as such, often defy adequate justification on a cost basis. One of the few measures which could be employed to evaluate effectiveness would be to suspend the function for a predetermined time period and note the outcome. The inherent dangers in this approach, however, do not permit its application on an extended basis. Suffice it to say that measurement rules are available and will be developed in subsequent discussion.

A first effort at conceptually defining quality costs is attributed to Dr. A. V. Feigenbaum, formerly with General Electric Company. Dr. Feigenbaum divided the cost of quality into three general areas: failure, appraisal, and prevention. The cost elements for each area follow.

Failure Costs

Losses, Errors, and Defects. These are usually accumulated in a special account and can readily be referred to for a cost figure.

Field Campaigns. These often result from engineering errors but can contribute heavily to the failure-cost dollar.

Repair Time. When allowed on a particular operation or product, it represents a departure from the optimum conditions and thus becomes another cost factor.

Warranty and Policy. Money spent in this category results from both engineering and manufacturing deficiencies and thus should be preventable.

Breach of Warranty and Liability. Although the cost figures for this are usually difficult to obtain, the engineer should consider the legal implications and costs involved in substandard quality and reliability.

Contact Engineering. This is the expense incurred because of inferior quality or other nonconformance to specifications which must be resolved at an engineering level.

Material Procurement. The expense involved in rejecting and/or reworking material should be recognized as another failure cost.

Appraisal Costs

Inspection. This element should include equipment and labor costs which comprise the largest inspection budget segment.

Test. Such testing as is required for final product acceptance, together with equipment costs, should be determined.

Quality Audits. These were mentioned previously in work elements and are an appropriate part of appraising product quality.

Laboratory Acceptance and Measurement Services. While these are not under quality engineering jurisdiction, services rendered for quality and reliability purposes are a part of appraisal costs.

Prevention Costs

Quality Control Engineering and Administration. These activity work elements have been defined previously, and the cost associated with the function is preventive.

Training. For any activity such as this to be completely successful, training must be conducted at all organization levels. Any money spent in this way can also be considered preventive. Failure prevention analysis (FPA) and failure mode and effects analysis (FMEA) are relatively new techniques used by engineers.

Generally, failure costs are high when product conformance to quality and reliability requirements is low, decreasing as better conformance is achieved. Prevention costs, however, usually rise when higher conformance is desired. Appraisal costs may involve both aspects. Those which are primarily sorting and segregating are reduced with improved conformance, while those which are preventive in nature tend to increase with better performance. The general relationships among failure, appraisal, and prevention costs are shown in Figure 10-3 and indicate that the optimum total cost occurs when the sum is a minimum.

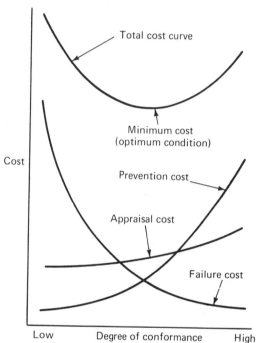

Fig. 10-3 Quality cost curves

While the curves are easily sketched, they are often difficult to obtain in practice. Utilizing others' knowledge in the quality field is one way to provide some guidelines. Dr. J. M. Juran at one time discovered that when quality costs are in the neighborhood of $500–$1,000 per productive employee per year or higher, a company may gain by spending more on prevention. Dr. Feigenbaum believes that quality costs exceeding 10 percent of sales are normally reducible. Also, if prevention costs are less than 10 percent of the total quality costs, failure and appraisal costs should be reduced by spending more on prevention. As stated, these are only guidelines. In actuality, the absolute magnitude should be the criterion for justifying the program cost to reduce failure and appraisal costs.

To determine effectiveness with an apparently adequate prevention budget, it is often advisable to compare quality-engineering-function activities against the following check list.

1. Is there a clear separation in responsibility between the people who perform the day-to-day activities and those who do the long-range planning and analytical work?

2. Is the team approach employed in problem solving, or is it some frustrated person's responsiblity?

3. Are prevention principles recognized and employed?
    a. Engineering approach:
        - Define the problem.
        - Study conditions.
        - Plan possible solutions.
        - Evaluate possible solutions.
        - Recommend a solution.
        - Follow up to assure action.
        - Check results.
    b. Separate the vital from the trivial.
    c. Obtain staff assistance.
    d. Coordinate others' activities.

4. Are chronic rather than sporadic problems tackled?

5. Are operator-controlled defects distinguished from management-controllable defects and an appropriate program developed for each?

6. Are relevant data, such as process capability studies, made available to those who can institute corrective action or employ this information most effectively?

7. Are quality plans developed well in advance in order to avoid trouble, rather than to effect cures?

8. On complex products, is there a separate design evaluation prior to its release to production?

Consideration should also be given to appraisal-cost magnitude, since in many situations it may amount to more than half the total cost. The measures usually employed are expressed as a ratio: inspection cost to manufacturing cost, or inspection head count to operator head count. Although many plants use such an index, it is fallacious to assume that inspection costs should vary with productive effort. The costs should actually depend on frequency, or potential frequency, of failure.

Appraisal costs normally arise from two basic situations: (1) costs incurred in sorting and segregating acceptable and nonacceptable material; (2) costs incurred in sampling either the process or the product. If the first cost constitutes the major portion, the cost for not removing the defects or defectives can readily be compared to the cost for removing them. The former cost will consist of repairs, wasted operations, teardown and repair, production line downtime, field failures, and customer returns. When these are compared to inspection costs, a rational economic decision can be made to either continue or replace the screening operation with a sampling system or to discontinue it completely. Examining frequency failures and the pattern in which they occur will indicate whether or not sampling can be utilized. Determining whether costs are excessive when they are primarily expended on sampling is much more difficult. It was previously suggested that one method for evaluating inspection effectiveness would consist in eliminating the activity. This could be analogous to not performing a surgical operation and noting whether or not the patient dies. A preferred approach would be to investigate each specific situation and note whether facts which would permit a significant reduction in inspection or control have been overlooked. Possible items to check are

1. Can rejected-lot recurrence be prevented? Where this involves screening material, a substantial decrease in cost should occur.

2. Does a material review normally accept rejected material anyway? If so, specifications may be changed to conform with existing practices.

3. Are these two conditions combined; i.e., is rejected material ultimately accepted and no action taken to prevent occurrence? If this is true, inspection is obviously a waste of money.

4. Is reduced or skip lot inspection used when the vendor has a good history and discrepant material is rarely encountered?

5. Is it possible to relocate the inspection station so that efficiency is improved by inspecting earlier or later in the system flow?

6. Can the operator perform the inspection and make decisions in the inspector's place?

7. Is there a better way to perform the inspection, i.e., a changed layout or installing automated equipment?

The minimum inspection required is that needed to verify that quality is, and continues to be, satisfactory. The ultimate would be an audit inspection for incoming, in-process, and outgoing product. If more than this is required, the ultimate has yet to be attained.

Two methods for assessing the cost problem in quality are those used by management consultants such as Dorian Shainin of Rath and Strong, Inc., and Harmon Bayer of Bayer, Kobert, and Associates. In the first, these men differentiate between those costs which can be classed as avoidable and those considered unavoidable. The unavoidable costs are those associated with making the product right the first time. All other costs are considered avoidable— inspection labor, scrap, rework, reoperation, customer service as applied to quality items, overtime hours caused by reruns or repairs on rejected material, downtime caused by interrupted schedules required to remake rejected parts, and all other similar costs. Admittedly, very few organizations will have records sufficiently complete to permit as detailed a cost analysis as this implies. However, it is usually possible to obtain an accurate approximation by sampling for a predetermined time period and recording the losses which occur. A record system should be established for the areas selected to include labor, material, and burden. Identification may be department, part number, operation number, operator name, dimension, or reason for rejection. The second method is often called the Pareto distribution or the Lorenz curve and involves ranking the costs connected with quality in order to select those which promise the major return for the effort expended. Ranking and cumulating the costs in descending order of magnitude usually reveal some maldistribution. It is often discovered that a condition exists whereby 3 out of 10 departments (machines, operators, defect types, dimensions) are responsible for approximately 70 to 90 percent of the total. Whether the major contributors are 3 or more, once they are isolated the quality control engineer can exert the major effort on these "vital few" as opposed to the "trivial many" others.

DESIGNING THE QUALITY INSPECTION SYSTEM[1]

A quality inspection system should be designed with controls which will maintain some specified quality level by regularly scheduling inspection for components and assemblies. The inspection may take place before, during, and/or after the machining and assembly operations. Its purpose may be to control, to sort, or to audit. It is most important to emphasize that "an ounce of prevention is worth a pound of cure." In other words, the system should be designed to prevent trouble, rather than to take action after the fact. A quality inspection system can operate effectively only through control and accurate problem diagnosis. This requires detecting defects when they occur and then providing information to those having authority in the area so that

[1]Adapted from F. R. Devic, *Methods for Design Reliability and Manufacturing Quality, Sec. 10;* ed. H. C. Charbonneau, GM Institute publication, 1972.

corrective action can be taken. The system must, therefore, monitor the man-machine-material-measurement variation in order to maintain the specified outgoing quality level. Inspection frequency, production rate, equipment, and operator characteristics and capabilities are all factors which will determine the requisite system scope and magnitude.

The system concept includes the following elements: personnel, job instruction, equipment, layout information system, and documentation. For discussion purposes, these will be considered under the headings (1) station location and work assignment, (2) personnel and training, (3) information system, and (4) station documentation.

Station Location and Work Assignment

The first element is done by planning where the inspection stations should be located, by deciding which part characteristics need to be checked, and by determining the frequency with which parts should be checked. It is logical to start at the receiving area and continue through the manufacturing process.

Receiving inspection can vary from none to the strict application of MIL-STD 105D, depending on part nature and importance. *First-piece inspection* consists of checking initial production for operations being set up to run where quality is dominated by the process and production-operator checks can maintain the quality. *In-process inspection* is done at points where the parts are leaving one department for another. *Finished goods inspection* in done at points where manufacturing or assembly operations are completed. *Roving inspection* is done at various locations as problems arise or are anticipated. Separate inspection points are set up on occasion to check results following repairs or salvage work on rejected stock.

Decisions with respect to what characteristics to check and how often may be made separately or jointly by the quality control engineer, the inspection supervisor, or the inspector. Interrelated factors considered are part design and criticality, equipment type and capability, and previous experience.

Part Design. Difficult-to-measure characteristics tend to require special gages and to take more time, resulting in reduced inspection frequency. Failure prevention analysis can assist in meeting design intent.

Part Criticality. Governmental and defense department classifications directly affect inspection frequency.

Equipment Type. Machines in different-type categories and yet performing the same basic operation will generate different output characteristics. For instance, metal removal on a lathe will produce different characteristic variations in size, taper, out-of-round, and surface finish than when done on a grinder. High-volume equipment may require automatic gaging as opposed to low-volume equipment with manual gaging.

Equipment Capability. Capability studies can provide necessary information on which characteristics are well in control, borderline, or constantly in trouble. Auditing will suffice when total spread is well within tolerance; statistical control is required in borderline situations; 100 percent inspection is required when the total spread significantly exceeds the tolerance.

Previous Experience. Only in this way can equipment having peculiar characteristics be guarded against. Special attention is called for when warranty problems have occurred previously. Failure mode analysis can anticipate potential problems even before they are experienced.

Once the above factors have been evaluated in totality, information will be available on part characteristics and checking frequency. Then, when gages and test equipment are specified, along with instructions for calibration and maintenance, it is possible to determine how many inspectors are needed. Actual gage placement, with necessary stands and storage cabinets, should be coordinated with the layout function to provide adequate space for instruments, inspectors, and unacceptable parts.

Correct part identification is also necessary for a successful system. Personnel must be completely acquainted with the various parts produced within each given area and the corresponding inspection procedures for the requisite specifications. Procedures must include identifying instructions as to accepted, rejected, scrapped, or stored as well as shift, machine, and operation. Other pertinent information requiring instructions would include defect type or other characteristics, recognizing part status (scrap, repair), and routing parts by status to the proper destination.

Instructions must include setting and reviewing the explicit or implicit standards needed in making decisions. Terms such as "commercially acceptable" are too vague to be unequivocally

Fig. 10-4 Typical instruction form

QUALITY CONTROL JOB INSTRUCTIONS

PART OR STATION NAME	Housing	MODEL YEAR 1971	DATE EFFECT. 9-22-70	SUPERSEDES ISSUE DATED 11-11-68	PART OR STATION NO.	FILE NO.
PREPARED BY	APPROVED BY		FACT. NO.	LOCATION	Section 2 Bay J	FILE ORIG. UNTIL

Characteristic	Type of Inspection	Defect Class	Quan. Chkd & Freq.	Equipment Used	Special Instructions
Dimensions checked by T-330200	Air Gage		1 of 10	T-320200	Master air gages at start of shift and as needed.
Hub O.D. 2.670/2.666 dia.	Air Gage		1 of 10	Col. No. 1	
Piston I. D. 5.896/5.901	Air Gage		1 of 10	Col. No. 2	
Top I.D. 6.062/6.210 dia.	Air Gage		1 of 10	Col. No. 3	
Hub I.D. 1.957/1.959 dia			1 of 10	T-330976	
Bearing dim. 2.125/2.110	Dial gage		2 P/S	T-332912	DWC 7-9-70
Concentricity from I.D. To O.D.	Concentricity gage		2 P/S	T-332919	DWC 7-9-70
Top ring groove 6.220/6.210 Dia.			2 P/S	T-328241	

DISPOSITION & IDENTIFICATION OF PART

Gage inspected, acceptable parts placed in tubs provided, identify with shift paint provided.

Rejected parts placed in roller conveyor, repair or scrap.

QUALITY CONTROL REPORT

Report showing defect, number of pieces, good pieces; total run will be made out at end of shift.

interpreted and should be replaced with exact specification limits if at all possible. In those cases where it is impossible, a visual display board showing acceptable and unacceptable parts as examples will assist in eliminating individual opinions. So-called *salvage limits*—limits which are at variance with specifications but used to accept parts as usable nevertheless—should be absolutely avoided.

An example instruction form is shown in Figure 10-4; an inspector assignment form is shown in Figure 10-5. The inspection system design must include initial instructions. Periodic instruction review is a necessity, with the review frequency specified in the original design.

GENERAL

☐ Set all gages with masters per instructions of your supervisor. Make certain locating pads, contact points, and masters are clean.
Use all gages as specified by your supervisor. Report any defective or inoperative gages.
Air gage filters are to be cleaned at start and middle of shift by opening air filter petcock.
Identify all stock as acceptable or rejected. Deipose of stock in the specified manner.

SAFETY

☐ Wear safety glasses at all times in areas where they are required.　　　Report any unsafe conditions to your supervisor.
Safety shoes are recommended.　　　Keep your area clean and neat.

REVISIONS

☐ Any revisions to this job instruction are subject to the approval of the quality control assistant superintendent.

INSPECTOR INSTRUCTION REVIEW
The Employees Listed Below Were Assigned to, and Orally Instructed in the Proper Method of Performing, This Job Operation.

Name	Soc. Sec. No.	Job	Date Instr.	Oper. No.	Regular	Relief	Utility	Repair	Foreman Signature	Remarks

Fig. 10-5 Typical inspector assignment form

It is sometimes the practice for an inspection foreman to have a utility man assigned with the responsibility for training new and transferred employees. An additional responsibility may be to check their work periodically for accuracy. A simple means to evaluate accuracy is given by Dr. J. M. Juran and C. A. Melsheimer†:

†*Quality Planning and Analysis*, p. 321 (see the references).

$$\text{Accuracy (percent correctly identified)} = \left[\frac{d - k}{d - k + b}\right]100$$

where $d =$ number of bad units reported by the inspector,

          $k =$ number of good units rejected by the inspector,

   $d - k =$ true number of bad units found by the inspector,

          $b =$ number of bad units missed by the inspector,

$d - k + b =$ true number of bad units originally in product.

Personnel and Training

Although there could be disagreement about the relative importance assigned to the different system elements, most would agree that the people selected to perform the function are the key to overall effectiveness and success for any endeavor. It is the inspectors themselves—in adequate number, properly trained, dedicated, and properly motivated—who are finally responsible for quality in the product. However, all the dedication and motivation in the world cannot overcome training deficiencies. Various methods for effective training may be summarized as follows:

1. Personal experience: It is obtained only by first-hand exposure to everyday problems on the job.

2. Guided experience: Guidance is acquired in dealing with fellow workers and supervisors who give advice on methods and actions. The value directly depends on the capability and experience of those giving the advice.

3. Independent study: The person may become involved in a formal educational program or may informally acquire information by attending technical meetings. The value depends on personal ambition and capability.

4. Company classes: Training which is tailored for a specific purpose and sponsored by the company has the greatest potential.

New model startup or midyear revisions involving new products and procedures or drastic changes will require guidance training or company classes. In all training, key emphasis is on the inspection work elements as well as on instructions for measuring instruments. Video tape is a relatively new concept being used successfully. Although proper training is essential to technical competence, it must be recognized that motivation and dedication will be greatly influenced by the attitudes shown by immediate supervisors and fellow workers.

Information System

Some might consider providing for information feedback as the most important element in the inspection system design. Certainly, much of the previous planning will be nullified unless information on past and present product performance is provided in such a way and at such a time as to expedite immediate corrective action when it is called for. It needs to be emphasized that inspection effectiveness is reduced when it is used simply for process control or for sorting. Status reports showing quantity accepted and quantity rejected, with specific information on rejection reasons, must be provided to supervision. Audit reports conducted on a regular basis also supply worthwhile information. A sample approval program performed by plate-room layout at the model-year end will provide quantitative data for the following year.

It must be stressed that reports are always after the fact, that generally there is more paper work than necessary generated in business, and that computers are many times used to generate a superabundance just that much faster. Unless means are devised to provide immediate information to someone assigned responsibility for corrective action, any report becomes no more than a performance record with only historical value. Just as a product can be overdesigned for its necessary function, so can an information system be overdesigned with respect to information utility. All reports need to be critically scrutinized for utility compatible with cost.

Station Documentation

A formal method is required to assure that the inspection system design has accomplished all necessary steps. This purpose can be handled by a check sheet such as that in Figure 10-6, which will ensure that all basic components for the system have been reviewed and will show what decisions were made with corresponding reasons. The form will then show detailed data useful for future system review and also for governmental and defense department documentation if necessary. The form can be modified as desirable to provide similar information for each inspection station.

Fig. 10-6 Typical inspection system checklist

INSPECTION SYSTEM DESIGN

Factory Number _____   Dept. Number _____
Part Number _____   Part Name _____
Station Name _____
Model Year _____

The following items are to be considered in designing the inspection station.
Documentation of each step is enclosed.

Check if Completed

1. List potential problems due to the design, and include how inspection system will handle these problems ☐

2. List potential problems related to the process, and include how inspection system will handle these problems. ☐

3. Warranty, scrap, repair, and inspection costs have been documented and considered in inspection system plans. ☐

4. List type of inspection needed on eacy characteristic (100% sampling, audit, visual gage test); show reason for selection. ☐

5. Manpower requirements have been established to adequately operate inspection system. ☐

6. Training program for supervision and hourly personnel on new requirements and potential problem areas has been formulated. ☐

7. Detailed job descriptions have been completed with provisions for recording those who have been instructed. System also provides for periodic reinstruction. ☐

8. System has been estblished to periodically verify the accuracy of masters and gaging equipment. ☐

9. Items to be covered by floor auditors have been estblished and audit forms provided. ☐

10. System satisfies all requirements for documentation required and/or federal motor vehicle safety standards. ☐

11. Reporting system has been defined, including the following forms: ☐
    a. Inspectors data sheets, OK pieces, rejects, scrap by ciritcal dims.
    b. Audit sheets.
    c. Special reports—sediment, roundness, etc.
    d. Summary reports, daily, weekly by part, department, etc.

Q.E. responsible for plan _____

Reviewed with _____ Q.C.   Date _____
              _____ Q.C.   Date _____
              _____ M.M.   Date _____
              _____ Prod.   Date _____
              _____ Rel.   Date _____

GAGE AND TEST EQUIPMENT REQUIREMENTS[2]

In general, all gaging and test equipment may be referred to as measuring devices. As such, only when product characteristics are expressed as numbers can these devices measure the degree to which a part meets the specified values. Lord Kelvin put this thought in words in 1883: "When you can measure what you are speaking about and express it in numbers, you know something about it." An extensive, but not exhaustive, list showing characteristics which commonly must be checked for conformity follows:

1. Size.
2. Weight.
3. Shape.
4. Dynamic and static strength.
5. Chemical and/or metallurgical material content.
6. Hardness.
7. Surface finish.
8. Volume.
9. Fatigue life.
10. Torque.
11. Thermal features.
12. Assembly fit.

Part Print Review

A part as simple as a piston pin (Figure 10-7) can be used to illustrate many characteristics. Size requirements are in the majority. The weight requirement is stated. The shape is implied to be cylindrical by the drawing convention, but nothing has been mentioned about taper, out-of-round, or concentricity. Static and dynamic strength requirements should be obtained from product engineering. The SAE 1019 material specification would be standard chemical and metallurgical requirements. Surface and core hardness specifications are stated. Surface finish is specified for the outside diameter. Fatigue life in cycles to failure would be required from product engineering. Thermal characteristics should be considered since the part is exposed to

Fig. 10-7 Piston pin

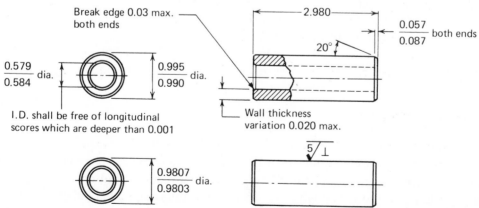

[2]Adapted from N. J. Campbell, *Methods for Design Reliability and Manufacturing Quality, Sec. 11;* ed. H. C. Charbonneau, GM Institute publication, 1972.

213

extreme temperature changes; this is again something to be obtained from product engineering. Assembly fit would be considered with respect to the piston and connecting rod and would be found on the assembly print. Common practice would call for segregation into several size classifications for assembly purposes. Thus volume and torque were the only two characteristics not involved in such a simple part. Questions considered in reviewing the print to make sure that nothing had been overlooked would be, Are all specifications understandable? Are additional specifications required? Are some specifications in conflict with others? Product engineering is the source for all the above information, which constitutes the "bible" insofar as everyone else is concerned.

Essentially, the procedural sequence is this: Product design information is received and specifications are evaluated; the gaging and test equipment are selected, and the inspection system is developed; a procurement schedule is established; equipment is ordered, designed, built, and shipped; received equipment is checked for compliance to specifications and put in operation; equipment is maintained in proper operating condition and in conformance with design changes.

Review with Other Engineers

It has been previously indicated that questionable, unstated, and implicit specifications are resolved in consultation with the product engineer. Occasionally, it will be discovered that there are errors existing which require a design change.

The gage engineer will next discuss the manufacturing process with the process engineer. This will start with receiving the purchased extrusion and will include design parameters, how the part is to be processed, what machines will be used, and what in-process gaging is planned. It must be determined that the in-process gaging is compatible with the final inspection gaging to avoid rejection as a result of differences between the two systems. Also, consideration should be given to the process control system at this time. It would seem desirable to have an automatic machine to gage the parts 100 percent, separating rejects from acceptable parts and separating acceptable parts into specified fit classifications. The process engineering review may uncover unrealistic characteristics or tolerances requiring design changes.

The gage engineer would discuss the failure mode analysis with the reliability engineer to make sure that special test requirements are considered. Meeting with the quality control engineer, as well as with floor inspection personnel, will assure complete consideration for the inspection system and controls. Quality on subsequent operations will be enhanced by discussion with the methods engineer responsible for the assembly operation involving the connecting rod, piston, and piston pin. Visits made to other companies manufacturing the same or similar parts can be a two-way street involving mutual information exchange.

This complete review with other engineers will provide sufficient preparation for a preliminary gaging plan covering specific design features and the corresponding gaging.

Equipment Selection

Prior to considering various aspects which affect the final selection, mention will be made of general equipment types which might be used. Standard gages would be micrometers, calipers, plain and thread plugs, plain and thread rings, and snap and indicating-snap gages. Unique custom gages having a specific design intent include flush-pin gages, dial indicators, fixed gages, and air gages. Test equipment items are hardness testers, optical comparators, surface-finish analyzers, non-destructive-testing eddy-current devices, and magnetic-particle and ultrasonic devices for surface and/or internal discontinuity checks.

Questions to be asked about specific aspects are

1. Is the part to be placed on the gage or vice versa?
2. Is it feasible to check more than one characteristic with a single gage?
3. Will some gages be used to audit for control purposes?
4. Will 100 percent or more inspection be required on certain items?
5. Is a go/no-go gage applicable, or is a specific readout necessary with the tolerance limits shown?
6. Will operator capabilities limit gage complexity?
7. What backup system is needed for certain situations? Will the backup readout be compatible (contact versus noncontact, automatic versus hand gage) with the primary system?
8. What about part location and orientation (three-point location versus full-contact ring)?

Possible equipment selected for the piston pin might be

1. Micrometers for outside diameters.
2. Plug gages for internal diameters.
3. Adjustable snap gage for received extrusion.
4. Air or electronic snap gage for finish-ground outside diameter.
5. Size snap gage with "V" locator to measure radius for outside diameter if generated by centerless grinding and subject to lobe characteristics.
6. Caliper gage for wall thickness.
7. Automatic size and classification gage for 100 percent inspect and identify sizes.
8. Scales to check finished weight.
9. Rockwell hardness tester.
10. Optical comparator to check lead form, a feature required for assembly.
11. Surface analyzer for microfinish.
12. Roundness checker for shape.
13. Automatic hardness tester using eddy currents to check material variation, skin hardness, and core hardness.
14. Dynamic durability test unit to functionally load and cycle for strength characteristics.

Equipment Procurement Schedule

The first thing to do is to determine the requirement dates. Assembly plant pilot schedules would be needed for assemblies and subassemblies. Machining plant schedules for pilot parts also would have to be procured from process engineering. Using delivery dates for sheet metal dies, the gage engineer would plan, preferably for tryout at the die manufacturer's facilities prior to delivery.

Next, the gage engineer must establish how much lead time is required for obtaining the various gages, considering that standard catalog items would frequently be available on an overnight basis, while sophisticated equipment might require more than a year to obtain. Additional lead time must be planned to verify conformity to specifications as well as to anticipate correction for errors in complex equipment. Also, the engineer will recognize that some items may require quotations from more than one source.

Typical lead times for the indicated piston pin equipment are

- Standard gages: 2 weeks
- Air and electronic hand gages: 4 to 8 weeks
- Rockwell hardness tester: 4 to 8 weeks
- Surface analyzer: 4 to 8 weeks
- Optical comparator: 4 to 8 weeks
- Roundness tester: 8 to 12 weeks
- Automatic hardness tester: 30 to 40 weeks
- Automatic gage for size and classification: 30 to 40 weeks, plus installation and debugging

Equipment Qualification and Control

Inspection for accuracy and compliance to specifications is done when the equipment is delivered. When required by governmental and defense department safety standards, documentation is done at that time. Any deviation from design specifications must be approved by the gage engineer. A check on application is made by using the gage on prototype parts which have been qualified by dimensional layouts. A qualified gage is released to the manufacturing department in time for the production run, with instructions given to quality control personnel relative to its use and why it is necessary. Then, complete and accurate records are essential to maintaining equipment in proper operating condition and current with design changes. Periodic scheduled review is desirable and is mandatory with safety standards.

A checklist to aid in determining gaging requirements is shown in Figure 10-8.

EVALUATING AN EXISTING QUALITY INSPECTION SYSTEM[3]

The following truism was stated many times in quality control's early days: "You can't inspect quality into a product—it must be built into it." Therefore it is entirely proper to concentrate on manufacturing and design when looking for the primary failure source whenever product failure occurs. However, the product engineers often say, "If they would only build them like we design them, everything would be perfectly OK." Consequently, it is also true that it was the quality inspection system which, as a secondary source, permitted the defective product to be accepted somewhere during the manufacturing process and to get in the customer's hands.

In introductory comments with regard to designing the quality inspection system, it was mentioned that controls are needed to maintain a specified quality level. Also, "a quality inspection system can operate effectively only through control and accurate problem diagnosis. This requires . . . providing information . . . so that corrective action can be taken." It will be apparent, then, that analyzing an existing system is concerned with two aspects: the control system and the information system. Even though the two will be discussed separately, it can be understood that this is only for the sake of convenience since they are inseparable in actual practice.

Evaluating the Control System

A logical approach to evaluation is to consider indicators which can identify problem areas, how to use the indicators, and problem area analysis.

[3]Adapted from E. R. Powers, *Methods for Design Reliability and Manufacturing Quality*, *Sec. 16;* ed. H. C. Charbonneau, GM Institute publication, 1972.

Fig. 10-8 Typical gaging requirements checklist

GAGING REQUIREMENTS

Part Name _____ Model Year _____
Part Number _____ Station _____
Factory Number _____
Department Number _____

The following should be considered in determining gage requirements.

Check if Completed

1. Examine product print for specified characteristics such as
   a. Size
   b. Weight
   c. Shape
   d. Strength (dynamic and static)
   e. Material content (chemical and/or metallurgical)
   f. Hardness
   g. Surface finish
   h. Volume
   i. Fatigue life
   j. Thermal features
   k. Assembly fit
   l. Torque
   m. Other
2. Relation to other parts
3. Consult product engineer to resolve any questions from 1 and 2
4. Consult production (process) engineer with regard to
   a. Machining process
   b. Machining equipment
   c. Process sheets
   d. In-process gaging (coordinate with final inspection gaging)
   e. Control system
   f. General information exchange
5. Consult methods engineer to acquaint him with proposed system
6. Consult reliability engineer in respect to special test requirements planned
7. Consult quality control engineer with respect to
   a. Inspection planning
   b. Inspection system and controls
8. Consult quality control or inspection department in area where part will be produced
9. Review commercially available gages and equipment such as
   a. Standard types
      (1) Micrometer
      (2) Caliper
      (3) Plain plug
      (4) Thread plug
      (5) Thread ring
      (6) Plain ring
      (7) Snap
      (8) Indicator snap
      (9) Other
   b. Custom types
      (1) Flush pin
      (2) Dial indicator
      (3) Fixed gage
      (4) Air gage
      (5) Other
   c. Test equipment
      (1) Hardness testers
      (2) Optical comparators
      (3) Surface analyzers
      (4) Eddy current
      (5) Magnetic particle
      (6) Ultrasonic
      (7) Other
10. Gaging method
    a. Gage positioned on part
    b. Part positioned on gage
    c. Single dimension gaged
    d. Multiple dimensions gaged
11. Gage use
    a. Auditing for sample or control charts
    b. 100 percent inspection
    c. Is limit gage adequate?
    d. Is readout required? (Consider expanded scale)
    e. Is backup gaging required?
12. Lead time or scheduling program
    a. Establish need date by
       (1) Pilot schedules in assembly and machining plants
       (2) Die delivery dates
       (3) Vendor sample dates
       (4) Other
    b. Estimate time to
       (1) Design
       (2) Evaluate or review design
       (3) Process prints
       (4) Obtain cost quotations
       (5) Build
       (6) Deliver
       (7) Qualify, certify and/or correct
13. Design features
    a. Functional part locating and holding
    b. Accuracy (10 percent rule)
    c. Speed and repeatability
    d. Overdesign
    e. Design layout sheets describing function
    f. Compliance to Gm and divisional standards
14. Initiate order through purchasing
15. Expediting program
16. Record system
17. Maintenance program

Problem Area Indicators

Indicators may be divided into two classes: internal indicators, which are generated internal to the manufacturing process and facilities, and external indicators, which provide information on products found defective external to the manufacturing plant. Indicators in common use are listed below:

1. *Internal:*
    a. Scrap percentages or scrap costs.
    b. Rework percentages or rework costs.
    c. Test rejects or test repairs.
    d. Audit data.

2. *External:*
    a. Warranty reports.
    b. Service reports.
    c. Customer complaints.
    d. Reliability test reports.
    e. Assembly plant rejects.
    f. Assembly plant returned parts.
    g. Field failed-parts returns.
    h. Audit data.

It can be seen that the internal ones provide evidence on what the system is finding and rejecting, while the external ones show what the system is failing to find and reject. Acute need for system revision is evidenced when both internal and external indicator values agree with respect to problem area identification.

The need for valid data as indicator information cannot be overemphasized since it is the foundation for system evaluation. It is possible that information system weakness may come to light when validity is being considered.

How to Use Indicators

Since the purpose of using indicators is to identify problem areas, it is wise to first arrange them in logical sequence. For instance, a summary form would have the major headings "internal" and "external." Then, the internal subheadings would be major component or assembly inspection points in flow sequence insofar as possible, while the external subheadings would be arranged in time sequence. Using the operation chart (Figure 10-9) as an example, the internal subheadings would be "flange," "plate," "weight," "pulley," and "assembly," showing external subheadings such as "reliability test," "assembly plant rejects," and "warranty."

With an internal combustion engine assembly as an example, the internal subheadings might be "block test rejects," "block test teardown," and "reliability test." In this case, the major components would then be listed vertically down the left-hand column as "block," "cam," "head," "exhaust manifold," "intake manifold," and "water pump." In either situation, each component would list as subheadings the associated failure causes. For example, head failure causes might be "valve seat eccentric," "valve seat shy stock," "sand hole," and "cold shut."

Once all headings are arranged and a specific indicator such as scrap percentage is chosen, data are obtained and listed on the summary by classification. It should be obvious that simply listing failure quantities does not provide the weighting characteristic for an indicator which is important in establishing corrective action priorities. However, percentages and costs serve as proper weighting functions.

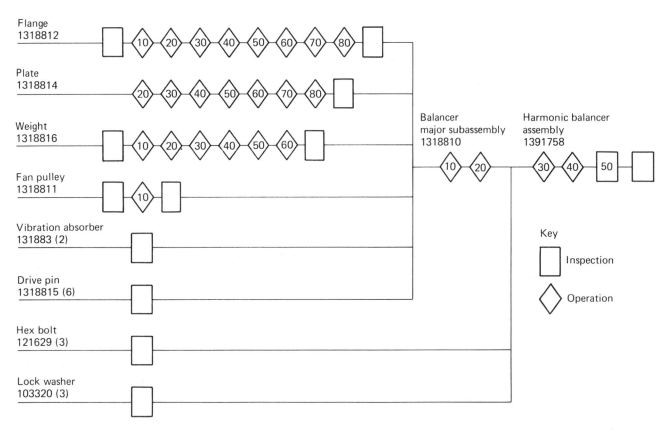

Fig. 10-9 Operation chart

Problem areas as identified on the summary will generally be observed to have much larger values than the specified quality level. Also, a sequence of low values for a failure cause followed by a high value will pinpoint a particular area. Additionally, a sequence extending all through internal and external is a *warning flag*. Further, values appearing only in the external category raise a question. Of course, the feature identifying a proper quality inspection system would be to show only figures which are consistent with the specified quality level.

Problem Area Analysis

Once the problem areas have been identified, each should be analyzed in turn on a priority basis.

Job Instruction Review. The first step in analysis is to review the written job instructions, to compare the periodic review reports with the job instructions, and then to interview the inspection personnel by shift to ascertain whether or not there is a need for revising the system itself or just the system operation. Included with the review should be consideration for the following items: adequate and up-to-date gaging and facilities, visual standards, personnel job instructions, specific accept-reject criteria, checking frequency, action expected, identifying rejects, reports, and repair procedures.

Classifying the Control System. By degree, the three classifications are

1. Complete control: 100-percent on-line testing, inspection, or gaging as well as sampling, sequential, or spot-checking which occurs frequently enough to detect defective units before they leave the production area.

2. Attempted control: sampling or spot-checking which does not determine break points to contain the defectives in the producing area.

3. Mere information: sampling or spot-checking for trend analysis or next-day feedback.

The three corresponding detection classifications resulting in written information are

1. Immediate: 100 percent inspection.
2. Short-term: frequent audit.
3. Daily: daily audit.

Inspection Effort Review. The final step in analysis is to evaluate the inspection effort with respect to the control system classification. Inspection effort ratios should be calculated for each problem area by dividing the failure percent by the inspection head count. These ratios may then be compared to those for some corresponding nonproblem area to see if inspection effort is consistent with the control system and detection classifications. However, inspection performed by receiving, manufacturing, and testing should also be taken into consideration. This review may reveal that effort deficiencies are resulting in problems.

Evaluating the Information System

It has been stressed previously that the purpose of an information system is to provide information feedback so that corrective action may be expedited in order to maintain a specified quality level. The procedure for evaluating this aspect of an existing quality inspection system will concentrate on the report origination and destination points.

Origination Point

To determine the status quo, examples should be obtained for all reports. Then information should be elicited from each originator with regard to the following items:

1. Issuing frequency.
2. Distribution list.
3. Known inaccuracies or assumptions.
4. Data source and validity.
5. Utilization.
6. Any way in which report data are used by receiver.
7. Subsequent summaries.

Next, all reports should be summarized by issuing frequency, by content, by the receiver's authority level, and by manufacturing or inspection sequence.

Destination Point

Considering that any report should convey information in order to obtain corrective action, each person on the receiving end should be interviewed with respect to actual report usage in terms of the following items, requesting suggestions for improvement:

1. Timeliness.
2. Trend analysis availability.
3. Time period comparison.

4. Summaries.

5. Base-line comparison.

6. Accuracy.

7. Exception reporting.

8. Action orientation.

9. Information only.

10. Goals.

11. Responsibility for corrective action.

12. Corrective action feedback.

13. Length.

14. Combining.

15. Eliminating.

System Analysis

Often it is found that reports simply convey information in the hope that corrective action will occur. A proper report would have a complete communication and feedback loop which would include designating the person responsible for action, require return information within a specified time with respect to action taken, and require information on preventive measures taken.

A report which sometimes sounds like a broken record from repetition is one listing the top 10 items for a complex assembly because it seems to stay the same for almost the entire model year. It is possible that there are economic and engineering reasons that corrective action is delayed or not taken. In such a circumstance, the only way to become aware that something unusual had occurred to significantly increase the percent defective would be to use statistical limits, arbitrary limits for weighted factors such as cost or safety, or predetermined goals.

Each report must be analyzed by itself and in conjunction with all others as they assist in implementing the quality inspection system.

Existing System Corrective Action

Once the control system and the information system have been analyzed for shortcomings and the reasons for these deficiencies have been established, it remains to do whatever is necessary to correct them. In some cases, assistance would be obtained by reviewing the material on designing a quality inspection system. At any rate, it would be wise to secure upper management support for necessary changes since cost and labor availability may well be involved. Should there be some restrictions which prevent a present optimal solution, then it will be necessary to find a temporary solution.

Follow-up

The person evaluating the system is probably best qualified to implement the corrective action and to perform the follow-up. Implementation requires expediting required action, auditing the outgoing quality, and debugging the revised system. Then periodic follow-up should be done to assure that the revisions remain effective. Complete system reevaluation is called for whenever any external indicator shows that the specified quality level is not being maintained.

Figure 10-10 illustrates a typical inspection system evaluation checklist, and Figure 10-11 shows a typical reporting systems evaluation checklist.

INSPECTION SYSTEMS EVALUATION

Check if Completed

1. Determine indicators
   a. Internal   _____
   b. External   _____

2. Tabulate indicators
   a. Major components and/or areas of assembly   _____
   b. Cause of failure   _____

3. Compute percent of each cause of failure by indicator
   (cause of failure/total failures)   _____

4. Review tabulations
   a. "Common information"   _____
   b. Effective and ineffective control points   _____

5. Compare percents of failure to inspection effort   _____

6. Document job instructions and their review with the inspector   _____

7. Document true system in effect (all shifts)   _____

8. Also review
   a. Facilities (gages, work area, repair handling)   _____
   b. Reject criteria (visual standards and job instructions)   _____
   c. Actions expected (frequency of check, tagging, and reports   _____

9. Classify type of inspection or control
   a. Inspection for control   _____
   b. Inspection for attempted control   _____
   c. Inspection for information   _____

10. Classify type of corrective action
    a. Rejection   _____
    b. Immediate feedback   _____
    c. Daily feedback   _____

11. Determine corrective actions
    a. Top management support   _____
    b. Lower-level suggestion   _____
    c. Quality engineering approach   _____

12. Follow-up   _____

Fig. 10-10 (**Left**) Typical inspection system evaluation checklist

REPORTING SYSTEMS EVALUATION

Check if Completed

1. Compile examples of all existing reports
   a. Determine report data sources   _____
   b. Determine distribution of reports   _____

2. Categorize reports into logical breakdown   _____

3. Interview cross section of report receivers   _____

4. Consider
   a. Timeliness   _____
   b. Availability of trend analyses   _____
   c. Time period comparison   _____
   d. Summaries   _____
   e. Base-line comparison   _____
   f. Accuracy   _____
   g. Exception reporting   _____
   h. Action oriented   _____
   i. Information only   _____
   j. Goal to be achieved shown on report   _____
   k. Responsibility for corrective action   _____
   l. Corrective action feedback   _____
   m. Length of report   _____
   n. Combining of reports   _____

5. Recommend corrective action
   a. Considering 4 above   _____
   b. Strive for exception-action-oriented reports   _____

Fig. 10-11 (**Right**) Typical reporting systems evaluation checklist

REFERENCES

AMERICAN SOCIETY FOR QUALITY CONTROL, *The Basic Work Elements of Quality Control Engineering*, ASQC, 161 West Wisconsin Ave., Milwaukee, 1960.

CROSBY, P. B., *Cutting the Cost of Quality*, Farnsworth Publishing, Inc., Boston, 1967.

FEIGENBAUM, A. V., *Total Quality Control*, McGraw-Hill Book Company, New York, 1961.

GRANT, E. L., *Statistical Quality Control*, McGraw-Hill Book Company, New York, 1964.

HANSEN, B. L., *Quality Control: Theory and Applications*, Prentice-Hall, Inc., Englewood Cliffs, N.J., 1963.

JURAN, J. M., and F. M. GRYNA, *Quality Planning and Analysis*, McGraw-Hill Book Company, New York, 1970.

QUALITY CONTROL DEFINITIONS AND SYMBOLS

Term	Symbol	Definition
	General Terms Relating to Control Charts	
Unit		One of a number of similar items, objects, individuals, etc.
Variables, method of		Measurement of quality by the method of variables consists of measuring and recording the numerical magnitude of a quality characteristic for each of the units in the group under consideration. This involves reading a scale of some kind.
Attributes, method of		Measurement of quality by the method of attributes consists of noting the presence or absence of some characteristic (attribute) in each of the units in the group under consideration and counting how many do or do not possess it. Example: Go and no-go gaging of a dimension.
Universe or population		The total collection of units from a common source; the conceptual total collection of units from a process, such as a production process. Also used in the sense of a "universe (or population) of observations." *Note: Universe, population,* and *parent distribution* are synonymous terms. Statistical methods are based on the concept of a distribution of an exceedingly large number of observations, termed an infinite universe or population. An individual observation, the $\bar{X}$ of a sample, etc., may be thought of as one coming from a parent distribution or infinite population of like items.

223

Term	*Symbol*	*Definition*

General Terms Relating to Control Charts (Cont.)

Term	Symbol	Definition
Sample		A group of units, or portion of material, taken from a larger collection of units, or quantity of material, which serves to provide information that can be used as a basis for judging the quality of the larger quantity, or as a basis for action on the larger quantity or on the production process. Also used in the sense of a "sample of observations."
Sample size	n	The number of units in a sample. Also used in the sense of the number of observations in a sample.
Assignable cause		A factor contributing to the variation in quality that it is economically feasible to identify. Assignable causes must be identified and removed to attain statistical control.
Subgroup		One of a series of groups of observations obtained by subdividing a larger group of observations; alternatively, the data obtained from one of a series of samples taken from one or more universes.
Rational subgroups		Subgroups within which variations may for engineering reasons be considered to be due to nonassignable chance causes only but between which there may be variations due to assignable causes whose presence is considered possible. (One of the essential features of the control chart method is to break up inspection data into rational subgroups.)
Statistical measure		A mathematical function of a set of numbers or observations. Common statistical measures are the arithmetic mean or average, the standard deviation, the range (for variables), and the relative frequency (for attributes).
Control chart		A graphical chart with upper and lower control limits and plotted values of some statistical measure for a series of samples or subgroups. A central line is shown frequently.
Control limits		Limits on a control chart which are used as criteria for action or for judging the significance of variations between samples or subgroups.
Central line		A line on a control chart representing the average or expected value of the statistical measure being plotted.
Control chart—no standard given		A control chart whose control limits are based on the data of the samples or subgroups for which values are plotted on the chart.
Control chart—standard given		A control chart whose control limits are based on adopted standard values of the statistical measure(s) for which values are plotted on the chart.

Term	Symbol	Definition

Terms Relating to Control Charts for Variables

(a) Statistical measures

| Observed value or observation | X | The measured value of a quality characteristic for an individual unit; specific observed values are designated X_1, X_2, X_3, etc. |

| Average | $\bar{X}$ (X bar) | The arithmetic mean; the average of a set of n numbers, X_1, X_2, . . . , X_n, is the sum of the numbers divided by n: |

$$\bar{X} = \frac{X_1 + X_2 + \cdots + X_n}{n}$$

| Standard deviation | σ (sigma) | The standard deviation of a set of n numbers, X_1, X_2, . . . , X_n, is the root-mean-square (r.m.s.) deviation of the numbers from their average: |

$$\sigma = \sqrt{\frac{(X_1 - \bar{X})^2 + (X_2 - \bar{X})^2 + \cdots + (X_n - \bar{X})^2}{n}}$$

or expressed in a form often more convenient for computation purposes:

$$\sigma = \sqrt{\frac{X_1^2 + X_2^2 + \cdots + X_n^2}{n} - \bar{X}^2}$$

| Range | R | The range of a set of n numbers is the difference between the largest number and the smallest number. (More precisely: the absolute value of the algebraic difference between the highest and lowest values.) |

$$R = (\text{Largest number}) - (\text{Smallest number})$$

(b) Terms relating to a sample (or subgroup)

Sample average	$\bar{X}$ (X bar)	The sum of the observed values in a sample divided by the number of observed values.
Sample standard deviation	σ (sigma)	The root-mean-square (r.m.s.) deviation of the observed values of a sample from their average.
Sample range	R	The difference between the largest observed value and the smallest observed value in a sample.

(c) Other terms

| Average value of $\bar{X}$, σ, or R | $\bar{\bar{X}}$, $\bar{\sigma}$, $\bar{R}$ (X double bar, sigma bar, R bar) | The average of the set of sample values of $\bar{X}$, σ, or R under consideration. For samples of unequal size, a weighted average is used. These values are used in computing control limits for the case "no standard given." |

| Standard value of $\bar{X}$ or σ | $\bar{X}'$, σ' (X bar prime, sigma prime) | The value of $\bar{X}$ or σ adopted as standard for computing control limits for the case "standard given." (These symbols are also used to designate the true or objective value of $\bar{X}$ or σ of the universe sampled.) |

| Factor for central line— standard deviation | c_2 | A factor, varying with sample size n, that is equal to the ratio of the expected value of σ for samples of size n to the σ' of the universe sampled; $c_2 = \sigma/\sigma'$. (Published values† are for a normal universe.) |

†*ASTM Manual on Presentation of Data*, p. 50, American Society for Testing Materials, Philadelphia, 1944; also *ASA Z1.3 Control Chart Method of Controlling Quality During Production*, p. 39, American Standards Association, 1942.

Term	*Symbol*	*Definition*

Terms Relating to Control Charts for Variables (Cont.)

Factor for central line—range	d_2	A factor, varying with sample size n, that is equal to the ratio of the expected value of $\bar{R}$ for samples of size n to the σ' of the universe sampled; $d_2 = \bar{R}/\sigma'$. (Published values† are for a normal universe.)
Standard deviation of $\bar{X}$, σ, or R	$\sigma_{\bar{X}}$ σ_σ σ_R	The standard deviation of the sampling distribution of $\bar{X}$, σ, or R.

Terms Relating to Control Charts for Attributes

(a) Statistical measures

Relative frequency, proportion	p	The ratio of the number of *events* to the number of *trials* under consideration, where only one *event* can occur per *trial*. An *event* may be any kind of occurrence, a failure, a defective condition, etc.; and a *trial* is a single instance of observing whether the event is present or absent.
	pn	The number of events, where only one event can occur per trial. (A single letter symbol is sometimes used for convenience in place of pn.)
	u	The ratio of the number of events to the number of trials under consideration, where more than one event can occur per trial, and a trial is a unit area of opportunity for occurrence of the event. An example is the number of pinholes per square foot; an event is the occurrence of a pinhole; a trial is the examination of one unit of area (1 square foot); and the number of trials is the number of units of area (number of square feet) under consideration.
	c	The number of events, where more than one event can occur per trial. (See explanation accompanying definition of symbol u.)

(b) Terms relating to a sample

Note: The following terms relate to events commonly called *defects* and *defectives* in quality control work. Other terms, such as failures, breaks, etc., can be substituted as necessary.

Defect		A failure to meet a requirement imposed on a unit with respect to a single quality characteristic; also an irregularity in material, surface, finish, etc.
A defective		A defective unit; one containing one or more defects with respect to the quality characteristic(s) under consideration.
Sample fraction defective	p	The ratio of the number of defective units in a sample to the total number of units in the sample; the number of defectives in a sample of n units divided by n. Sometimes referred to as the sample *proportion defective*.

Term	Symbol	Definition

Terms Relating to Control Charts for Attributes (Cont.)

Term	Symbol	Definition
Sample number of defectives	pn	The number of defectives in a sample. (A single letter is sometimes used for convenience in place of pn.)
Sample defects per units	u	The ratio of the number of defects in a sample to the total number of units in the sample; the number of defects in a sample of n units divided by n; $u = c/n$.
Sample number of defects	c	The number of defects in a sample.
(c) Other terms		
Average value of p, pn, u, or c	$\bar{p}$ $\bar{p}n$ $\bar{u}$ $\bar{c}$	The average of the set of sample values of p, pn, u, or c. Values of $\bar{p}n$ and $\bar{c}$ are computed for samples of equal size. For a set of samples of unequal size, $\bar{p}$ and $\bar{u}$ are weighted averages, usually obtained as follows: $\bar{p}$ is the total number of defective units found in the set of samples divided by the total number of units in the set; $\bar{u}$ is the total number of defects in the set divided by the total number of units in the set. These values are used in computing control limits for the case "no standard given."
Standard value of p, pn, u, or c	p' $p'n$ u' c'	The value of p, pn, u, or c adopted as a standard for computing control limits for the case "standard given." (These symbols are also used to designate the true or objective value of p, pn, u, or c for the universe sampled.)
Standard deviation of p, pn, u, or c	σ_p σ_{pn} σ_u σ_c	The standard deviation of the sampling distribution of p, pn, u, or c: $$\sigma = \sqrt{\bar{p}(1-\bar{p})/n} \quad \text{or} \quad \sqrt{p'(1-p')/n}$$ $$\sigma = \sqrt{\bar{p}n(1-\bar{p})} \quad \text{or} \quad \sqrt{p'n(1-p')}$$ $$\sigma = \sqrt{\bar{u}/n} \quad \text{or} \quad \sqrt{u'/n}$$ $$\sigma = \sqrt{\bar{c}} \quad \text{or} \quad \sqrt{c'}$$

General Terms Relating to Acceptance Sampling

Term	Symbol	Definition
Acceptance sampling		The art or science that deals with procedures in which decisions to accept or reject lots or processes are based on the examination of samples.
Sampling plan		A specific plan which states (a) the sample sizes and (b) the criteria for accepting, rejecting, or taking another sample, to be used in inspecting a lot.
Inspection lot		A specific quantity of similar material, or a collection of similar units, offered for inspection and acceptance at one time.
Lot size		The number of units in the lot.
Sample		A portion of material or a group of units, taken from a lot, which serves to provide information for reaching a decision regarding acceptance.
Sample size	n	The number of units in the sample.
Single sampling		Sampling inspection in which a decision to accept or to reject is reached after the inspection of a single sample.

Term	*Symbol*	*Definition*

General Terms Relating to Acceptance Sampling (Cont.)

Term	Symbol	Definition
Double sampling		Sampling inspection in which the inspection of the first sample leads to a decision to accept, to reject, or to take a second sample and the examination of a second sample, when required, always leads to a decision to accept or to reject.
Multiple sampling		Sampling inspection in which, after each sample, the decision may be to accept, to reject, or to take another sample but in which there is usually a prescribed maximum number of samples, after which a decision to accept or to reject is reached. *Note:* Multiple sampling as defined here is sometimes called *sequential sampling* or *group sequential sampling*. The term *multiple sampling* is preferred.
Sequential sampling		Sampling inspection in which, after each unit is inspected, the decision is made to accept, to reject, or to inspect another unit. *Note:* Sequential sampling as defined here is sometimes called *unit sequential sampling*.
Curtailed inspection		Sampling inspection in which, as soon as a decision is certain, the inspection of the sample is stopped. Thus as soon as the rejection number for defectives is reached, the decision is certain, and no further inspection is necessary. *Note:* Commonly a first sample is always completed for the purpose of estimating the process average.
Normal inspection		Inspection in accordance with a sampling plan that is used under ordinary circumstances.
Reduced inspection		Inspection in accordance with a sampling plan requiring smaller sample sizes than those used in normal inspection.
Tightened inspection		Inspection in accordance with a sampling plan that has more strict acceptance criteria than normal inspection.
Process average quality		Expected quality of product from a given process, usually estimated from first sample inspection results of past lots.
Acceptable quality level	AQL	The maximum percent defective (or the maximum number of defects per 100 units) which can be considered satisfactory as a process average.
Probability of acceptance	P_a	Probability that a lot or process will be accepted.
Operating characteristic curve for acceptance sampling plan	OC curve	A curve showing the relation between the probability of acceptance and either lot quality or process quality, whichever is applicable.
Consumer's risk		The probability or risk of accepting a lot, for a given lot quality or process quality, whichever is applicable; usually applied only to quality values that are relatively poor.
Producer's risk		The probability or risk of rejecting a lot, for a given lot quality or process quality, whichever is applicable; usually applied only to quality values that are relatively good.

Term	Symbol	Definition

General Terms Relating to Acceptance Sampling (Cont.)

Term	Symbol	Definition
Average sample number	ASN	The average number of sample units inspected per lot in reaching a decision to accept or to reject.
Average total inspection	ATI	The average number of units inspected per lot including all units in rejected lots (applicable when the procedure calls for 100 percent inspection of rejected lots).

Terms Relating to Attribute Sampling Plans

Term	Symbol	Definition
Acceptance number	Ac	The largest number of defectives (or defects) in the sample or samples under consideration that will permit the acceptance of the inspection lot.
Rejection number	Re	The smallest number of defectives (or defects) in the sample or samples under consideration that will require the rejection of the inspection lot.
Average outgoing quality	AOQ	The average quality of outgoing product after 100 percent inspection of rejected lots, with replacement by good units of all defective units found in inspection.
Average outgoing quality limit	AOQL	The maximum average outgoing quality (AOQ) for a sampling plan.
	$p_{95}, p_{50}, p_{10},$ $p_{05},$ etc.	Lot quality or process quality for which the probability of acceptance is 0.95, 0.50, 0.10, 0.05, etc., respectively, for a given acceptance sampling plan.

PRACTICE
PROBLEMS AND
CASE STUDIES

CHAPTER 1

Problem 1

Considerable variation is often encountered in the miles per gallon (mpg) obtained when driving. A great many factors contribute to this variation, such as the type of vehicle, city driving, expressway driving, time of year, driver, whether the tank is filled each time, plus other factors too numerous to list. Because of this, miles per gallon calculated on the basis of one or two trips cannot be considered a valid indicator of performance. (This is further substantiated by the differences between EPA figures and actual results.) Extensive records of mileage figures for several different vehicles follow.

A. 1956 Buick Special

Date		mpg	Date		mpg	Date		mpg
1960			Mar.	3	16.0	Aug.	1	15.9
Oct.	29	15.5		13	13.4		9	14.5
Nov.	11	12.6		27	15.0		17	12.2
	28	14.3	Apr.	10	12.2	Sep.	1	21.7
Dec.	8	13.2		27	14.1		5	16.5
	16	12.4	May	9	14.5		6	15.0
1961				15	13.9		7	19.1
Jan.	9	12.2		24	15.5		11	13.8
	18	11.9	Jun.	12	15.0		18	14.7
	24	14.3		19	17.3		27	13.0
	30	11.6		27	15.3	Oct.	2	14.4
Feb.	5	13.9	Jul.	6	Error		10	14.7
	14	15.0		19	Error			
	23	12.3		25	14.9			

B. 1959 German DKW

Date		mpg	Date		mpg	Date		mpg
1959			Feb.	7	21.9	May	26	51.2
Dec.	29	22.0		11	24.7	Jun.	2	39.2
	30	28.4		16	26.0		14	32.6
	31	33.5		21	24.0		20	31.6
	31	24.0		26	42.4		24	18.0
1960				27	11.8	Jul.	2	29.3
Jan.	1	29.4	Mar.	4	41.4		13	29.3
	1	31.7		6	13.6		24	31.3
	13	25.2		10	20.1	Aug.	1	28.8
	18	40.2		16	26.2		8	28.5
	19	15.6		29	28.9		22	31.9
	23	21.2	Apr.	9	25.6	Sep.	20	31.2
	28	26.3		21	31.2		26	75.0
Feb.	4	26.2		30	31.1		27	13.1
	5	28.6	May	10	54.6			
	7	38.2		17	17.9			

C. 1960 Corvair

Date		mpg	Date		mpg	Date		mpg
1960			Jul.	14	24.5	Oct.	27	21.7
Mar.	19	17.6		19	22.2		27	23.5
	23	17.4		25	24.4		28	22.1
	30	19.6		30	23.3		31	21.9
Apr.	3	17.3	Aug.	4	23.4	Nov.	4	20.7
	10	21.2		9	23.2		11	19.1
	15	20.6		13	24.0		17	21.3
	21	24.1		22	23.8		20	20.6
	28	21.3		31	23.9		29	19.9
May	4	20.9	Sep.	6	24.1	Dec.	5	19.3
	9	20.1		8	24.6		9	19.0
	14	20.5		8	25.6		14	17.8
	21	22.5		17	23.4		19	18.8
	24	21.8		18	25.9		22	17.8
	31	23.0		19	25.7		26	17.8
Jun.	5	23.3		21	25.3		26	21.2
	11	23.4		22	23.9		26	23.5
	18	23.4		27	24.8		27	22.6
	26	23.1	Oct.	10	23.3		27	24.5
Jul.	2	22.2		18	22.6			
	9	24.2		24	20.2			

D. 1963 Renault

Date		mpg	Date		mpg	Date		mpg
1963			Jan.	9	32.9	Sep.	18	33.0
Jul.	31	36.0		20	31.5		29	35.8
Aug.	7	39.2	Feb.	3	31.0	Oct.	6	35.5
	13	37.2		12	22.5		14	32.5
	21	32.8		24	33.8		20	37.1
	26	39.0	Mar.	9	32.2		28	34.5
Sep.	16	35.3		24	32.2	Nov.	7	35.1
	25	34.8	Apr.	3	32.6		14	35.6
Oct.	2	36.5		10	35.1		21	30.6
	8	35.2		30	35.9		30	34.0
	14	37.0	May	14	35.0	Dec.	4	27.9
	20	34.6		28	36.9		15	28.8
	28	36.0	Jun.	8	37.0		21	30.3
Nov.	4	34.7		17	34.3	1965		
	12	34.0	Jul.	2	37.3	Jan.	2	28.8
	23	31.3		14	42.6		9	31.4
	30	33.4		24	31.3		19	31.9
Dec.	7	33.4	Aug.	4	35.7		27	26.0
	19	28.2		25	35.2	Feb.	3	26.4
1964			Sep.	2	34.3		9	30.1
Jan.	2	31.4		11	38.7			

E. 1965 Cadillac Coupe de Ville

Date		mpg	Date		mpg	Date		mpg
1965			May	3	13.65	Jul.	5	11.05
Feb.	28	10.0		6	11.82		11	12.02
Mar.	4	11.58		11	12.40		17	11.41
	7	11.40		19	11.87		22	10.98
	15	11.36		22	11.39		22	12.40
	26	10.98		26	12.13		24	12.36
Apr.	4	10.54	Jun.	2	10.76		30	11.16
	7	13.13		7	11.55	Aug.	18	10.43
	14	10.81		8	13.14		21	12.40
	18	12.29		16	10.90		23	11.83
	26	10.73		20	11.28		29	11.09
	30	12.33		29	11.42			

Assignment

1. Select one or more sets of the preceding data.

2. Construct a histogram. Use actual frequencies on the left vertical axis and relative frequencies on the right.

3. Construct an ogive. Again use actual frequencies on the left vertical axis and relative frequencies on the right.

Problem 2

A study was made of the 1.896–1.915-inch dimension in the machining of a steering knuckle. Machining was done on a six-station Bullard. Each head acted essentially as a separate machine, and a capability study would take this into consideration. The tools are set in slides and can be moved in or out as adjustment is required. The part is located on the head by matching centers.

Sample No.	Head Numbers					
	1	2	3	4	5	6
1	1.914	1.934	1.925	1.929	1.928	1.9155
2	1.9145	1.933	1.934	1.916	1.925	1.915
3	1.9135	1.928	1.935	1.9235	1.924	1.926
4	1.911	[1]1.934	1.9345	1.925	1.927	1.9175
5	1.9135	1.9305	1.933	1.930	1.927	1.9265
6	1.907	1.917	1.923	1.927	1.927	1.918
7	1.9175	1.916	1.9255	1.9325	1.9265	1.9165
8	1.911	1.911	1.934	1.9275	1.9245	1.916
9	1.918	1.9085	1.9275	1.929	1.930	1.929
10	1.9155	1.9205	[2]1.9165	1.922	1.925	1.920
11	1.9175	1.917	1.907	1.924	1.932	1.9265
12	1.920	1.9155	1.913	1.930	1.931	1.9185
13	1.9165	1.9145	1.9125	1.9235	1.9265	1.9265
14	1.9155	1.910	1.911	1.9125	1.930	1.9255
15	1.918	1.915	1.914	1.926	1.9295	1.9175
16	1.912	1.9155	1.9125	[3]1.928	1.9235	1.923
17	1.9185	1.9185	1.901	1.932	1.929	1.928
18	1.913	1.9205	1.9145	1.940	1.927	1.922
19	1.914	1.916	1.9135	1.936	1.927	1.9235
20	1.9165	1.9135	1.908	[4]1.937	1.9165	1.918
21	1.9135	1.918	1.916	1.910	1.920	1.9285
22	1.914	1.918	1.9175	[5]1.9115	1.940	1.929
23	1.9135	1.912	1.906	1.9215	1.9335	[6]1.9305
24	1.917	1.9175	1.915	1.906	1.931	1.939
25	1.919	1.917	1.917	1.914	1.927	1.915

Explanation of notations: 1: Operator moved tool in.   4: Relief operator moved tool in.
                                2: Operator changed tool.   5: Operator returned.
                                3: Operator relieved.   6: Operator changed tool.

Assignment

1. Set up a frequency table, combining data from all six heads.

2. Construct a histogram. Use actual frequencies on the left vertical axis and relative frequencies on the right.

3. Construct a separate histogram for each head on one sheet of graph paper. Does there appear to be any difference among heads?

Problem 3

A study was made over a period of several days of the paint film thickness on the fenders of a certain vehicle manufactured by a large corporation. Readings are in mils, with specifications requiring 2.0–3.2 mils.

Date		Samples					
		1	2	3	4	5	6
2/1	10:00 A	2.7	2.7	2.6	2.7	2.8	2.8
2/4	8:30 A	2.6	2.5	2.7	2.7	2.4	2.4
2/4	1:00 P	2.8	2.6	2.6	2.7	2.2	2.7
2/5	8:30 A	2.4	2.8	2.3	2.7	3.0	2.7
2/5	2:30 P	2.7	2.5	2.8	3.0	2.3	3.2
2/6	8:30 A	2.5	2.8	2.8	3.2	2.8	3.5
2/6	2:30 P	3.2	2.7	2.8	2.8	2.8	3.3
2/7	10:30 A	2.6	2.7	2.4	3.0	2.4	2.7
2/7	3:00 P	3.0	3.1	2.7	2.8	2.7	2.8
2/8	8:45 A	2.9	2.9	2.5	2.8	3.0	2.9
2/8	1:30 P	3.0	2.7	3.5	3.2	3.2	3.2
2/11	8:45 A	3.2	2.9	3.3	2.8	3.6	3.4
2/11	2:45 P	3.0	3.0	2.9	2.8	2.8	2.7
2/12	8:30 A	2.8	2.8	2.5	2.4	2.9	3.0
2/12	2:30 P	2.8	2.4	2.8	3.0	2.7	2.4
2/13	8:15 A	2.8	2.4	2.7	2.5	2.7	2.5
2/13	9:30 A	2.9	3.0	2.9	3.0	2.6	2.6
2/13	2:00 P	2.8	2.6	3.2	2.7	2.3	3.0
2/14	8:20 A	3.2	3.2	2.7	2.4	2.8	2.6
2/14	2:00 P	2.5	2.3	2.9	2.8	2.3	3.1
2/15	8:30 A	2.8	2.8	2.9	2.5	3.0	2.8
2/15	2:30 P	2.8	2.8	2.9	2.9	2.7	3.0
2/18	10:30 A	2.8	2.7	2.5	2.7	2.8	2.4
2/18	2:45 P	2.7	2.8	2.8	2.8	2.6	3.1
2/19	8:30 A	2.5	3.2	2.8	2.8	2.7	3.2

Assignment

1. Set up a frequency table.
2. Construct a histogram, using actual frequencies on the left vertical axis and relative frequencies on the right.
3. Construct an ogive, using actual frequencies on the left vertical axis and relative frequencies on the right.

Problem 4

Plant efficiency figures are a frequently used guide in evaluating area or overall operational effectiveness. Comparisons may be also made between shifts and between areas. The following data represent 6-month, two-shift operation:

Date	First Shift	Second Shift	Date	First Shift	Second Shift
Nov. 8	104.6	64.8	Feb. 13	140.9	82.3
9	83.9	78.8	14	100.7	80.2
10	46.4	73.8	15	65.2	100.9
11	63.9	82.2	16	74.2	184.7
14	85.2	69.0	17	173.8	
15	51.1		21	102.3	92.6
16	57.2	68.8	22	76.1	53.2
17	43.6	54.9	23	59.8	
18	132.3	78.0	24	107.9	48.1
21	60.0	73.6	27	115.7	63.2
22	39.5	58.3	28	68.4	114.8
23	84.4	89.7	Mar. 1	102.5	114.5
25	59.0	29.8	2	165.7	
28	173.5	59.4	3	44.4	35.6
29	99.5	53.8	6	113.6	
Dec. 9	119.7	98.9	13	120.8	63.3
12	58.5		14	86.4	61.7
13	64.2	90.2	15	94.2	
14	57.7	72.3	16	27.8	
15	85.2	90.4	17	75.5	131.0
16	83.6	73.7	20	89.3	60.3
19	82.5	103.3	21	98.2	
20	70.1	22.8	22	60.0	88.6
21	10.0		23	111.8	169.2
Jan. 9	100.1	88.3	24	88.8	71.8
10	115.6		27	103.9	152.3
11	122.8	68.0	29	152.7	116.9
12	95.0	99.0	30	120.8	
13	90.3	43.2	Apr. 3	86.3	63.6
16	83.4	219.1	4	99.8	44.2
17	60.3		5	59.2	76.2
18	107.5	82.6	6	102.9	106.9
19	62.3	74.0	7	98.0	133.6
23	79.7	86.0	10	108.7	78.0
24	33.7	76.1	11	118.1	124.7
25	128.9		12	32.5	
26	69.5	42.2	13	61.7	
30	276.7		14	65.7	152.7
31	93.9		19	62.7	
Feb. 3	96.9		20	56.0	
6	43.0		21	55.3	222.5
7	45.7	61.8	24	91.8	109.9
8	114.9	99.0	25	86.1	99.2
9	63.6		26	98.5	118.6
10	95.8	117.8	27	60.9	91.4

Assignment

1. Set up a frequency table.

2. Construct separate histograms for the first- and second-shift operations, using actual frequencies on the left vertical axis and relative frequencies on the right.

3. Construct ogive curves. Use actual frequencies on the left vertical axis and relative frequencies on the right.

Problem 5

A study was made in a foundry to determine if camshaft inoculation alloys were within established specifications. The following data are the result of 50 random checks during 1 month on manganese, chromium, nickel, and molybdenum content.

Alloy Concentrations in Camshaft for 1 Month

Mn	Ni	Cr	Mo	Mn	Ni	Cr	Mo
0.72	0.26	1.00	0.45	0.87	0.25	1.06	0.45
0.81	0.26	1.05	0.49	0.88	0.24	1.02	0.48
0.79	0.27	1.01	0.50	0.92	0.26	1.02	0.47
0.75	0.25	1.05	0.48	0.85	0.25	0.98	0.44
0.65	0.24	1.02	0.48	0.83	0.28	1.10	0.46
0.78	0.25	0.98	0.46	0.93	0.26	1.04	0.47
0.75	0.24	1.00	0.49	0.81	0.20	1.05	0.44
0.87	0.25	1.09	0.51	0.89	0.26	1.06	0.47
0.75	0.22	1.05	0.47	0.98	0.19	1.11	0.51
0.80	0.24	1.07	0.45	0.85	0.25	1.03	0.46
0.79	0.20	1.02	0.46	0.87	0.23	1.12	0.51
0.79	0.24	1.03	0.42	0.82	0.26	1.15	0.47
0.82	0.24	0.96	0.41	0.82	0.23	0.12	0.46
0.85	0.27	1.15	0.57	0.79	0.24	0.88	0.35
0.79	0.24	0.90	0.38	0.95	0.25	1.10	0.50
0.78	0.25	1.12	0.53	0.88	0.25	1.07	0.47
0.92	0.27	1.03	0.46	0.78	0.27	1.12	0.48
0.90	0.23	1.07	0.50	0.89	0.25	1.08	0.44
0.84	0.22	1.00	0.50	0.75	0.25	1.14	0.51
0.88	0.23	1.02	0.47	0.88	0.27	1.17	0.49
0.80	0.22	1.06	0.45	0.88	0.29	1.21	0.56
0.90	0.20	1.06	0.42	0.87	0.26	1.15	0.50
0.75	0.25	1.02	0.49	0.82	0.22	1.13	0.47
0.79	0.24	0.97	0.47	0.96	0.25	1.17	0.53
0.82	0.24	1.07	0.48	0.76	0.24	1.06	0.43

Alloy Specifications:

Mn:	0.60–0.90	Cr:	0.85–1.20
Ni:	0.20–0.40	Mo:	0.40–0.60

Assignment

1. Set up a frequency table for one element.
2. Construct a histogram. Use actual frequencies on the left vertical axis and relative frequencies on the right.
3. Construct an ogive. Use actual frequencies on the left vertical axis and relative frequencies on the right.

Problem 6

To determine the runout on a transmission output shaft, a study was conducted on the preroll grinding operation. Specifications require a maximum 0.0015-inch T.I.R.

Sample No.	X_1	X_2	X_3	X_4	X_5
1	23	20	30	9	43
2	7	10	6	20	7
3	30	39	10	19	13
4	18	25	34	15	38
5	4	1	3	1	3
6	1	5	2	2	5
7	3	4	2	3	2
8	24	7	14	15	25
9	30	23	21	6	18
10	7	25	20	8	1-2
11	7	6	9	27	11
12	8	14	9	8	17
13	3	3	8	12	11
14	12	3	2	14	16
15	9	18	11	9	10
16	13	12	19	3	6
17	21	58	6	41	19
18	17	4	24	10	20
19	10	65	11	12	57
20	14	18	22	3	9
21	12	15	10	8	20
22	11	9	7	19	21
23	14	17	9	20	22
24	8	9	17	23	30
25	22	12	14	21	23

Assignment

1. Set up a frequency table.
2. Construct a histogram, using actual frequencies on the left vertical axis and relative frequencies on the right.
3. Construct an ogive, using actual frequencies on the left vertical axis and relative frequencies on the right.

Problem 7

Find the mean, median, mode, and standard deviation for the data in the following problems:

a. Problem 1-A, B, C, D, E.
b. Problem 2.
c. Problem 3.
d. Problem 4.
e. Problem 5.
f. Problem 6.

CHAPTER 2

Problem 1

An operator of a carnival has several games of semiskill designed to bring in (naturally) more money than is paid out in the form of prizes. One of the games involves putting a golf ball into a cylindrical depression. Past experience has indicated that the probability of accomplishing this on one stroke is about 1 in 5. Based on this information, the operator decides to sell a chance for 10 cents. This entitles the customer to three putts. If he sinks one putt, he wins a 10-cent prize; if he sinks two putts, he wins a 20-cent prize; if he sinks three putts, he wins a 30-cent prize. On any series of putts only one prize is given. If this is going to be a one-night stand and approximately 200 people are expected to participate in the game, how many prizes of each should be purchased, and what would be the expected profit or loss?

Problem 2

A product is made up of two parts, A and B. The manufacturing process for each is such that the probability of a defective part A is 0.05 and the probability of a defective part B is 0.05. What is the probability that the assembled product will not be defective?

Problem 3

If the probability of a defective door lock on an automobile is 1 out of 10,000, what is the probability that both doors on a two-door sedan have defective locks?

Problem 4

A common game at carnivals involves tossing a coin (usually a penny—3/4-inch diameter) at a board ruled in 1-inch squares. The player wins if his tossed coin does not touch any lines and loses if it does touch a line. What is the probability of winning? If the payoff is 10 to 1, what is the expected return to the operator?

Problem 5

An experiment is performed using a bag and two boxes. The bag contains three numbered balls, two with the number one and one with the number two. The boxes are designated Box No. 1 and Box No. 2. Box No. 1 contains one black ball and three white balls. Box No. 2 contains four black balls and one white ball. The experiment E consists of two consecutive draws of the balls. A ball is first drawn from the bag and then a second ball is drawn, either from Box No. 1 or No. 2, dependent on the number on the ball drawn from the bag. Compute the probability that the second draw in the experiment will yield a black ball.

Problem 6

A plant currently conducts 100 percent inspection on a transmission part which arrives in the assembly area in lots of 25 pieces. If defective items are assembled in the transmission, tear down and repair are required. Anticipating a reduction in labor time, management investigates the possibility of using a sampling plan of 5 pieces, rejecting the lot if 1 or more defective pieces are found in the sample. Past records indicate a process fraction defective of 0.12.

Would you recommend that this inspection scheme be instituted, or should the current method be continued? Substantiate your answer statistically.

Problem 7

Highly effective, repeated inspection has reduced the probability of shipping to a customer a spark plug with no base threads to 0.00005. The probability of a cracked insulator is 0.00040, and the probability of a missing electrode is 0.00008.

a. What is the probability of no threads and a cracked insulator?

b. What is the probability of no threads and a missing electrode?

c. What is the probability of a spark plug with all three defects?

d. What is the probability of a good plug?

Problem 8

A man walked home in the dark eating roasted chestnuts. Arriving at home after having consumed 20, he discovered upon opening the remaining 10 that 7 contained worms. What is the probability that none of the 20 contained worms? Or, stated differently, if there were only 7 wormy chestnuts among the original 30, what was the probability of drawing all of the first 20 free from worms?

Problem 9

A product is assembled in five stages. At the first stage there are five assembly lines; at the second stage, four; at the third stage, three; at the fourth stage, three; and at the fifth stage, two. In how many different ways may the product be routed through the assembly process?

Problem 10

A car manufacturer offers his customers their choice of the following:

Body styles	6	
Engines	5	
Paint	15	
Transmissions	4	
Differentials	3	
Tires	3	
Radios	3	
Air conditioning	2	
Heaters	3	
Options	10	(can select any 4)

How many completely different cars may be produced?

CHAPTER 3

Problem 1

Refer to the 1956 Buick Special mileage data in Problem 1 for Chapter 1. What is the probability of exceeding 16.5 mpg? The probability of less than 11 mpg? (Use the mean and standard deviation calculated in Problem 7-a for Chapter 1.)

Problem 2

Refer to the 1959 German DKW mileage data in Problem 1 for Chapter 1. What is the probability of exceeding 30.0 mpg? The probability of less than 22 mpg? (Use the mean and standard deviation calculated in Problem 7-a for Chapter 1.)

Problem 3

Refer to the 1960 Corvair mileage data in Problem 1 for Chapter 1. What is the probability of exceeding 24.5 mpg? The probability that the mileage is less than 20.0 mpg? (Use the mean and standard deviation calculated in Problem 7-a for Chapter 1.)

Problem 4

Refer to the 1963 Renault mileage data in Problem 1 for Chapter 1. What is the probability of exceeding 37 mpg? The probability that the mileage is less than 28 mpg? (Use the mean and standard deviation calculated in Problem 7-a for Chapter 1.)

Problem 5

Refer to the 1965 Cadillac mileage data in Problem 1 for Chapter 1. What is the probability of exceeding 13.0 mpg? The probability that the mileage is less than 10.5 mpg? (Use the mean and standard deviation calculated in Problem 7-a for Chapter 1.)

Problem 6

Refer to Problem 2 for Chapter 1. Using the mean and standard deviation calculated in Problem 7-b for Chapter 1, what percentage of steering knuckles are within specifications when all six heads are combined? Does this vary for different heads?

Problem 7

Refer to Problem 3 for Chapter 1. Using the mean and standard deviation calculated in Problem 7-c for Chapter 1, what percentage of readings are outside the specifications of 2.0 to 3.2 mils?

Problem 8

Refer to Problem 4 for Chapter 1. Using the mean and standard deviation calculated in Problem 7-d for Chapter 1, what percentage of each shift's efficiency figures exceed 100 percent? What percentage is less than 80 percent?

Problem 9

Refer to Problem 5 for Chapter 1. Using the mean and standard deviation calculated in Problem 7-e for Chapter 1, what percentages of the various alloys specified for analysis are within their specifications?

Problem 10

Refer to Problem 6 for Chapter 1. Using the mean and standard deviation calculated in Problem 7-f for Chapter 1, what percentage of the readings exceeds the maximum runout specifications?

Problem 11

Use the mirror image technique on the data in Problem 6 for Chapter 1. Calculate the standard deviations for each side. Estimate the probability of exceeding the maximum specification using the appropriate standard deviation. How does this compare with the results in Problem 10?

Problem 12

Select one or more of Problems 1 through 6 for Chapter 1. Plot the data on normal probability paper. Determine the means and standard deviations from these plots. Compare these with the means and standard deviations calculated in Problem 7-a through f for Chapter 1. Also estimate the probabilities of exceeding the values specified in problems 1 through 11 for Chapter 3.

CHAPTER 4

Problem 1

In tossing coins, the probability of a head is one-half. If 10 coins are tossed simultaneously ($n = 10$), use the binomial distribution to calculate the probability of $0, 1, 2, \ldots, 10$ heads. Plot the results on a graph.

Problem 2

A process has a constant probability of 0.05 of producing a defective unit. Find the probability of a sample of 15 containing $0, 1, 2, \ldots, 15$ defective units. Graph the results.

Problem 3

The probability of a defective head lamp being received in an assembly plant is 0.10. Assuming that the lamps are not tested and sorted but sent directly to the assembly line, what is the probability that a car would have 0, 1, 2, 3, or 4 defective lamps?

Problem 4

In a bank of four machines performing a similar operation, the probability that a machine will require servicing is 0.20. What is the probability that in any given period of time,

   a.   None of the machines will require servicing?
   b.   Two of the machines will require servicing?
   c.   Three or more of the machines will require servicing?
   d.   All four machines will require servicing?

Problem 5

A machine set up to manufacture bolts turns out defective bolts (on the average) at the rate of 1 defective per 200 bolts. Bolts are packed in boxes of 100. What is the probability that a box will have 1 or more defective bolts?

Problem 6

Knowing that the average rate of defective assemblies from a production line is 0.10,

   a.   Determine the probability that if 5 assemblies are taken from the line, all are good.
   b.   What is the probability that at most 1 of the 5 is defective?
   c.   What will be the average number of defectives in a lot of 50?

Problem 7

Work Problems 1, 2, and 3 above using the Poisson distribution. If there is a difference in answers, what can the difference be attributed to?

Problem 8

Work Problem 5 above using the normal approximation to the binomial. Is there a difference in results? Why?

Problem 9

If the probability of a defective door lock on an automobile is 1 out of 10,000, what is the probability that both doors on a two-door sedan have defective locks?

241

Problem 10

A receiving inspector will accept a lot of 100 parts if a sample of 5, picked at random and inspected, contains no defectives. What is the probability that the lot will be accepted if it is 10 percent defective?

Problem 11

A certain assembly consists of four parts, so connected that the assembly functions only if all four parts work properly. If the probability that each part functions properly is 0.90, what is the probability that the assembly functions properly? (Assume independence.)

Problem 12

You attempt to predict how a coin will fall during each of several independent tosses. If you are not clairvoyant, but only guessing,

a. What is the probability of correctly predicting 4 out of 4 tosses?
b. What is the probability of correctly predicting 6 out of 8 tosses?
c. What is the probability of correctly predicting, at most, 2 out of 10 tosses?

Problem 13

Defects in the zinc plating of sheet steel occur on the average of one defect per 10 square feet of area.

a. What is the probability that a 5- by 8-foot sheet will have no defects?
b. Will have at most one defect?

Problem 14

A telephone switchboard gets on the average 500 calls per hour. The maximum number of connections that can be made is 12 per minute. What is the probability that the switchboard will receive more calls than it can handle in a given minute?

Problem 15

If the reliability of a missile is 0.80, what is the probability of

a. Six successes in 10 missile firings?
b. Nine successes in 10 missile firings?

Problem 16

Records of an airline owning a fleet of four-engine aircraft show that on the average an engine fails 3 times in 10^4 operating hours. What is the probability of two or more engines failing on an aircraft during an 8-hour flight?

Problem 17

The 100-hour reliability for an alternating-current generator is determined to be 0.98:

a. What is the probability of 1 failure in a sample of 10 for the same period of time?
b. What is the probability of more than 1 failure out of 10?

CHAPTER 5

Problem 1

The following are the fractions defective of shaft and washer assemblies during the month of April, in samples of 1,500 each:

Date	Fraction Defective	Date	Fraction Defective
1	0.11	17	0.04
3	0.06	18	0.07
4	0.10	19	0.04
5	0.11	20	0.04
6	0.14	21	0.04
7	0.11	22	0.03
10	0.14	24	0.06
11	0.03	25	0.06
12	0.02	26	0.04
13	0.03	27	0.03
14	0.03	28	0.04
15	0.03		

Assignment

1. Plot the above data as a fraction defective chart.
2. Calculate the mean and control limits.
3. If any points are out of control, assume an assignable cause exists, and recalculate the limits.
4. What limits would you recommend for the next time period?
5. What is your general analysis of the chart?

Problem 2

The data at right show the results of 100 percent inspection of an electrical assembly:

Assignment

Set up a p control chart for the next period's operation based on these data. What might be suspected about the first 6 days? (Assume assignable causes for this week's activity, and then proceed from there.)

Day	Sample Size	Number Defective
1	1,361	161
2	1,278	118
3	1,328	220
4	710	67
5	735	85
6	726	82
8	803	78
9	850	74
10	700	60
11	670	45
12	680	54
13	801	64
15	717	53
16	722	52
17	691	51
18	756	53
19	652	46
20	701	62
22	741	66
23	754	46
24	703	38
25	682	47
26	719	44
27	713	57

Problem 3

A recurring problem in any assembly plant is stripped threads on bolts. The following data show the number of anchor bolts stripped daily for a 40-day period. The average sample size was 1,200. Use the first 20 days' data to calculate the mean and control limits. Assume assignable causes for any out-of-control points. After plotting this 20-day period, project the limits and plot the succeeding 20 days. What is your analysis?

Date	Number Defective	Date	Number Defective
9/16	46	11/12	18
9/17	28	11/13	18
9/18	37	11/16	16
9/22	56	11/17	19
9/23	32	11/18	36
9/24	23	11/19	22
9/25	119	11/20	32
9/27	110	11/21	29
10/28	60	11/23	23
10/29	35	11/24	14
10/30	71	11/25	34
11/2	54	11/27	22
11/3	17	11/30	54
11/4	47	12/1	34
11/5	31	12/2	22
11/6	54	12/3	35
11/7	127	12/4	35
11/9	17	12/5	62
11/10	16	12/7	70
11/11	12	12/8	79

Problem 4

At one time many automobile and truck manufacturers packed and shipped components to small overseas assembly plants where the parts were assembled into finished vehicles by local labor. The subgroupings that made up a shipping case were referred to as material layouts. Figure 5P4-1 is a quality analysis chart for the passenger and truck chassis metal line spanning a 25-day time period. During this period this line, with a normal crew (one foreman, one production checker, and eight production workers), produced 6,299 material layouts to complete 241 cases for overseas shipment.

Of the 6,299 completed layouts, the production checker rejected 97 for missing or incorrect parts. Had any one of these rejected layouts been shipped, as many as 24 vehicles could have been delayed in assembly at the destination point. Obtaining either correct or missing parts frequently resulted in assembly delays of from 3 to 12 weeks' duration. Although the 97 rejected layouts appear small compared to the 6,299 correct layouts, it should be noted that both the shipping plant and the overseas organizations incur additional cost and difficulties in issuing shipping orders, in obtaining customs releases, in obtaining and boxing materials, in air freight, plus in possibly having orders canceled due to delays in car delivery.

Fig. 5P4-1

QUALITY AND ACCURACY CHART

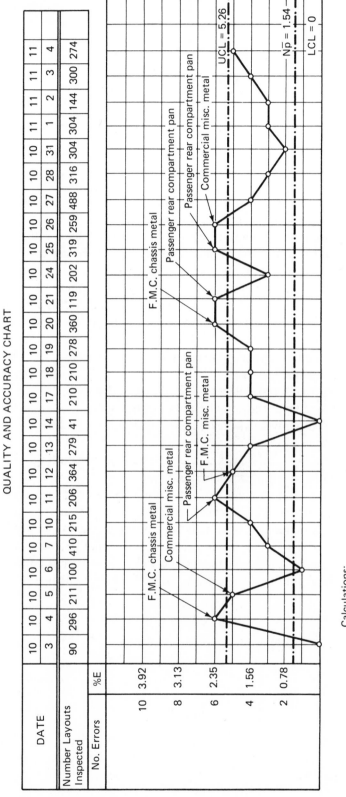

Calculations:

Total items   6,299

Average items/day   266

Total errors   97

$$\overline{Np} = \frac{\text{Total no. errors}}{\text{No. items}} = \frac{97}{6{,}299} = 1.54$$

$$UCL = \overline{Np} + 3\sqrt{\overline{Np}} = 1.54 + 3.72 = 5.26$$

$$LCL = \overline{Np} - 3\sqrt{\overline{Np}} = 1.54 - 3.72 = 0$$

The quality and accuracy chart shown indicates the line had trouble each time truck cases were run, due to a similarity in two models. In addition there was also an increase in defective layouts whenever passenger cases were packed. This was also attributed to part similarity on four different models.

Corrective action consisted of designing foolproof layout fixtures and using bright-colored paints to mark distinguishing features on similar items. The chart referred to was submitted both as an assigned exercise and to aid in error reduction.

Assignment

Analyze the chart for accuracy of technique and interpretation of results.

Problem 5

Quality control techniques have many diverse applications. The following illustrates an application to upholstery cloth in a receiving inspection area.

When cloth is woven at the mill, it is inevitable that the process will produce some defects. When a flaw does occur in the material and is detected, rather than cutting it out, the vendor makes an allowance for it by supplying extra yardage to make up for the loss. The minimum yardage allowed per flaw is 0.125 yard. Vendors indicate where these flaws, or defects, occur by tying either red or yellow strings at the material's edge. If the defect is created by only one flaw, the minimum allowance (0.125 yard) is permitted, and the flaw is marked with a red string. If, however, the defect is created by several flaws, exceeding a distance greater than 0.125 yard, the allowance is made for whatever yardage is necessary, and the defect area is bounded by yellow strings at the material's edge.

Assuming that the vendor(s) detects all the flaws and makes the appropriate allowances, the premise might be made that the actual number of flaws which occur is of little consequence. Such is not the case. Too many flaws create losses over and beyond the allowance permitted by the mills.

To fully understand how these flaws create material loss, the cutting process must be understood. Anywhere from 50 to 100 plies are laid out and cut at one time. When laying this material out on long tables, *splices* can be made only at limited locations. For example, if a flaw occurs halfway between two splice areas, the yardage lost is often greater than the allowance for the flaw. In addition to this material loss, time is lost by the workers who lay the material out.

The vendee's material specification for cloth requires that defects shall not exceed one in 12 yards. One red string counts as one defect and two yellow strings count as one defect.

The following data represent the results from checking two different vendors and three different materials:

Vendor X, Cloth A			Vendor Y, Cloth B			Vendor Y, Cloth C		
Sample No.	Yd/ Roll	No. Defects	Sample No.	Yd/ Roll	No. Defects	Sample No.	Yd/ Roll	No. Defects
1	36.875	4	1	63.750	8	1	78.375	3
2	28.000	3	2	63.250	8	2	71.000	3
3	35.125	2	3	70.125	6	3	60.500	6
4	36.500	0	4	70.000	7	4	70.625	3
5	35.373	5	5	65.625	7	5	70.000	1
6	36.000	2	6	71.250	5	6	73.125	2
7	25.625	1	7	65.500	10	7	72.125	2
8	33.875	4	8	64.000	5	8	68.875	2
9	36.000	3	9	52.125	4	9	64.625	3
10	40.250	2	10	49.500	2	10	71.000	0
11	39.250	2	11	65.500	3	11	61.875	1
12	48.500	0	12	53.125	3	12	72.375	4
13	33.750	5	13	70.000	9	13	72.250	1
14	37.250	1	14	62.000	6	14	68.625	2
15	39.375	4	15	54.250	4	15	65.750	0
16	37.625	0	16	63.875	7	16	73.500	2
17	39.875	6	17	66.875	8	17	71.875	6
18	32.625	0	18	52.875	5	18	76.375	2
19	35.750	8	19	65.375	7	19	69.125	2
20	33.245	10	20	34.250	1	20	74.500	1
21	36.000	4	21	62.125	3	21	74.250	0
22	33.875	5	22	61.500	7	22	71.375	0
23	35.500	12				23	70.625	2
24	40.625	5				24	61.375	3
						25	66.625	1
						26	66.375	5
						27	76.250	6

Assignment

1. Decide what type of charts would be appropriate for portraying this information.
2. Plot these charts and construct the means and limits.
3. Analyze the following:
   a. Are vendors in control?
   b. Are some materials better than others?
   c. Are specifications adhered to? If not, what percent of the product would be expected to be out of specifications?
4. Would there be a better way to handle these data?

Problem 6

The accompanying data sheet summarizes the results of final inspection on a plated article. Fifty pieces were checked every hour for burrs, poor plate, poor finish, untapped holes, and undersize holes.

a. Plot the total number of defects by hours through 1/12/70.

b. Based on these data, calculate $\bar{C}$ and control limits. Extend these limits and the average line as a guide to decisions regarding future quality levels.

c. Due to the quality level shown on this chart, certain changes were made in the process. These were made on 1/13/70. New racks were developed to hold articles for plating. They were designed to provide a better finish on the plated articles. Countersinking attachments were added to the die-cast cores to help eliminate plating buildup around the tapped holes. A control chart was placed on the tapper in an attempt to reduce the number of undersize and untapped holes. You have been assigned to follow this job and note the effect of these changes. Plot the hourly results of checks after 1/13/70 on the control chart to observe the quality level after the changes.

d. The following cost figures were obtained relative to the defects which were being tabulated:

Repair on untapped holes	$0.015
Repair on undersize holes	$0.010
Poor finish	$0.015
Poor plate	$0.050
Burrs	$0.005

Using these figures, determine appropriate weighting factors for each defect. Using these factors, plot a weighted C chart for the total period. It is not necessary to use limits on this chart.

e. Analyze these charts to determine the effect of the changes.

Data for Number of Defects Chart

Date	1/10/70							
Hour	1	2	3	4	5	6	7	8
Holes not tapped	15	21	26	15	22	20	30	26
Holes U/S—tap	6	5	18	16	14	12	10	9
Holes U/S—plate	0	1	2	2	1	0	1	0
Poor finish	7	8	7	9	8	7	8	6
Poor plate	5	6	7	6	7	3	6	4
Burrs	5	4	10	3	5	6	4	3
Total	38	45	70	51	57	48	59	48

Date	1/11/70							
Hour	1	2	3	4	5	6	7	8
Holes not tapped	24	20	22	23	26	22	15	16
Holes U/S—tap	14	12	13	12	15	16	10	16
Holes U/S—plate	1	0	1	0	1	1	0	1
Poor finish	7	7	5	6	5	6	5	6
Poor plate	5	4	6	7	4	6	3	4
Burrs	6	5	4	5	5	4	4	3
Total	57	48	51	53	56	55	37	46

Date	1/12/70							
Hour	1	2	3	4	5	6	7	8
Holes not tapped	18	18	19	22	22	25	18	28
Holes U/S—tap	12	15	14	18	13	15	12	16
Holes U/S—plate	0	3	1	2	1	0	0	2
Poor finish	6	5	7	6	4	5	5	4
Poor plate	5	3	4	5	6	5	5	6
Burrs	5	6	3	5	4	4	5	4
Total	46	50	48	58	50	54	45	60

Date	1/14/70							
Hour	1	2	3	4	5	6	7	8
Holes not tapped	20	18	25	19	28	22	18	18
Holes U/S—tap	15	14	19	16	17	16	12	10
Holes U/S—plate	1	0	0	1	1	0	0	0
Poor finish	7	6	6	5	4	7	6	5
Poor plate	5	8	4	5	5	7	9	10
Burrs	4	3	5	2	5	5	4	3
Total	52	49	59	48	60	57	49	46

Date	1/15/70							
Hour	1	2	3	4	5	6	7	8
Holes not tapped	16	15	14	13	12	16	18	18
Holes U/S—tap	9	8	6	5	4	6	5	10
Holes U/S—plate	0	0	0	0	0	0	0	0
Poor finish	4	4	6	7	7	8	6	5
Poor plate	11	11	12	14	11	12	15	10
Burrs	3	6	5	5	4	6	5	3
Total	43	44	43	44	38	48	49	46

Date	1/16/70							
Hour	1	2	3	4	5	6	7	8
Holes not tapped	10	9	12	11	8	15	12	12
Holes U/S—tap	5	6	5	3	1	2	4	3
Holes U/S—plate	0	0	0	1	0	2	0	1
Poor finish	4	3	4	4	4	5	4	5
Poor plate	14	16	12	10	12	15	17	15
Burrs	4	3	8	6	5	4	5	6
Total	37	37	41	35	30	43	42	42

Data for Weighted Chart

Date	1/10/70							
Hour	1	2	3	4	5	6	7	8
Holes not tapped	45	63	78	45	66	60	90	78
Holes U/S—tap	12	10	36	32	28	24	20	18
Holes U/S—plate	0	2	4	4	2	0	2	0
Poor finish	21	24	21	27	24	21	24	18
Poor plate	50	60	70	60	70	30	60	40
Burrs	5	4	10	3	5	6	4	3
Total	133	163	219	171	195	141	200	157

Date	1/11/70							
Hour	1	2	3	4	5	6	7	8
Holes not tapped	72	60	66	69	78	66	45	48
Holes U/S—tap	28	24	26	24	30	32	20	32
Holes U/S—plate	2	0	2	0	2	2	0	2
Poor finish	21	21	15	18	15	18	15	18
Poor plate	50	40	60	70	40	60	30	40
Burrs	6	5	4	5	5	4	4	3
Total	179	150	173	186	170	182	114	143

Date	1/12/70								
Hour	1	2	3	4	5	6	7	8	Totals
Holes not tapped	54	54	57	66	66	75	54	84	1539
Holes U/S—tap	24	30	28	36	26	30	24	32	626
Holes U/S—plate	0	6	2	4	2	0	0	4	42
Poor finish	18	15	21	18	12	15	15	12	447
Poor plate	50	30	40	50	60	50	50	60	1220
Burrs	5	6	3	5	4	4	5	4	112
Total	151	141	151	179	170	174	148	196	3986

Date	1/14/70							
Hour	1	2	3	4	5	6	7	8
Holes not tapped	60	54	75	57	84	66	54	54
Holes U/S—tap	30	28	38	32	34	32	24	20
Holes U/S—plate	2	0	0	2	2	0	0	0
Poor finish	21	18	18	15	12	21	18	15
Poor plate	50	80	40	50	50	70	90	100
Burrs	4	3	5	2	5	5	4	3
Total	167	183	176	158	187	194	190	192

Date	1/15/70							
Hour	1	2	3	4	5	6	7	8
Holes not tapped	48	45	42	39	36	48	45	30
Holes U/S—tap	18	16	12	10	8	12	14	10
Holes U/S—plate	0	0	0	0	0	0	2	0
Poor finish	12	12	18	21	21	24	18	21
Poor plate	110	110	120	140	110	120	150	150
Burrs	3	6	5	5	4	6	5	6
Total	191	189	197	215	179	210	234	217

Date	1/16/70								
Hour	1	2	3	4	5	6	7	8	Totals
Holes not tapped	30	27	36	33	24	45	36	36	1104
Holes U/S—tap	10	12	10	6	2	4	8	6	396
Holes U/S—plate	0	0	0	2	0	4	0	2	24
Poor finish	12.	9	12	12	12	15	12	15	384
Poor plate	140	160	120	100	120	150	170	150	2550
Burrs	4	3	8	6	5	4	5	6	112
Total	196	211	186	159	163	222	231	215	4662

CHAPTERS 7 AND 8

Problem 1

To determine if it was feasible to use a control chart, an initial study was made on a machine cutting operation. Five consecutive measurements were taken each hour, over a 14-hour period. Measurements were recorded in thousandths, from a zero setting of 0.450 inch. Specifications were 0.460 ± 0.005 inch.

Hour	X_1	X_2	X_3	X_4	X_5
1	5	6	6	7	8
2	5	6	7	8	8
3	7	7	8	8	9
4	8	8	9	10	11
5	9	10	10	10	12
6	10	12	12	13	14
7	13	13	14	14	15

Machine stopped and cutting edge ground

8	5	5	6	7	8
9	6	6	7	7	8
10	6	7	8	9	10
11	7	7	8	9	10
12	8	9	10	10	12
13	10	10	11	12	13
14	12	12	13	14	15

Machine stopped and cutting edge ground

15	5	6	7	8	9
16	6	6	7	7	9
17	6	7	8	9	9
18	7	8	8	8	10
19	9	9	9	10	11
20	10	10	11	11	12
21	11	11	12	14	15

Assignment

1. Can the process be considered in control? If not, what corrections are necessary?

2. What type of control limits might be placed on this operation?

3. What are the control values if no defective product is tolerated?

Problem 2

A frequently recurring problem in an engine plant is trying to maintain torque readings to specifications. The following data was collected on bolts holding the rocker arm cover to the engine (eight readings represents eight bolts). Both first and second shift readings are given. Print specifications are 30 to 50 in-lb.

Date	Shift	X_1	X_2	X_3	X_4	X_5	X_6	X_7	X_8	Totals
10–15	1st.	42	43	40	46	46	50	42	44	349
//	//	44	44	50	42	46	40	42	44	342
//	2nd.	48	46	46	48	44	48	48	44	372
//	//	40	48	46	46	48	46	46	44	364
10–16	1st.	44	40	41	44	43	44	40	38	334
//	//	46	44	46	45	45	45	42	46	359
//	2nd.	46	46	50	48	48	50	44	46	378
//	//	46	48	46	45	46	44	46	44	365
10–17	1st.	44	44	44	46	46	40	44	42	350
//	//	45	44	46	44	42	44	45	46	356
//	2nd.	46	46	44	44	44	40	46	42	352
//	//	46	48	46	46	46	44	43	46	367
10–18	1st.	43	44	43	45	46	44	44	46	355
//	//	44	44	46	48	44	43	44	40	353
//	2nd.	44	43	46	46	45	46	46	45	361
//	//	44	44	43	42	41	46	44	44	348
10–19	1st.	46	48	48	48	46	48	46	48	378
//	//	46	46	48	48	46	46	48	48	376
//	2nd.	42	44	42	44	46	44	44	45	351
//	//	46	46	44	46	47	46	44	45	364
10–22	1st.	45	45	46	48	46	48	46	48	372
//	//	48	48	46	46	48	50	46	46	378
//	2nd.	48	48	50	46	44	46	44	46	372
//	//	48	48	46	48	50	46	50	46	382
10–23	1st.	44	46	43	44	44	44	45	44	353
//	//	42	45	46	44	40	38	38	40	333
//	2nd.	46	44	48	44	45	48	44	48	367
//	//	48	45	44	50	45	45	46	46	369

Assignment

1. Calculate the average and range values for each subgroup.
2. Plot these values on an average and range chart.
3. Compute the control limits for both charts and plot.
4. Analysis:
   a. Is a *state of control* exhibited?
   b. What are the control limits for individual values?
   c. What is the probability of getting torque readings out of specifications?
   d. What limits would you recommend for the next chart?
   e. Would there be any particular reason for operating as shown on this chart?

Problem 3

A study was undertaken at the request of production engineering to determine the process capability of a new Churchill Grinder BT-8041. The operation performed by this grinder involved grinding a pilot diameter on a transmission main drive gear, Part No. 8A-7017. Specifications for the diameter were 0.6682 to 0.6688 inch. A carborundum No. 60JX5 (English) grinding wheel was used for the following set of 50 readings. The readings were taken continously as the parts were produced. Readings are in 0.0001-inch increments from a zero setting of 0.6685 inch.

Sample No.	X_1	X_2	X_3	X_4	X_5
1	0	−1	−2	−1	−1
2	0	0	0	−1	0
3	0	+1	+1	0	0
4	+1	+2	+1	+1	+2
5	0	−1	0	−1	−1†
6	+1	0	0	+1	0
7	+2	+2	+2	+2	+2
8	+2	+2	+2	+3	+2
9	+3	+4	+3	+4	+4
10	+3	+4	+3	+3	+3

†Drift from samples 5 to 9 involved a time interval of 15 minutes.

For a comparison the grinding wheel was changed to a Universal No. 60M (English), and another set of 50 readings was taken:

Sample No.	X_1	X_2	X_3	X_4	X_5
1	−3	−2	−3	−3	−3
2	−2	−1	−3	−3	−1
3	−2	−2	−2	−3	−2
4	−2	−2	−1	−2	−1
5	−2	−1	−2	−2	−2
6	−2	−2	−1	−2	−2
7	−1	−2	−2	−1	−2
8	−1	−1	−2	0	−2
9	−1	0	−1	−1	−1
10	0	0	−2	−1	0

Assignment

1. Calculate the mean and standard deviation ($\bar{X}$ and s) for both sets of data, using either a histogram (root mean square) or normal probability paper (NOPP).

    a. Do both wheels indicate a similar capability?

    b. Do both wheels meet acceptable capability requirements? (Is the ratio of six standard deviations to the tolerance less than or equal to 0.75?)

    c. What percentage of parts is outside specifications?

2. Determine the range for each subgroup in each set, calculate the average ranges ($\bar{R}$), and estimate the standard deviation ($\hat{\sigma}$) for both grinding wheels.

    a. Compare these deviations to those calculated in 1. What can the differences be attributed to?

    b. Using these standard deviations, do the wheels meet the capability requirements specified in 1-b?

3. Calculate the following and plot an average and range chart for each grinding wheel:

$$\bar{\bar{X}}, \qquad 3\sigma_{\bar{x}}, \qquad \text{UCL}_{\bar{x}}, \qquad \text{LCL}_{\bar{x}}, \qquad \text{UCL}_R, \qquad \text{LCL}_R$$

    a. Analyze these charts and recommend what action should be taken, based on the state of control exhibited.

    b. Estimate the number of pieces that should be run, prior to resetting the grinder.

Problem 4

This study concerned an input sun gear, a gear used in an automatic transmission. See Figure 7/8P4-1.

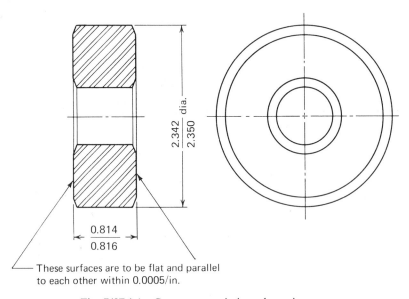

Fig. 7/8P4-1 Gear—transmission planet input sun

Excessive scrap and rework was attributed to the inability to hold specifications on a grinding operation. This was a double-face grinder where both gear faces were ground simultaneously by two grinding wheels rotating in opposite directions. These wheels also have a slight toe-in angle to facilitate grabbing the blank and imparting a spinning motion which is required to obtain a uniform grind.

In making the dimensional checks, it was discovered that a taper existed across the face of some of the pieces. This was obviously attributable to an uneven removal of material and was considered a potential problem source. Observations made while the parts were being ground revealed that in some instances the gear did not spin. Figure 7/8P4-2 shows distributions of overall length and measured taper.

Additional information for average and range charts is shown in Figure 7/8P4-3. These conditions are shown for both before and after changes were instituted. *Note:* Data for both 'before' and 'after' taken at random times during the days indicated.

| Overall Length | | Taper | | | |
| | | * Part spinning | | ! Part not spinning | |
Midpoint	Frequency	Midpoint	Frequency	Midpoint	Frequency
0.8172	1	0.00037	2	0.0029	4
0.8157	7	0.00032	2	0.0026	13
0.8142	13	0.00027	4	0.0023	4
0.8127	3	0.00022	3	0.0020	1
0.8112	1	0.00017	11	0.0017	2
		0.00012	2	0.0014	0
		0.00007	1	0.0011	1

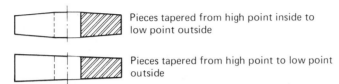

Pieces tapered from high point inside to low point outside

Pieces tapered from high point to low point outside

Fig. 7/8P4-2   Distributions—size and taper

Date	X_1	X_2	X_3	X_4	X_5	Totals
			Before Data			
2/5	+15	+15	+13	+13	+12	+68
2/5	+11	+12	+11	+12	+15	+61
2/5	+1	+1	+2	+2	+1	+7
2/5	−14	−16	−17	−20	−23	−90
2/5	−10	−10	−13	−9	−15	−57
2/8	−10	−10	−13	−13	−15	−61
2/8	+3	+3	+4	+5	+6	+21
2/8	+27	+30	+35	+37	+40	+169
2/8	+11	+11	+17	+17	+17	+73
2/9	+2	+3	+7	+6	+4	+22
2/9	−30	−30	−32	−45	−50	−187
2/9	+16	+16	+18	+17	+19	+86
2/9	+15	+15	+15	+15	+15	+75
			After Data			
3/16	+5	+5	+5	+5	+5	+25
3/16	−5	−5	−5	−5	−5	−25
3/16	0	0	0	0	0	0
3/16	−10	−10	−5	−5	−5	−35
3 16	0	0	0	0	0	0
3/16	0	−5	−5	0	−5	−15
3/16	−10	−10	−5	−5	0	−30
3/16	0	+5	+5	0	+5	+15
3/16	+5	+5	0	+5	0	+15
3/16	−5	−10	−10	−5	−10	−40
3/16	0	0	0	−5	−5	−10
3/16	0	+5	+5	0	0	+10
3/16	−5	−5	0	0	−10	−20

Fig. 7/8P4-3   Before data—After data

Assignment

1. Analyze the information shown in Figure 7/8P4-2. Does this indicate the ability to meet specifications?

2. Use the 'before' data in Figure 7/8P4-3 to set up an average and range chart. Plot these data, calculate all required limits, and extend into the next time period.

3. Plot the "after" data. Has the change accomplished the intended purpose? What limits would be proposed for the next period?

Problem 5

This problem concerns torque requirements on the vertical movement on an inside glare-proof mirror. (See Figure 7/8P5-1.) The design specified 8 to 14 inch-pounds of torque on the vertical movement and a slightly higher torque on the horizontal movement (not considered in this study).

Fig. 7/8P5-1   Cross section—inside rear view mirror

In attempting to correct the problem, $2,500 had been expended over a 2-year period on die maintenance in an effort to control one dimension on the ball. In addition, during periods when extreme difficulties were encountered with the tools, production on the assembly line had to be stopped until die changes could be made.

Repairing a high-torque mirror costs considerably less than repairing one with low torque. A tight ball can usually be repaired by oiling and rotating it until the oil is between the ball and ball seat. The operation was performed by an assembly line repairman and costs approximately $0.007 per mirror.

The cost for repairing a loose ball is much higher, since it cannot be repaired on the line. It has to be sent to the salvage department, the glass removed, and the ball taken out. Removing the glass costs $0.0063 per mirror. In addition, there is a 10 percent glass breakage which costs $0.0065 per mirror. Other costs were

Disassembling ball	$0.014 per mirror
Reassembling ball	$0.058 per mirror

To determine what percent of each defect was being produced, an average and range chart was used to record torque measurement. A five-piece random sample was taken each hour over a 20-hour period. Results are shown in Figure 7/8P5-2. As can be observed, the average torque is well below the print mean. An investigation revealed that this had occurred to remedy assembly plant complaints concerning high-torque effort. At the same time, there were also complaints about low torque. Further inquiry disclosed that the torque checking method varied between the production and inspection departments. When the prints were critically examined, the reason for the assembly plant misinterpreting the checking method was understood. The engineering department was contacted and agreed to issue new prints to clarify the appropriate method.

The next step involved the tooling department. Data from the study were used to show what torque existed. It was explained that if the ball seat could be held toward the high limit, the torque would be toward the high side (14 inch-pounds). Further, if the processing department could hold the ball seat within 0.001-inch roundness and within 0.003 inch on location, torque specifications could be held. The die was reworked to bring it to the required dimensions, and another torque study was instituted. (See Figure 7/8P5-3.)

Assignment

1. Do the control charts show evidence of statistical control?
2. Estimate the standard deviation for individual torque values for both data sets, i.e., before and after change. Use the average range from the charts shown in Figures 7/8P5-2 and 7/8P5-3.

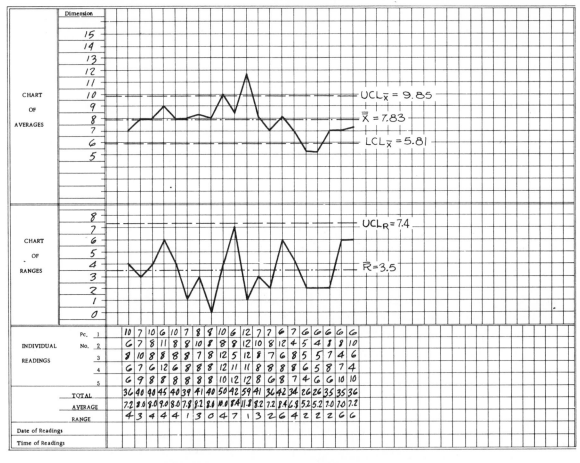

Fig. 7/8P5-2 *(Above)* Torque readings before change

Fig. 7/8P5-3 *(Below)* Torque readings after change

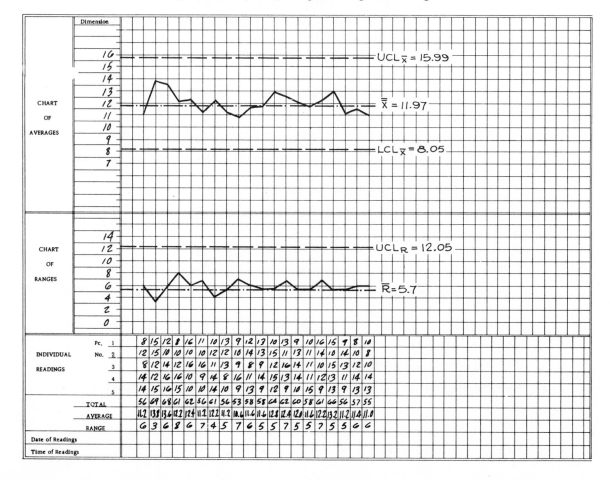

3. Using these standard deviations, estimate the percent that are out of specifications. Plot these data on normal probability paper, and compare.

4. Using the cost figures given and the rework percentages from 3, determine if the overall cost has been reduced by the change.

5. Construct a minimum cost curve, utilizing the data in Figure 7/8P5-3, by assuming the mean can be shifted. What is the optimum mean torque and the minimum cost?

Problem 6

Management has become concerned about a rise in warranty costs on the radiators produced in your plant. The latest figures released show that these costs, for a comparable period, have increased nearly 40 percent over last year. Production volume is approximately the same as last year.

The radiator line was recently moved to a new building and was directly in front of the main factory doors. Since these doors were frequently open, one engineer believed that the draft could be chilling the solder too rapidly, with resultant leaks reported as warranty items. To eliminate this condition, a large barrier was erected to block the drafts. This seemingly had little or no effect on improving the situation, other than providing a more comfortable environment for the workers.

At this point, the quality engineering department decided to study the situation more thoroughly and as an initial effort collected the data portrayed on the chart in Figure 7/8P6-1. On this chart the defects found at water test are listed by area, i.e., top header, lower header, upper solder off, lower solder off, inlet, outlet, tube, filler, oil cooler, and drain. The upper solder off, lower solder off, inlet, outlet, and filler are hand operations, while the others are done on a molten solder machine. Leaks generally occur at random on the headers, although slightly more occur on the ends. It can be observed from the chart that for the period March 7 to May 8 the percent defective is approximately 22 percent higher than last year.

Since the two highest individual defects were leaks at the top and bottom headers, the quality control engineer decided to concentrate on these two areas in an effort to lower the percent defective.

The header to tube assembly is performed on a molten solder machine. This is the machine that was recently moved to a new location and it is set up to run all high-production radiator cores. Current output is 900 units per shift, 2 shifts per day. Volume in 2 years is predicted to be 3,200 units per shift.

The many different dimensions specified for these cores create problems such as different preheat temperatures and varying amounts of solder deposited per core. The operation of the molten solder machine is as follows:

1. Assembled cores are loaded into fixtures on the machine.

2. Cores pass across a stream of flux.

3. The header is preheated by a row of 40 burners.

4. Solder is applied to the header by means of a nozzle supplied by a constant head of solder. A recirculating system which flows solder over a weir maintains this constant head.

5. Solder deposited on the header is remelted by a series of 6 burners to ensure a good tube to header bond.

6. The core is steam-cleaned.

7. The core is automatically turned over, and the process is repeated on the other header.

DEPT. RADIATOR   PART NAME RADIATOR CORE   OPERATION WATER TEST

Date	3/7	3/8	3/9	3/10	3/11	3/14	3/15	3/16	3/17	3/18	3/21	3/22	3/23	3/25	3/28	3/29	3/30	3/31	4/1	4/4	4/5	4/6	4/7	4/8
No. pct. Inspected	100	100	100	100	100	100	100	100	100	100	100	100	100	100	100	100	100	100	100	100	100	100	100	100

Defects

Defects																								
1 TOP HEADER	17	6	41	16	13	19	18	16	13	29	42	16	17	23	26	19	12	12	10	16	4	13	11	
2 LOWER HEADER	25	15	11	12	7	14	15	23	21	19	29	9	8	7	12	8	18	13	34	5	4	15	21	
3 UP SOLDER OFF	3	3	5	2	3	1	5	5	5	4	1	2	3	2	1	7	6	3	1	3	4	6	5	
4 LOW SOLDER OFF	2	3	4	3	3	1	1	10	2	10	1			1	4	1	1		2	2	9	6	1	
5 INLET		1		2								1	2	2	1	3		3	1	3	2			
6 OUTLET	2		2	2	2	8	19	2	5	3			1	5	4	2	3	2	2	10	3	3		
7 TUBE	5	1	2	2	3	6	6	2	2		5	2	5	2	2	5	3	3	1		10	3	1	5
8 FILLER						6	1		6	1		6		2		3	8		3	3			2	
9 OIL COOLER	2		4		7	6	4	5							32				5		5	2		1
10 DRAIN																								
Total No. Defects	56	41	67	45	38	54	64	61	61	66	87	45	35	42	54	44	48	30	62	38	60	29	44	44
Total No. Defectives	50	38	61	40	33	49	48	53	57	58	73	42	35	42	50	43	46	29	59	37	59	26	44	43
% Defective	50	38	61	40	33	49	48	53	57	58	73	42	35	42	50	43	46	29	59	37	59	26	44	43

1965 AVG.

Part No.: *3007703*   Part Name: *RADIATOR CORE*   Plant: _____

Characteristic Measured: *WEIGHT OF SOLDER DEPOSIT.*   Date Received _____

Unit of Measurement: *OUNCE* _____   Zero Setting: _____

NOZZLE DIAMETER —0.060″

Sample No	Date (And hour)	Measurements of Each Item in Sample						Total	Average for Sample	Range for Sample
		1	2	3	4	5	6			
1	4/11	6.75	6.50	7.25	7.00	7.25	7.00	41.75	6.96	0.75
2		6.50	6.25	6.25	6.75	7.00	6.50	39.25	6.54	0.75
3		6.00	6.50	6.25	6.75	6.25	6.00	37.75	6.29	0.75
4		6.00	6.50	6.25	6.25	6.75	5.75	37.50	6.25	1.00
5		5.25	6.00	6.25	5.75	5.50	6.75	35.50	5.91	0.75
6	4/12	5.75	6.25	5.25	6.50	6.50	5.25	35.50	5.91	1.25
7		5.25	4.75	5.00	5.00	4.50	4.75	29.25	4.88	0.75
8		5.00	4.25	4.00	4.25	4.50	4.25	26.25	4.38	1.00
9		7.00	7.50	6.50	7.25	6.25	6.25	40.75	6.79	1.25
10	4/13	6.75	7.00	6.75	6.50	6.25	6.50	39.75	6.63	0.75
11		6.00	6.00	5.75	6.50	6.25	6.00	36.50	6.08	0.75
12		6.25	6.00	5.75	6.00	6.00	5.50	35.50	5.92	0.75
13		6.00	6.25	6.75	6.25	6.25	7.00	38.50	6.42	1.00
14		6.00	6.00	5.25	7.50	5.75	5.50	36.00	6.00	2.25
15		5.75	5.50	5.50	5.25	6.00	5.75	33.75	5.62	0.75
16	4/14	5.25	5.00	5.25	5.00	5.75	5.25	31.50	5.25	0.75
17		5.00	4.75	5.25	4.50	4.75	4.50	28.75	4.79	0.75
18		7.50	7.50	5.75	6.00	6.00	5.75	38.50	6.42	1.75
19		6.00	6.00	6.00	5.75	6.25	5.75	34.75	5.79	0.75
20		5.50	5.75	5.25	5.75	5.50	5.75	33.50	5.58	0.50
21	4/15	5.25	5.75	5.75	5.00	5.25	5.00	32.00	5.33	0.75
22		5.25	5.50	5.50	5.50	5.25	5.00	32.00	5.33	0.25
23		4.50	5.00	5.00	4.75	5.00	4.50	28.75	4.79	0.50
24		4.50	4.50	5.75	5.25	4.50	4.50	28.50	4.75	0.50
25										
26			Totals						138.59	21.00
27			Grand Average (X̄)						5.775	0.75

Fig. 7/8P6-2 Solder deposits (ounces)

At a meeting held with representatives from the tool engineering and quality engineering groups, it was decided to investigate the header leak areas and, specifically, to determine the amount of solder applied in these areas. The results of this study are shown in Figure 7/8P6-2. The average weight of solder deposited on the header was 5.775 ounces. Previous checks of a competitor's cores revealed that 10.73 ounces of solder were deposited in these areas. The obvious solution in reducing leaks appeared to involve depositing additional solder. Since the molten solder machine maintains a constant head, the flow rate of the solder is governed by the size of the nozzles. The original nozzles had a diameter of 0.060 inch, resulting in the previous average weight of 5.775 ounces (Figure 7/8P6-2).

To determine the validity of this hypothesis (additional solder reduces leaks) the nozzles were removed and drilled to an 0.070-inch diameter. Samples were again taken as shown in Figure 7/8P6-3. The results at water test are given in Figure 7/8P6-4. This appeared to indicate that the investigation was progressing in the right direction, so a further step was taken. The nozzles were again removed and drilled to an 0.081-inch diameter. Results are shown in Figure 7/8P6-5. Although additional warranty information was not available at the time this study was completed, the general opinion was that the problem was satisfactorily resolved.

RECORD SHEET FOR MEASUREMENTS

Part No.: _3007703_____ Part Name: _RADIATOR CORE_ Plant: _____

Characteristic Measured: _WEIGHT OF SOLDER DEPOSIT_ Date Received _____

Unit of Measurement: _OUNCE_____ Zero Setting: _____

NOZZLE DIAMETER −0.070″

Sample No.	Date (And hour)	Measurements of Each Item in Sample					Total	Average for Sample	Range for Sample
		1	2	3	4	5			
1	4/18	6.75	6.25	6.25	6.00	6.25	31.50	6.30	0.75
2		5.75	5.50	6.50	5.75	5.75	29.25	5.85	1.00
3		7.25	7.00	7.25	6.50	6.50	34.50	6.90	0.75
4		5.75	6.50	6.50	6.25	6.50	31.50	6.30	0.75
5	4/19	5.75	5.50	6.00	5.50	5.00	27.75	5.55	0.50
6		6.75	6.75	7.50	7.00	5.75	33.75	6.75	1.75
7		6.50	6.00	5.75	6.00	6.00	30.25	6.05	0.75
8		5.25	5.50	4.75	5.00	4.75	25.25	5.05	0.75
9	4/20	5.75	6.00	7.25	5.50	5.75	30.25	6.05	1.75
10		6.00	5.00	5.50	5.75	6.00	28.25	5.65	1.00
11		4.75	5.00	5.25	5.25	4.75	25.00	5.00	0.50
12		6.00	5.50	5.25	5.50	5.25	27.50	5.50	0.75
13		8.00	7.25	7.75	6.75	7.75	37.50	7.50	1.25
14	4/21	6.00	6.25	5.50	6.25	6.00	30.00	6.00	0.75
15		6.00	6.50	6.25	6.25	6.50	31.50	6.30	0.50
16		7.50	7.25	6.50	7.00	7.00	35.25	7.05	1.00
17		5.25	4.50	4.50	5.25	5.25	24.75	4.95	0.75
18		5.50	6.00	6.75	6.50	6.50	31.25	6.25	1.25
19	4/22	5.00	5.50	5.50	6.00	6.25	28.25	5.65	1.25
20		6.25	5.50	5.00	5.75	6.50	29.00	5.80	1.50
21		6.75	5.50	6.00	6.75	6.00	30.90	6.18	1.25
22		6.75	5.00	5.50	5.00	6.00	28.25	5.65	1.75
23									
24			Totals					132.28	22.25
25			Grand Average (X̄)					6.013	1.011
26									
27									

Fig. 7/8P6-3 Solder deposits (ounces)

Fig. 7/8P6-4 Leaks at water test after first change

Date	4/18	4/19	4/20	4/21	4/22					
No. Pcs. Inspected	100	100	100	100	100					
Defects										
1. Top Header	4	10	3	22	8					
2. Lower Header	13	3	10	6	3					
3. Upper Solder Off	3	12	2	3	4					
4. Lower Solder Off	4	1	11	1	7					
5. Inlet	0	1	0	1	0					
6. Outlet	0	4	1	1	4					
7. Tube	4	3	2	3	3					
8. Filler	0	2	0	0	0					
9. Oil Cooler	0	0	8	1	1					
10. Drain	0	0	0	0	0					
Total No. Defects	28	36	37	38	30					
Total No. Defective	27	34	36	35	27					
Percent Defective	27	34	36	35	27					

Date	4/25	4/26	4/27	4/28	4/29	5/2	5/3	5/4	5/5	5/6
No. Pcs. Inspected	100	100	100	100	100	100	100	100	100	100
Defects										
1. Top Header	4	0	4	3	5	2	0	7	2	4
2. Lower Header	5	3	6	4	1	3	4	3	1	0
3. Upper Solder Off	3	2	1	3	2	6	2	2	4	4
4. Lower Solder Off	3	0	4	1	0	3	11	7	1	0
5. Inlet	0	0	0	1	0	0	0	0	1	4
6. Outlet	0	1	1	0	1	3	0	1	3	0
7. Tube	8	4	1	0	3	2	4	7	6	7
8. Filler	1	3	1	1	1	1	0	0	4	0
9. Oil Cooler	2	2	0	0	0	0	4	2	0	0
10. Drain	0	0	0	0	0	0	0	0	0	0
Total No. Defects	26	15	20	17	13	20	25	29	22	19
Total No. Defective	25	13	19	16	12	19	23	28	19	18
Percent Defective	25	13	19	16	12	19	23	28	19	18

Fig. 7/8P6-5 Leaks at water test after second change

Assignment

1. Determine control limits for the data in Figure 7/8P6-1. Extend these to a new chart and plot the data from Figures 7/8P6-4 and 7/8P6-5. What conclusions can you draw?

2. Set up average and range charts for Figures 7/8P6-2, 7/8P6-3, and 7/8P6-5. Do each of these appear to be in statistical control?

3. What is your opinion of the approach followed in resolving this problem?

Problem 7

A certain dimension on a molded plastic housing is known to be causing problems at final assembly. The dimension has a specification of 53 ± 0.6 millimeters. The assembly operation is such that the undersize housings will not assemble and thus can be "sorted out" at the assembly station. It has been estimated that the cost of such a sorting process amounts to $0.12 per undersize housing reaching the assembly area (time loss, extra handling, etc.). The salvage value of an undersize housing is $0.05. If an oversize housing reaches the assembly area, it cannot be detected by the assembly operator. The resulting assembly will, however, be rejected at final test. The value (production cost) of an assembly is $6.53. Teardown costs are $0.75, and the salvage value of the components (including housing) is $2.43.

If the housings are inspected prior to assembly, it has been determined that 90 percent of the defectives (undersize and oversize) will be detected. The cost of a housing at this point is $0.35. Since they cannot be reworked, defective housings must be scrapped, with a salvage value of $0.05 each. An inspector with an hourly cost of $6.00 per hour can inspect approximately 200 housings per hour.

It is known that the variation on the 53- $\pm$ 0.6-millimeter dimension on the housing results from a poor sliding core configuration in the mold. Recent experience with a revised core mechanism on a similar part indicates that a capability of 0.8 millimeter (6σ spread) is attainable. Tooling costs for such a modification to the mold are estimated at $4,700.00, and time is no problem.

The remaining production requirements for the assembly are 100,000 units (i.e., 100,000 *good* housings are required).

The results of a daily five-piece check on the troublesome housing dimension for the last 2 weeks are shown in Figure 7/8P7-1. This dimension seems to follow a normal distribution.

Sample No. (Days)	X	R	Sample No. (Days)	X	R
1	52.4	0 4	6	52.8	1.4
2	53.0	0.8	7	52.8	0.6
3	52.8	0.8	8	53.0	0.4
4	53.0	0.6	9	52.6	0.6
5	52.6	1.0	10	52.8	1.2

Fig. 7/8P7-1 Five-piece sample check

Three alternative courses of action are being considered:

1. Run the mold as is and catch defectives at assembly and final test.
2. Run the mold as is and set up 100 percent inspection prior to assembly.
3. Revise the core configuration at a cost of $4,700.00 (the mold has no value at the end of the production run).

Assignment
What would you recommend?

CHAPTER 9

Problem 1

Rivets are received in lots of 40,000. The specified AQL = 6.5 percent. What is the single sampling plan that would be specified? General inspection level II is to be used. What plan would be required if level I were used? Level III? If lots are submitted at AQL quality, i.e., 6.5 percent, what is the probability of acceptance with each of these plans? Construct the OC curves for each of these three plans.

Problem 2

Trim moldings are packed in cartons containing 4,000 pieces. Determine a single sampling plan to use as an audit procedure if the desired AQL = 2.5 percent. Construct the OC curve. If the lot quality was actually 5 percent defective, what is the probability of acceptance?

Problem 3

Hinges are inspected using a double sampling plan. The lot size is 2,400 pieces, with a specified AQL = 1.5 percent. What is the correct sampling plan? An inspector, using this plan, discovered 3 defectives in the first sample. In the second sample he found 4 additional defective hinges. What decision should he make?

Problem 4

A double sampling plan is to be employed to check 1,000 parts for a safety characteristic. Due to the nature of the device, the AQL has been set at 0.1 percent, general inspection level III. What plan would be used?

Problem 5

For a continuing audit inspection, a multiple sampling plan with an AQL = 2.5 percent is required. Material is submitted in 1,400-piece lots. Specify the appropriate plan. The following results were obtained on the first audit:

First sample	1 defective found
Second sample	1 defective found
Third sample	3 defectives found
Fourth sample	5 defectives found
Fifth sample	0 defective found
Sixth sample	1 defective found
Seventh sample	2 defectives found

Evaluate the auditor's procedure and determine the correct final decision. Does he need additional instruction?

Problem 6

Refer to Problem 1 above. For general inspection level II only, specify the corresponding double and multiple sampling plans to use. If all material is submitted at AQL quality (6.5 percent), what would the average sample size be? Based on this, which plan would be recommended?

Problem 7

Refer to Problem 2 above. What conditions would pertain that would require tightened inspection? Assume that receiving inspection would like to use a reduced inspection plan. In the last 10 lots inspected, a total of 126 defective moldings were found. Does this qualify for reduced inspection? If this qualifies, what is the correct plan? Draw the OC curves for these tightened and reduced plans. How do they compare with the "normal" inspection plan curve constructed previously?

Problem 8

Find a single-sample fraction defective sampling plan that has $p_1 = 0.03$, $p_2 = 0.08$, $\alpha = 0.05$, and $\beta = 0.10$. Construct the OC curve for this plan. How closely does it match the specified values?

Problem 9

Find a single-sample fraction defective sampling plan that has $p_1 = 0.02$, $p_2 = 0.04$, $\alpha = 0.10$, and $\beta = 0.10$. Construct the OC curve for this plan. How closely does it match the specified values?

Problem 10

It was decided that a variable sampling plan would be used on the dimension shown in Figure 9P10-1. The part is a secondary piston. Shipments are made in cartons containing 250 pieces. Inspection level IV is to be used, with an AQL = 1.0 percent. Referring to MIL-STD-414, code letter H is specified. Initially it was decided to use the double specification limit plan, variability unknown, one AQL value for both upper and lower limit combined. This requires a sample of 20 pieces. The results were as follows:

$$0.637, \quad 0.633, \quad 0.635, \quad 0.635, \quad 0.637, \quad 0.638, \quad 0.638, \quad 0.638,$$
$$0.637, \quad 0.638, \quad 0.637, \quad 0.638, \quad 0.637, \quad 0.638, \quad 0.636, \quad 0.634,$$
$$0.632, \quad 0.636, \quad 0.635, \quad 0.636$$

Follow the procedure for applying this plan and determine the lot's disposition.

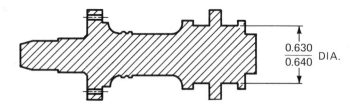

Fig. 9P10-1   Cross section—secondary piston

Some doubt was expressed as to the validity of this approach, and the calculations required to make a decision seemed cumbersome. Concern was also voiced as to the capability of the inspection personnel to perform the analysis. For comparative purposes, it was decided to try the double specification limit plan, variability unknown, average range method, single AQL value for both upper and lower limit combined. Code letter H is again needed, but the sample size is now 25 pieces. The results follow:

Sample No.	X_1	X_2	X_3	X_4	X_5	Totals
1	0.637	0.635	0.637	0.632	0.637	3.178
2	0.633	0.635	0.638	0.636	0.638	3.180
3	0.637	0.638	0.637	0.635	0.636	3.183
4	0.638	0.638	0.638	0.636	0.634	3.184
5	0.638	0.635	0.636	0.635	0.636	3.180

Follow the procedure for applying this plan and determine the lot's disposition. Is it the same as the standard deviation plan? Which plan is simpler? Would the inspection personnel be capable of performing this analysis? How does this compare to a comparable attribute sampling plan? Is there sufficient information to compare results?

Problem 11

A tail lamp contact terminal is made from steel. It is described as multislide built and is then heat-treated and cadmium-plated. In operation it completes the circuit from the "hot" lead to the bulb. If the terminal is soft, i.e., not heat-treated, the bulb will usually fail to function.

In the heat-treating operation, a buildup of salt on the *drop shoot* can cause slow cooling rather than the desired instantaneous quench. The result can be a small percentage of soft parts. Currently the auditing procedure specifies taking 125 pieces from each pan of 10,000. The acceptance number is zero. Each piece in the sample is physically inspected for hardness by opening the rocker portion and checking whether it returns to its original position.

Despite this audit, numerous complaints have been received from the assembly plant that lots have contained a small percentage of soft terminals, resulting in nonfunctioning bulbs. Figure 9P11-1 shows the rejected lot record for three months—July, August, and September.

Fig. 9P11-1   Rejection data

Sample Size	Number Defective	Frequency
125	1	138
125	2	81
125	3	12
125	4	3
125	5	0
125	6	1
125	7	2

The quality control engineer decided to determine the effectiveness of the 125-piece sample, considering that the percent defective could be adequately estimated based on the information in Figure 9P11-1. Essentially there was a feeling that a larger sample might result in preventing these defective lots from being shipped.

Using these data, the average percent defective was estimated as 1.24 percent. With the 125-piece, $c = 0$ plan, the probability of acceptance was 0.212. Figure 9P11-2 shows further calculations which were made to justify using a larger sample. (Poisson tables were used.)

Sample Size	np'	Probability Acceptance	Inspection Time and Cost			
			Min	Hr	Hr/Yr†	$/Yr
125	1.55	0.212	10	0.17	1.105	$5,525.00
200	2.48	0.082	13	0.22	1,430	7,150.00
250	3.10	0.045	15	0.25	1,625	8,125.00
300	3.72	0.024	17	0.28	1,820	9,100.00
400	4.96	0.007	21	0.35	2,275	11,375.00

†Audit cost per year based on 10,000 pieces/lot, 25 lots/day, 125 lots/wk, 6,500 lots/yr; labor cost = $5.00/hr.

Fig. 9P11-2   Cost calculations

Based on this analysis, the engineer recommended that the sample size be changed to 400 pieces and that production engineering be notified that an additional $11,375.00 per year be spent to detect defective lots. With this approach they could improve the process and eliminate the problem.

Assignment

1. What is your opinion of the analysis performed by the quality control engineer?
2. Is the statistical approach correct?
3. What would happen if the quality level deteriorated—if it were 3 percent defective, for example?

Problem 12

An assembly commonly used on small gasoline engines is the throttle shaft and outer lever (Figure 9P12-1). The lever, shaft, and brazing ring are to be purchased from outside sources. Due to the assembly's critical nature and standards promulgated by various government agencies, specifications require that the joint where the shaft and lever are brazed together be capable of withstanding a minimum 2000-pound axial load. The proposed processing sequence is

1. Fluxing the lever hole and shaft.
2. Assembling the lever and shaft.
3. Placing a brazing ring on the shaft.
4. Brazing the assembly with an induction heater.

Four different vendors have expressed interest in bidding on this job. Only two items will be considered—the shaft and the lever—since the brazing rings will be purchased as off-the-

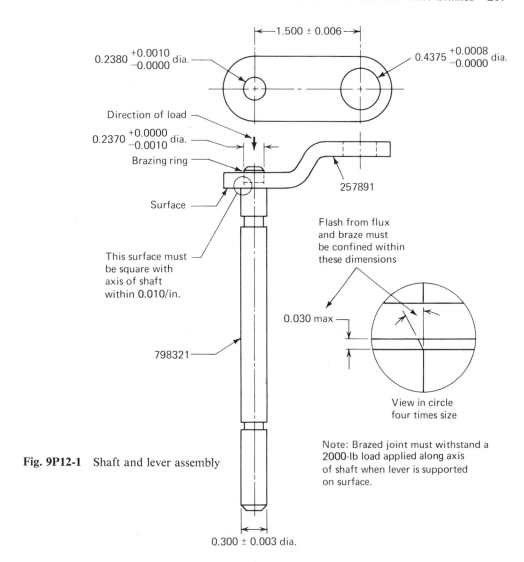

Fig. 9P12-1 Shaft and lever assembly

shelf items. For purposes of evaluation, each vendor has submitted 20 sample parts, which have been inspected dimensionally, brazed, and destructively tested to determine conformance to the axial load requirements. Data for each significant dimension and the destructive test, by vendor, are shown in Figures 9P12-2, 9P12-3, 9P12-4, 9P12-5, and 9P12-6.

Anticipated yearly requirements are 2 million pieces each, i.e., shaft and lever. Various costs for inspection and test are

a.	Hole, 1.500 ± 0.006 center to center (lever)	$0.010 per piece
b.	Hole, 0.2380 (+0.0010 or −0.0000) diameter (lever)	$0.004 per piece
c.	Hole, 0.4375 (+0.0008 or −0.0000) diameter (lever)	$0.004 per piece
d.	0.2370 (+0.0000 or −0.0010) diameter (shaft)	$0.006 per piece
e.	0.300 ± 0.0035 diameter (shaft)	$0.006 per piece
f.	0.010-per-inch squareness	$0.007 per piece
†g.	Brazed joint (assembly)	$0.050 each

†Destructive test.

Sample results from vendor A:

Shaft sizes

0.2364, 0.2362, 0.2365, 0.2366, 0.2360, 0.2365, 0.2368, 0.2363, 0.2366, 0.2364, 0.2365, 0.2366, 0.2363, 0.2366, 0.2364, 0.2367, 0.2366, 0.2364, 0.2363, 0.2365.

Lever hole sizes

0.2386, 0.2386, 0.2387, 0.2386, 0.2388, 0.2386, 0.2385, 0.2388, 0.2386, 0.2386, 0.2385, 0.2386, 0.2382, 0.2382, 0.2387, 0.2389, 0.2386, 0.2387, 0.2385, 0.2386.

Sample results from vendor B:

Shaft sizes

0.2362, 0.2368, 0.2366, 0.2365, 0.2372, 0.2364, 0.2365, 0.2368, 0.2368, 0.2366, 0.2354, 0.2372, 0.2368, 0.2358, 0.2367, 0.2360, 0.2365, 0.2362, 0.2364, 0.2364.

Lever hole sizes

0.2375, 0.2378, 0.2381, 0.2386, 0.2377, 0.2391, 0.2379, 0.2396, 0.2378, 0.2370, 0.2389, 0.2387, 0.2379, 0.2392, 0.2386, 0.2391, 0.2376, 0.2386, 0.2388, 0.2395.

Sample results from vendor C:

Shaft sizes

0.2362, 0.2359, 0.2365, 0.2365, 0.2361, 0.2363, 0.2366, 0.2368, 0.2370, 0.2365, 0.2367, 0.2364, 0.2360, 0.2368, 0.2366, 0.2365, 0.2365, 0.2362, 0.2362, 0.2368.

Lever hole sizes

0.2384, 0.2389, 0.2386, 0.2382, 0.2386, 0.2389, 0.2385, 0.2386, 0.2386, 0.2387, 0.2386, 0.2386, 0.2382, 0.2388, 0.2387, 0.2386, 0.2385, 0.2384, 0.2384, 0.2385.

Sample results from vendor D:

Shaft sizes

0.2370, 0.2371, 0.2367, 0.2372, 0.2368, 0.2367, 0.2371, 0.2363, 0.2364, 0.2364, 0.2364, 0.2369, 0.2364, 0.2361, 0.2369, 0.2359, 0.2365, 0.2369, 0.2362, 0.2363.

Lever hole sizes

0.2388, 0.2388, 0.2388, 0.2381, 0.2383, 0.2388, 0.2381, 0.2387, 0.2383, 0.2387, 0.2384, 0.2379, 0.2384, 0.2383, 0.2387, 0.2386, 0.2384, 0.2385, 0.2388, 0.2380.

Shaft dimension: 0.2370 (+0.0000 or −0.0010)

Lever hole dimension: 0.2380 (+0.0010 or −0.0000)

Fig. 9P12-2 Vendor data

A	B	C	D
1.499	1.495	1.495	1.496
1.499	1.491	1.500	1.504
1.499	1.498	1.494	1.504
1.501	1.496	1.502	1.505
1.500	1.500	1.497	1.508
1.503	1.495	1.501	1.508
1.499	1.494	1.501	1.499
1.500	1.496	1.500	1.498
1.501	1.498	1.502	1.504
1.500	1.500	1.495	1.500
1.499	1.499	1.499	1.502
1.499	1.496	1.503	1.496
1.500	1.495	1.502	1.502
1.502	1.496	1.501	1.506
1.504	1.494	1.503	1.501
1.502	1.498	1.503	1.502
1.498	1.496	1.506	1.505
1.499	1.499	1.502	1.502
1.497	1.492	1.502	1.503
1.499	1.495	1.501	1.503

Fig. 9P12-3 Vendor data—sample data on 1.500 ± 0.006 center distance between holes on lever

A	B	C	D
0.4379	0.4378	0.4381	0.4375
0.4380	0.4381	0.4381	0.4378
0.4380	0.4377	0.4380	0.4380
0.4379	0.4380	0.4382	0.4378
0.4378	0.4379	0.4383	0.4376
0.4379	0.4380	0.4381	0.4378
0.4380	0.4380	0.4381	0.4376
0.4380	0.4382	0.4381	0.4377
0.4379	0.4382	0.4382	0.4375
0.4379	0.4382	0.4380	0.4375
0.4381	0.4381	0.4381	0.4377
0.4380	0.4378	0.4383	0.4372
0.4379	0.4377	0.4381	0.4381
0.4380	0.4382	0.4382	0.4377
0.4381	0.4380	0.4383	0.4374
0.4379	0.4381	0.4381	0.4378
0.4380	0.4379	0.4382	0.4379
0.4378	0.4378	0.4382	0.4372
0.4379	0.4379	0.4383	0.4378
0.4379	0 4381	0.4380	0.4381

Fig. 9P12-4 Vendor data—sample data on 0.4375 ± 0.0008 diameter hole on lever

Fig. 9P12-5 Vendor data—sample data on minimum 2000-pound axial load test

Fig. 9P12-6 Vendor data—sample data on 0.300 ± 0.003 diameter on shaft

A	B	C	D
4,300	1,900	3,300	4,100
4,700	2,700	2,600	3,000
3,700	2,300	3,200	3,100
3,600	1,700	3,300	2,500
3,200	2,100	3,700	4,000
3,800	2,400	3,600	2,900
3,800	2,200	3,400	3,900
2,300	2,500	2,900	2,800
3,000	2,200	3,600	2,500
3,600	2,900	3,500	4,000
3,000	2,700	4,200	3,300
3,400	2,200	3,400	1,700
3,400	2,300	3,400	1,900
3,200	2,000	4,700	4,100
3,000	2,800	3,600	2,900
3,600	2,200	3,700	2,700
4,400	2,700	4,000	3,500
4,400	2,100	4,000	4,600
3,300	2,000	3,500	3,500
3,800	2,700	3,400	3,300

A	B	C	D
0.299	0.300	0.301	0.297
0.300	0.303	0.301	0.302
0.298	0.301	0.302	0.298
0.299	0.302	0.300	0.300
0.299	0.303	0.300	0.301
0.299	0.303	0.303	0.298
0.300	0.302	0.302	0.303
0.297	0.301	0.303	0.299
0.298	0.300	0.302	0.303
0.300	0.303	0.302	0.299
0.299	0.299	0.302	0.299
0.300	0.299	0.303	0.298
0.300	0.304	0.299	0.298
0.299	0.302	0.302	0.301
0.298	0.302	0.300	0.300
0.297	0.300	0.302	0.303
0.301	0.302	0.302	0.299
0.300	0.303	0.303	0.300
0.298	0.299	0.299	0.301
0.300	0.302	0.300	0.299

Other pertinent information, which may or may not be relevant, includes the following:

1. Parts will be shipped in boxes containing 1,000 pieces.
2. Cost to return rejected shipments to source:

Vendor A $12.00 per 1,000 pieces
Vendor B $2.00 per 1,000 pieces
Vendor C $10.00 per 1,000 pieces
Vendor D $7.00 per 1,000 pieces

3. To conform with the company's policy, at least two vendors must be selected.
4. If the brazed joint fails in the field (within the 1-year warranty period), the repair cost is $10.00 per unit. There is also the possibility of product liability suits if failures occur.
5. Bids submitted by vendors are

Vendor	Shaft	Lever	Shipping
A	$0.060	$0.048	$10.00/1,000 pcs
B	0.040	0.031	1.50/1,000 pcs
C	0.055	0.045	8.00/1,000 pcs
D	0.052	0.043	6.00/1,000 pcs

Assignment

1. By examining the information shown in Figure 9P12-1, decide what AQL's would be specified for the dimensional and test characteristics shown.
2. Use an attribute sampling table and specify the appropriate sample size and acceptance number, using the AQL's from 1. Reproduce the OC curve(s) for the plan(s).
3. Use a variable sampling table and specify the appropriate sampling plan and procedure to follow. Reproduce the OC curve(s) for the plan(s).
4. Statistically analyze all the information in Figure 9P12-2. Consider each dimension and its specified tolerance and predict the percentage of parts, by vendor, that would be out of specification.
5. Using the results from 4 and the curve(s) in 2 and 3, what percent of submitted lots would be rejected (by vendor)?
6. Again, analyzing by vendor, would it be less expensive to 100 percent inspect the rejected lots or simply return them to the source? If they were 100 percent inspected and mixed with accepted lots, what AOQ would be expected?
7. How does the cost of 100 percent inspection compare with sampling inspection? Would you recommend using an attribute or a variable sampling plan?
8. By using a table of random numbers and the data on the mating lever hole and shaft diameter, randomly assemble the 20 parts from each vendor. This will result in a distribution of clearances. Calculate the mean and standard deviation and determine the percentage that exceeds the specified clearance. Does this seem consistent with previous results?
9. Is there evidence that the results in 8 have any relationship to the axial load test results?
10. Summarize all the information and recommend what vendors would be selected.

INDEX